THE GREAT WAR

THE

Cyril Falls

GREAT
WAR

A PERIGEE BOOK

Perigee Books
are published by
G. P. Putnam's Sons
200 Madison Avenue
New York, New York, 10016

*Published simultaneously in the Dominion of
Canada by Longmans Canada Limited, Toronto.*

Eleventh Impression

SBN: 399-50100-2

Library of Congress Catalog
Card Number: 59-7851

*I am grateful to Mr. Leonard Barnes for his kindness
in permitting me to make two quotations from his
little verse sequence* Youth at Arms, *which I have
admired and often read since its publication in 1933.*

*To friends and companions, those growing
old and those to whom long life was denied*

But roll-call works a change. Name after name
Of comrades gone recaptures bit by bit
The battle for minds which thus can pause on it
With infinite compassion and no shame.
Thus do they focus sense diffused of grief
On the particular dead, and thus derive
From pity and envy mixed a child's relief
That they themselves incredibly survive.

LEONARD BARNES: *Youth at Arms.*

Contents

8   CONTENTS

Preface

WHEN I had made good progress on this history I confided to a few friends what I was doing. They differed in age and interests, but all asked in virtually the same words: "What's your thesis?" I was taken aback. I had not started with a thesis consciously in mind. I was, as I always had been, intensely interested in the subject. Having devoted to its study some twenty years of my life, not counting my modest participation in it, I could not doubt that I knew more about it than most. I hoped that a fair number of survivors would welcome a condensed account in what I trusted would be readable form, and that younger people would echo Southey's young Peterkin with:

> Now tell us all about the war,
> And what they fought each other for.

Before long I felt gratitude to those who had asked the question. They had helped me to clear my own mind. I began to realize that there had always been a thesis at the back of it. I wanted to show what the war had meant to my generation, so large a part of which—and so much of the best at that—lost their lives in it. I wanted to commemorate the spirit in which these men served and fought. The modern intellectual is inclined to look upon the ardor with which they went to war with impatience. To him it is obsolete. If so, I must be obsolete too. Looking back, the intensity, and I dare add the purity, of that spirit still moves me deeply. I speak particularly of the combatants, including leaders and staffs. In the circumstances of that war a large proportion of men in uniform might almost as well have been company directors, clerks, grocers' assistants, or street cleaners at home, for the most part useful, but martial only in appearance and not always even that.

I find in the soldiers other virtues besides courage and self-sacrifice. Though their ardor became blunted, their comradeship never died. Then, though barbarity enters into all wars, they were in general remarkably free from this wickedness which soils the name of patriot. They were called to the colors as volunteers or conscripts on a scale greater than had ever been known; yet, though this was a war of nations in which the scum was swept along beside the finest elements and the far larger average, it was not where Britain was concerned a savage or cruel war. Its most abominable episodes, such as the Armenian massacres perpetrated by the Turks, do not match the cold cruelty of the Second World War.

Next I wanted to do all I could to demolish a myth as preposterous as it is widely believed. For the first time in the known history of war, we are told, the military art stood still in the greatest war up to date. Theoretically and historically this appears impossible. I believe reality reflects theory and history. The only grain of truth in the myth derives from the very fact that this was the greatest war: commanders were often baffled by its size and the masses engaged in it. Most of the belligerents, however, threw up leaders notable for skill and character, though Russia found none of the highest apart from Brusilov and Yudenich, and it is hard to rank the Italians Cadorna and Diaz as more than capable organizers. France, Germany, and Britain produced many. Joffre, Foch, Pétain, Franchet d'Esperey, and Mangin; Falkenhayn, Ludendorff, Otto von Below, Gallwitz, and Hutier; Haig, Rawlinson, Plumer, Maude, and Allenby—all these were great figures. Near them stood more junior leaders of merit, several of whom would have risen in stature with bigger responsibilities. Take one on whom fortune unexpectedly smiled. Lord Cavan, when a corps commander on the Western Front, was known only as a sound general with the steadfast qualities often seen in British Guardsmen; as army commander in Italy under the Italian commander in chief, he revealed himself to be also an imaginative soldier and endowed with political flair and tact, masterly in dealings with allies. The American Pershing and Liggett, the Austrian Conrad von Hötzendorf and Krauss, the Serbian Putnik and Mišić were outstanding figures. Of all, Haig and Pershing would have been the most difficult to replace in their roles.

I doubt whether naval leadership matched the best among the

soldiers, except in the case of Hipper. To me he is the most attractive figure among the admirals, and his handling of his battle
cruisers at Jutland bears the stamp of genius. Jellicoe, Beatty,
Wemyss, Scheer and von Reuter all possessed professional skill and
were personalities in their different ways. The young air service
was training leaders rather than producing them within the span
of the war, and the figures who really stand out are Trenchard and
John Salmond.

I have striven to find space for impressions on generalship, especially that of Haig, and given more to it than I would have but for
the myopia of the English-speaking races where it was concerned.
The Germans have not been equally myopic.

The conception which I have called a myth is based on conditions on the Western Front. It is an erroneous view that the stag-
nant type of warfare between the autumn of 1914 and the spring of
1918 was reflected in other theaters of war. It is true the opposing
forces went to ground in all the European theaters, in Asia Minor,
in Palestine, and in Mesopotamia. Yet in these theaters there were
rapid movements and changes of fortune revealed by large—sometimes vast—gains and losses of ground. The explanation is as simple
as it well could be: the Western Front was regarded as the principal
and vital front. In consequence it was held by more troops, more
artillery, more machine guns, per mile, and stronger fortifications,
than any other. Thus there was less room for maneuver and a
larger reserve force available to close breaches. A kindred fallacy,
almost peculiar to Britain and also created by conditions on the
Western Front, is that the First World War was far more ghastly
than the Second. It was for Britain, but mainly because she was
driven off the European continent early in 1940, did not become
established upon it again in Italy until late 1943, or in the vital
French theater until halfway through 1944. The Second was worse
for Russia and for Germany. The dead, measured by millions, seem
to have numbered about the same.

Yet one difference between the two wars is clear. The earlier saw
the defensive in the ascendant; in the later it was the turn of the
offensive. The reasons for the change are many, but three are of
immense importance: the tank, only in its childhood in the First
World War; the increased power of aircraft both in close support
of land forces and as a strategic method of attack; the increase in
mobility brought about by the improvement in mechanical trans-

port. In the First World War the trench network, reinforced by concrete fortifications, shielded behind barbed wire, and protected by curtains of artillery fire and overlapping zones of machine-gun fire, gave the defensive its strength, while reliance on indifferent mechanical transport and slow-moving animal transport made the offensive weak in such conditions.

Here we come on another fallacy: that the machine gun was the biggest killer. The means by which men died were not recorded, but the means by which they were wounded were, by the British medical services. The shell accounted for over 50 per cent of the wounds. Now the bullet came from the rifle as well as from the machine gun, and especially in the early stages of the war when there were only two machine guns per battalion, vast losses were caused by rifle fire. Again, common sense tells us that men hit by a shell or a fragment of shell are more often killed than those hit by a bullet. Therefore the proportion of killed to wounded must be considerably higher from artillery than from machine guns and rifles combined. Artillery was the biggest killer, but at the start of a great offensive, when a high proportion of the defending artillery had generally been knocked out, the machine gun, being harder to knock out, was the best defensive weapon.

The gun was the best offensive weapon. It was not seriously challenged by the tank until the last twelvemonth of the war, and the tank was not a destructive so much as a moral weapon. Battles are won by moral rather than material effect, as Napoleon remarked, but destructive weapons were always needed in this age of field fortification. The number of guns went on increasing to the end even on the Western Front, and tanks were scarcely used elsewhere. The disadvantage of the colossal bombardments of the second half of the war was that they cut up the ground—especially when the soil was wet and heavy—so much as to hamper the attacks which they were intended to support.

I have denied the allegation that the leadership was mentally barren. There can be no doubt, however, that it was baffled by the sealing up of the war in France and Belgium and the extreme difficulty in loosening it again. Yet skill and intelligence were applied to the task. I think the Germans outshone their foes in infantry tactics. Between 1915 and March, 1918, they launched only one major offensive, that of Verdun. In this battle, however, and in several minor attacks they showed that by elasticity, by probing before assault, by reinforcing success and not failure, the problem of penetrating a trench system was partially soluble. In 1918 they advanced at a greater pace than their foes could ever equal, though it proved to be to their own destruction.

A German attack meeting stout resistance was often a remarkable spectacle. Cooperation between infantry and artillery by fireworks was more detailed than the British or French could achieve. The sky was at times so full of yellow, red, and green rockets that the observer wondered how anyone could make head or tail of the signals. Yet time after time the artillery would lengthen or shorten its fire or carry out a rebombardment of varying duration. This may be Greek to the infantryman of the Second World War because, having other means of communicating with the artillery, he finds it hard to realize how vital rocket signals might be.

Regarding battle-winning gadgets, the Germans were surpassed in inventiveness by the British and French. The tank in itself was a conception of genius to the credit of the former. The creeping artillery barrage, copied everywhere and often used in the Second World War, was a French contribution. Though the Germans made the better start with hand and rifle grenades, the Allies caught them up and went ahead. Identification of batteries by sound-ranging and flash-spotting was British; so also were the remarkable devices for the rapid bridging of rivers and canals.

German writers have been prolific in excuses for defeat. The principal one is that their superior skill, endurance, and bravery had to bow before weight of metal. They talk as if there were something unfair, even treacherous and contemptible, in waging a war of material. In fact, they made use of their superior material strength with the utmost complacency while they had it. So contemptuous were they of their enemies that they started unrestricted U-boat warfare, the "sink at sight" policy, in face of the certainty that it would bring the United States in.

They denounce the blockade, which has always been the weapon of great naval powers, and in order to take the responsibility for defeat off the back of their army, lay on the blockade even more weight than it actually carried. German generals of the Second World War have been criticized for putting all the blame on Hitler. At least they never deny defeat, which is what Hitler did in regard to the First World War. Though many honest writers had earlier told the truth, there already existed a legend that the army had never been defeated. This became a firm belief with millions of Germans under Hitler. It is wholly untrue. By late September, 1918, Germany, having then concentrated virtually her whole strength on the Western Front, was utterly defeated there. Many divisions collapsed. Many men were sent to the rear in empty supply trucks and railway cars because they were themselves useless and infected others with their readiness to bolt at sight of an enemy. Good units remained, of course, but by the end the whole army had been defeated and a large part of it had become demoralized. The easy armistice terms contributed to the birth of the legend. Pershing thought the terms were too soft and was convinced that the Germans would accept any. Whatever the verdict is on the first point, we know that he was right on the second.

The French army, on the other hand, retrieved its spirit in a striking way after being nearly down and out in the summer of 1917. I neither support nor oppose the theorists who tell us that the Teutonic races hold out in adversity longer than the Latin, but that when the former's morale cracks the damage is fatal, whereas the latter's morale can be patched up with surprising speed. It is a highly speculative theory, yet it does fit the case here. The French outlasted the Germans. Even though the French troops may not have got back to their best and though Britain bore more than her share of the final victorious offensive, this was a gallant recovery on the part of France. She had carried a far greater weight than Britain in the first half of the land war. One factor in her endurance, half forgotten today but which at the time the Germans realized to their cost, was the part played by colonial troops, especially from North and Central Africa. I doubt whether she would have survived without them.

The effects of the First World War on France have a significance extending beyond its immediate political results. The trend of military thought between the wars, the doctrine of extreme caution, the bridling of initiative in junior leaders, the tying of tanks to infantry, the Maginot Line and still more the Maginot mentality, the conception of *la guerre à la bourgeoise* (a respectable, moderate, sort of war); and above all the wave of horror when the specter of another bloody war, neither respectable nor moderate, loomed up: all this was the aftermath of the slaughter of the First World War and France's toll of over a million of her dead. The rout of 1940 was the product of the years 1914 to 1918.

For the first time in her history Britain fought a war with a mass conscript army on what had become the continental pattern. For the first time too she fought as the central power in a commonwealth of free nations: Canada, Australia, New Zealand, and South Africa. Their contingents were among the finest troops in the world. Their senior commanders—the highest being Canadian and Australian corps commanders—bore a double responsibility, to their own governments and to the higher British commanders under whom they served. The system led to occasional difficulties, but not to many. The British soldier sometimes grumbled that, to judge by press reports, the ten divisions of Australians, Canadians, and New Zealanders did more fighting than the fifty or so British. The dominion troops were extremely good, but it is only fair to add that their countries did not dig so deeply into their manpower as the United Kingdom. As a consequence their average physique was better and they never filled their ranks with youths as the United Kingdom was compelled to do in 1918. Nor did they follow its example in reducing divisions from twelve to nine battalions. India made a larger contribution than any of the Dominions, but, except for two divisions early in the war, Indian infantry was not employed in France. Indian troops played a great part in the Palestinian and Mesopotamian campaigns. They were capable of standing the northern French winter, as was proved by the fact that by the end of the war the drivers of the horse-drawn divisional ammunition columns were all Indian: infantry could not, however, stand the combined cold and wet of the trenches in winter.

I shall say little here of British endurance. I have done my best to show in Book V how splendid it was. From August, 1918, onward the British Army played the predominant role in the series of offensives. This great army, so largely composed of young soldiers, lacked the stamina of their predecessors. It was less steady in face of counterattacks. Nevertheless, a short apprenticeship to the more open type of warfare made the young soldiers cannier fighters on the offensive than those predecessors. They often outmaneuvered as well as outfought the Germans. But they had ghostly allies. The men who had gone before had worn the polish off the German army in those terrible battles of attrition. The dead rank high among the victors of the war on land.

The other British contribution to victory was equally great. The Royal Navy was the framework within which victory was won and without which it would have been lost. The French, Italian, American, and Japanese navies played gallant and invaluable parts, but, even counting the magnificent role of the French navy in the Dardanelles campaign, they were secondary. Germany and Austria would not have survived as long as they did but for their conquest of the rich granaries of Rumania and the Ukraine. These resources saved them from being strangled by the blockade long before November, 1918. As it was, the blockade was not the primary cause of their overthrow, but it helped to bring this about. The armies did not suffer as badly as the people at home, but even they were underfed, and the hunger of the civilians—on the very brink of starvation in Austria—hampered the waging of a national war. The armies were also handicapped by a shortage of horses, and that too was largely due to lack of grain. The navies of Britain and her allies brought food across the oceans for themselves and denied it to their enemies. They made possible the importation of munitions from the United States and of horses and mules from many countries of the New World and prevented their enemies from imitating them. They enabled Britain to feed her troops in Mesopotamia to a large extent, and in Palestine to a considerable extent, from Australia, New Zealand, and Africa by routes avoiding waters infested by submarines. The Royal Navy took the foremost part in these activities. It was the mainstay of the antisubmarine war; in fact, few U-boats were accounted for except by British ships, aircraft, and mines. All operations against the enemy's main naval force, the German High Seas Fleet, were carried out by Britain.

In the air the British were handicapped by aircraft designs and performances nearly always somewhat inferior to the German. For all that, they ended the war with the most powerful air force of either of the opposing coalitions, and the most effective. What younger readers need to be reminded of is that all air forces in this war were chiefly adjuncts to land armies and in rather lesser degree to navies. Not until the last year did they begin to be forces in their own right and even then they moved only a short distance along that road.

I have a deep admiration for the deeds and the spirit of the United States Army. It appeared, fresh if for the greater part inexperienced, when Russia had been driven out of the war and Germany had transferred all the best of her forces to the Western Front. It found the French and British war-weary. It went into battle on a small scale but with remarkable results when the Germans were in the ascendant. It helped to turn the tide. Early in its expansion it began to take part with its French and British allies in the series of final offensives. Its thrusts were always shrewd and determined. In the most difficult sector of the whole front, the Argonne, it fought with wonderful tenacity and endurance. It raised spirits wherever it was engaged, notably among the French, under whose commander in chief all but a few of its divisions served in these campaigns. Apart from its achievements, the very fact that it was on the spot and continually growing removed an enormous weight of anxiety from the shoulders of Foch, Pétain and Haig.

Fortunately for itself and for the cause in general the United States Army was commanded by a strong-willed man. The policy of filling up shattered French and British divisions with American infantry regiments would have been calamitous. The Americans would have felt that they were being treated as mere cannon fodder and each nationality would have lost confidence in the other. Pershing inflexibly refused this proposal. To cajolery and anger alike he returned an uncompromising "No!" On the other hand, when the French were in desperate straits he always sent them what aid he could, though he loathed splitting up his forces. It is impossible to find fault with his policy: blank refusal to split up formations on any plea; generous aid to allies in adversity; the earliest possible concentration of the bulk of his forces under his own command.

The extreme view of the Americans' part in the war, that France and Britain muddled it for eleven-twelfths of the time and that the United States put things right in the last twelfth is moonshine. It would have been impossible unless the men had been demigods. The United States high command had not in fact any great influence on the *conduct* of the war, apart from its representation on the Supreme War Council. That body had a fair amount of influence on theaters outside the principal one, France and Belgium, but curiously little there. The reason was that the French prime minister, Clemenceau, was prepared to give Foch a very free hand, while the British prime minister, Lloyd George, who distrusted Haig's judgment and would have liked to alter the strategy of the war, if not to remove Haig from his command, was shackled by his colleagues, especially the Conservatives, who put their trust in Haig. Lloyd George as a national leader, an inspirer, was almost as effective in the First World War as Winston Churchill in the Second, but never possessed the latter's power in military affairs. The strategy of the final offensive was dictated by Foch and Haig, by Foch because he had been created generalissimo, by Haig because on the few occasions when his views differed from those of Foch the Scot managed to bring the Frenchman round to his opinion. He could not have done so, however, had he not commanded the hardest-hitting army. The contribution of the United States Army was its first-class fighting qualities, but it was only during the last two months that it was engaged on a considerable scale.

This is not a political history. I have, however, dealt with the political situations which counted most. The causes of the war, the entry into it of Turkey, Italy, Bulgaria, Rumania, and especially the United States—the only combatant to come in after the outbreak without striking a bargain for itself—and the Russian revolution, are all examined. Other incidents, such as the stand of the German Emperor and his Chancellor against unrestricted submarine warfare and their surrender to the admirals and generals, the curious relations of the French and British governments with the government of Greece, the defeatist campaign in France, peace negotiations, and British motives in Mesopotamia have their place. But a week-to-week study of policy and diplomacy would take nearly all the room. Anyhow it was not politicians who decided the issue of the war.

C. F.

THE GREAT WAR

Book One—1914

Chapter I

VULTURES IN THE SKIES

THE Archduke Francis Ferdinand, heir to the Austrian and Hungarian thrones, was, for him, in happy mood when he came to Sarajevo on Sunday morning, June 28, 1914. He had been following maneuvers, and his heart had always been in the army. The weather was lovely; the town was beflagged, though doubtless on official orders; and his dear wife had come to join him. Her position was always easier anywhere away from Vienna. She was not of royal blood and their marriage had been reluctantly permitted by the Emperor only on condition that their children should be debarred from the succession. The rigid "Spanish" etiquette of the imperial court barely recognized her existence.

Francis Ferdinand was a lonely, reserved, haughty man, not lacking, however, in the strength of character often appearing in the house of Hapsburg. He exhibited, too, gleams of statesmanship. He was associated with an idea undoubtedly bold, possibly unattainable, reconstitution of the dual monarchy as a triad: Austria, Hungary, and the Slav southern provinces of the latter linked with predominantly Slav Bosnia and Herzegovina, instead of Austria and Hungary alone. This attitude made him relatively popular with the Bosnian bourgeoisie. To the ultranationalist or "Irredentist" South Slavs of Bosnia, however, his very moderation made him dangerous. Should he succeed in establishing a contented South Slav state on an equality with Austria and Hungary, their hopes of union with the little kingdom of Serbia would be ruined. He was naturally disliked in Hungary, whose territory he proposed to lop.

As the Archduke and the Duchess of Hohenberg drove to the town hall, along the Appel Quay beside the river Miliača, a bomb was thrown at their car. It either rolled to the ground or was brushed out of the open hood by the Archduke, but the explosion wounded several people. Francis Ferdinand reached the town hall in a not unnatural bad temper. The burgomaster had not heard what had happened. He soon learned. "Mr. Burgomaster," the Archduke said gruffly, "I come to visit you and I am greeted with bombs. What do you mean by talking of loyalty?"

His lady appeased him. The burgomaster said his piece and the Archduke's reply was gracious enough. Some talk of changing the program then took place. General Potiorek, the governor of Bosnia, is said to have made the comment that he knew his Bosnians and that they did not attempt assassination twice in one day. The Archduke decided to visit first Potiorek's wounded aide-de-camp in the hospital. He and his wife were fearless, and one of the traditional virtues of royal personages is good manners and consideration for those who serve them closely. They set off again.

Francis-Joseph Street, leading off the Appel Quay, had been left open because it was on the original itinerary. The leading car entered it, and the Archduke's driver was following when Potiorek pointed out the error. The car slowed, then stopped. Before it could reverse, a man in the crowd shot both the Archduke and his consort with a pistol. Both died shortly afterward.*

All over Europe telegrams sped. The British vice-consul at Sarajevo was quick, but his brief message took a long time to get through.

CONSUL JONES TO SIR EDWARD GREY. SERAJEVO JUNE 28, 1914 DESPATCHED 12.30 P.M. RECEIVED 4.0 P.M.
ACCORDING TO NEWS RECEIVED HERE HEIR APPARENT AND HIS CONSORT ASSASSINATED THIS MORNING BY MEANS OF AN EXPLOSIVE NATURE.†

Almost up to the moment when the crisis burst, the murder, though shocking news everywhere, had small political significance for the world at large, even for the money markets; but by Monday morning every foreign ministry, every chancellery, and every war office in Europe was buzzing. The grave factor was the strong suspicion, amounting to a moral certainty, that the plot had been hatched on Serbian soil. It may be said at once that there was no

* Serajevo, pp. 13-18. Conrad, IV, 21.
† Gooch and Temperley, XI, 12.

difficulty in confirming this belief and that the murderer's Browning had been given to him by the chief of the intelligence section of the Serbian general staff. The crime was never traced to the Serbian government, though in 1924 a member of the 1914 Cabinet, Lyuba Yovanović, stated that the then Prime Minister had told him that he believed there was a plot to kill the Archduke. Many students of the subject discredit the story. If it was true, the Serbian government sinned by conveying no warning.* There is not a jot of evidence that it was involved in the plot or approved of it. Serbia, impoverished and strained by two Balkan wars, desired peace. At the same time, a government whose director of military intelligence connived at the murder of the heir to a great neighboring empire was in those days exposed to heavy reprisals. Everyone expected the Austro-Hungarian government to act sternly and decisively.

But how sternly and decisively? That was the dilemma. Russia was the patron of Serbia, not merely from sympathy for fellow Slavs but because the reduction of Serbia to the position of an Austrian appanage—we might say today satellite—would bring Austria closer to the Dardanelles. On the Black Sea Rumania was already Austria's ally. Russia was allied to France; Austria to Germany and Italy; Britain had an entente, or understanding, with France, though no alliance. Austria's dealing with Serbia would jangle sensitive nerves running to every European capital, but most sensitive of all in St. Petersburg, Paris, Rome, and London. Statesmen realized at once that they were in for complex negotiations. Most of them, indeed, expected the affair to blow over; and yet—supposing it did not! Then there might be a war greater than any the world had known for almost exactly a century.

Before outlining these negotiations it will be well to glance at the state of Europe on the day that the fanatical consumptive Gavrilo Prinzip pulled out his Browning in the Appel Quay at Sarajevo. Both subjects have a literature big enough to fill many bookshelves.

It might be thought that industrialization, ease of travel, the growth of literacy and of the press would have damped down nationalist fervor, but in fact it had become particularly fiery. On the one hand, great powers were rivals for the acquisition of undeveloped areas outside Europe as sources of raw materials and as markets. Bismarck had shrewdly encouraged France to become a colonial

* Schmitt, I, 232 ff. A. J. P. Taylor (*The Observer*, November 16, 1958) speaks of "an obscure warning" to civil authorities in Vienna.

nation in order to turn her thoughts away from revenge for the defeat of 1870. But France had, recently with the friendly concurrence of Britain, proved herself too adept in stepping into places where no claim had been staked to please Bismarck's successors. Germany wanted to be a colonial power too, and the tropical lands she had picked up merely whetted her appetite for something worthier of her prestige. On the other hand, in Europe itself fierce nationalism was created by the desire of subject races to be freed from alien overlords. This was particularly the case in the Austro-Hungarian Empire. Prinzip was an Austrian subject.

In the fencing, intrigue, and uneasiness prevalent in Europe, in which few nations, certainly none of the great powers—Britain, Germany, France, Russia, Austria-Hungary, and Italy—can be absolved from selfishness at the least, one influence had been outstanding. This was the arrogance which disguised Germany's anxieties. On the face of it her position was splendid. She had routed her Austrian and French rivals. Her commerce and wealth were expanding with astonishing speed. The future appeared to glow in a bright dawn of promise. The people were enterprising and industrious. Her army was first-class. Yet she suffered from a neurosis which originated in one particular danger and at the same time aggravated it. She feared no single nation. The combination of France and Russia was another matter. If it came to war this would involve "war on two fronts." The prospect presented certain strategic advantages over that of fighting two nations side by side because forces could be swung quickly over Germany's good communications to one flank or the other; but in the long run it might involve the deadly peril of a squeeze from both at once. This peril Germany helped to bring closer by a series of threats which destroyed all sense of security.

While Bismarck held office her policy was prudent. In 1883 he expanded Germany's alliance with Austria-Hungary into the Triple Alliance of Germany, Austria-Hungary, and Italy. He then sought to bring about a "League of Three Emperors," the German, Austrian, and Russian, but in this he was balked by the unfriendliness of Austria and Russia. One cornerstone of his system was good relations with Britain. After his dismissal a less wise policy developed, and at the same time new stresses came into operation.

Two years later, in 1892, that which Bismarck had consistently tried to stave off came to pass: France and Russia signed an alliance. German relations with Britain began to deteriorate, though slowly.

The announcement in 1900 of Germany's intention to build a strong battle fleet helped to bring about the Anglo-Japanese alliance of 1902. Yet Germany had still little reason to worry. So far Britain's relations with her had been better than those with France. Now the British Secretary of State for Foreign Affairs, Lord Lansdowne, approached France to put an end to differences. An agreement signed in 1904 gave Britain a free hand in Egypt and France one in Morocco. Britain had emerged from isolation.

Step by step the opposing camps were fortified. The Triple Alliance was confronted by the Triple Entente of France, Russia, and Britain, though Britain entered into no alliance with the other two. Japan's defeat of Russia in 1905 strengthened Germany because it left Russia weakened and in peril of internal revolution. Franco-German rivalry over Morocco came to a head when the German Emperor made an inflammatory speech at Tangier on March 31, 1905. The upshot was humiliation for unready France and the sacrifice of her foreign minister, Delcassé. But another consequence was that the British Liberal Prime Minister of 1906, Sir Henry Campbell-Bannerman, authorized staff talks—without commitments —with France.

The next milestone on the bleak road to war was the sudden annexation of Bosnia and Herzegovina by Austria in 1908. Austria had in fact administered them for just thirty years as nominally Turkish provinces confided to her charge, but her action infuriated Serbia and nearly sparked off war between Austria and Russia. Up bobbed the German Emperor again to tell the world that Germany stood behind her ally "in shining armor." Russia backed out. The Kaiser was pleased as a peacock. He did not realize how rash it was to humble and mortify two great powers in succession.

In 1911 the German government, which had a genuine case over Morocco, blundered again. It sent the gunboat *Panther* to Agadir and opened a press compaign for concessions. No one flinched this time. Lloyd George, the British Chancellor of the Exchequer, a fiery left-winger who had tried to balk the armament plans of his colleagues, made a sensational speech which warned Germany that Britain supported France. Now it was Germany that climbed down, but war looked likely that summer.

Germany made a sinister impression of eagerness for war on an unbiased outsider. Colonel Edward M. House, after visiting Berlin in early June, 1914, as emissary of the President of the United States, came to England shocked. "It only needs a spark to set the whole thing off," he said.*

Meanwhile the German naval program had expanded and a race with Britain had developed. In 1906 Britain launched the *Dreadnought*, an "all-big-gun" battleship. This ship not only made her predecessors obsolescent but set Germany a poser. She must build her own dreadnoughts, but such warships could not pass through the Kiel Canal to emerge from and return to the Baltic. She did not hesitate, and even the Social Democrats voted for the credits needed to widen and deepen the canal. The sharpest threat from Germany came in 1908, when she decided to lay down between that year and 1911, inclusive, twelve battleships of dreadnought type. Here was something understood by the British man in the street. Britain was an island power and a naval power. Her army was small, trifling in size compared with the conscript hosts of the continent. Her very life, it seemed, depended on the Royal Navy. If she lost command of the sea in war she would starve. Tennyson had written:

> The fleet of England is her all-in-all;
> Her fleet is in your hands,
> And in her fleet her Fate.

The question stirred the country. On no other subject did it show anxiety during these prodromes to the world conflict. Britain kept her head, however. The building increases which answered the German challenge were actually opposed by many supporters of the Liberal government, and by most of the Liberal press. To cut short a long and intricate story, by August, 1914, the British Grand Fleet comprised twenty-four dreadnoughts and battle cruisers and the German High Seas Fleet, seventeen.

The building race was not disastrous to relations with Germany. Britain on her side was good-tempered about it. The German Emperor, an intelligent, quick-minded lightweight, had a genuine admiration for the Royal Navy. He deliberately sought to model his officers on the British, who for their part appreciated the naval standards of the Germans. Yet they watched each other carefully. Britain withdrew her battleships from the Mediterranean to concentrate her strength. The fleet visited the coast of Spain only when the Germans were carrying out winter refits. Even coaling and

* Hendrick, I, 299.

leave after grand maneuvers were so arranged that the Royal Navy should always be ready to meet a sudden blow. It was a case of living close to the lip of an active volcano, near enough to smell the acrid fumes.

The Austrian foreign minister, Count Berchtold, was a debonair society figure, delightful as host or guest, an expert diplomatist, but frivolous and usually unwilling to abandon his pleasures for affairs of state. He worked hard now. His first impulse was to send a force straight into Serbia to demand satisfaction. Here he was opposed by the Hungarian prime minister, Count Tisza, who advised prudence, and by the brilliant chief of the general staff, General Conrad von Hötzendorf. Conrad declared that an army such as the Austrian could not move without mobilization, that is, the issue of war equipment and the calling up of reservists, which would take roughly sixteen days. To move units on peace establishments into Serbia now would, he said, make a mess of any future mobilization. But it was all a simple matter, he went on. Order mobilization against Serbia at once and send her an ultimatum. Berchtold was unwilling to mobilize at once.*

Again and again we find this conflict between soldier and statesman. The statesman knows the adage "mobilization means war" and shies off it even while following a warlike course. The soldier knows that if his government threatens but does not make ready, a war may be lost. He would not be human if he did not realize that the blame then falls on him. In this case Conrad was itching to chastise Serbia. The soldier may or may not be a warmonger, but we should not conclude that he is one merely because he wants to put his machine in motion when he sees that it may be needed.

What Berchtold did was clever. He sent an emissary to Berlin to ask for advice. If he were counseled to go ahead he could force Tisza's hand and would be covered by the alliance; if not, he could avoid recourse to arms and emerge with an air of statesmanlike moderation. The emissary, Count Hoyos, reached Berlin on July 5. The Emperor, who was setting out on a cruise to Norway, gave him the green light. The Chancellor, Theobald von Bethmann-Hollweg, told him that Austria must decide what was to be done, but that she could be sure of finding Germany on her side. Is there any excuse for this lack of responsibility? The only one is that the Ger-

* Regele, pp. 232-239. Mobilization by armies would result in variation in the time taken.

man Kaiser and the Chancellor may have believed that failure to take action would be so ignominious that it would break up the ramshackle Austro-Hungarian empire, Germany's only sincere ally.

Berchtold still had to convert Tisza to warlike action, and Tisza was a tough character. Yet on July 14 he hauled down his colors. No one knows exactly why, but two factors were lack of support from the Emperor, and Conrad's argument that long-drawn-out diplomatic exchanges would give Austria's foes time to take military measures. As for the old Emperor, he had hesitated, but chiefly from doubt whether the senior partner, Germany, would march. While Germany's reply to the mission of Count Hoyos was still awaited, Conrad asked him: "If the answer shows that Germany stands on our side, do we then go to war with Serbia?" "*Dann ja*," said Francis Joseph.*

The Austrian government drafted a note to Serbia. The most significant clauses laid down that Serbia should officially condemn anti-Austrian propaganda and express regret that Serbian officials had taken part in it; should accept collaboration *in Serbia* from Austrian representatives "for the suppression of the subversive movement directed against the territorial integrity of the monarchy"; and should institute judicial proceedings against abettors of the murder plot—"delegates of the Austro-Hungarian Government will take part in the investigation relating thereto." † These demands were made in the expectation that they would be refused and after Austrian investigations in Sarajevo had found no trace of complicity on the part of the Serbian government. It was arranged to deliver the note on July 23 at 6 P.M. The late hour was an afterthought. The reason was that by that time the President of the French Republic, Raymond Poincaré, and the Prime Minister and Minister of Foreign Affairs, René Viviani, who were on a state visit to Russia, would have embarked at Kronstadt and would be unavailable for consultation in St. Petersburg. Neat work!

And then—on July 25, Serbia virtually accepted the demands. Her chief reservations were about Austrian collaboration in suppressing the subversive movement and participation in legal investigations. She would agree to such collaboration as was consistent with international law but could not allow agents of a foreign government to take part in her judicial affairs. She ended by stating

* Conrad, IV, 36.
† Fay, II, 272.

that she would be prepared to submit the question to the International Tribunal at The Hague or to the great powers.

Berchtold, like most others, was astonished by this meekness. As for the German Emperor, his first reaction was: "A great moral victory for Vienna; but with it every reason for war disappears." He did not hold that view long, and on the same day the Austrian ambassador in Berlin telegraphed to Berchtold: "We are urgently advised to act at once and present the world with a *fait accompli*." *

At 3 P.M. on the same day, July 25, actually before the pacific reply was delivered, the Serbian government inadvisedly ordered mobilization. This was playing into Berchtold's hands. The Austro-Hungarian minister quitted Belgrade that evening and at 9.23 P.M. the Emperor ordered the mobilization of the corps required to deal with Serbia to begin on July 28.

The beam has so far been shifted between Vienna, Berlin, and Belgrade. Meanwhile St. Petersburg and Paris had been deeply affected, and London in only slightly less degree. Russia was, to put it briefly, desirous of avoiding war but prepared to fight. France was more pacific than her ally and had no intention of fighting for Serbia, but was ready to fulfill her treaty obligations. Britain was the least committed member of the Triple Entente and therefore rightly the most active in efforts to mediate in the quarrel. The foreign secretary, Sir Edward Grey, worked with all his might to induce Germany to take part. Germany promised that she would, but it is clear that she was disingenuous. If Grey's motto was "mediation," Bethmann-Hollweg's was "localization" of the conflict. In fact, the object of the proposal of "localization" was to keep France and Britain quiet. Germany could afford to stand back longer than other continental powers because her mobilization would be swifter. When Grey thought his proposals were being urged upon Vienna by the good offices of Berlin, Bethmann was assuming the role of mediator without mediating. One responsible German who emerges with a clean slate is Prince Lichnowsky, the ambassador in London. His Emperor hoodwinked him, he said later, and caused him to deceive the British.

In his unceasing and high-minded battle for peace Grey was fettered. The British government was, as the writer who has become the most famous of its members, Winston Churchill, has since

* Schmidt, II, 5.

declared, "a veiled coalition." Grey could not say to Germany that if she attacked France, Britain would go to war, because neither the government nor Parliament would have backed him. The most he could do was to tell Germany not to count on her standing aside. It may be that if he could have spoken out earlier the war would not have occurred. Britain has been reproached on this score. Everyone is entitled to his own opinion, but it is here maintained that in all probability Germany would not have been deterred. What enabled Grey to act and carry the government with him—though even then there were resignations—was Germany's determination to violate the neutrality of Belgium, guaranteed by herself as well as by other great powers.

The Entente had other embarrassments during the negotiations. Britain faced an astoundingly ugly situation in Ireland, which had looked like bursting out into civil war; Russia was worried by angry strikes; France was dangerously convulsed—trivial though the business should have been—by the trial of Madame Caillaux, wife of a minister, for the murder of a newspaper editor, and her scandalous acquittal.

Now for the sequence of action, as apart from debate and correspondence.

On July 26 the British fleets in home waters, after a normal test mobilization and exercises, were ordered not to disperse. On the same day the German High Seas Fleet was ordered home from a cruise off the Norwegian coast. The Austrian rupture with Serbia and partial mobilization have been mentioned. In consequence, Russia ordered partial mobilization, on the Austrian frontier, on the twenty-ninth, and on the thirtieth general mobilization. Austria followed suit next day. Germany then moved, ostensibly in favor of her "brilliant second," with an ultimatum to Russia, requiring her to demobilize within twelve hours. The demand was disregarded, and Germany issued a declaration of war on August 1.

Earlier, on July 31, Germany had launched another ultimatum, demanding of France a definite statement whether or not she would remain neutral in a Russo-German war. Should the French reply be favorable—a remote contingency—the ambassador, Baron von Shoen, had been instructed to demand the handing over, as a pledge, of the fortresses of Toul and Verdun. Germany knew that no French government could agree to that; she meant it to be war either way. On August 1 France replied that she would consult her own interests.

That afternoon France and Germany ordered mobilization almost simultaneously. Germany's declaration of war followed on August 3.

During the night of August 1, in breach of treaty, German troops entered Luxembourg to seize the railways, needed for the invasion of Belgium. On the second, Germany demanded from Belgium free passage for her troops, dragging in as excuse lying rubbish alleging that France intended to violate Belgian neutrality. The Belgian reply was magnificent. For the best part of half a century phrases from it have rung out.

> This note has made a deep and painful impression upon the King's Government.... Belgium has always been faithful to her international obligations; she has accomplished her duties in a spirit of loyal impartiality.... Were the Belgian Government to accept the propositions conveyed to it, it would be sacrificing the nation's honour and betraying its engagements to Europe.*

On the afternoon of August 4 Grey sent the German government an ultimatum on Belgium. Now it was that Bethmann used, to Sir Edward Goschen, the British ambassador, the famous words "scrap of paper" with reference to the solemn engagement of Britain, France, Prussia, Austria, and Russia to maintain Belgian neutrality. War followed at midnight.

Italy declared that the quarrel did not come within the terms of the Triple Alliance and declared her neutrality. Rumania followed suit. An ironic anticlimax saw Austria, the starting point of the trouble, pushed by Germany into war with Russia as late as August 6. Conrad was still worrying about those mobilization tables, asking that the whistle should not blow till he was ready.

* Schmitt, II, 390.

Chapter II

PLANS—ARMIES—LEADERS

Now commanders and staffs had taken over from diplomatists and foreign ministries. Every belligerent had its plan. The war plan is as important a job for a general staff as the raising and training of its forces and the study of those of other nations. It would go over the plan year by year in the light of changing circumstances. Thus the French had reached Plan XVII, the seventeenth variation. In Germany Waldersee had planned to knock out Russia first; Schlieffen had planned to knock out France first; and the younger Moltke had modified Schlieffen's plan. Staff officers followed politics closely. "Foreign Office says X-land isn't as reliable as we thought. Flirting with Y-land." "Is she, by God? I wouldn't put it past her. And, by the same token, Z-land looks more likely to come in on the wrong side. Well, suppose we—"

The outstanding plan was that of Germany. It was the work of many men, of whom one, Count Schlieffen, had been something like a genius: outstanding by bold and yet objective thought, by quick mobilization and deployment, and by the lack of scruple which founded it on the violation of Belgian neutrality. The design would have been impossible but for this feature. Behind the French frontier with Germany was a chain of fortresses, and between them the French field armies would be thick on the ground. Head-on attack looked unpromising. Schlieffen's master plan was to concentrate his main strength on the right wing, wheel through Belgium and the Dutch province of Maastricht—the south-jutting strip which the jargon of the strategists called "the Limburg appendix"—swing west of Paris and then southeast, to drive the French into neutral Switzerland or into the arms of the German armies in Lorraine.

Schlieffen's successor Moltke made certain changes. He cut out the invasion of Holland, so leaving himself with one fewer enemy to fight and the use of neutral Dutch ports in case of a British naval blockade. He didn't, as often alleged, reduce the strength of the marching right wing, but he reinforced that of the left. Now, he hoped, the left would also be able to advance as the left arm of a pair of pincers in which the French would be caught. He had borrowed this notion from an afterthought which had come to Schlieffen, who had been reading and writing about Hannibal's great victory of envelopment at Cannae.*

Against Russia, German policy was to stand on the defensive to start with. Only one out of eight armies was allotted to the eastern front, where the Austrians would have to bear the main responsibility. That was rather worrying, but, after all, you had to take risks somewhere and this was not all that great. In six weeks France would be routed and German reinforcements would stream eastward—at least, assuming all went well.

The French, pledged not to violate the integrity of Belgium, had to mold their plan on what they supposed the German to be. They had got it nearly correct, but unfortunately for themselves had not expected the German wheel to extend beyond the Meuse. As the German columns moved westward the French would strike northward and smash them. It was to be as simple as that. The British, who could send only a very small contingent to start with, merely agreed to take their place on the French left.

The Austrians hoped to crush Serbia before Russia intervened in strength. At least one would have expected Austria to stand on the defensive against Russia while the great Schlieffen drama was performed at top speed in the west. But Conrad was a thruster and Austria was, at this time, a very loyal ally. When one thinks it over one realizes that she owed Germany a pretty big debt from the diplomatic phase. Austria would advance northeastward through Galicia against that tempting objective, the great salient of Russian Poland, jutting westward between East Prussia and the Carpathians. Conrad, the real commander in chief, though nominally chief of staff to the Archduke Frederick, had a promise that the German army in East Prussia would simultaneously strike southeastward, but it lacked the strength and got no instructions to this end.

* Ritter, p. 75. See also Kessel, p. 15. He condemns the charge that Moltke "watered down" the plan.

Russia also intended to use the Polish salient. In the north, two armies, one striking north from Poland, the other west, were to envelop the Germans in East Prussia. In the south the salient was to play a similar part in the envelopment of the Austrians north of the Carpathians.

Belgium's aims were purely defensive. The Belgian field army planned to fall back into the fortress of Antwerp, unless the French were successful enough to enable it to attack the enemy with a good prospect of success. The Serbians likewise prepared to fight on defensive lines, but they were roughhewn, vigorous men who could be relied on for a hearty counteroffensive if they saw the slightest glint of a chance.

Naval plans could not be cut and dried like plans for land warfare. Britain undertook operations in the North Sea, for which purpose the Grand Fleet was based on Scapa Flow in the Orkney Islands. The Royal Navy adopted the principle of "distant" blockade from necessity, not choice. The submarine made it much too dangerous to cruise off the enemy's ports in the style of St. Vincent and Nelson. Britain also undertook commerce protection in the Atlantic. The Mediterranean was in the main the responsibility of the French, though Britain had a battle cruiser squadron in these waters. Defense of the Straits of Dover was shared.

The size of the hosts marching to battle was colossal. Take first the opposing forces together. They mustered 335 infantry divisions, call it from five to five and a half million men. Add about fifty cavalry divisions, corps and army troops, and odds and ends, to bring the figure to well over six millions. Garrisons of fortresses did not march to war, but they counted. Then there were the recruits in depots; thousands of drill sergeants were barking and bellowing all over Europe. Naval strengths are less easy to estimate because they are normally counted in ships, not men, but they must have amounted to a good half million. And yet virtually every belligerent was to expand its forces; some, like Britain, enormously. Japan was to enter the war within a few days, and Turkey within three months.

The biggest army was the Russian, with 114 infantry divisions. This large force, however, lacked leadership; only a small proportion of the officers were good and some were ludicrously bad. The rank and file were largely illiterate and could hardly execute the simplest maneuver. They were, however, brave and hardy.

The French mustered sixty-two divisions. All except the reserve divisions, which were badly disciplined and shaky, and a few from the south, were first-class troops, intelligent and skilled in the use of ground. A disastrous doctrine had, however, been spread among them. It was a sort of fanaticism, a veritable *mystique* of the offensive. Colonel de Grandmaison, a gaunt Peter the Hermit with flaming eyes, preached the new crusade: "For the attack only two things are necessary: to know where the enemy is and to decide what to do. What the enemy intends to do is of no consequence."

Artillery support was hardly taken into account by this high-minded and selfless but crack-brained seer. It is impossible to calculate how many men were sent to their deaths through his agency, but the roll must have been a long one. His seniors who allowed him to preach must share the responsibility.

The British would have been the best of the lot on the Entente side if there had been enough of them. Military critics talk airily of the superiority of small professional *armées d'élite* over "armed conscript hordes." Very good; but in the first place, the main enemy had a magnificent army, and in the second, small armies feel losses more sharply than big. *Armées d'élite* would be invincible if wars were fought without casualties. Things being what they are, *armées d'élite* are unlikely to remain so long. To begin with, Britain could send to France only the expeditionary force of six divisions created by the able secretary of state, Richard Burdon Haldane.

Of the two small allies Belgium had six not very well-trained divisions. Serbia had the equivalent of eleven, some of them one might say armed off the scrap heap. In their own rugged land these equally rugged troops, who had emerged from two victorious wars, were very formidable.

Germany put into the field eighty-seven divisions. Hers was a peace-trained army, but a very efficient one. German troops had as much bite as French in attack and were just a fraction—but a fraction that counted—steadier in defense. They were wedded as firmly to the offensive, but they had no raving Colonel de Grandmaison in their outfit.

Austria-Hungary, with forty-nine divisions, was marked with a note of interrogation by friend and foe. Some ten nationalities marched in her armies, and thousands of their underofficers knew no German but for eighty words of command. The Czechs were disaffected; the Serbo-Croats were ranged against their own countrymen—but, it must be added, made no bones about shooting them down in the earlier phases. Officers were apt to be easy-going and insouciant. The army—by comparison with Germany's and Austria-Hungary's own resources—had been starved. Yet the best Austrian formations were excellent.

Cavalry strength varied between about one cavalry division to three infantry in the Russian army and one to eight in the German. A sentimental outlook on cavalry, together with the social prestige of cavalry officers, did much to exaggerate its role, which was very limited in the west after the first few months. Yet it was useful on the plains of Russia and ended triumphantly in Palestine.

The richer belligerents had good modern field artillery. The French 75mm. gun had a wonderful reputation and the highest rate of fire of any, distinctly higher than that of the British 18-pounder, though the latter was slightly harder-hitting. In modernized armies like the French, British, and German, and to some extent the Austrian, there were in principle three transport echelons: the rearmost, which drew food, ammunition and stores from the railhead, of motor-vehicles, the other two of vehicles drawn by horses or mules. It was a war of horses. Man had from remotest times taken his "best friends" to war, but had seldom slaughtered them on such a scale.

Counting of battleships depends on which ships already launched and nearly completed are to be included. For practical purposes we may put the Royal Navy at twenty-four modern battleships, the German Navy at seventeen, the French at six, and the Italian at three. The air forces were very small and, but for a few reconnaissance reports, did not influence the war in its first stages. It is the naked truth, though hard to realize, that the armament of an "airplane" or "machine"—never an "aircraft" in those days—was a rifle, perhaps even a revolver.

Hardly any of the chief commanders of these legions survived the war in high command. They were cast, like horses, for age or unsoundness; occasionally one would have to go for an offense not committed by horses, that of talking out of turn.

The best strategist at the outset, probably of the war, was Conrad von Hötzendorf, later raised to the rank of field marshal. A man of sixty-one, vigorous and farseeing, his schemes were often brilliant. Alas for him, the instrument in his hands did not match his brain in strength and vigor! The *Kaiserliche und Königliche Armee* was too brittle for the calls he made upon it. The Germans often founded their plans for the eastern theater of war upon his.

Next must come the French commander in chief, General Joffre —"Papa Joffre" to admirers. A big man, carrying a big paunch, Joffre was, despite his weight, immensely strong physically but intellectually past his best. That best had been high when he was a young engineer officer. He was generally placid, his critics said bovine. His mind moved slowly and seemed to miss a lot altogether, but when it reached essentials it produced a great deal of common sense. He was never perturbed and he possessed that combination of courage and stamina that the English prizefighters of bare-knuckle days called "bottom."

The German chief of the general staff and virtual commander in chief, Helmuth von Moltke, lived and rose on the ladder of a great name, that of his famous uncle, and, what was worse, knew that he was unworthy of it. The younger Moltke was something of an intellectual and professionally competent, not a brainless courtier, as often alleged. He was, however, sixty-six, rather old for war— even with a strong constitution, and that he did not have. He was a notably bad rider, enough to damn any general in those days of the cult of horsemanship. This was silly: Turenne had been a timid rider; Stonewall Jackson's seat had been incredibly awkward; and anyhow a car was by now a commander in chief's means of transport. Still, it is disquieting to see the man destined to command in war taking tosses on maneuvers. Moltke lacked confidence in himself in an office chair as well as in the saddle. He did not last long.

The Russian commander in chief, the Grand Duke Nicholas, is something of an enigma. We know that he was patriotic and devoted to his profession, that he was popular in the army, and that he was credited with a good military mind. We are, however, confronted by the fact that his control was always loose and that he failed consistently to coordinate the movements and actions of his senior subordinates. It is difficult to rate him highly, beyond acknowledging that he was a man of character.

Field Marshal Sir John French, the British commander in chief, born in the same year as Conrad and Joffre, had not weathered as well as either. He was a good commander, but not what his countrymen called an "educated" soldier. A far more remarkable character was one of his two corps commanders, General Sir Douglas Haig, nine years his junior. There will be much more to be said about him.

One leader of a little army deserves a place among these sketches. The Serbian *voivode* (marshal) Putnik was to prove, like Marshal Saxe and the Swedish Torstensson, that spirit and ability may overcome even the disability of crippling ill health. Putnik had established a brilliant reputation in the two Balkan wars. On the eve of the world war he was under medical treatment in Austria, his own country's doctors not being notable for their skill. The Austrians arrested him during the crisis and then very honorably put him on a train for home—honorably but not prudently. Putnik conducted the campaigns of 1914 from a superheated room, which he quitted as seldom as possible. Inside that room he was more formidable than many a mediocrity in the pink of condition dutifully visiting his troops in all weathers.

Four admirals only will be mentioned at this stage. The commander in chief of the Grand Fleet was Admiral Sir John Jellicoe; the commander of the First Battle Cruiser Squadron in home waters Vice-Admiral Sir David Beatty. Twelve years separated them, and Beatty at forty-three was held to be absurdly young for his post. Yet in 1916 he was to succeed Jellicoe in command of the Grand Fleet. Jellicoe was a man of character, but not outwardly striking. He was a profound student of naval tactics and strategy and a good organizer. He created trust rather than inspiration. Beatty was of a very different type. He was wealthy, devoted to sport, and a hard rider in the hunting field. Many seniors and contemporaries thought that he neglected business of the duller kind for sport and social pleasures. Yet the First Lord of the Admiralty, Winston Churchill, did not err in seeing in him flashes of the golden quality of genius or in picking him for his command. Their first German opposite numbers were failures, but Admiral R. Scheer, commander in chief of the High Seas Fleet from January, 1916, and Vice-Admiral F. Hipper, commander of the Cruiser Squadrons, were leaders of a very high standard, notable figures to find in so young a fleet. With inferior forces they had to aim at surprise blows, and the best they could hope for was to weaken the Grand Fleet and get back to port without themselves suffering disaster.

The forces of all the nations involved went to war with good morale. Only Russia had suffered recent defeat, and that in a war in which she had been unable to deploy her full strength, whereas her Japanese foe had done so. No troops knew what they were in for and in some cases they found even their earliest experiences shaking.

No "great war" had taken place for a century and none which cut into the vitals of nations for over forty years. Very few, whether soldiers or civilians, saw, like Edward Grey, a vision of the lamps going out in Europe one by one. Some time later the recently appointed Secretary of State for War, Field Marshal Lord Kitchener, startled his countrymen by talking of a war of three years.

If morale was good throughout, the mood differed. The British regular soldier, Thomas Atkins, thought little about the matter. He knew he could fire his fifteen to eighteen rounds or more a minute and that no one else could. The nations in arms represented national feeling more fully. The French were sober. There were no shouts of "À Berlin!" this time. The German troops and people were far more excited. They were supremely confident and physically superior to the French because Germany had called up a lower proportion of her manpower so that no weaklings were included. That would come. What has already been said about the Austrian army will suggest that its sentiments were mixed. The vast majority of the Russian troops knew only that the little Father was going to war against his enemies, but to them his war was a holy war. The Russian soldier was obedient and uncomplaining. The world took this for granted. Even political students, who were well aware of the unrest and revolutionary violence which had followed the Russo-Japanese War, had no suspicion of the virulence of the poison then engendered, any more than they foresaw the fate of the little Father.

It is an arguable thesis that all war is madness. The First World War is looked on with particular abhorrence by many people because it seems to them to have been waged with unexampled clumsiness and to stand for a picture of slaughter and misery unrelieved by the genius and the drama which make certain other wars interesting. The question of how the war was waged and why it took the form it did will be constantly reviewed in this narrative. Yet, for good or ill, the world of those years witnessed the upsurge of an enthusiasm for ideals, of determination and bravery in face of death and suffering, of generosity of spirit, which may not reappear on so wide a scale. There was something sublime in the endurance of these men. What a man was the battalion runner, carrying messages through the barrage, falling asleep in the mud between tasks! Nor was all human decency stifled by hatred and cruelty. Men did atrocious and abominable things: the terrible treatment of British prisoners of war by the Turks, the murder, rape, and torture in the campaigns between

Austria and Serbia, do not stand alone. Yet prisoners were better treated than in the Second World War. There was little looting in the west, and after the fighting was over the British in their occupation of the Rhineland hardly took a shoe button from the defeated Germans. Would that the same could be said of 1945! It was a gallant and high-hearted generation. The losses suffered in the ranks of its best were a grave loss to the world, and in some parts of it the effects have still not ceased to be felt.

Chapter III

THE CLASH IN THE WEST

THERE was one good reason why hostilities should start earlier in the west than in the east. It has been pointed out that Germany's mobilization would be the speediest in Europe. Regarding the immediate future, there was a still more important factor. On the Belgian frontier Germany had a force of six brigades of all arms, kept at fighting strength in peace just for the job of seizing the Belgian fortress of Liége, which blocked the gap between "the Limburg appendix" of Holland * and the Forest of the Ardennes and formed a bottleneck for the railways. There these troops had been stationed for no other purpose than that of raping a small, inoffensive state, in pledge of whose integrity Germany, like Britain, had signed a "scrap of paper." Such was the penalty for living behind a frontier conterminous with that of imperial Germany. This was why Germany began hostilities against Belgium on August 4 before any others took place in the west, or indeed in Europe, apart from a bombardment of Belgrade by the Austrian Danube flotilla starting on July 29.

The clutching hands were rapped. A night attack on August 5 failed to take a single one of the forts which ringed Liége, and collapsed with heavy loss. Major General Erich Ludendorff then appeared on the scene. He was a thick, undistinguished-looking officer, with something of the air of a middle-aged quartermaster sergeant beginning to go to seed, but with a very good brain. He had felt that something would go wrong—he had that sort of military sensitivity, strangely belying his appearance. He rallied fleeing troops, laid hands on one brigade, led it in the dark between forts, entered Liége itself, and induced the garrison to surrender. Still, there could be no

* See p. 32.

general advance till the forts had been dealt with by the heaviest howitzers. The last held out until August 16, and the German right wing had penetrated only ten miles deep by then. The great movement may be said to have started on August 18. Here and to the southwest at Namur the Belgians had made a magnificent contribution. However, the field army, apart from giving valuable temporary aid to the fortress troops at Liége and Namur, was not heavily committed by King Albert, only too conscious of its weaknesses. It fell back into the fortress of Antwerp on the twentieth, and made a brief sortie toward Brussels on the twenty-fourth.

The German staff work was at its best when the advance began. On the extreme right the whole of the First Army under General von Kluck had to brush along the Dutch frontier and defile through the streets of Aachen. Yet neither here nor on the rest of the heavily weighted right wing was there a hitch that mattered. Day and night the columns poured westward, Kluck beginning his wheel to the southwest from the level of Brussels. By September 1, the great wheel was expected to take the German armies to the line Amiens, La Fère, Rethel, Thionville. Despite the resistance of the Belgian fortresses and the intervention of the French, it did so. And though September 1 was the thirty-first day from mobilization, it was only the fifteenth marching day from the frontier. In that time Kluck on the right wing covered roughly 180 miles. The maximum day's march of a cavalry division is said to have been just 30 miles—and the attached Jaeger (light infantry) battalions kept up on foot.

In front of this advancing host fled throngs of refugees, which would have been larger but for the pace of the advance. The internal combustion engine was still young in 1914. In the towns only a few of the well-to-do and a handful of professional people possessed "motors"; in the country practically no peasant farmer had one. The exodus was partly by train but chiefly in horse-drawn vehicles. The most familiar sight was the big farm wagon, moving at a walk, piled high with household goods: beds and mattresses, chairs and tables, among which children were perched, with perhaps a grand-mother in black bonnet dominating all. If the family were large, the younger women and the older children had to walk with the men and the dogs. These people were not the most miserable. The poorest, who were often the oldest, pushed their wretched chattels on hand-carts. This flight from invaders took place on the whole front in 1914, on a small scale in Flanders in 1915, and on four or five occasions in

HOLLAND

Rhine

Scheldt

Maas

BELGIANS

1

Brussels

Maastricht

Lille

Tournai

Aachen

Cologne

Mons

Charleroi

Meuse

Liége

2

Le Cateau

Sambre

Namur

B.E.F.

Dinant

3

Amiens

Guise

LUXEMBOURG

La Fere

4

Moselle

Oise

Soissons

5

Rethel

Meuse

Reims

Verdun

Thionville

Marne

4

Metz

5

Paris

3

Morhange

2

Nancy

Toul

GERMAN OFFENSIVE

1

Meurthe

6

1914

Épinal

1

Scale of Miles

0 10 20 30 40 50

Langres

7

Saône

Allies

Germans

Dijon

Besançon

Fortresses

SWITZERLAND

1918. The Belgian exodus had as one result the provision of recruits without which the army would have melted away.

While this was going on the French did not stand idle, but their intervention was strangely feeble to start with. Moltke—the great one, not the nephew who now enjoyed his brief period of fame and triumph as his armies swept forward—once remarked that when a commander did not know what to do he ordered a reconnaissance in force, a probe or feeler to find out what the other side was doing. It would perhaps be unfair to say that Joffre did not know what he was doing, but his reconnaissance in force on the extreme right, into Alsace, was a meaningless advance and withdrawal. On September 11 the French attempted a real invasion, with six divisions. Mulhouse was taken but was recovered by the Germans.

On the fourteenth Joffre set his plan in motion. As previously stated, it was to strike at the German columns from the south. It was not an easy offensive to mount—the Germans had had forty-three years to make it difficult. Since Lorraine had been ceded to them, together with Alsace, after their victory in the war of 1870, they had modernized the fortresses of Metz and Thionville. The First French Army on the right wing lay southeast of the Metz ring of forts, the Second Army to the south, and the other three west and northwest, up to the Belgian frontier south of Maubeuge. In order to strike at the German host wheeling through Belgium the French forces had to be split, the two right-wing armies moving east of Metz, the others to the west. The Second French Army in particular had a risky task. It had to march past and expose its left to the fortress, moving through country broken by abrupt wooded hills, many streams, and occasional lakes and marshes, blind country well suited to an ambush or a surprise counterstroke. Moreover—though this the French could not know till they had moved—the German Sixth Army had been ordered to give way to start with. Later on the German left wing was to strike back. It was, in fact, to form the short arm of the pincers in which the French were to be enveloped.*

On August 14 the French started, crossing the frontier in face of trifling opposition. It was a thrilling moment. To countless Frenchmen the soil of Alsace-Lorraine, wrenched from France in her last war with Germany, was sacred, a symbol of great days. The troops advanced in high spirits. Before they had moved very far, however,

* See p. 33.

they came under damaging artillery fire, some of it from guns and howitzers of longer range and greater weight than their own. The movement was not rapid.

The First Army, which had a long line of frontier to cover to the south, moved very cautiously and employed only its left. General de Castelnau's Second Army showed more enterprise, especially the Twentieth Army Corps on the left under the orders of General Foch. He had been commandant of the School of War and was regarded as one of the leading lights of the French army, but had been blocked in promotion as a "clerical" after the Dreyfus case and was now sixty-two years of age. He was a man of ardent spirit and unflinching will, but inclined to impetuosity and touched by the headlong, head-down tactical doctrine of Colonel de Grandmaison, though not nearly as much as has been alleged. It need hardly be said that his corps was well ahead when the German commander in front of him, Crown Prince Rupprecht of Bavaria, struck back at Morhange on August 20.

The punch was a hard one, and the Twentieth Corps was rocked on its feet. It was, however, not a grave setback, though a nasty one, where Foch was concerned. True to type, he was contemplating a counterattack when he received orders to fall back. "If ever I was tempted to disobey, it is today," he said to his chief of staff. "You don't know what is happening to the neighboring corps," Colonel Duchêne answered.*

He was soon to find out. The two corps in the center and on the right had been worse mauled than his and were shaken. Their southern troops had not the stability of his men of the Meuse. The two French armies fell back towards the frontier. The German pursuit was slack.

On August 21, the day after the German counteroffensive against the two right-wing French armies, two more, the Third and Fourth, began their advance northward on the westward side of the Metz-Thionville fortifications. Their mission was to strike the marching columns of the enemy in flank, cut through them, and rout them. It was what Napoleon had done to Blücher in the Campaign of France in 1814. This time matters did not go the same way. What happened was a series of clashes on August 22 between forces of the German Fourth and Fifth Armies and the French Third and Fourth: not one battle but actions amounting to one, named Virton, Ethe, Rossignol, and Neufchâteau, all unhappy for the French.

* Falls, *Marshal Foch*, p. 49.

The French divisions taking part in the first three and the single mixed brigade at Neufchâteau behaved magnificently. The last-named, marines of the highest quality, fought with almost fantastic heroism against heavy odds. Its orders were "to attack the enemy wherever met." Like the other columns, it advanced into the Ardennes, thickly wooded, poor in communications—especially lateral, so that touch with neighbors was difficult, at times impossible—broken with hills and valleys creating dangerous defiles. Long-range reconnaissance by Sordet's Cavalry Corps was generally blocked by better-armed German cavalry and cyclists, and where news got through it filtered down too late. For close tactical reconnaissance the attached cavalry was hopelessly inadequate—the brigade marching on Neufchâteau had twenty-five reservists mounted on soft requisitioned horses. Consequently each French column, thinking it had only German mounted troops in front of it, bumped into strong German forces of all arms, with calamitous results. Had the Germans not been also to a great extent in the dark, the defeat of the French would have been crushing. The Germans fought very cautiously but stoutly. They missed fine opportunities, but successfully covered their march.

It was ferocious fighting in great heat, more trying, because stuffier, in the woodlands than in the sun. In many cases it came to revolvers and bayonets. At Ethe, French field guns swept the street, while the Germans rooted themselves in the western end, some three hundred yards from the muzzles.* At one moment at Neufchâteau about a hundred French survivors, lying at ten-yard intervals on a thousand-yard front, were all that faced five German battalions.† It ended inevitably in a general French retreat. Yet the Germans acknowledged that they had been in a critical situation, threatening the whole of their wheeling wing.

The effect was unpleasant for the next French army, the Fifth, which had advanced to the south bank of the Sambre facing Charleroi. What was even more so was the fact that this army was the French left wing, with only a handful of troops to the west and north, and that the German wheel appeared to be well outside its flank. General Lanrezac, its commander, was more than a little worried about his position.

The commander of the German First Army on the right, which

* Grasset, *Ethe*, p. 87.
† Grasset, *Neufchâteau*, p. 45.

had the longest distance to cover and the biggest task, was General von Kluck, a sour, bad-tempered old soldier of sixty-eight, but a thruster. His information was scanty. He thought he had a wonderful chance to outflank the French. He knew the British Expeditionary Force had landed, but, as he approached Mons, believed it to be at Tournai, thirty miles northwest. Actually it lay in his path.

At the moment it numbered only four of its six divisions. Another was on its way and the sixth had been held up in England by brief and needless anxiety about a German invasion. The B.E.F. had crossed, mainly to Havre, under the protection of the Royal Navy. The German navy had made no attempt to interfere with its passage; in fact it had been told by Moltke that he did not particularly want it stopped and would prefer to deal with so small a force straight away and put it into the same bag as the French in the great victory that was forthcoming.

The British had a fair amount of protection behind the Mons-Condé Canal but could not prevent the enemy's crossing this obstacle east of Mons because the French were somewhat in rear and barely in touch, so that the British right flank had to be refused. Hastily the force took up position amid the engine-house chimneys, black shale heaps, and pit headgears of a vast coalfield. Squadrons and regiments of the cavalry division maneuvered in front, charging the German cavalry when they saw a chance and bringing in news of the German advance. Battery commanders hunted desperately for a field of fire. One battery was hoisted onto a knoll called the Bois La Haut, a mile southeast of Mons, with a commanding view, but an ugly spot to get caught in. It was August 23, a Sunday. The bells rang and people went to church, ignorant of what was coming.

Kluck could have outflanked the British, and with his superior numbers it might have been disastrous for them if he had. Unluckily for him, he had been placed under the Second Army commander, General von Bülow, and that nervous old man ordered him to keep close touch and absolutely forbade him to swing wide. So Kluck came at the British like a bull, head down.

The Germans tried the standard tactics: to build up a strong firing line and then rush their enemy. Instead, something they had never dreamed of hit unit after unit. The leading ones were shot to tatters. The survivors could not understand it. For long they believed they had faced a "machine-gun army," but in fact the British, like themselves, had only two machine guns per battalion. It was musketry, rapid fire such as no mass conscript army could produce. Let a German tell the story in his own words: "The rushes became shorter, and finally the whole advance came to a stop.... With bloody losses the attack came gradually to an end." *

However, German determination had pushed superior numbers to pretty close quarters and the British had suffered loss in a salient formed by a loop in the canal north of Mons. It was decided to withdraw by night to a position two and a half miles south of the town. At midnight, however, Sir John French learned from General Lanrezac that he had ordered a retreat by his Fifth Army to begin in the small hours of April 24. He had been heavily engaged all day; he had to face danger from the east and the north simultaneously; and the withdrawal from the Ardennes of the armies on his right made his position still uglier. Sir John French could only issue similar orders. There could be no question of fighting on the second position. So the last of the French armies to hold its ground was now to fall back, and with it the little B.E.F. And it would be a long retreat.

The B.E.F. disengaged itself and drew off without the loss of a gun. The troops were already weary and were worried by a retirement which they could not understand. Most of them were convinced that they had been victorious. The French Fifth Army also drew off in fairly good shape, though not as good. Kluck's and Bülow's First and Second Armies followed hard on their heels. Behind the British lay the big Forest of Mormal. The two corps split to pass on either side of it, ill-advisedly, because in fact the roads through it would have been adequate to take the First Corps. Against the isolated Second Corps Kluck pressed his pursuit so hard that its commander, General Sir Horace Smith-Dorrien, decided to halt and fight a rear-guard action at Le Cateau, thirty miles south-southwest of Mons, on August 26. He had now been joined by the Fourth Division from England.

This was a hotter and for the British a more costly affair than Mons. Again British musketry punished the Germans heavily, but they used their artillery to far better effect than at Mons. The British succeeded in holding them off and withdrawing in generally good order, and there was no serious pursuit. The Germans, however, took thirty-eight guns from batteries which had sacrificed themselves to cover the retreat.

The French armies had suffered both tactical and strategic defeat.

* Edmonds, *Short History*, p. 29.

That is to say, they had in almost every case been beaten when they clashed with the Germans, and the Germans had exploited these tactical victories to keep their great strategic plan alive, so far practically unaffected by the presence of the French armies in the field. If that plan could be maintained, the virtual destruction of the French was certain. Yet their situation, perilous and agonizing as it was, was not as hopeless as it looked on the map. All of the tactical victories on which the German strategic success was based had fallen short of being disastrous in themselves. Moltke realized this. Great victories, he remarked, were signalized by great hauls of prisoners and guns. Where were the prisoners and guns? In truth, their numbers had no relation to the progress made by the German armies. If the French spirit had been broken, then indeed all was well. The prisoners and guns would come in soon enough. Yet though the French were in some cases shaken, there were no signs of general demoralization. They were indeed fighting a good rear-guard action in the center and counterattacking in Lorraine. Their armies had lost heavily, but, if their morale survived, they had for practical purposes to be reckoned as intact. The Germans were not. The right wing had had to detach two corps to mask the Belgians in the fortress of Antwerp. Worse still, news of a defeat suffered at the hands of the Russians induced Moltke to order two corps to pull out and move to the eastern front. He maintained this order even when he learned that the situation had been reversed and that a great victory had been won in East Prussia. This was one of the fatal decisions of the war.

Joffre was in fact seeking time and room for regrouping. His slow mind was so far unable to keep up with events, but he had, on the day of the action of Le Cateau, created a new army on his left wing to strike at the German right flank, from the region of Amiens. This plan fell through, but was rebuilt farther in the rear, with Paris substituted for Amiens. He also took one small but admirable measure to ease the danger in which the British stood. On August 29, the French Fifth Army turned about and hit Bülow's Second Army hard in the flank in the Battle of Guise, then cleverly disengaged itself and slipped away. The effect was to make Bülow halt for two days and shout for aid from Kluck.

Still the retreat went on. The spectacle caused astonishment and depression far and wide. In Britain the public, searching maps for unfamiliar names, could scarcely credit the reports. Could the French pull themselves together, and if so when? Could Paris be saved? In some cases, though few, similar doubts had affected senior commanders. The men in the ranks were probably too weary to think out the matter. The heat, the dust, the eternal marching, the shortness of the halts, the proportion of the troops who had to cover their sleeping comrades during these halts, and some stiff rear-guard actions constituted a fearful strain. The Germans suffered too, but there is a great difference between the exertions of pursuing and retreating armies. For Bülow, the only bad consequence of giving his men an extra hour in billets was that the pursuit slackened by that much. For Sir John French it might involve being overrun and scattered to the winds.

The infantry marched in a daze caused by fatigue and lack of sleep. Even mounted men slept in their saddles and often crashed to the ground. French was so appalled by the state of his troops that he wanted to withdraw them from the front for reorganization and was stopped from doing so only by a visit from the Secretary of State for War, Lord Kitchener, who strongly forbade anything of the sort. And now the Germans were entering the very heart of France, that vital, lovely, and almost sacred region where so many rivers converge toward Paris.

Meanwhile affairs were going better for the French right wing. We left it falling back across the frontier. Beyond that, between the fortresses of Epinal and Toul, ran an unfortified gap known as the Trouée de Charmes, forty miles along the valley of the Moselle. Prince Rupprecht made for this opening. Now the Germans displayed the most astonishing indecision and the most atrocious staff work, which must at least in part be attributed to the breakdown for which Moltke was heading. In turn Rupprecht was ordered to strike south toward Epinal, west into the Trouée de Charmes, and northwest against the fortified Grand Couronné of Nancy. The first and second efforts were gradually bogged; the attempts to take the Grand Couronné broke down completely—and this though its defender, Castelnau, was sending troops away toward Paris. To the east the door had been slammed in the faces of the Germans. Up at Verdun the new commander of the Third Army, General Sarrail, clung to the fortress and hit the flank of the German Crown Prince when he tried to pass it. The question the Germans had been asking themselves, whether the French were still fighting fit and in fighting mood, was answered.

The general comment on this fast-moving campaign must be that, on the whole, German staff work and tactics had been superior to French, but that, though the Germans reacted skillfully to the kind of accidents they expected, they blundered in face of the unexpected. This tendency was to be observed also in early September. It would be unfair not to mention one handicap, which the older at least will easily recognize. Wireless was in its infancy, unreliable, and not even as effective as later in the war. Long-distance telephony was uncertain. The speed of the advance made it difficult to maintain cable communication, and in any case to make a call without interruption or inability to hear on one side or the other over a distance of two hundred miles—roughly that, as the cable ran, between Moltke and his right wing on the eve of the Battle of the Marne—was in those days something of a feat.

Yet, when all is said and done, most of the responsibility must fall on Moltke. He did not make use enough of staff officers in cars. He carried to extreme the doctrine of his famous uncle that army commanders should be given the freest possible hand—"an élite let loose." It did not pay in 1914 as it had in 1870.

Chapter IV

MIXED FORTUNES IN THE EAST

THE Western Front is left at a moment when a critical decision had been made certain by what had already happened, though this had not included anything which could be called a great battle. On the Eastern Front the early fighting was bloodier and on a bigger scale.

On July 11, 1914, seventeen days before the assassination of the Archduke, he had entertained at his Bohemian palace of Konopic the German Emperor, accompanied by Moltke and the head of the Admiralty, Admiral von Tirpitz. There, amid the world-famous rose gardens, then at their best, a conference had been held. After that was over Moltke and Conrad von Hötzendorf went off to Carlsbad, where the Germans took baths. A less spectacular but more business-like conference was held between these two. Moltke dotted i's and crossed t's of German strategy in a war on two fronts.

Germany must first send the bulk of her army against the French. Moltke hoped to overwhelm them in six weeks. Then a strong section of the German army would be sent east. Till then Austria-Hungary, possibly with the support of Rumania—but that, as we know, had not been obtained *—would have to bear the main weight of the Russian attack.

Conrad von Hötzendorf thus knew what was in store for him, though he did later send Moltke a plea not to leave him too long *in der Tinte* (literally "in the ink," but it may be translated "in a nasty mess"). There was, however, a prospect that the Germans might find themselves in a worse mess than the Austrians in this theater. The commander of the German Eighth Army in East Prussia, General von

* See p. 31.

Prittwitz, had nine divisions, whereas it was estimated that the Russians could bring twenty-two against him. Yet at the last moment he was bidden to take the offensive. The Russians had the same intention where he was concerned and also meant to attack the main Austrian armies. Conrad was equally determined to attack the Russians. Everyone was offensively minded.

We must not, however, forget what had started the war. The chastisement of Serbia and her little Montenegrin ally was a part of the Austrian program which could not be neglected. Here the planners had got themselves into a curious muddle. They had planned the campaign against Serbia as though it were an isolated affair, or at all events as if it could be disposed of before the Russians came on in strength into Galicia, where roads and railways alike were bad and sparse. The Russians, however, had sprung one surprise, an accelerated mobilization, and they marched light. It became clear that they were coming on quicker than Conrad had allowed for and that he would have to milk the Serbian front. This was a serious matter because the milking had to be done in the Austrian Second Army standing on the Save west of Belgrade, and this was the best army, with the best communications. It was split in two, and half was sent to Galicia. So the main attack had to be carried out by the two small armies facing east on the Drina.

The Serbians had a far worse risk to face. If Bulgaria, a country with which they were on bad terms, came in against them, there was no hope for them. They would be assaulted simultaneously from west, north and east, and annihilated. Even if Bulgaria kept quiet they had to scrape up troops to watch her. In actual numbers Austrians and Serbians were similar in strength, about 180,000 rifles on either side, not counting Serbia's Montenegrin allies. The Serbian commander in chief has already been named, the *voivode* Putnik. The Austrian was the governor of Bosnia, General Potiorek, who had not greatly distinguished himself by his security measures during Francis Ferdinand's visit to Sarajevo.

On August 12 the Austrians crossed the Drina, so to speak whip in hand, to make Serbia realize that an archduke's murder had to be paid for. But, to the astonishment of the world, there was no time to use the whip. The Serbians threw themselves on their foes and drove them back over the river.

Now began a series of fierce blows and counterblows. The Serbians got a footing over the Save, but were then held. Potiorek renewed his attacks and established bridgeheads over the Drina. On the thin southern front the Serbians impudently invaded Bosnia, but were thrown out by October 25. Both sides fought furiously and recklessly. Both practiced horrible barbarity. What does it matter who was the first sinner when reprisal followed crime and was followed by counterreprisal *ad infinitum?*

At last Potiorek really got moving. He drove back the Serbians step by step. On the banks of the Kolubara, fifty miles east of the Drina, what appeared to be the decisive battle was fought—and won by the Austrians. No regrouping for Potiorek. He pressed on for the kill. Then Putnik spurred his weary and depressed troops into a counteroffensive.

The result was curious. Victory had kept the Austrians on their feet, though in some cases they had marched the soles off their boots. Now was the moment when they found they could take no more. Physically and spiritually they were finished. Potiorek ordered a retreat and was lucky to have the Austrian monitors to cover his troops as they poured back over the Danube and Save. Not that the Serbians were in any state to press the pursuit. Both sides were fought out and reduced almost to the level of rabbles. The last Austrian soldier crossed the Danube on December 15. The Austrian losses were more than half the number of troops brought in from first to last, 227,000 out of 450,000. The Serbian were about 170,000. Potiorek was relieved of his command and replaced by the handsome and popular Archduke Eugen—an archduke was generally the first remedy that occurred to Vienna when things went wrong. The moral humiliation was almost worse than the physical disaster. It was not to be long before German officers would say, brutally and indeed unfairly: "Allies? Why, we're shackled to a corpse."

We may deal next with East Prussia, where the campaign began a little earlier than that in Poland. The action of the Russians was typical of their best and worst: their best because it showed their generosity of spirit—strange how getting rid of tsarism and introducing all the benefits of Stalinism seems to have been accompanied by a loss of this quality; their worst because it was so careless and amateurish. In answer to the plea of their French allies they came on before they were ready, before they had fully mobilized their transport, which was scanty even on its full establishment. And the northern army under General Rennenkampf moved alone, but for one corps of the southern, because General Samsonov was unable to start. To move alone was a risky business when the theater of operations was split in two by the great barrier of the Masurian Lakes.

However, Rennenkampf started fairly well. He crossed the frontier on August 17, had the better of a combat there, dawdled on a few miles a day, and on the twentieth clashed with the Germans at Gumbinnen. It was a touch-and-go battle. Finally, however, the German corps commanded by Mackensen, one of the most overadvertised generals of the war,* fled in panic. The Russians took 6,000 prisoners.

Samsonov had started to move also by now. But the two Russian armies were not in touch—perhaps because their leaders disliked each other. The German commander, Prittwitz, was a worried man. In the long series of war games played by the general staff one of the solutions to meet the case if things went awry was to retreat behind the Vistula. Prittwitz telephoned to Moltke that this was what he thought he would have to do. Moltke decided that he was not up to his work. The Germans have a fancy for old generals— who admittedly have served them well—and the successor chosen was a retired officer of sixty-seven, Paul von Hindenburg, brother-in-law of the man he was to displace. He was given as staff officer the fashionable one of the moment, Ludendorff, now a major general and wearing the *Pour le Mérite* won at Liége.

Before they had arrived they were at work on a scheme to take advantage of the wide separation of the two Russian armies, of the slowness and caution of Rennenkampf and the impetuosity of Samsonov. The idea was to leave only a screen in front of Rennenkampf's northern army and shift all possible strength southward to fall upon Samsonov's. It was a daring conception because if Rennenkampf followed up his victory at Gumbinnen and came on at even a fair pace he would take the Germans in the rear before they had dealt with Samsonov in front.

In order to support and magnify the prestige of the Hindenburg-Ludendorff combination it was afterward intimated and long believed that they were the joint authors. This thesis was the more easily established because of the general assumption that strategy is a profound mystery only to be conceived by genius. In a case like this and most others it calls for a competent and experienced eye, a bold

---

* He used to boast of his descent from a Highland chieftain, a Mackenzie. When this became unsuitable it was given out that his name was derived from the village of Mackenhausen.

heart, and some nice calculations about how it is to be worked, especially on the administrative or logistic side. Precisely the same idea had come to Lieutenant Colonel Max Hoffmann, chief operations officer of the Eighth Army. He had taken it to Prittwitz, who had approved it. And while Hindenburg and Ludendorff were still in the train the first moves took place. The danger proved less than had been expected when it was found that the Russians were obligingly sending wireless messages, even orders, in clear.*

The plan was to leave only the attached cavalry division facing Rennenkampf and to move three corps, two by road and a third in a wider sweep by rail, via Königsberg and Marienburg, to meet Samsonov. When Hindenburg reached Marienburg, headquarters of the Eighth Army, on August 23, the troops of this corps, commanded by General von François, were detraining near Tannenberg —a wooded hill, not a town—to support the single German corps in the south, which had been facing odds of over six to one. Even now it was a pretty critical situation for the Germans, whose two marching corps had ninety miles to cover. The Russians had the best of it till these two corps suddenly appeared from the north on August 27. Two of Samsonov's corps were hemmed in on the east, north, and west, and Rennenkampf was too far off to help.

It was like herding stock into a corral, and the head cowboy was François. Regardless of his orders to stand fast, he spread out a thin net into which the two Russian corps marched or reeled, too dazed and hungry to fight. He took two-thirds of the 90,000 prisoners taken by August 30. Samsonov went alone into the woods and shot himself.

Now reinforced by the two corps which Moltke had insisted on sending east, Hindenburg turned on Rennenkampf. He tried, but failed, to pin him to the shore. Though there was no envelopment, there was another great success in the Battle of the Masurian Lakes, and by September 15 the Russians had fallen back out of reach, leaving behind them some 30,000 more prisoners.

This was one of the most brilliant campaigns of the war, and will always find a place in the annals of war. It freed East Prussia, inflicted enormous losses on the Russians, and raised German self-confidence in the east. It created from the rugged bulk of Hindenburg a sort of god, a truly Germanic deity, a Wotan. "Well, well," wrote Max Hoffmann in his diary, "up to now, with our inferior numbers, we

* Edmonds, *Short History*, p. 33.

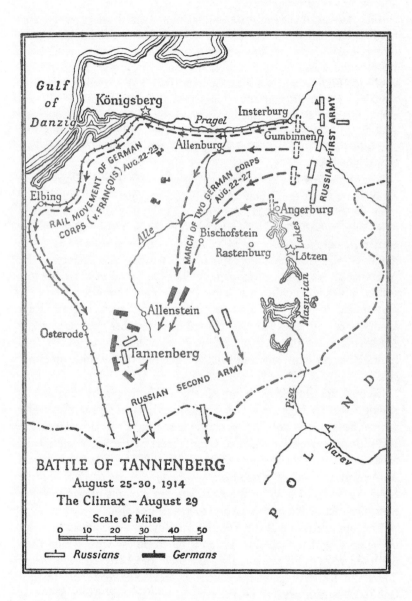

Gulf
of
Danzig

Königsberg

Insterburg

Pragel

RUSSIAN-FIRST ARMY

Allenburg

Gumbinnen

RAIL MOVEMENT OF GERMAN CORPS (v. FRANÇOIS) AUG. 22-23

MARCH OF TWO GERMAN CORPS AUG. 22-27

Elbing

Angerburg

Alle

Bischofstein

Masurian Lakes

Rastenburg

Lötzen

Allenstein

Osterode

Tannenberg

RUSSIAN SECOND ARMY

Pisz

P O L A N D

Narew

BATTLE OF TANNENBERG

August 25-30, 1914

The Climax — August 29

Scale of Miles

0   10   20   30   40   50

⊏⊐ *Russians*   ◼ *Germans*

have defeated about 15 Russian army corps and 8 cavalry divisions, and we are not finished yet."

The Russian main body of four armies formed an army group—the Russians called it a "front," one of the terms handed down by the imperial army to the Communists—under the command of General Ivanov. He was a man of humble origin, living only for his profession, but limited and wanting in initiative. There was at least one very fine soldier in that advancing host, the commander of the left army, General Brusilov, but he was bad-tempered and insubordinate and, typical of the Russian army, the reaction to these faults was petty intrigue, such as omitting his name from reports, which made him wilder still.

The Austrians had three armies, right to left Third, Fourth, and First, apart from the Second which was being gradually transferred from Belgrade to the extreme right. The nominal commander in chief was the Archduke Frederick, but it was the Chief of the General Staff, Conrad von Hötzendorf, who mattered. The force deployed on a frontage of 175 miles, right flank on the Dniester north of Stanislau, left south of Lublin. As had happened in the Ardennes battles in France, neither side knew much about the other. The Russians failed to use their cavalry except to fill gaps between their armies, with the unexpectedly favorable result that the enterprising Austrian cavalry met Russian infantry, who shot its patrols flat and let it gather little information. Aircraft got practically none on either side.

Conrad was thus nearly blind. He started, however, by taking hair-raising risks. He side-slipped his armies northward, without knowing where the Russians stood but actually marching across their front. He also split dangerously his Third Army, directing part of it northward to support the other two and part northeast.* The first battle began on August 23, when the northernmost armies, those of Evert on the Russian side and Dankl on the Austrian, ran straight into each other near Krasnik, which gives its name to a very hot fight.

The opponents made up for their failures in reconnaissance by the energy with which they hit and the stoutness with which they accepted blows. Three days they charged and battered each other. Then the Russians gave the Austrians best and made off toward Lublin, Austrian cavalry on their heels, and leaving 6,000 prisoners

* Conrad, IV, 508.

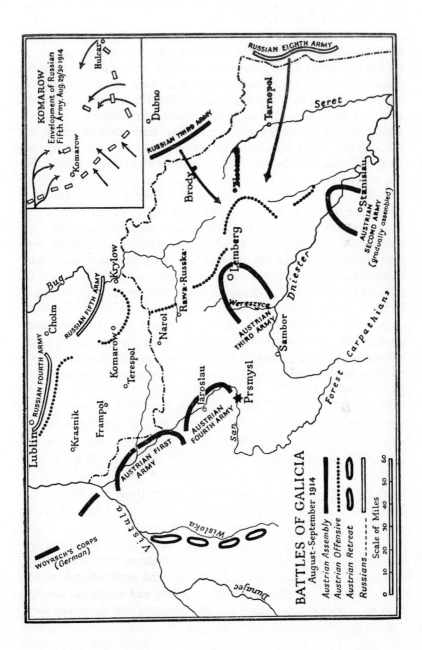

RUSSIAN EIGHTH ARMY

Seret

KOMAROW
Envelopment of Russian
Fifth Army. Aug.29/30 1914

Hulcar

Dubno

°Tarnopol

RUSSIAN THIRD ARMY

Brody

Żł...

AUSTRIAN
SECOND ARMY
(gradually assembled)

°Stanislau

°Lemberg

Dniester

Krylow

Bug

Rawa-Russka

RUSSIAN FIFTH ARMY

Cholm

Wereszyca

AUSTRIAN
THIRD ARMY

Sambor

°Narol

Komarow °

°Terespol

RUSSIAN FOURTH ARMY

°Lublin

Krasnik

Frampol

Forest Carpathians

°Jaroslau

★ Prsmysl

AUSTRIAN
FOURTH ARMY

San

AUSTRIAN FIRST
ARMY

Vistula

WOYRSCH'S CORPS
(German)

Wistoka

Dunajec

BATTLES OF GALICIA
August–September 1914

Austrian Assembly ▬▬▬
Austrian Offensive ●●●●●
Austrian Retreat ◯◯◯
Russians- - - - - -

Scale of Miles
0 10 20 30 40 50 60

behind. Round one to Conrad, though for so able a soldier the victory had a somewhat accidental air about it.

Another army battle started on August 26, when the Austrian Fourth Army under Auffenberg got to grips with the Russian Fifth under Plehve. The first engagement had lasted three days, but this went on for a week. By the end of that time Auffenberg had practically enveloped the Russians opposed to him. He was starting the process of mopping up his victims when evil news and unwelcome orders came from Conrad. The Third Army (General von Brudermann) had suffered a heavy defeat. Auffenberg must bring him aid. To do so he had to loose his grip on Plehve. So the Battle of Komarow was only half an Austrian victory.

Brudermann was unlucky. The Russians had "a man over," and on August 25 he discovered that very heavy Russian columns were bearing down on his small army. On the right these came from Brusilov's Eighth Army, and on the left from Ruszki's Third. On Brudermann's right the Austrian Second Army from the Serbian front was only assembling and could give him little aid to start with. Like Conrad and all the Austrian army commanders, Brudermann was bold to the point of rashness. He paid for it now. He wrung from Conrad leave to attack, did so without concentrating as he was bidden, and was beaten at Zlotchow.*

By the twenty-eighth Conrad's eyes were opened and he realized what trouble his right wing was in. He ordered it back to a north-south line in front of Lemberg, but he had no thought of a further retreat. On the other side Ivanov was still in the dark and thought he was faced by the main Austrian strength in front of Lemberg. His intelligence service must have been deplorable, since by this time he had certainly captured plenty of documents as well as prisoners. He therefore made no attempt to exploit his victory at Zlotchow, but ordered a halt for reorganization. However, the Grand Duke Nicholas, who presumably had a better staff, was certain that Ivanov was wrong and ordered him to resume his advance. The result was another handsome victory for the Russians, when Brusilov and Ruszki broke the Austrian front covering Lemberg on August 30.

Conrad was as buoyant and jaunty as ever. He was planning, not to get away, but to hit the Russians a staggering blow. His program was as follows: Second and Third Armies on the right to stand fast; Auffenberg's Fourth Army to march south from Komarov—where

* Conrad, IV, 516.

he thought Plehve's Russian Fifth Army had been so hard hit that it would be disorganized for some time—and strike the southern Russian armies in flank; then a renewal of the offensive by the Second and Third Armies to smash the Russian left. On paper it was a fine maneuver, as brilliant as that of Tannenberg, but his troops were not German and his communications were not as good as those of the Germans in East Prussia. On the evening of September 1 a Hungarian division and some cavalry north of Lemberg fled in panic and this time the Russians found the gap. Conrad ordered his two right-hand armies back behind the Wereszyca, a northern tributary of the Dniester.

The Grand Duke saw the whole situation quite clearly now, and he thought that the destruction of the Austrian right was at hand. Very heavy close fighting occurred again on September 6. Plehve showed signs of hearty revival by fighting a hard but untidy and inconclusive battle with Auffenberg at Rawa-Russka, while the two southern armies tried to envelop the Austrian Second and Third on the Wereszyca. Once more the indefatigable Conrad ordered a counteroffensive. Ivanov did the same. The two great forces, weary, in some cases shaken, reduced by vast losses, running short of shells, collided along the whole front on September 10. Brusilov, on the Russian left, was driven back twelve miles and records in his memoirs that he was outnumbered two to one, which is far from the truth. The Austrians were indeed outnumbered everywhere. Otherwise neither side had much to show for great efforts and sacrifices.

The Grand Duke Nicholas now prepared to play his ace of trumps. Brusilov and Ruszki on the left wing were ordered to keep the Austrian Second and Third Armies well occupied on the Wereszyca, but not to push them so hard as to make them decide to fall back from the river. Meanwhile the other two Russian armies and the vast mass of Russian cavalry were to sweep behind them. This would be practically the end of the Austrian armies, a very small proportion of which would get away.

It might have come off too, but, staggering as it may sound, Russian wireless messages in clear began on this front also and showed Conrad that he was indeed *in der Tinte*, with Plehve almost in his rear. This habit of sending out top-secret material in clear has been much debated and it has generally been agreed that it was not deliberate treachery but rank carelessness. A third alternative reason, seldom put forward, seems more probable than either: that higher staffs considered lower so stupid that they were unlikely to be able to decode cipher messages or would take so long about it that they would not be in time to act upon them.

It was on the morning of September 11 that Conrad ordered his whole force to fall back to the San, a distance of over sixty miles. It was a symbolic withdrawal. Though the San is not among the greatest of European rivers, no other so clearly marks a boundary. On the west bank the country and the architecture are Western, on the east side Eastern. The Austrians had been driven out of their eastern Polish lands.

Actually they had to go back farther. Hardly had they got behind the San than Conrad learned—more messages in clear!—that Evert from the north was round him. Back he went again and did not finally halt till he had reached the Dunajac on October 3. He was 140 miles west of Lemberg now.

Though many Austrian-formations had been victorious all through, this terrific fighting, followed by a long and trying retreat and much sickness, led to a lowering of Austrian morale, particularly among the soldiers of the subject nations. The troops had given of their best and the disappointment was crushing. Henceforth very great demands had to be made on the German-Austrians, who numbered only 25 per cent of the army, and on first-line Hungarian troops. A second effect was to force the Germans to begin at once a process which was to be developed to a vast extent, that of providing military aid for their allies. And this aid was to be given, not, as had been arranged in Schlieffen's program, to overwhelm the Russians, but simply to hold them. With all his weaknesses—which were, after all, more in his leadership than anywhere else—the Russian soldier had begun well.

Chapter V

THE LOVELY MARNE

THE writings of the sacred book were disregarded. The Schlieffen plan, already tampered with, was now virtually abandoned. It enjoined the German right wing to pass nearly forty miles west of Paris and wheel southeast only when it had crossed the Seine below the city. The headstrong leader on the German right, Alexander von Kluck, did not hesitate to strike out his own path, even if it meant giving up the plan. What were plans, however sacred, to Kluck if he could get his fangs into the French? The French left wing was retreating southward. He would go after it, find its flank, drive it eastward from Paris. To do so he would himself have to march some forty miles east instead of forty miles west of the capital. His colleague Bülow urged him on. "A wheel inwards of the First Army," he wired on August 30, was "urgently desired." And Moltke, who had that day moved forward some eighty miles from Coblenz to Luxembourg—still too far from the vital part of the front—and who was hardly initiating anything himself, agreed. "The movements of the First and Second Armies conform to the intentions of the Supreme Command," he radioed.* As Bülow remarks, Kluck does not seem to have sent in any report about the considerable numbers of French troops who were outside his right flank—that is, to west of him—and at this stage the luckless Moltke probably knew nothing about them. To do him justice, he had more brains than Kluck and would have been more alive to their significance.

General Joffre, the French commander in chief, had set about forming a new army, the Sixth, under General Maunoury. It con-

---

* Koeltz, p. 51. Schlieffen had given some consideration to moving east of Paris.

tained only one high-class division—from Alsace—and three reserve divisions to start with, but as it fell back toward Paris another good division from Algeria and a Moroccan brigade, both of which had recently crossed the Mediterranean, were added. It was thus a hastily improvised army, more than half of it of doubtful quality; it had suffered a few smart knocks from Kluck as he pushed it out of his path or brushed past it; it had been involved in the general French retreat in depressing circumstances; and most of its divisions reached the fortified camp of Paris in a state of exhaustion. However, as it moved back it was outside Kluck, by reason of the flattening of his wheel, and clearly had some possibilities. What would the French make of it?

The military governor of Paris was a veteran colonial soldier named Galliéni, recalled from retirement to hold this appointment. For a brief period he had been Joffre's superior in Madagascar, and the commander in chief had great respect for him. He had now become a very important figure because not only was Paris under threat of attack but the government had quitted it on September 2 to establish itself at Bordeaux, having placed the Sixth Army under his orders for the defense of the capital. On the third, both British and French air reconnaissances discovered Kluck's change of direction. When this news reached Galliéni he inquired of the Grand Quartier General * whether he should move Maunoury's Sixth Army north of the Marne in the direction of its tributary, the Ourcq.

Joffre answered that some of Galliéni's field troops might "at any time from now on" be moved northeast to threaten the German right and encourage the British—a phrase which did not suggest any loss of morale on the part of the troops but was occasioned by the marked pessimism of Sir John French which Joffre had noted. It must be confessed that this is not the sort of message one expects from a highly trained soldier. He had not really made up his mind. He was toying with the notion of letting the Germans move more deeply into the net. Curious or not, his delay proves his spirit and his nerves. Nothing could scare Father Joffre. Disaster made no difference to the excellent appetite with which he sat down to the two main meals of the day, served according to timetable, whatever was going on.

* Given in future as G.Q.G. (in speech always "Grand Q.G."). British General Headquarters will be written as G.H.Q. and German Obersteheeres-Leitung as O.H.L. The German Grosses Hauptquartier was the Kaiser's General Headquarters, with a vague authority over both sea and land forces.

His extraordinary mixture of ruthlessness and softness of heart is worth mentioning because it brings upon the scene another of the great figures of the war. The Fifth Army commander, General Lanrezac, was one of the most distinguished officers in the service and an old friend. But he seemed to be strained and fatigued. Joffre had noted how much of the good work done by the Fifth Army had been due to one of the corps commanders, General Franchet d'Esperey, and that he had practically run the operations of the Battle of Guise. He decided to offer him the command of the army. And he would make the offer before he spoke to Lanrezac because he feared that if he did not present himself with a *fait accompli* he would not be able to bring himself up to scratch. This was the man who was knocking over and dismissing generals like ninepins. He had no time to visit Franchet d'Esperey at his headquarters and would not waste the latter's time by summoning him to the G.Q.G. He therefore gave him rendezvous at a village between the two. Out of the blue he made his proposal:

"I shall be obliged to replace Lanrezac. I have thought of you. Do you feel yourself capable of commanding an army?" "As well as anybody else, my general," replied the astonished but supremely self-confident man.

Joffre asked some questions about the state of Franchet d'Esperey's corps, which was good, and others in the Fifth Army. He then departed as abruptly as he had come without a word about his plans, drove to Fifth Army headquarters, informed Lanrezac of his decision, and again summoned Franchet d'Esperey, this time to take over.*

Louis Felix Marie François Franchet d'Esperey, future Marshal of France, was fifty-eight years of age. He had, like Foch, been blocked in his promotion as a clerical, and, unlike Foch, had royalist associations—his father was the godson of King Louis XVIII. At least a dozen lieutenant colonels had passed over his head. Every one of these, he used to say in after life with great delight, was sacked between 1914 and 1918. He was short and sturdily built, with a splendid head above a thick neck. At once headstrong, loyal, and shrewd, his spirit and nerves were matched by a frame of steel. He lived to the age of eighty-six. He was accounted severe, and few of his troops realized his solicitude for them. The one thing he seemed to dread was any sign of seeking popularity. Most people feared

* Azan, p. 105.

him. Only a few loved him, but these were the men who knew him best.

Early on September 4 the march of the German First Army southeastward across the Marne was reported by cavalry reconnaissances. Galliéni set the French Sixth Army moving forward and telephoned to Joffre that a grand opportunity to hit the enemy in flank had appeared. Even then Joffre did not immediately issue orders for a general counteroffensive. It was a hot day, and he spent almost the whole of it—not, of course, missing his meals—sitting astride a chair under an apple tree in the school playground at Bar-sur-Aube. His admirers say he was in deep thought. His detractors declare that he gave this impression and that it would have been correct had he been capable of deep thought. Let them have their fun. Yet how contemptible are most of these detractors! In his place they would by now have suffered a nervous breakdown. Still, the birth throes of ideas was slow with him, it must be admitted, even though he had in Commandant Gamelin a competent midwife. The orders did not go out till after 8 P.M.

If he could have managed to get them out even an hour or so earlier he would have saved an invaluable day. The telegrams were not deciphered at the army headquarters until, on an average, 3.30 A.M. on September 5. Owing to the great heat the troops were on the move southward very early, so that it proved impossible to put the orders into effect that day.

The Germans were now taking precautions. Moltke realized the situation and did not like the look of it. He concluded that the French were "concentrating superior force in the region of Paris to protect the capital and threaten the right flank of the German array." He therefore issued orders to his First and Second Armies on the right wing to face the eastern side of Paris—that is, to wheel right and then halt—in order to cover the rest of the armies against French attacks from that quarter. The other armies were to continue their progress, but the Third was to halt when it reached the Seine.

Like the French orders, the German were not issued in time to be wholly effective on September 5. But fighting began. In the course of the afternoon Maunoury's advanced troops collided with Kluck's corps serving as right-flank guard. The German corps commander, finding himself outnumbered, fell back rapidly half a dozen miles. This was the first day of the Battle of the Ourcq, the first engagement in the Battle of the Marne, which was to explode or flicker up and down the front from Verdun to Compiègne, a distance of over a hundred miles, for four days or six, according as you choose to reckon.

Books as long as the present one have been written about this battle, which is one of great complexity in detail, as must always occur when such large forces are on the move, alternately clashing and disengaging. It can, however, be simplified.

Its main episode was the continued stripping of Kluck's First Army by one corps after another, to face Maunoury's attack from Paris. Three had been thus withdrawn from their original front by the morning of September 7. Their absence created a void on the right of Bülow's Second Army, filled only by cavalry, a single infantry brigade, and odd battalions of Jaegers. And into the gap—which it did not at first realize in this heavily wooded country—marched the British Expeditionary Force, now six divisions strong, and the left wing of the Fifth French Army, now under the lively leading of Franchet d'Esperey. The right wing of this army threw itself on the remaining two corps of the First Army, which had now passed under Bülow's command.

Farther east, on the Petit Morin, fierce fighting occurred between the German Third Army and a new French Army, the Ninth, under the command of Foch. On balance the French got the worst of it here, so that Foch called on Franchet d'Esperey for aid. Unfortunately, this caused the latter to divert his right northeastward instead of north, where the great prize was to be won. Meanwhile his army was at all events extending the gap and forcing Bülow to yield ground.

Most British historians have done their utmost to make as good a story as possible of the B.E.F.'s advance. In fact it was a crawl. The chief blame must undoubtedly fall upon the head of Sir John French, who never seems to have sensed that he was moving into what was virtually a void, and never drove his troops forward. Undoubtedly too there was among French and British troops alike a certain caution, degenerating at times into timidity. Commanders could not believe that the tide had turned and kept wondering whether or not they were walking into a gigantic ambush. If they could have overheard German discussions they would have realized how fantastically far from the truth were their impressions. Anyhow, the British infantry's advance measured only about eight miles a day from September 7 to 9, when half as much again, a mere 12 miles, would have been enough to sever Kluck's three corps from the rest of the German array and enable the British to attack them in rear while Maunoury was attacking them frontally. It may be urged in Sir John French's defense that he did not know this was the case. The answer to that is that by September 8 the situation was becoming pretty clear and that in any case very few men have been accounted great soldiers if they have not been ready to act on inferences and if their inferences have not ordinarily been right.

Meanwhile Moltke brooded and fretted. To make any soldier under forty understand his plight is barely possible because modern means of communication are so much better than his. All that can here be said is that these were now at their worst and that such messages as had reached Moltke had an ugly air. One spoke of the threat of a hostile breakthrough on the Marne. Moltke had lost his nerve. Finally he decided to send one of his staff officers, Major Hentsch, on a round trip of some four hundred miles to the western army headquarters.* An extraordinary feature of this mission, which almost suggests a state of panic, was that Hentsch was given no written instructions. He himself declared that he was given full powers to order, in case of necessity, a withdrawal behind the Vesle. This story has been contested by German military propagandists in search of an excuse for defeat, but there seems little reason to doubt it. He set out at 11 A.M. on September 8.

Hentsch visited the headquarters of the Fifth, Fourth, and Third Armies in the afternoon of that day. He found them all reasonably satisfied with their situation. When he got to Montmort, north of the Petit Morin, he found the atmosphere different. The commander and staff of the Second Army were worried about their right flank. Bülow already believed a retreat inevitable. Before they both retired for the night it was agreed that if the Allies crossed the Marne in strength the right wing of the army must be pulled back.

Hentsch set out again at 7 A.M. on September 9. He was repeatedly held up by transport hastening north and had to get out of the car to force a passage. He witnessed one panic resulting from an air attack. It took him the better part of five hours to cover thirty-seven miles. He never saw Kluck, but discussed the situation

---

* We must not measure his importance by the *folie des grandeurs* of the British or United States Armies of today, in which he would have been a major general or two-star general. Hentsch was actually chief of the intelligence service at O.H.L.

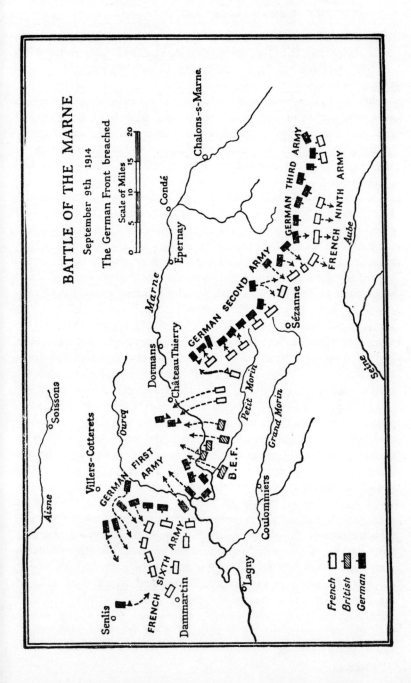

BATTLE OF THE MARNE

September 9th 1914

The German Front breached

Scale of Miles
0   5   10   15   20

French ☐
British ▨
German ■

with his chief of staff.* However, he found that orders had already been issued for the first stage of a retreat. He then fulfilled his instructions from Moltke by indicating the direction which it should take.

Such is, in brief, the story of the Hentsch mission, about which so many gallons of ink have been spilled. It only remains to add that a court of inquiry declared his action to have been entirely in accordance with the instructions given by Moltke, and that he afterward held important appointments. He died before the end of the war.

German writers have poured forth venom upon his memory. It is true that Kluck was doing quite well against Maunoury and that the Frenchman also was thinking of retreat. It is true that the Germans were nowhere really beaten—as apart from being out-maneuvered—except in Alsace-Lorraine, where after their disastrous failure to take the Grand Couronné, they broke off the battle and went back behind the frontier. But the German claim that Kluck ought to have gone straight forward and thrashed Maunoury is a pretty tall one and is based on the typical German theme that whenever German troops are beaten it is because they have been badly led or even "stabbed in the back." Every step forward taken by Kluck would have removed him farther from Bülow. Bülow's own flank was completely turned and he was in grave danger himself.

The Marne was, however, as the victors have never denied, a strategic, not a tactical, victory. The number of German prisoners taken in the fighting was not great; in the subsequent pursuit to the Aisne and Vesle it was small, and even so was to a considerable extent made up of drunks who had raided champagne cellars. And yet, by a strange irony, it is one of the vital battles of history. The Germans had come within an inch of bringing off a set plan of great length and ending it with the annihilation of their foes, and then lamentably failed. They had lost the opportunities of the first blow and the violation of neutrality, and these would never recur. And their defeat was largely moral, not in the rank and file but in the higher leadership. In Moltke, Bülow, and Kluck they did not produce leaders of the mettle and guts of Joffre, Foch, and Franchet d'Esperey.

In the pursuit to the Aisne and the Vesle the hesitations which had appeared during the battle itself were witnessed once more.

* Kluck, p. 137.

Foch might write in his own hand at the foot of his orders the Napoleonic *"Vitesse! Vitesse!"*; might call for the outflanking and envelopment of rear guards; Franchet d'Esperey might send out the call, *"En avant, soldats, pour la France!"* It was hard to get a move on. The men were weary in their very bones; the cavalry horses could hardly raise a walk. The weather had turned wet and the chalky roads were slippery. Yet Foch was probably correct when he wrote in his memoirs that the soldiers would have marched forward, despite their fatigue, if the leaders had not been content to enjoy the return of fortune and had shown more decision and skill in swelling, while success was still easy, the results of the hard victory.* On September 12 the whole of Bülow's Second German Army crossed the Aisne. Kluck's First Army was already over the river west of Soissons. That night British troops clambered across a broken bridge at Venizel and established the first bridgehead. A Franco-British holding on a wide front north of the river was quickly secured.

The goddess of chance, whose favors may mean so much in war, now granted them to the Germans. At this critical moment, when it looked as though their position on the Aisne might collapse, there turned up almost simultaneously, and in time by about two hours, a corps which had been plodding round from Alsace and another hitherto engaged in the siege of Maubeuge, where the French garrison had capitulated on September 7. Until now the Germans had never been able to fill the gap between their First and Second Armies; now they could, and they created on the spot a new army, the Seventh, to take over these corps and some oddments. Very hot fighting followed, but the progress of the Allies was gradually brought to a halt and they even lost a few parcels of ground to counterattacks. The Germans had been ready to go right back to the Oise, over twenty miles between Soissons and La Fère, if they could not form a front on the Aisne.

A new hand now guided their destinies. On September 14 an emissary of the Emperor informed Moltke that, since his health appeared to unfit him for his present appointment, he was to be replaced by the Prussian Minister of War, a tall and fine-looking infantryman aged fifty-three, and therefore by German reckoning almost an infant prodigy, Erich von Falkenhayn. Some German historians consider him a disastrous figure, but, whatever the verdict

* Foch. *Mémoires*, I, 142.

on his strategy, he was clearly a strong-minded man and his assumption of command brought to an end the recent series of blunders.

The new commander at once attempted to rebuild the Schlieffen plan on an improvised and diminished basis by massing a strong force on his right wing and rolling up the Allied left. The French naturally extended to meet the threat. So, even before the stubborn and bloody struggle on the Aisne had closed in deadlock, there developed what is known as "the Race to the Sea." It is not a logical title. The two sides were not in fact racing each other to the sea but racing to outflank each other. Division by division, corps by corps, army by army, they spread out virtually due northward, meeting, clashing violently, then forced to dig in and lie motionless, till open fighting continued only between Armentières and the coast at Nieuport. This phase included the rudimentary beginnings of trench warfare, the move of the British Expeditionary Force to the north, the fall of Antwerp and the escape of the Belgian army from the fortress, and the appointment of Foch as *adjoint* (assistant) to Joffre in coordinating the build-up northward.

His was no easy assignment; for, though in unquestioned command of all French troops engaged, his control of the other allies depended on his personality and the French reinforcements he could put in.* He had more of the former than the latter.

His hasty tongue seemed a doubtful asset for a coordinator of allies, but he had the virtues of open-hearted candor and loyalty. Shortly before his death he uttered words which are inscribed on his equestrian statue outside Victoria Station in London: "I am conscious of having served England as I served my own country."

His must have been one of the quickest promotions in military history. Thirty-seven days earlier Foch had led a corps in the Second Army under the command of General de Castelnau. Now he was virtually an army group commander and Castelnau was under his orders. He was, moreover, chiding and exhorting Castelnau and putting in as his chief of staff his own former chief of staff, Duchêne, as a stiffening influence in the hot fighting in which the

* When the present writer was engaged on a short biography of the Marshal in 1937 and visited Brittany in search of local color and family papers, he was shown a letter from Foch to his wife's aunt, Madame Bienvenüe, to whom he was devoted, in which he remarked that the English and Belgians obeyed him when they were in such trouble that they had to.

Second Army was engaged in the Race to the Sea. He himself had acquired a new chief of staff, Maxime Weygand.

The British were indeed in a sense racing to the sea. Sir John French had pointed out to Joffre that the Channel ports were their particular interest and that they ought in any event to fight on or near the left flank for the sake of their communications. They left the Aisne during the first fortnight of October, the cavalry corps marching, the infantry divisions moving by rail.

Antwerp was one of the ring fortresses fashionable at the end of the nineteenth century, established on the theory that the fire of the ring of forts would prevent a besieger bringing his batteries within range of the city. The trouble was that ranges had increased, and, far more important, that the heaviest modern howitzers—and the Austrians were able to lend their allies some monsters—could account quickly for the forts. When these howitzers opened fire on September 27 the forts were doomed, and with them the fortress, that is, unless the Belgian field army could drive away the second-line German forces investing it. King Albert was conscious that his army was too brittle for such a task, though it behaved gallantly in brief episodes and made a fine second sortie during the Aisne fighting which cost it 8,000 casualties.

Indeed, it seemed so likely to collapse that Britain reinforced the garrison by sea with three half-equipped marine brigades, hastily organized by the First Lord of the Admiralty, Mr. Churchill. He visited them on the spot and cabled home to propose that he should take command of the whole outfit. Mr. Asquith, whose sense of humor was on the quiet side, replied that his services were too urgently needed at the Admiralty for this arrangement to be possible. King Albert hung on till the last possible moment in order not to set free the German besiegers, but his hand was forced by a panic among the civil population which gravely affected the troops.* The retreat began on the night of October 6, and the whole force got away but for one luckless British brigade which was pushed over the Dutch frontier and interned. Antwerp fell on the tenth, having rendered to the Allies services of inestimable value.

* Cammaerts, p. 197.

Chapter VI

MANEUVER AND SLOGGING MATCHES

SOMETHING, the Germans saw now, had to be done to keep Austria on her feet. Indeed, this way of putting it was a euphemism; their own foothold in the east was unstable. Conrad accompanied his plea that they should extend southward by pointing out that their Silesian coal field was in danger. So Hindenburg was bidden to close down operations on the East Prussian front, leave minimum strength with the Eighth Army to protect the province, and take four good corps down to Silesia. This body, the new Ninth Army, picked up two scratch German corps already on the spot and took up a position on the Austrian left in the last week of September, 1914. Hindenburg brought with him Ludendorff as chief of staff and Max Hoffmann as what the British army would call G.S.O.1.

The Kielce province west of the Vistula had been the scene of little fighting and lightly held by either side; in fact there had been something like a void of seventy-five miles. If Hindenburg, with the Austrians on his right thrusting northeastward from Cracow, could get in his blow by surprise, he was likely to sweep forward, across the Vistula, and capture Warsaw. However, on September 25, the Russian cavalry discovered the new dispositions. Now the Russians had to move north to bar the way. Their cautious command would not take the risk of doing this west of the Vistula. So they had to depend on their cavalry to check the German-Austrian advance while the infantry, making a circuitous march, struggled and floundered northward over the bottomless roads of the Lublin province east of the river. Somehow they accomplished the long side-slip, which few other troops in the world could have made in the time. One division is said to have gone without bread for six days. Three armies lined the Vistula. But by now, October 9, the Germans were along the west bank and farther south the Austrians had advanced to the San and relieved the fortress of Przemysl.

The very few foreigners who, like the British military attaché, Colonel Knox, saw the Russian infantry divisions on the Vistula believed that they were worn out. A few days, however, sufficed to restore the strength and energy of these hard and primitive men. Behind them fresh divisions, not yet engaged but containing many veterans of the Japanese war of a decade back, were pouring from the railheads: flat-faced, narrow-eyed Siberians, coming to the rescue of western Russia not for the first time—nor for the last. Neither command nor troops were defensively minded. They had won great successes. They were in considerably superior strength and full of confidence. As Conrad had foretold, they meant to invade Silesia.

But the old clownish performance was repeated. Hindenburg learned by intercepting wireless messages and capturing written orders what the Russians were at and what he was running into. The man supposedly made of iron broke off the fighting that had already begun outside Ivanograd and bolted, to the ironical accompaniment of Austrian protests against the abandonment of Poland. Hoffmann penned venomous attacks in his diary against Ludendorff, who, he declared, had lost his nerve. More ironically still, Conrad had to rush northward Austrian troops—who did well in some terrific fighting—to take over a considerable portion of the German front. The Hindenburg-Ludendorff combination had not been notably successful in the role of rescuer.

Conrad did the Germans another good turn when he advised them to launch a counteroffensive from near Lodz into the Russian flank. This operation led to one of the most famous incidents of the war, in a romantic tradition which seemed to have deserted the battlefields. Three German divisions were enveloped and cut off from their comrades. The Russians actually ordered up trains to take them away as prisoners, but they botched the business and the German divisions broke out. Evidence points to Rennenkampf as the culprit. What army could carry such an incubus as he and his like and survive a war against German professionals? The counteroffensive halted the Russian advance, but the opposing forces dug in for the winter much closer to the German frontier than at the beginning of Hindenburg's offensive.

On the extreme wings the fate of the Central Powers was a good deal worse. In the north the German Eighth Army was driven back to the Masurian Lakes, and once more the Russians trod East Prussian soil. Some officers returned to their old billets and were courteously greeted by landlords and landladies. When they kept sober the Russians of the Tsar were the kindliest and gentlest of all occupying forces, and anyhow, if there were Russian officers in the schloss, it would not be burned out, or the daughters and maids raped, by the Cossacks. In the south the Russians drove the Austrians to the crest of the Carpathians. They even captured the celebrated Dukla Pass, but were unable to penetrate it. Considering that they regularly revealed their plans to the enemy and were already perilously short of shells and even of small arms, the Russian armies had again done well.

The fighting had been fierce and sanguinary. The German Ninth Army lost well over 100,000 men, 36,000 of them killed. The Austrian First on its right suffered at least 30,000 casualties. Russian losses, as almost always, are unknown, but the Germans claimed 135,000 prisoners, mostly in the Lodz counteroffensive.

In one sense the Russian achievement had actually been too great. It had compelled the Germans to reverse their strategy. As has been stated, Falkenhayn took over from Moltke with the intention of repairing the damage done at the Marne, so far as that was possible, by a new envelopment of the French left. A great battle or series of battles now to be described was fought between Armentières and the sea. When that was over Falkenhayn had to bring his offensive in the west to a stop. The Germans had been thoroughly scared on three counts: the two invasions of East Prussia, which represented a grave loss of prestige and a considerable loss in beef, wheat, and root crops; the threat to Beuthen, the center of the Silesian industrial and mining area; and the risk that Austrian arms might suffer decisive defeat followed by a Russian march through the Carpathians and an invasion of Hungary.

Others besides the Austrians called for aid now. Hindenburg was shouting for it. The big businessmen were warning the Emperor how disastrous would be the loss of Beuthen. Falkenhayn was forced to send eight German divisions eastward during the latter part of November. Little by little he had to do far more than that: to make the Eastern Front the principal theater of the war for the year 1915. In fact O.H.L. spent much of the year on that flank, leaving only the shred of a staff in the west. Russia's unexpectedly high fighting qualities brought correspondingly heavy blows upon her.

Meanwhile in the west another tremendous battle had been fought, the last phase of the Race to the Sea. Both sides sensed, while not admitting it to themselves, that if they did not win a decisive victory between La Bassée or Armentières and the Channel coast the deadlock now appearing farther south was likely to grip the whole front. Here the Allies owed much to the stubborn determination of the saintly, tongue-tied king of the Belgians, whose worth few of their leaders appreciated and whose tattered, weary, and shaken army they were disposed to regard as little better than a uniformed mob. They were also deeply in debt to Winston Churchill and his marines, whom they had not taken seriously. If the King had not held out until the last possible moment in Antwerp, risking the loss of his whole force against the professional advice tendered to him, the investing German troops would have been thrown into the fighting correspondingly earlier. It might then have proved impossible to hold the enemy in front of Ypres and on the Yser.

As it was, the Germans had formed a great mass of cavalry, eight divisions first concentrated near Lille, which spread out westward and got as far as Hazebrouck on the line of least resistance. The B.E.F., moving up from the Aisne, had therefore to detrain well to the west. When, however, the infantry left their trains and set about the German cavalry they swept it back. It was proved, as indeed it had been in the east also, that cavalry armed with carbines had little power even to check good infantry. This was still more the case when the infantry was well supported by cavalry. The B.E.F. was aided to begin with by a French cavalry corps, then by its own cavalry, now a corps of two divisions, first covering the infantry and then moving into a gap between Armentières, the left of the newly formed Third Corps, and the First Corps moving on Ypres. And the British cavalry troopers did not carry a carbine but the short rifle which was standard throughout the army—a great boon.

The Germans, however, had no longer to rely entirely on forces already engaged. They had prepared an ugly surprise, though it was penetrated before they struck. Eight newly formed divisions had joined the forces released by the fall of Antwerp and with a marine division had been formed into a new Fourth Army, under the command of Duke Albrecht of Württemberg. These new divisions were made up of 75 per cent volunteers under military age, or not yet called up, the rest being trained reservists. The British and French did not at first realize what they were up against. It was the flower of the youth of Germany, middle- and upper-class students, flaming with patriotism and enthusiasm, ready for any sacrifice. They had little power of maneuver because their training had been so scanty, but they were absolutely determined to win or fall. For the most part they fell. It was madness on the part of the Germans to send these lads into action, since a large proportion of them were potential officers, of whom there was to be a shortage later on, but they were dangerous troops to meet. At practically the same moment the Germans brought up, on their Fourth Army's left, the Sixth Army with all the best troops from Lorraine, still under the command of Crown Prince Rupprecht of Bavaria.

On the British side few reinforcements were expected. The Indian Corps of two divisions, had, however, landed at Marseilles just before the battle began, and the British Eighth Division, made up of troops from oversea stations, arrived just before it came to an end.

The campaign in the north opened with a British advance between La Bassée and Armentières on October 12. Still there was only German cavalry to be dealt with. It was pushed back, though by no means as fast as when it had first been encountered because, in this flat, water-logged region, the drainage dikes had to be bridged, and the smoke shells or bombs which would have been used to cover such an operation in the latter part of the war were not yet available. However, it would have come to much the same thing however fast the advance. When Rupprecht's infantry divisions were met it was another matter. The British were quickly brought to a halt. Indeed they fell back a mile or so to a position prepared in advance, but there they stood like a rock. The effect of British shooting with both field gun and rifle was greater than ever in country devoid of cover. The Germans were shot to a standstill and the Battle of La Bassée ended quickly.

This battle is accounted part of the Battle of the Yser, which extended from the sea at Nieuport to the La Bassée Canal, nearly forty-five miles as the crow flies and far longer on the curving front. The German attack was launched on October 20, the very day that Haig's First Corps reached Ypres and took up a position on the ridge east of it. On the northern flank, between Dixmude and the coast, the Belgians, by no means restored after their retreat from Antwerp, lined the Yser, a wide stream creeping to the sea and tidal on their whole front.

After bombardment lasting throughout October 21 the fighting on the Yser reached its most furious next day. Time after time the Germans came on; time after time they were beaten back. The Belgians put up a resistance no one had expected of them. In a bridgehead at Dixmude a French marine brigade proved steadfast. But Foch was worried. The Belgians had thrown in their last reserves and were exhausted. The men were often so coated with clay that they were hardly recognizable as human. Would they hold?

Not on the Yser. By the night of October 24 the enemy was across the river on the whole front between Dixmude, where the French marines stood fast, and Nieuport, where a crack French division sent by Foch had just arrived. The Belgians fell back to the Dixmude-Nieuport railway—a very slight obstacle, but better than nothing. Then a staff officer, Commandant Nuyten, after consulting the head lock-keeper at Nieuport, brought in a bright proposal. If, he declared, the culverts in the embankment, standing only three to five feet above the dead flat plain, were first blocked, and then the sluices were opened to let in the sea, the water would flood the ground to the east and lap the embankment without crossing it. This was done on October 29.* But the sea came in so gently that men cursed it in their impatience. Eager German battalions waded through the water while a smashing bombardment fell on Ramscappelle, and seized the village, which stood high and dry beyond the inundation. The French division at Nieuport turned on them savagely and slew them or drove them out. The final winner, however, was the sea. The Germans had to withdraw and this front became silent.

A more prolonged and bloodier battle was fought east of Ypres. British and French attempts to advance made little progress and were soon halted. On October 31 the second phase opened on a narrower front, from the Messines Ridge to Gheluvelt, five miles east of Ypres. The Germans drove the British Cavalry Corps off the ridge after heavy and bitter fighting. Further north, where the blow fell largely on Haig's First Corps, it was touch and go. The

* Cammaerts, p. 214.

Germans broke through at Gheluvelt, but a fierce counterattack by a mixed force of battalions from different brigades drove them out again. Then and on other days the young German volunteers came on like men possessed, and at times the roar of a patriotic song would reach the defenders through the din of battle. Incredible numbers of dead were counted by British patrols who crept out at night when the fighting had died down. The Germans themselves have used the phrase *Der Kindermord von Ypern* to describe the sacrifices of these reserve divisions.* Yet these youths attacked so furiously that on two or three occasions when they got to close quarters they overran and virtually annihilated British battalions. In such cases there were seldom reserves available on the spot and the only way of plugging the breach in the front was to pull out a battalion from another sector where the pressure was less severe and hurry it to the scene. The battlefield thus became incredibly confused, especially as British and French also tended to become intermingled. It seemed to make little difference to Haig and his French colleague Dubois, commanding the Ninth Corps. They kept control of their respective fronts and supported each other loyally. Foch fed in such French reinforcements as he could lay his hands on, and finally Sir John French used the Indian Corps to relieve British troops of Smith-Dorrien's Second Corps down in front of Béthune and brought them up to thicken the Ypres front.

The reinforcements came none too soon. After a number of local attacks another great offensive was launched on November 11. It was on a wide front, but its main weight was astride that famous highway, the Menin Road. The reserve divisions which had borne the brunt of the early attacks had now been nearly shot to pieces, and this thrust was made by two splendid regular divisions. South of the road British shrapnel and musketry time after time broke up the waves of the attack and foiled every effort to re-form them. North of the road a division of the Prussian Guard punched a hole, and its troops began to pass through. There was nothing in front of them but the British gun line, some batteries firing at them point-blank.

At the critical moment the troops who had broken through hesitated. A ragged counterattack in which cooks and orderlies

* "The Murder of the Children at Ypres," but as *Kindermord* is the word used to describe Herod's slaughter of the infants, the phrase may be translated, "The Massacre of the Innocents at Ypres."

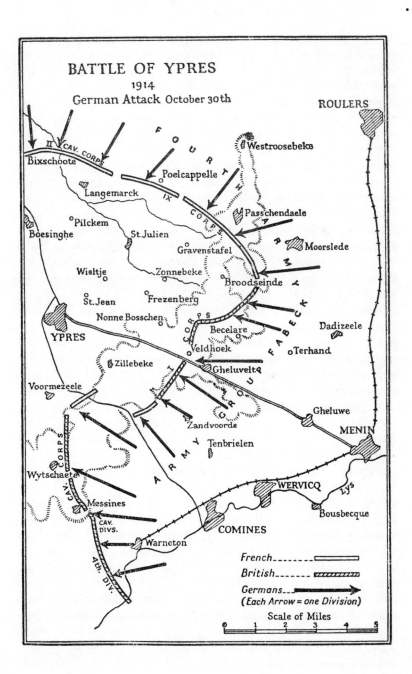

BATTLE OF YPRES

1914
German Attack October 30th

ROULERS

II CAV. CORPS

Bixschoote

Langemarck

FOURTH

Poelcappelle

Westroosebeke

IX

Pilckem

St.Julien

CORPS

Passchendaele

Boesinghe

Gravenstafel

Moorslede

ARMY

Wieltje

Zonnebeke

Broodseinde

St.Jean

Frezenberg

CORPS

FABECK

Dadizeele

Nonne Bosschen

Becelare

YPRES

Veldhoek

Terhand

Zillebeke

Gheluvelt

GROUP

Voormezeele

Zandvoorde

Gheluwe

MENIN

ARMY

Tenbrielen

CORPS

Wytschaete

CAV.

Messines

WERVICQ

Lys

CAV.
DIVS.

Bousbecque

Warneton

COMINES

4th. DIV.

French _ _ _ _ _ _ _

British _ _ _ _ _ _

Germans _ _ _
(Each Arrow = one Division)

Scale of Miles

0   1   2   3   4   5

took part closed the breach. As a captured Prussian Guards officer was being taken back past a British battery he asked his escort: "What have you behind that?" "Divisional headquarters," he was answered. "Almighty God!" was his summing up.

Much more fighting followed, but the crisis ended that day, and with it open warfare virtually ended too, not to reappear in the west until the year 1918, and only in a limited form then. The British had lost some 50,000 men killed, wounded, and missing at Ypres. French accounts do not distinguish losses in the Battle of Ypres from others, but there were more French troops engaged, though in general not quite so heavily, and casualties must have been as high or higher. German losses in this phase of the war have never been published, but figures which are partial in regard to time and place point to their having been greater than those of the three Allies combined. In one sense Britain was the most cruelly hit. Her small and precious regular army was fast melting away and she had nothing behind it but good raw material.

Joffre still hoped to break through into the open. In December he attacked in Artois, north of Arras, with little or no success. A few days later he launched an offensive in Champagne which did no better and was enormously costly on both sides—a mere killing match, in fact. From time to time the word "Hartmannswillerkopf" —a peak in the Vosges—appeared in communiqués, few who read them realizing that in the bloody little combats fought 3,000 feet up, probably in snow and ice, certainly under the heavy snow-laden skies that cap the Vosges in winter, gains and losses could be measured by yards.

Gradually the bits of trench, scratched in the ground, irrespective of tactical siting, wherever an advance had come to an end, were linked together, deepened, and when possible drained. Dugouts which were at least splinterproof appeared in them. Telephone cable in almost inextricable tangles ran along their sides. Reserve lines were dug, though nothing like the great systems, several thousands of yards deep, of the latter part of the war. In front stretched curtains of barbed wire on wooden stakes and later iron corkscrew pickets. The opposing forces became well nigh invisible to each other, though observers on high ground with fixed telescopes saw occasional movement in the enemy's lines. An infantryman might spend half of six months in the trenches—the other half being spent in billets, generally barns if he were a private soldier—without seeing a single enemy. And from the Swiss frontier to the English Channel this long snakelike excavation was being photographed from aircraft and reproduced on maps of $\frac{1}{5,000}$ or even $\frac{1}{2,500}$, on which the very latrines could be depicted.

Virtually no one, barring a Jewish scientist unheard of before the war and forgotten since, had expected this to occur. And yet the Russo-Japanese War might have served as a warning, for in it the opposing armies dug themselves in fairly thoroughly. There had been much entrenchment in the American Civil War, but the proportion of men to front or fronts was very much lower. In the First World War it was nearly always the case that the fewer the men to the mile, the more open was the warfare.

Why did not one side or the other break through these defenses, which remained very flimsy until at least the end of 1915? This book might be devoted entirely to the problem and then leave more to say. Writings on the subject, if typescript be included, would fill a library. The essence can, however, be given in a few words. The assault could never be driven through into open country fast and cleanly enough to prevent new lines of resistance being established and the defense congealing about the bulge, as skin reestablishes itself about a wound. The break-*in* could not be converted into a break-*through*. It seems a simple conundrum, and a hundred times men thought it solved, but it never was wholly solved.

Chapter VII

OPENING OF THE WAR AT SEA

NEITHER French friends nor German foes fully understood the significance of the Royal Navy. The French were, not
unnaturally, critical of the meager strength of the B.E.F.; by the end
of 1914 it still numbered only ten divisions, including two Indian.
French soldiers and politicians were inclined to believe, and say,
that Britain was taking only a small part in the war.

Her role was in fact already a big one. So long as the Royal Navy
could hold open the Atlantic trade routes it made Britain virtually
invulnerable. The risk of invasion was there, but it was slight. And
the Royal Navy—with aid from the French—placed France in the
same position as Britain, except that it could not make an island of
her. While Britain survived, France—anyhow more nearly self-sufficing in food than Britain—could not be starved; could not be deprived of arms, equipment, horses and mules obtained in the western
hemisphere; and could not be defeated, except by land armies.

At the same time, the denial of the seas to German freighters, the
blockade of Germany, and the control of goods consigned to European neutrals was as much to the benefit of France as of Britain.
Command of the sea enabled Britain and France to bring to the
Western Front important land forces from overseas with a minimum
of danger. Germany had none to summon home, but she would
have been glad to send small bodies of troops to her colonies in the
hope of tying down larger numbers of Britons, Frenchmen, and Belgians. She never could do so, though it must be owned that, even
without that power, she tied down a large number at small cost.
Command of the sea enabled the Entente to send its land forces

where it would, whereas the Central Powers could send theirs only to destinations to be reached by land routes.

Yet too many British historians and self-styled experts in strategy have, especially when dealing with this war, made preposterous claims for sea power, claims both contrary to common sense and founded on distortion of history. Britain, they say, should not have gone so deeply into this continental war; she should not have created a mass conscript army; she should have stood off, kept the seas, and blockaded the enemy. This, they add, was her traditional policy.

It may have been the policy she had hankered after in selfish moments, but it had never been pursued for long. Time after time Britain—a country with a small population, and therefore a small army, before the nineteenth century—had been forced to send land forces to the continent to prevent her allies from collapsing. It was not merely that they might be routed and driven out of the war by sheer force of arms. They might walk out. They might decide that it would be better to take such terms as the enemy would give rather than see their people condemned to all the sufferings of war while their partner fought her war sitting on a cushion and keeping her boots clean. There can be no shadow of doubt that, if Britain and the British Empire had not raised the vast armies which they did build up, France would have been crushed and forced to surrender.

The war opened with a striking exhibition of the value of sea power. It has already been mentioned that the B.E.F. was transported to France without interference—and chiefly to Havre, nearly 120 miles from Southampton, as against the twenty-eight miles from Dover to Calais. In fact no troopship or leave-boat was attacked in the Channel from the start of the war to the finish. The passage of the Mediterranean of troops from the ports of Algeria and the Moroccan protectorate was equally successful. France drew good Arab and Berber infantry from these sources. Later on she brought over a large number of battalions of Negroes, known by the name of "Senegalese," though coming from other regions of tropical West Africa also: stout shock troops but without the rudiments of education and so ill-suited to the climate of northern France that their employment at the front in winter had to be abandoned.

The main British naval force, by far the strongest in the world, was the Grand Fleet, of four battle squadrons, a battle cruiser squadron, two cruiser squadrons, and a light cruiser squadron. It was stationed at Scapa Flow, a miniature inland sea in the Orkney Islands, and at Rosyth, near Edinburgh. This position was suitable for engaging the German High Seas Fleet if it put to sea. It could not be engaged otherwise because its bases from the Jade to the Elbe were strongly fortified and the island of Heligoland was full of long-range artillery. At Harwich was a cruiser squadron and on the south coast the Channel Fleet, including the Fifth Battle Squadron. No convoy system in the Atlantic was established for a long time to come. However, cruisers ranged out widely for the protection of trade, and before the end of 1914, twenty-three "patrol areas" were organized in home waters, four with bases in the Channel and eight with Irish bases. The British battle cruiser squadron in the Mediterranean was based on Malta. Its area was the eastern basin; that of the main French fleet was the western, with base at Toulon.

The Austrian navy was in a difficult situation after the declaration of Italian neutrality. It was based on Pola, near the head of the Adriatic. Outside that sea it could scarcely hope to venture far; indeed it could not move far from its base unless assured that the main Franco-British forces could not intercept it. The main Russian fleet in the Baltic was no better off. Russia's allies were prevented by German submarines from sending naval forces into the Baltic—except a few British submarines—and, without a single modern battleship completed, the Russians had to be very wary. The Germans employed little strength in the Baltic, though they did for a time strongly escort their East Prussian convoys.

One early incident of the naval war stung instructed British opinion like a whiplash and was long and angrily debated. In the Mediterranean were two German warships, the cruiser *Goeben* and the light cruiser *Breslau*. On the eve of war between Britain and Germany they were very much the concern of the British commander, Rear Admiral Sir Christopher Berkeley Milne.

It was an amazing affair, a nightmare of naval war. On the British side the confusion was appalling, yet much of it was unavoidable, and it is all but impossible to fix the final responsibility for the rest. Delay in the transmission of messages played a part. The news of Italy's declaration of neutrality came late to Milne; this was a big factor because until then it seemed that the Allies might have to face the combined Austrian and Italian fleets. Milne was also late in learning what his French colleague, Admiral Boué de Lapeyrère, was doing; this was another big factor because Milne's first duty was to aid in the protection of the French troop transports from North

Africa, the sailing of which had actually been postponed by the French admiral owing to the presence of the German cruisers.

The German Admiral von Souchon was in a pretty fix. His chances of getting out of the Mediterranean were not worth a red cent. However, he was a mettlesome man, very bold, very keen to do all the damage he could, even if his ships were sent to the bottom. The *Goeben* was a fine modern cruiser, at her best after an overhaul in the Austrian naval dockyard at Pola. The *Breslau* was also modern and fast. Souchon was, like other German commanders who gave trouble on the open seas, from Graf von Spee downward, a masterly handler of colliers, and tactical skill in coaling at sea was a great asset in this sort of war. On quitting the Adriatic, Souchon sailed west to bombard Algerian ports in order to damage transports and delay the sailing of the troops. The gods were laughing at this naval comedy. Souchon had no more need than Milne to worry about the colonial troops. Boué de Lapeyrère was not going to start them until he had made up convoys.

Then came the climax of the drama. At 6 P.M. on August 3, as his ships sped through the water for their dash at the Algerian ports, Souchon received a wireless order to make for Constantinople. There had been an arrangement with Turkey. He did not turn back. No, he had set out to bombard Bone and Philippeville, and he held on through the night to do it. He did it early on August 4. The results were trifling.

Then he turned east. The comedy changed to farce when he met two British ships. Neither side saluted—but neither opened fire. Yet Souchon came red-handed from bombarding French towns, where he had at least killed a fair number of civilians. To put the situation straight, we have to go back to dates and times.* Germany had declared war on France at 6.45 P.M. on August 3—and Souchon knew it. Britain had sent her ultimatum to Germany on August 4, to expire at midnight. Therefore the United Kingdom and the German Empire were not at war when their ships met, though France and the German Empire were.

In the rest of the strange story there are only two further outstanding points. The light cruiser *Gloucester* (Captain Howard Kelly) tracked the *Goeben* with great skill and courage, alone and at deadly risk to herself, on August 7. And just when Souchon thought he had a fine chance of reaching safety he was refused a

* See p. 31.

passage through the Dardanelles because of opposition within the
Turkish government. He hung about the Aegean. Once more he
seemed to be doomed. Yet nothing could go wrong for this bold
man. The pro-German Turks triumphed and the *Goeben* and *Breslau* entered the Dardanelles at 8.30 P.M. on August 10. Milne's
senior subordinate was brought before a court-martial. He was
acquitted on the ground that he had acted in accordance with his
orders and instructions.

The significance of the incident was not so much the escape of
the German cruisers as the part played by their admiral in bringing
Turkey into the war three months later. Yet, as will appear, Turkey
was already pledged to fight on the German side. She might conceivably have defrauded Germany, as she failed her allies in a later
war, but the probability is that the Germans, who were troubled
by few scruples, would have ended her shivers on the brink by
pushing her in, even had Souchon and his cruisers not been present.
At all events it was he who did push her in.

No fighting beyond the exchange of a few salvos had occurred
in this affair. The next was an extremely hard-fought naval action.
Its only resemblance to the other was confusion, which was equally
plentiful on a larger scale. Now, as in the Mediterranean, the confusion proved to be to the advantage of the man who was trying to
do something definite rather than of those who were trying to
prevent it. The man was Vice-Admiral Sir David Beatty. He was as
bold as Souchon and a far greater personality.

Beatty had before him a general and a special object. He was to
assert British command of the North Sea "right up to the enemy's
gates." * The second object was a naval "ambush." It was designed
to take advantage of the practice of German light cruisers meeting
the returning destroyer guard about daybreak. Beatty with the
battle cruisers was ready to intervene. Submarines were also to take
part. They might hope for some fine opportunities, but their
presence might, on the other hand, lead to accidents. The whole
conception was daring, since Beatty risked facing not merely the
German battle cruisers, which he outnumbered, but the battleships
of the High Seas Fleet, though his speed was superior to the latter.

Few had fully foreseen the disorder and obscurity likely to occur
in naval warfare owing to the increased speed of warships, the
increased range of guns and torpedoes, the vast area covered by

* Corbett, I, 99.

fleets, and the frequent use of smoke for concealment. On August 28 the North Sea was, moreover, overcast and gloomy. A great deal that could go wrong went wrong at one time or another. British submarines were troublesome to their own side, which was scared of sinking them and nervous lest they should attack British surface ships in error. Constant errors of identity, some of them hair-raising, occurred, and, needless to say in the circumstances, many chances were lost.

At first contact the British were outnumbered and outgunned. The situation changed completely when the Admiral appeared with his battle cruisers. By then British superiority was crushing. Yet the risks Beatty accepted in pressing into the Heligoland Bight to aid his flotilla would have daunted many an admiral whose country's fate was so tightly bound to that of her fleet. Three German light cruisers, the *Cöln*, *Mainz*, and *Ariadne*, and one destroyer, were sunk in the action. On the British side only one cruiser, the *Arethusa*, was at all badly hit. The moral effect was splendid. The Germans might declare with truth that their cruisers were fought with great gallantry, but they also had to admit that the leadership had been faulty and that the cruisers had not supported the destroyers quickly enough. The German battle cruisers did come out, but after a delay owing to low water over the bar at Wilhelmshaven, and they were not even seen by the British.

The comfort brought to the British was needed and indeed did not go very far to meet the depression caused by events which followed this brilliant raid. On September 22 the old cruiser *Aboukir* was sunk by a torpedo off the Dutch coast. The same U-boat then sank the *Hogue* and *Cressy*. Losses were huge, especially in the case of the *Cressy*, because her boats were some way off, picking up survivors of the other two. On October 27 the battleship *Audacious* struck a mine off the Ulster coast and sank. There was little to show on the British side in repayment, but for the sinking of four torpedo boats seeking to mine the Thames estuary.

Then came another affair arousing widespread controversy. Though this debate has in the nature of things been generally forgotten, it still creates differences of opinion among those who recall it. The German squadron on the China Station under Admiral Graf von Spee had crossed the Pacific. He had no base, but as he approached the Chilean coast along latitude 32 he coaled from colliers at the lonely island of Más Afuera, 500 miles west of Valparaiso.

Meanwhile Vice-Admiral Sir Christopher Cradock had been ordered "to be prepared to have to meet" the enemy and to "search" for him.* He had picked up the *Canopus*, an obsolete battleship, but armed with 12-inch guns. If he kept her with him, however, she would reduce his speed to 15 knots and to bring Spee to action would be out of the question. The First Lord, Mr. Churchill, afterward contended that Cradock would have been safe with the *Canopus* in company, but this argument was questioned. The Admiralty's final message to him was that he was being sent another cruiser and was not expected to act without the *Canopus*. This message did not reach him. And, at the critical moment, the old tub needed a twenty-four hours' repair job and was left behind.

On the afternoon of November 1 the two squadrons sighted one another off Coronel, on the Chilean coast. Cradock doubtless believed that his orders left him with no alternative but to fight. His flagship, the *Good Hope*, carried two 9.2-inch guns, but they were opposed to sixteen of the most modern 8.2-inch in Spee's heavy cruisers, the *Scharnhorst* and *Gneisenau*. Cradock must have known that, barring incredible luck, he was facing destruction. The odds were greater than he realized because the German gunnery was the better and Spee secured the inshore station, so that the afterglow of the sunset outlined the British ships. He naturally extended the range when Cradock strove to close it. The *Good Hope* and the 6-inch cruiser *Monmouth* were sunk. It was pitch dark and blowing so hard that the Germans could not lower boats, but in any case they saw neither ship go down. The light cruiser *Glasgow* ran for it on the Admiral's orders and escaped. The *Scharnhost* was hit twice and the *Gneisenau* four times, with trifling damage.

For Britain it was a disaster, not in the loss of the two cruisers, which could be replaced, but in their loss with not a single survivor, which struck people with horror at that early stage of the war. It also brought with it a grave loss of prestige. Germany, of course, "went to town" on her victory, the results of which were spread all over the world without one out of ten of those who received the news realizing the disparity in the strength of the opponents.

However, it was no good mourning or even tilting at Mr. Churchill. The thing was to repair the damage. That he and his new First Sea Lord, the ebullient Admiral Sir John Fisher, proceeded to do, so far as it lay in their power. With admirable resolution they

* Corbett, I, 179.

detached two battle cruisers, the *Invincible* and *Inflexible*, under command of Vice-Admiral Sir F. Doveton Sturdee and sent them out to wring victory from Germany's hands. Spee's squadron, after being feted by the Germans at Valparaiso, rounded the Horn at midnight, December 1/2. He intended to cross the South Atlantic, but on December 8 could not resist the bait of the wireless station in the Falkland Islands and the docks and stores at Port Stanley, which he decided to destroy. Sturdee was coaling within.

Some critics have suggested that if Spee had attacked forthwith after this surprise—brought off by pure chance—he might have won a victory. It is unlikely, though he would assuredly have caused greater loss than he did. As it was, he fled. Sturdee came out in almost leisurely pursuit and did not draw level till it suited him. His superiority was as great as Spee's had been over Cradock and he kept the range extended to favor his 12-inch guns. The only difference in the results of the two actions was that the German cruisers got more hits than had those of Cradock. Even so, British casualties were minute in numbers. Both the German heavy cruisers were sunk. The same fate awaited the small cruisers *Nurnberg* and *Leipzig*, which were caught by the British cruisers. The only one to escape was the fast *Dresden*. She was the last German cruiser at sea and survived until March, 1915, when she was sunk off the island of Juan Fernandez, not far from Más Afuera, where the German squadron had coaled before the action of Coronel.

The lesson was that superior range and weight of shell were overwhelming in the then relation between gun and armor. Graf von Spee, a capable commander, had behaved recklessly. To be ambushed by a foe in port is odd, but to be ambushed by a foe seeking nothing of the kind is fantastic. He may have thought it unlikely that reinforcements of superior gun-power had been sent, but at least there had been ample time to do so since the news of Coronel had reached the British Admiralty.

Had he so chosen, Spee might have done far more damage by dispersing his squadron. Before crossing the Pacific, he had sent one little cruiser, the *Emden*, into the Indian Ocean. Her haul of prizes had been amazing and her cheeky bombardment of Madras and Penang had provided fine material for German humorists at British expense. There was nothing humorous about her end. She was caught by the Australian cruiser *Sydney* in the Cocos Islands and quickly turned into a slaughterhouse.

Other naval events of 1914 include the destruction of the light cruiser *Magdeburg*, which grounded in the Baltic and was caught by the Russian Fleet; the shelling of Scarborough and the Hartlepools on the English east coast by German battle cruisers on December 16; and the loss of the new French battleship *Jean Bart*, sunk in the Straits of Otranto by an Austrian submarine on Christmas Day. The exploits of the *Goeben* and *Breslau* in the Black Sea belong to another chapter.

Lay opinion on the Allied side and among neutrals found this record unimpressive, with the Heligoland Bight the one bright spot. German naval officers did not. The German flag had been swept from the seas. All over the world German freighters had taken refuge in neutral ports, whereas British were going about their tasks. And between British and French ports the vital traffic was uninterrupted. The transports, cargo boats and leave boats could ply "as securely as the motor-buses between Fleet Street and the Fulham Road." * The British Navy had done its work.

* Pollen, p. 14. Note that "motor-buses" were still new enough to be so described.

Chapter VIII

OVER THE WIDE WORLD

THE military chiefs had not been caught napping, even in the states most averse to war—the captains were to meet their surprises later. On the civil side it was otherwise. Nobody had experienced a war on this scale. Other conflicts had been preceded by longer warning, so that adjustments could be made. Cushions such as the rise of money rates had softened the shock. In this case bank rates in London, Paris, and Berlin stood at 3, 3½ and 4 per cent, respectively, a week before the invasion of Belgium. In the first week the British bank rate rose to 10 per cent. The export of gold was prohibited and—a striking measure in "a nation of shop-keepers"—a moratorium on debts was declared. The Stock Exchange closed on July 31. That of every great city in the world followed suit. In the neutral United States it remained shut until the following April. All belligerents went onto paper money.* All put into force a series of wartime regulations.

Britain rapidly increased her fighting strength, in the army above all. The regular units overseas were brought home to form five divisions and replaced either by British Territorial or by local forces. The Territorial divisions and mounted Yeomanry brigades, fourteen of each, were mobilized. Instead of expanding on this basis, however, Lord Kitchener, almost a stranger to his own country and doubtful about the Territorial principle, raised thirty divisions in three "new armies," formed one after another. Recruits poured in so fast that the manufacture of equipment and munitions was handicapped.

The volunteers included the prime of the nation's youth. Their spirit was amazing. The like of it had not been seen before. Men

* Noyes, pp. 53-57.

barged and jostled to get into the recruiting offices. For young and old, belief in the justice of the cause was no convention but a clear reality. To begin with, a few foolish and unworthy exhibitions of excitement and spleen occurred—for example, wrecking of German bakers' shops—but they were not widespread. A characteristic of university students was a combination of eagerness to dedicate themselves and a gaiety based on peace of mind, rejoicing in an aim beset by no doubts. For many this was to be "a war to end war."

Expansion was simpler for other belligerents than for Britain. In her Territorial divisions there were commonly about half a dozen professional officers—the commander and staff. In the new armies retired officers and a handful on leave from the Indian army filled gaps. Foreign armies, on the other hand, built new units on a nucleus of about 25 per cent trained officers and men. Only Russia suffered comparatively or even worse, from shortage of equipment. In the British camps dummy rifles made by carpenters and dummy guns of piping were used.

The United Kingdom could call on one magnificent reinforcement, the Empire—that institution which the Germans had expected to break up in war. There was no guarantee that the United Kingdom would be supported by contingents of specified strength from the Dominions. In 1911 the then Prime Minister of Canada, Sir Wilfred Laurier, had said that she was not bound to fight in any and every "British war," though the government was legally bound to recognize a state of war with the enemies of the United Kingdom. Now Laurier, in opposition, said that there was in Canada "but one mind and one heart." The first Canadian contingent (mainly the First Division), 33,000 men and 7,000 horses, left the St. Lawrence on October 3. It was the largest armed force yet to cross the Atlantic as a unit. It reached Plymouth without a casualty.* (Pace the critics, the Navy must have been doing something.)

The Anzac Corps, made up of the First Australian and the Australian and New Zealand divisions, began arriving in December in Egypt, the station in which the British government desired to see it. South Africa relieved the British troops, but could not accomplish much more until a revolt had been disposed of. The rebels were in a sense pro-German, but the primary sentiment behind the business was anti-British feeling in veterans of the South African War. The

* Stanley, p. 310.

revolt was extinguished by South Africans, whose leaders had fought against the British. It lasted until January, 1915.

India's first contributions were invaluable, though small by comparison with what was to come. As already stated, a corps (two divisions) arrived in France at a critical moment. In November two newly formed divisions arrived in Egypt and in the course of the same month another division reached the Persian Gulf. The proclamation of a *jihad*, or holy war against the infidel, in Turkey caused some anxiety in view of the large numbers of excellent Moslem soldiers in the Indian Army. A handful of desertions did in fact occur, but virtually all the Indian Moslem soldiers remained true to their salt. In this war there was no equivalent to the "Indian National Army" in Japanese pay which appeared in the Second World War—and it was Hindu, not Moslem.

Before the year was out Britain and her Russian ally had to face a new foe. On August 2 a secret Turco-German treaty involving the entry of Turkey into the war had been signed in Constantinople. Britain's unexpected appearance on the other side, the German defeat on the Marne, and the Austrian defeats at the hands of Russia and Serbia caused the Turks to hesitate. They did not mind fighting, but it must be on the winning side. The Germans put an end to this dallying by a plot in which Enver Pasha, the Turkish war minister, collaborated. Since the German cruisers had arrived in the Bosporus they had, by a transparent fiction, formed part of the Turkish fleet, and Admiral Souchon had gone through the motions of entering the Turkish service. On October 28 he led the combined fleet into the Black Sea and next morning, on a false and even ridiculous pretext, bombarded Odessa, Sebastopol, Theodosia, and Novorossisk. The *Goeben* sank a transport and Turkish destroyers a gunboat. The object, which was war with Russia, was attained. The method was infamous as regards Russia, but it served the Turks right and was almost justified by the probability that they would break their word.

Enver was an adventurer with plenty of personality, but, despite the fact that he was a soldier, ignorant of how to manage any kind of war. Turkey's only enemy immediately to hand was represented by the Russian forces in Caucasia. Enver came forward with one of those colossal plans dear to the dreamer who fancies himself an Alexander or a Napoleon. It was based on the roads—and there at least did not err, for the generally scanty communications are the key 'o mountain warfare. In brief, it depended on a lightning stroke which would place a powerful Turkish force between the Russians and their main bases at Ardahan and Kars, destroying their Caucasian army and opening the way for invasion of Georgia, where all the "Turanian" people would rise against Russia. It disregarded the fact that the troops would have to live on the country in winter; night temperatures twenty degrees below freezing point; bitter winds, amounting to gales on the higher ground; the inadequacy of a mere 50 per cent superiority in infantry for such an ambitious venture.

Both sides fought like savage heroes. Death came quickly in the cold to the wounded left lying out. The fate of thousands of stout Turkish askars touches the emotion of him who contemplates it even today. One division with 8,000 rifles, after four days' marching in the mountains, numbered 4,000. The rest were frozen as hard as boards, but for stragglers who had found shelter in hamlets on the slopes. In the whole army these two causes, frost and desertion, reduced Enver's force of 95,000 to 70,000 in the phase of deployment alone. The decisive Russian victory was won at Sarikamis, halfway between Kars and Erzurum, during the first days of 1915. By mid-January, when the Turkish defeat was acknowledged and Enver had fled from the scene of his destruction of his own army, the 95,000 had fallen to 18,000. How many died is unknown; the Germans heard that 30,000 were buried. The campaign brought to light one fine Russian soldier, Yudenich, at the outbreak of war staff officer to the Viceroy of Caucasia, later in command of a corps. The scope of this Turkish disaster was wide. Turkish strength and fighting power were affected for the rest of the war.

Turkey had mobilized and brought more or less up to strength by the end of September, a month before she entered the war, a force of thirty-six divisions. The reorganization of the army after the disastrous Balkan Wars was the work of a German military mission headed by a capable officer, General Liman von Sanders, supported by German subsidies, weapons and equipment. The modernization and military value of the forces varied, largely with the distance from the capital and the workshops. In Syria, Mesopotamia (roughly the modern Iraq), and southern Arabia, equipment was primitive, and, into the bargain, there were strong reasons to suppose that unrest in the Arab world would render Arab troops unreliable. The communications with these outposts were weak. Tunnels needed to carry the Constantinople-Baghdad railway through the Taurus and Amanus mountains had not been pierced, and the railway extended only to Ras el Ain, halfway between Aleppo and Mosul.

The farthest corps was in the Yemen, in southwestern Arabia. Here and even in the Hejaz the troops still dozed and the officers smoked on divans in the old style, whereas under the eyes of Liman von Sanders and his ever-growing staff all was bustle and modernity. The fundamental strength of Turkey lay, however, as always, in the fighting qualities of the Anatolian peasant, disciplined, frugal, hardy, and brave, normally quiet and good-tempered, but savage when his blood was up.

The reinforcement of the Turkish garrison in Syria was the cause of the parallel reinforcement of the British garrison in Egypt, though it would have been strengthened in any case. In place of a reinforced brigade, there were now four divisions and some other troops, amounting early in 1915 to 70,000 men. The Suez Canal was of immense importance to the British Empire, which reacted violently throughout the war to every hint of a threat to its security. For the moment this precious waterway helped to provide for its own defense, playing the humble part of a moat behind which its defenders lined up. However, the besetting sin of British politicians and their military advisers in this war, that of going a little further, step by step, without any clear appreciation of why they were doing so or what they were heading for, was to carry the advanced guard of a great army nearly a thousand miles northward before the war was done.

A somewhat similar train of events were now being prepared at Basra, on the Shatt-al-Arab, which carries the waters of three great rivers, the Euphrates, the Tigris, and the Karun, into the Persian Gulf. It started with a suggestion from the India Office that a reinforced brigade should be sent "to encourage the Arabs to rally to us and confirm the local sheiks of Mohammerah and Kuwait in their allegiance"; * also, less vaguely, to protect the Anglo-Persian oil installations on Abadan Island. The government of India agreed and the force arrived on October 23. This was before Turkey had entered the war, but the navy virtuously and prudently waited until she was in before bombarding a fort which covered the landing place. On November 6 the landing took place under long-range fire. The Turks were so slow in bringing up their force at Basra, rather stronger than the brigade which had landed, that the remainder of

* Edmonds, *Short History,* p. 377.

the Sixth Indian Division arrived in the interval. With the aid of naval guns the Turkish force was routed on November 17 and disappeared upriver.

Then leave was given to go as far as Basra—quite a sensible move, as it was a good place for a base. Next the government thought the division might as well go as far as Al Qurna, at the confluence of the Euphrates and Tigris, and that such a move would look well in Arab eyes. Perhaps it did, but the Arabs did not appear vastly impressed when Al Qurna was occupied on December 9. But nobody must suppose, said the government earnestly, that any project for an advance on Baghdad could be entertained. It remained to be seen how long this restraint would last.

"In order that he might rob a neighbor whom he had promised to defend," wrote Macaulay of Frederick the Great, "black men fought on the Coromandel, and red men scalped each other by the Great Lakes of North America." In order that a more virtuous man than Frederick, Theobold von Bethmann-Hollweg, might violate the integrity of a neighbor whom his country was pledged by "a solemn testimony" to support, men of variously colored skins fought far and wide, though the main battlefields were in Europe. The modern historian Keith Feiling has rivaled Macaulay with: "So the circle widened until a war, begun by a squalid murder in Bosnia, ended with British soldiers fighting in Syria, on the Caspian, at Archangel, in East Africa, the Alps, and the Caucasus."

Japan entered the war on the side of the Entente on August 23. British and American commentators have dwelt upon the self-interest which inspired her, but nations do not commonly join in wars, once the wars have started, out of pure idealism. Japan had certain aims, and apart from them she meant to play a limited role and resist all attempts to draw her soldiers to Europe. Yet her contribution was valuable and whole-hearted within its bounds. Some of her cruisers and destroyers accompanied British troop convoys as far as Marseilles, and the keenness and efficiency of the crews created a good impression.

Japan was determined to get the Germans out of Kiaochow, their holding in the Shantung province of China. To do this she had to take the fortress-port of Tsingtau, held by a German garrison—excluding Chinese—not far short of 4,000 strong. The Japanese army and navy took the job very seriously, assembling two fleets, which included six battleships, and a large land force. On October 31 they started their bombardment, and on the night of November 6 they assaulted and took a line of redoubts in Port Arthur style. Next day the German governor ran up the white flag. Losses on both sides had been fairly high.

In the Pacific the Japanese navy secured the Marianas, the Carolines, and the Marshalls, which the Germans had no means of defending. Meanwhile a New Zealand force had occupied Samoa. The Australians had landed on an island which Germany had renamed Neu Pommern, soon to become again New Britain. They occupied its so-called capital, a place few had heard of and no one expected to hear of again—there they were wrong, for it was Rabaul, so famous in the Second World War. The governor's surrender involved the downfall of German authority throughout German New Guinea, the Bismarck Archipelago, and possessions in the Solomons. The German holdings in the Pacific had been a façade, with no defensive power except at Tsingtau, a show of prestige without foundation. It collapsed without prestige.

The delay in starting in German Southwest Africa, which has been mentioned, was atoned for by the vigor of the campaign when it was started. The commander was the South African prime minister, General Louis Botha, who had acquired useful military experience in fighting the British. This country, some 800 miles from the Orange River in the south to the frontier of Portuguese Angola in the north, was semidesert and had, like some other German territories, been acquired largely because so vast a block of land looked imposing. It had turned out to possess a more material and satisfactory asset—diamonds in great quantity.

Though the Germans had only about 2,000 regular troops in the colony, a force numerically increased to about threefold on mobilization, its subjugation was no easy matter. The worst difficulty was the extreme scarcity of water, which involved the use of long columns carrying it and of tanks on the railways which ran inland from Lüderitz and Swakopmund. Some 60,000 South African troops entered the territory from first to last, but it need hardly be said that the administrative "tail" was a long one and that but a small proportion ever came under fire. Botha used mounted riflemen in the traditional Boer style on a large scale, and these troops, fighting in a country which was a very bleak version of their own veldt, proved very suitable. The railways also proved valuable, permitting a simultaneous advance in the south halfway up the country.

Botha, thanks to his strength in cavalry, succeeded in preventing the Germans from getting away into Angola, which they would have had almost at their mercy in view of the weakness of the Portuguese garrison. On July 9 Major Franke, the German commander, capitulated. Counting men previously captured, over 5,000 Europeans laid down their arms.

Of the other German colonies, nothing need be said of Togoland, where the garrison surrendered surprisingly quickly to British and French forces. The campaign in the Cameroons may be dealt with entirely here, though it was eighteen months before the last German post surrendered. This great territory, larger than Germany, mainly grassland but containing also scrub and forest, was picturesque enough but possessed a bad climate and a horrible assortment of diseases. Among its plagues was the tsetse fly, though this was not universal. Three allies took part in the reduction of this German colony: the British occupiers, the French from Equatorial Africa, and the Belgians from the Congo. All these troops were natives, excepting officers and noncommissioned officers—the British also employed a handful of Indian and West Indian troops. The total was around 24,000 men, the French contingent being the biggest. There is no figure for porters, but at least 40,000 is the estimate.

The Allies soon found they had bitten off more than they could chew. The waves of malaria and dysentery—with other diseases on a smaller scale—which swept over the troops, and the virtual absence of roads, brought the grandiose scheme of a concentric advance on Yaoundé to a dead stop. The French were the first to get on the move again, but the general advance was not resumed until October, 1915. The German commander bolted southward and, with over 6,000 troops, was interned by the Spanish garrison of Río Muni. British soldiers facetiously accused the Royal Army Medical Corps of using fearsomely heavy needles, so that a shot of antitoxin was as bad as a stab with a bayonet, but the corps knew something by now about tropical diseases. Six Britons only died from disease in this campaign and eighty-four askaris. The porters were less fortunate.

Command of the sea was the decisive factor in overcoming the local difficulties of these campaigns. On balance they were well conducted. German East Africa—today Tanganyika—was another affair altogether. It started with a humiliating British blunder, and the German force remained at large throughout the war. The campaign is a fascinating story, which must be followed year by year. It includes a naval struggle for control of a chain of great lakes. A brilliant soldier, Lieutenant Colonel von Lettow-Vorbeck, stamped it with his name.

West of the coast plain the country was a high plateau, in parts, especially on the frontier of British East Africa, mountainous. The famous peak of Kilimanjaro is not far short of 20,000 feet. The greater part was typical African bush, but there were also large and dense forests. Motor roads were almost nonexistent. The assessment of horse and mule casualties was simple. One hundred per cent would die from the bite of the tsetse fly, though care might keep a proportion alive for a year or so. Human beings faced a long list of tropical diseases. Yet the Germans had to be dealt with for the sake of the neighboring British and Belgian colonies.

The German garrison was small but homogeneous, a dozen little companies of askaris, afterward expanded to perhaps 16,000, a quarter of them white. The British in Uganda and British East Africa to the north and the Rhodesias and Nyasaland to the south, the Belgians in the Congo, gradually built up what amounted to a considerable army. South Africa, as has appeared, had its hands full at the outbreak of war, so India was asked for aid. It sent, among other troops, a force of half a dozen Indian battalions and one British, with one battery. This was ordered to capture the little port of Tanga, between Mombasa and Zanzibar, by a landing from the sea.

The British sometimes become unscrupulous in their wars, but they start them with a purity halfway between innocence and fatuity. A project for keeping the Negroes of African colonies out of the war had been discussed and it was therefore thought right by the naval commander to give warning of hostilities. In other ways, minesweeping and the like, time was provided for the bustling von Lettow to run a few reinforcements—including his own valuable person—down the railway from Moshi at the foot of Kilimanjaro. The leading Indian battalion walked into the fire of the German askaris, and then took to its heels. After three days' fighting, during which Indian morale was not improved by attacks from colonies of wild bees, the troops were reembarked. They had been outfought by a small fraction of their numbers. Tanga stands for a fruitful lesson on how not to start a colonial campaign.

Book Two—1915

Chapter I

THE WEST IN 1915

THE five months of war in 1914 had been filled with virtually continuous fighting, nearly all in the open. By the close of the year, however, the Western Front had coagulated. As yet the fortifications had not become anything like as strong or as deep as they were to be later, but they were already formidable obstacles.

They exercised a profound influence on the struggle throughout the year 1915. The results of the biggest battles were scarcely perceptible on any but large-scale maps. Between battles, trench warfare became a routine. On some parts of the fronts, the Lys valley, for example, "trench" was not the correct word. The subsoil water lay so close to the surface that trenches filled almost as fast as they were dug. Here the line was often held in breastworks. And in wet weather, sometimes all through the winter, many trenches were apt to fill to a depth of two feet or more, making the existence of their occupants miserable. Frost brought relief, and men put up with the cold because it kept them dry. But frost paid off badly. Thaw brought collapse, on a big or small scale according as the trenches were well or badly revetted.

The year 1915 was one of expansion. In its course the B.E.F., ten divisions strong at the outset, was raised to 37 (including two Canadian and the Guards Division), the French strength in the home country to 107, and the German to 94, out of a total of 159. Russia was the only belligerent whose military growth was sharply checked by lack of arms, and her rate of enlistment in proportion to her total manpower was by far the lowest. Britain was, however, heavily handicapped. Her position would have been desperate but for the resource of her private armament firms, which in peace had subsisted mainly on foreign orders and had been reviled in consequence. It was they rather than the government's armament works or the new national factories that delivered the goods. The figures for the whole war are quite extraordinary. Just 90 per cent of the 28,750 guns issued to the army and 97 per cent of the output of 55,000 aircraft came from them.* Large orders were now placed in the United States, despite a protest from Congress, but these were mainly for ammunition.

Output increased in 1915, but very slowly, as must be the case when plants have to be built and tooled up to start the process. Another factor was excessive enlistment of skilled labor in the forces—nothing would hold back men in the early and ardent phase. Getting wind of the shell shortage, with details from Sir John French himself, the powerful newspaper proprietor Lord Northcliffe launched violent attacks on Lord Kitchener. They were generally unpopular, since he was looked on as the greatest man in the country, far more important than any other cabinet minister. Yet the shortage was one of the causes of the setting up of a coalition government and the sole cause of the establishment of the Ministry of Munitions, with Lloyd George at its head. Later on opinion attributed the improvement entirely to him, and though he must have realized that this was nonsense, he did not disclaim the laurels. Undoubtedly, however, his energy was useful in clearing away obstacles from the path of his subordinates.

The British Royal Flying Corps was divided into a Military and a Naval Wing. The division between their functions was, however, a wide one, with the result that the Naval Wing quickly became known as the Royal Naval Air Service and then the title Royal Flying Corps came to stand for the Military Wing alone. The growth was in each case less rapid in numbers than in design and armament. By August, 1915, the B.E.F. had increased from four to thirty divisions but the R.F.C. only from four to eleven squadrons. On the other hand, aircraft types had advanced and new equipment or tactics had made the general picture very different from that of August, 1914.

Photography, mentioned once or twice already, had made great progress. Cameras were now fixed to the aircraft and fitted with a plate-charging device. The use of wireless had extended and the quality of the equipment had improved. Wireless was not, however,

* Edmonds, *Short History*, p. 98.

and never became, reliable enough to do away with the need for simpler means of communication between troops on the ground and aircraft during a battle. Smoke candles, flares, cotton strips, and small mirrors worn on the back—or fixed to packs when these were carried in action—could only indicate infantry positions, but that much amounted to a good deal. Signaling lamps could do more, but they were dangerous instruments anywhere near the firing line. The flares, strips, and lamps appear to have been first used by the French in their autumn Champagne offensive. Another big development was the ranging of artillery from the air. Squared maps, on which objects could be pinpointed, were used by the R.F.C. for this purpose as early as October, 1915.

The growing success of aircraft in these functions inevitably led to a struggle for mastery of the air, and it in turn led to better armament. To begin with, aircraft suitable for fighting were included in squadrons, but in July, 1915, the first homogeneous fighter squadron joined the B.E.F. in France. Squadron encounters began to replace single-handed encounters, and in the latter part of the war these battles swelled till sometimes a hundred or more aircraft maneuvered and fought in a small area.

To begin with, the best fighter was held to be the "pusher," that is, an aircraft with the propeller in the tail. In these machines the French generally took the lead. Then the Germans produced something startling. It was the Fokker, the name being that of its Dutch inventor. The first Fokker was a monoplane, still something of a rarity. It was also a "tractor"—with the propeller in front—and had a gear which synchronized the flow of machine-gun bullets with the engine propulsion, so that they passed between the propeller blades. The aircraft was fast and handy. It appeared in October, 1915, and was superior to all others until the following May. Synchronizing gear came into general use, but few British aircraft were fitted with it even during the Battle of the Somme in 1916.

Tactically, the most striking combat-winning trick was the long-famous "Immelmann turn." Max Immelmann, finest of the Fokker pilots, observed that they seldom got a second chance because, having dived on their opponents, they maintained the dive if it had failed, in order to avoid being attacked from above. His expedient was to make his aircraft rear up, as though to loop, turn sideways, and flatten out in the opposite direction, thus regaining height and reversing course simultaneously. Many victories were won by him and his imitators by this means.*

The young men of the air forces, national and racial characteristics apart, resembled each other closely. They returned from their expeditions to comfortable billets beside airfields in the heart of the countryside. For them the battlefields were not as depressing as for the land forces who slept there. The airmen were adventurous, high-spirited, and gay, though they passed through bad phases when the other side exploited superior aircraft. In general they suffered big losses in proportion to their numbers. Death being always so near, they tried to make the most of life. Life often meant for them *Wein, Weib, und Gesang* and parties ending with smashed glass, crockery, and furniture.

Most of the great fighter pilots died. Among the survivors several, like the Frenchman Charles Nungesser, lost their lives soon after the war in civilian flights. Though formation flying became more and more the rule, theirs was a war of individual warriors, Lancelots and Tristrams who worsted one individual foe after another. Rittmeister Freiherr von Richthofen shot down five British aircraft in a single day, April 29, 1917, one of them being his fiftieth victim. Captain J. L. Trollope shot down six German aircraft in about four hours on March 24, 1918.†

One service tried earnestly to avoid advertisement or even identification of individuals. The British, as usual, failed to realize that heroic deeds were a national tonic. Even they, however, could hardly keep quiet about the winning of a Victoria Cross, and Albert Ball, V.C., of Britain became as famous as Georges Guynemer of France. Hero worship was inevitable when the feats of such "aces" became known. Even now, as we look back upon them, there is something magical, superhuman, about them. Guynemer and Fonck, Ball and McCudden, Boelcke and Richthofen appeal all the more to us because some of their secrets elude us. It does not suffice to say that Ball was fantastically brave, that his reflexes were uncannily rapid, and that he was a deadly shot. Their methods differed widely. Guynemer, gentle and delicate but with never a word of pity for a slain foe, was wildly reckless and returned again and again with his aircraft peppered with bullet holes. Fonck, icily cool, is said to have brought his back nearly always unmarked. Guynemer died over Passchendaele; Fonck lived

* Jones, *War in the Air*, II, 149-150.
† Jones, *War in the Air*, IV, 317.

to be a businessman and an unprepossessing right-wing politician at the time of the Second World War. The distinctive characteristics of all the leaders in combat and of fighter pilots were an intense concentration, extraordinarily quick thinking, and unquenchable activity. Ball, whose spelling did not match his marksmanship, put it that he liked life a "bussel." This was the sort of life they lived, while it lasted.

Despite the growth of the B.E.F., the weight of the war in the west was still borne mainly by the French. Control went with responsibility. In theory the British were not under French command; in practice the demands of General Joffre were almost always met. Sir John French's actions were governed by his loyalty to the Alliance. It was his finest quality. It instilled into his mind the principle that, since he commanded a relatively small contingent, he must act as Joffre desired even when he would rather have done something different. He might have nursed and seasoned his young troops for future opportunities, but just as Joffre felt bound to launch offensives in support of Russia and because the Germans had shifted forces to the east, so the British commander in chief felt bound to take part up to the limit of his resources, sometimes beyond them.

The end of open warfare had left between the sea and the Meuse a front bulging westward in a big blunt-nosed salient with its apex near Compiègne. Joffre's strategy was to attack one side of it eastward from the Artois plateau and the other northward from Champagne. He believed he could finally break the German defenses on both fronts. Then, when the enemy was floundering, he would launch a third offensive from Verdun, to threaten and if possible cut the enemy's only good railway south of the Ardennes. The lines north of the forest would not suffice to maintain a fighting front, and the Germans would be compelled to quit French and Belgian soil.

It was good strategy on paper. It was, in fact, essentially the strategy of 1918, by means of which the Germans were forced not merely to abandon their hold on France and Belgium but to sue for peace. The strategic aim, however, depended on tactical success. Strategy is the art of conducting a war; tactics the art of fighting. "Tactics, weapons, and supply are the master-keys which alone can open the door to strategy." * And in 1915 tactical defense, based on

* Falls: *Marshal Foch*, p. 88.

the machine gun and barbed wire and the high quality and resolution of German troops, proved to be very strong.

After a pause of a month in January and February, the French renewed their offensive in Champagne. Once more the fighting was fierce and bloody; once more the gains were very small and the losses vast, some 90,000 men killed, wounded, and prisoners of war on either side. The attack was broken off on March 17, but Joffre was determined to try again in that quarter.

He had also decided to launch in March another offensive—the second half of the plan—in Artois, to capture the commanding height of Vimy Ridge and if possible exploit success by thrusting at the German road and rail network in the plain of Douai. To assemble the necessary strength he had to demand of the British the relief of French forces in the Ypres salient. This relief was delayed owing to the slow arrival of British reinforcements and the demands of the Gallipoli campaign. Moreover, Sir John French did not consider that after the relief he would be strong enough to give much support to the Artois offensive. He therefore decided to attack first independently. This was carrying loyalty to excessive lengths. However, he chose his place well: opposite the village of Neuve Chapelle, where the Germans were very thin on the ground. General Sir Douglas Haig, commanding the recently created First Army, massed four divisions in secrecy on a frontage defended by only one German division, and the Royal Flying Corps photographed the whole position, so that large-scale maps showing every trench and work could be printed and issued to the troops.

The affair started brilliantly on March 10. The Germans were surprised and their position was overrun. Men's spirits soared. They believed the enemy had little left, and they were pretty nearly right. But delays, minor hitches, and uncertainty proved fatal to their high hopes. The Germans rushed up reinforcements. The drive petered out. At the end of three days no more than a dent, a mile and a quarter wide and a thousand yards deep, had been made. The Germans had suffered severely in an abortive counterattack and the losses were about equal. The British were disappointed, but their spirits remained high. They knew a gaping hole had been punched and that their errors had been largely responsible for failure to exploit the victory. They vowed to repair those errors and to do better next time.

The Germans were committed to the defensive in the west, now

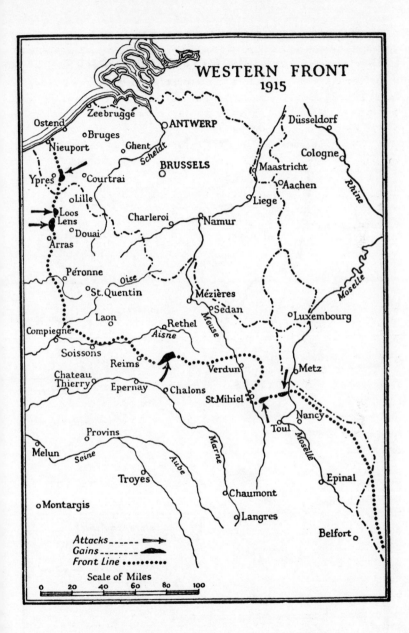

WESTERN FRONT
1915

Ostend
Zeebrugge
ANTWERP
Düsseldorf
Bruges
Nieuport
Ghent
Cologne
Scheldt
BRUSSELS
Maastricht
Ypres
Courtrai
Aachen
Lille
Liege
Loos
Charleroi
Namur
Lens
Douai
Arras
Péronne
Oise
St.Quentin
Mézières
Laon
Sedan
Luxembourg
Rethel
Compiegne
Aisne
Meuse
Soissons
Reims
Verdun
Metz
Chateau
Thierry
Epernay
Chalons
St.Mihiel
Nancy
Toul
Provins
Moselle
Melun
Seine
Aube
Epinal
Troyes
Marne
Montargis
Chaumont
Langres
Belfort

Rhine

Moselle

Attacks _ _ _ _ _
Gains _ _ _ _ _
Front Line • • • • • • •

Scale of Miles
0   20   40   60   80   100

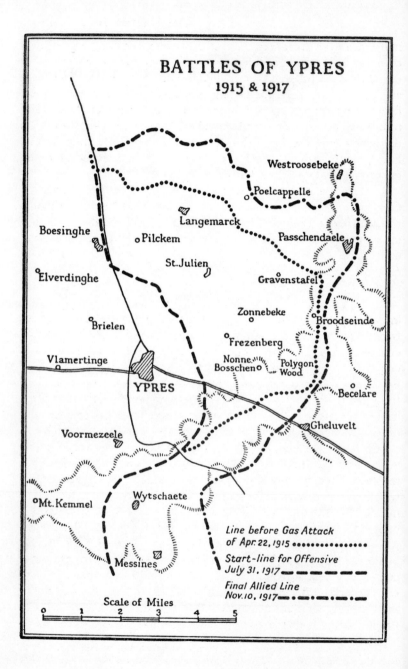

BATTLES OF YPRES
1915 & 1917

Westroosebeke

Poelcappelle

Langemarck

Boesinghe

Pilckem

Passchendaele

St. Julien

Elverdinghe

Gravenstafel

Zonnebeke

Brielen

Broodseinde

Frezenberg

Vlamertinge

Nonne
Bosschen

Polygon
Wood

YPRES

Becelare

Voormezeele

Gheluvelt

Mt. Kemmel

Wytschaete

Line before Gas Attack
of Apr. 22, 1915 ••••••••••

Start-line for Offensive
July 31, 1917 ----

Final Allied Line
Nov. 10, 1917 --•--•--

Messines

Scale of Miles

0   1   2   3   4   5

more than ever because in the east they were mounting a great new offensive. Falkenhayn had, however, been persuaded to try the effect of chlorine gas released from cylinders and to make the experiment at Ypres, where the experts told him favorable winds were most likely. It was purely an experiment and no reserves were held ready to exploit success; but round the salient there were eleven German divisions facing the five British and two French defending it. The French were on the left flank. Reports of German preparations to use gas had reached the Allies, but were neglected.

April 22 was a beautiful spring day. At 5 P.M. a short but fierce German bombardment opened. Soon afterward French Algerian riflemen were seen fleeing in flocks toward Ypres and the canal running north from it. Some vomited; some pointed to their throats and uttered the word "gaz," but were otherwise unintelligible to British officers who encountered them. Their flight was soon copied by the French Territorials—troops of the oldest classes—on their left. A mist was seen drifting along close to the ground. It was gas from cylinders in the German trenches. The discharge hardly involved the British front, but west of that held by the First Canadian Division it had collapsed; indeed it had disappeared. The Germans followed up for a couple of miles; then their troops ran into their own gas and halted. By dawn on the twenty-third the British had strung out battalions from three divisions to fill the gap, but by the twenty-fifth the highest ground had been lost together with nearly half the breadth of the salient. The rest, under fire from three sides, was untenable.

Foch, now commanding the Groupe d'Armées du Nord,* intervened with reinforcements and orders for a counteroffensive, but the local French commander did nothing. Practically the whole weight of the defense fell on the British. Their Second Army commander, Sir Horace Smith-Dorrien, therefore proposed to withdraw two and a half miles to a position covering Ypres. Sir John French was so angered that he sent him home and replaced him by Sir Herbert Plumer—and then, when the latter declared for the same course of action, agreed. After several postponements the retirement was carried out during the first three nights of May. On the eighth the Germans, after advancing their artillery, attacked the Frezenberg Ridge. For six days there was terrific fighting, a real soldiers' battle

---

* The Russians had from the first formed army groups, which, as in a later war, they called "fronts." French, Germans, and Austrians imitated them. The British, with a maximum of five armies in the west, did not.

which the higher commands could influence hardly at all. The British lost valuable ground on the ridge. In the early hours of May 24, the Germans released gas on a bigger scale than on April 22, entirely against the British, and followed it up by an infantry attack. There was no surprise this time and the defense was magnificent. The troops did not flinch, though they had as yet only the most primitive protection against the gas. The Germans gained very little further ground, and at a heavy cost.

"Second Ypres" was, for its size, one of the most murderous battles of the war. The total casualties, including those due to gas, exceeded 100,000, those of the Allies being slightly the greater. By using poison gas in defiance of the convention, the Germans gained the biggest success of the year in the west. They reduced the Ypres salient to a flat curve just east of the city and secured all the commanding ground. Yet, because their action had been experimental and they had so slender a reserve, they missed a far greater victory before the effect of surprise wore off. Leaving morality out of it, their action was imprudent. It laid them open to heavy reprisals because the prevailing winds were westerly.

Perhaps the most important advantage they got out of it was that it had involved seven Allied divisions due to take part in the Artois offensive which had meanwhile been launched and in the expenditure of a vast amount of shell. On May 9 the French Tenth Army attacked, with nine divisions in first line and another nine in reserve. The main assault in the center was made by a corps commanded by General Pétain. The troops were good, intrepid, determined that nothing should stop them. They smashed through the German defense and penetrated two and a half miles, at one point almost to the crest of Vimy Ridge. And then—how often has the tale to be told!— reserves were held too far back; the Germans were reinforced; the footing on the crest was lost; the battle degenerated into one of attrition, lasting till May 15 and renewed for four days on June 15. It was attrition the French could not afford. In most of the great battles losses were roughly equal, but here the French suffered four to three, 100,000 to 75,000. In the face of this appalling slaughter the French General Staff concluded that a breakthrough followed by exploitation of the victory could be achieved only after the enemy had been so worn down that he had no reserves to reinforce his front. This came near to making naked attrition the sole aim.

The plight of the British in regard to ammunition is grimly illustrated by the fact that, whereas the French had carried out an artillery preparation lasting five days, General Haig considered he could only afford one of forty minutes. The objective was a slight swelling of the low ground of the Lys valley dignified by the title of Aubers Ridge. This was a bigger-scale venture than Neuve Chapelle and aroused high hopes. The result was calamitous, one might say a fiasco. The strength of the defenses and the lack of heavy shells to smash them—largely due to the demands of the Gallipoli campaign—made the task impossible. The British command had at least the strength of mind to break it off that evening. Yet, under ceaseless pressure from Joffre, it tried again a little farther south at Festubert on May 11. This time it had husbanded enough ammunition for a four-day bombardment and opened with a night attack. The results were a great improvement on the last effort, but still very disappointing, the maximum advance being only three-quarters of a mile at the end on May 27.

None the less, amazing as it sounds, optimism continued. It was not only that of the higher command. The officer commanding the Second Gordon Highlanders, returning soon after the battle on recovery from a wound received earlier, recorded that he found his battalion "as pleased as Punch." * The command knew that German reserves which would otherwise have faced the French had been drawn in. It believed that with more and better ammunition far more could have been achieved. Many shells had failed to explode.

A pause in major operations followed, broken by a long series of minor ones of little value, as well as raids for identifications. A new British army, the Third, was formed, and in July and August took over fifteen miles of the French line astride the Somme, where it was separated from the remainder of the B.E.F. by the twenty-mile front of the French Tenth Army astride the Artois battlefield. At a conference between the two ministers of munitions, Mr. Lloyd George and M. Albert Thomas, with military advisers, the British advocated shutting down the offensive till the spring of 1916, when more heavy howitzers and ammunition to meet this new kind of warfare, as well as more divisions, would be available. Joffre would not hear of it, and once more the British gave way. It was all very well for Joffre to demand aggression: he could use in Champagne well over twice, and in Artois nearly twice, as many guns per mile as the British had available in their next battle.

* Falls, *The Gordon Highlanders in the First World War*, p. 44.

Joffre had originally hoped to renew the offensive quickly, but delays, mainly due to a lag in the relief and to roadmaking in barren Champagne, caused a long postponement. Inevitably, German intelligence got a rough idea of what was brewing. The German command had time to make ready. It brought over four divisions from Russia, where the summer offensive of the Central Powers had won an outstanding success. Even more to the point, it constructed a second position, two to four miles behind the first. This was something new, the first big development in defense.

The double offensive, the greatest since the front had been stabilized, was launched on September 25. The major effort was in Champagne. Here the Eastern Group of Armies of General de Castelnau attacked on a front of fifteen miles halfway between Reims and Verdun, with two armies (Pétain and de Langle de Cary). The Germans had available only twelve divisions in line or local reserve, little more than a third of the French resources. The highest hopes accompanied the enterprise. Here, and in Artois too, cavalry stood ready to exploit a breakthrough. Buses were parked at hand to carry infantry in support. The French were all out for victory. Cloud gas was used on a large scale.

There was no breakthrough. Initial success was considerable, with progress up to a mile and three-quarters at one point. The Germans were shaken, and only the insistence of Falkenhayn—who had hurried back from the Eastern Front—stopped a precipitate retreat.* It was the new German second line that decided the issue. For the first time the Germans exploited the principle of defense in depth, having withdrawn part of their artillery behind the second line before the attack began. Deadlock having been reached, the French broke off the offensive on September 28. They had taken 18,000 prisoners and given the enemy a scare to remember.†

Their Artois offensive by d'Urbal's Tenth Army, in the Northern Group of Foch, accomplished less. It began badly, though Crown Prince Rupprecht of Bavaria had little more than two divisions in first line to meet it. On September 28 a determined and gallant attack reached the crest of Vimy Ridge. Then the weather broke and the venture ended. The French took over a short sector of the British front south of Loos. The offensive would have been renewed but for the demands of a new theater of war, Macedonia.

* Falkenhayn, p. 141.
† Weltkrieg, X, 11.

Sir John French had objected to the battlefield allotted to him, largely a coal field with *cités ouvrières* of miners' cottages. Lord Kitchener, however, intervened to support the demands of Joffre and Foch that the attack should be made alongside the French instead of farther north. Again that uncompromising British loyalty! The First Army commander, Haig, attacked with six divisions in line. Three were regular divisions, the other three new, though one of them, a Territorial division, possessed the dubious experience of having fought at Festubert; the other two were Scottish divisions of the new army. They were full of enthusiasm and they fought like lions.

Here also gas was used, but not very successfully. On the left it once blew back and was largely responsible for the complete failure on that flank. In the center it started all right but near the end of the discharge drifted back and caused a number of casualties. The other five divisions carried the German first line and at one point penetrated the second. Counterattacks were generally repulsed, but darkness fell with the main British line about halfway between the two defense positions.

Sir Douglas Haig had no army reserve. If the G.H.Q. reserve of three divisions had been available in good time it might conceivably have broken through at the point where the second position had been reached. Sir John French, however, released it too late. Two of its divisions were raw. They were a march in rear and tired by three previous night marches. The final approach march was also made in the dark for the sake of concealment and was chaotic, with traffic blocks due to poor march discipline. Some arrived hungry because they had been unable to make contact with their transport. They were moved up to the fringe of the battle, but their attack had to be postponed until 11 A.M. on the twenty-sixth. One of them was broken by a counterattack, and soon afterward men of both began to stream rearward. The third G.H.Q. division, the Guards, and a cavalry division were rushed up to fill the void. The battle was renewed after a pause and on October 8 a counterattack was smashed. The whole thing petered out and was abandoned on November 4.

On December 15 Field Marshal Sir John French was superseded, as was inevitable. His successor was General Sir Douglas Haig.

The French casualties for the campaign were over 190,000; those of the British at Loos and a couple of useless subsidiary thrusts little short of 60,000. The German losses, compiled on a different method, were put at 178,000.* This frightful hecatomb was rewarded with little or no strategic gain.

The German view is that a substantial, perhaps a great, success might have been won if the offensive had been carried out as originally intended in July or even in August. Then the Western Front had been drained of reserves. It may be so, but the defensive was in the ascendant. A well-mounted offensive could always break in at first, but was always quickly blocked. Even the progress was almost unchanging: a depth of one mile and a half to about one and three-quarters was usual. This was roughly the utmost range of field artillery before moving forward.

In his surveys of the Artois offensive Foch wrote of the need for more heavy artillery and of trench artillery for short-range fire. Turning to tactics, he threw doubt on the possibility of a swift breakthrough.

"The headlong, violent onset, aiming at a breakthrough," he wrote in his private notebook, "has not given the results we expected of it. It can be resumed when we have corrected it, to obtain successful results, by consecutive actions, each including an artillery preparation and an infantry assault." And to the G.Q.G.: "We must abandon the brutal assault in masses more or less deep and dense, with the reserves on the heels of the leading line, ready to capture several successive objectives in a single bound. It has never reached its goal." †

The argument was cogent. Yet it was to be found that this controlled, continuous, and gradual action brought its own disadvantages. It gave the enemy more time—time to reinforce, to mount counterattacks, to dig. Now the battlefield seemed to be governed by the machine gun, the coil of barbed wire, and the slab of concrete, which shattered the infantry again and again, whatever the tactics employed. But there was no sign of flagging on either side.

* Unlike those of the western allies, German official casualty lists did not include men treated in the corps hospitals and returned to their units without being evacuated, still less those "wounded—at duty," that is, very lightly wounded and remaining with their units. To relate the two systems, at least 20 per cent must be added to German totals. With this adjustment the German losses would stand at 213,000 against an Allied figure of 250,000.
† Weygand, p. 129.

Chapter II

THE EAST IN 1915

THE Germans were as keen as the more directly threatened Austrians to drive the Russians away from the Carpathians. An invasion of Hungary would in the long run be no more pleasant for Germany than for Austria. The Russians were already over part of the crest. The barrier was less strong than the height of the peaks suggests, because they rise from a lofty tableland, but winter warfare in snow is never welcome to large armies.

German reinforcements were transported from the Western Front to make, first, the bulk of a new force called the South Army, the rest being Austrian; second, another German army in East Prussia. Here, it will be recalled, the Russians had brought off a second invasion at the end of 1914. A double offensive was planned for early 1915. In the Carpathians Linsingen's South Army was to break through by the Beskiden Pass, advance northeast in the general direction of Lemberg, and wheel outward to roll up the Russian front. On its left the Austrian Third Army under Borojević was to force the Russians to raise the siege of Przemysl. On the extreme right the Seventh Army under Pflanzer-Baltin was to aid the main drive. The other half of the offensive was to be made by the Germans in East Prussia.

The Carpathian offensive, starting on January 23, proved a failure. Cold, snow, and lack of roads in the mountains hampered the attack so greatly that progress was small, losses heavy, and suffering tragic. The diversion on the right proved far more successful than the main operation. Freiherr von Pflanzer-Baltin, whom Conrad considered his best army commander, struck out through yard-deep snow, smashed the opposition, and drove the Russians back some sixty

miles. Czernowitz, on the Prut, was taken on February 17 with 60,-
000 prisoners and Stanislau on the twentieth; the latter place was
regained by the Russians, but the front was stabilized a day's march
to the south. This was one of the most brilliant feats of Austrian
arms, but while Linsingen stuck in the mountains, where, says
Conrad bitterly, he "did nothing but shout for reinforcements," *
Pflanzer-Baltin was out on his own.

On March 22 the fortress of Przemysl, isolated for the second
time, surrendered to the Russians, thus setting free the three corps
besieging it. With their aid the Third Russian Army creditably
pulled itself together, with the aid of the Eighth. Here shone one
of the finest qualities of the Russian armies. They might seem to be
fought to a finish, hammered to a jelly. While the pressure was
maintained they showed no sign of recovery, but if they were
afforded half a chance through its slackening they were ready to
batter away once more. Indeed, the bearing of both sides was
wonderful. If it takes courage to fight as they did in any circumstances, it takes yet more to keep on fighting in the misery of snow
and frost, when the wounded perish before they can be found and
the luckier ones may lose a limb from exposure to cold. The Russians
recovered the ground lost in the mountains. On the left of the
South Army the Austrians found themselves in such trouble that
Hindenburg had to send more German reinforcements southward.

His own offensive had been far more successful. The Eighth and
Tenth Armies advanced from the Masurian Lakes on February 9:
Cannae, Hannibal's envelopment of the Romans in 216 B.C., still
haunted German military minds—oblivious of the fact that the
original Cannae had been won, not in an offensive, but by taking
advantage of the enemy's impetuosity, and that this method was the
easier to work. The advance was to be fastest on the outer wings
of the two German armies and to put the Russian Tenth Army into a
bag.

That army had no ground as favorable to defense as the Carpathians. The shortage of shell was approaching its worst—and 1915
was for Russia the worst year of the war. In the trench warfare
which had begun in the east a little later than in the west, batteries
were often limited to four rounds a gun per day. More crippling
still, there was a shortage of rifles. Some reinforcements arrived without them. These troops were not only unable to fight; they could

* Regele, p. 343.

not be properly trained, or only very slowly by sharing rifles. The Japanese had provided 200,000, but the Russians had hoped for a million, and orders placed elsewhere abroad had not yet borne fruit. In leadership the Germans held a strong advantage. From armies down to brigades they maneuvered fast and boldly because leaders trusted both their colleagues and the higher command. On the Russian side leaders trusted neither. Besides armament and leadership the Germans had a third advantage in the superiority of the rank and file. Some Russian formations were still magnificent in spirit—though even then behind the Germans in intelligence—but others had deteriorated sadly owing to their enormous losses in officers and underofficers. Here are two pictures from the pen of the British military attaché, a friendly observer, of troops moving into action on the Narev, just south of the main battlefield:

"They made a bad impression. Most of them seemed listless, of brutally stupid type, of poor physique and stamina. . . . Not an inspiriting spectacle. The men crowded all over the pavements, and the officers rode or else slouched along without making any attempt to enforce march discipline. The corps had only three-battalion regiments and only about twenty officers a regiment. The bulk of the men had never been under fire, and they looked quite untrained." *

In these circumstances the Russians fell back in face of the German attack. But their withdrawal was not fast enough. The enemy pressed hard on their heels. Many units were overrun. Finally the bulk of the Tenth Army was enveloped, as the Germans had planned, in the forest between Augustow, Suwalki, and Grodno. The Germans claimed 90,000 prisoners, but a great number broke out. Once more the Russians revealed that they could come back into the fight when they seemed to be down and out. A new army, the Twelfth, under the waspish and unpopular but hard-fighting sexagenarian General Plehve, began on February 22 to strike back between the Narev and the East Prussian frontier. Plehve won no outstanding success, but the German advance was brought to an end. To show how different were the Eastern and Western Fronts, the German offensive from Masuria had led to an advance of some seventy miles in a fortnight and yet was not accounted a great

---

* Knox, I, 255. The normal complement of officers to a three-battalion regiment would be at least sixty.

strategic victory. Such an advance at such a pace on Brussels, Namur, or Mezières might have brought the end of the war in sight.

"We are stuck fast on the whole front," Max Hoffmann wrote in his diary on April 3.* This would not do. A bigger effort must be made. And it was because the Masurian offensive had not won an adequate victory, while the Carpathian offensive had miscarried, that Falkenhayn decided to give the Eastern Front priority in 1915 and that he had no reserves to exploit the one breakthrough of the year in the west, the Ypres gas attack.

Two plans were presented. One came ostensibly from the bullet head of Hindenburg, actually from his staff; the other came from the more intellectual and imaginative head of Conrad. Hindenburg's plan was, naturally, for an advance from East Prussia. He wanted to thrust southeast toward the Narev and then behind Warsaw. Conrad looked to the northern foothills of the Carpathians and the Vistula. There, he insisted to the Germans again and again, was the place to strike. Success there meant the collapse of the Russian Carpathian front at the very least. François, a shrewd judge, doubted if Hindenburg's plan would have worked.†

Falkenhayn agreed with Conrad. He was a "westerner." ‡ He believed that the war could be won only in the west; he had indeed begun preparations there for offensives in 1915. If he must involve himself more deeply in Russia, however, he would do it properly. That Russia could be driven right out of the war he thought impossible. But it would be possible not merely to halt the Russian advance but to subject the enemy to such a *Lähmung* (crippling) that forces would be made available to obtain a decision in the west. But what did Falkenhayn mean by a decision? Not quite what soldiers generally mean. He himself said he wanted "a good peace." This should be every wise man's goal in war, but a good peace entails a correct calculation of the extent of the victory needed to obtain it. A number of German soldiers, including at that time Ludendorff, and Hoffmann always, thought that Russia could be knocked out. This was also the view of Conrad. The fate of the Central Powers depended mainly on him and Falkenhayn, but the

* Hoffmann, *War Diaries*, I, 55.
† François, p. 251.
‡ The terms "westerner" and "easterner" are English, created in the controversy in Britain as to whether the aim should be to win the war in the west or in the east.

Austrian had to take the subordinate place. We have a picture of their meeting at this time.

> Beside the driver sat Falkenhayn with his inevitable cigar, his sharply cut intellectual features half hidden by goggles, his tall, slim figure covered by a driving dust-coat.*
>
> Falkenhayn sprang out and greeted the waiting Conrad with animation. The Austro-Hungarian chief was small and elegant, almost girlish in figure. His clever face with its white imperial was agitated by a nervous twitch of the mouth and eyelids. His uniform was clothing, not adornment; seldom was there an order on his jacket; indeed on ceremonial occasions he often forgot such decorations. So they stood together, the two men whose decisions set thousands in motion. The first was the more of a soldier; the second the more deeply instructed soldier. Over one there remained something of the bloom of his days as a lieutenant; over the other the irritable air created by mental toil.†

This time Falkenhayn did not succumb to the temptation of a double major offensive. Conrad's or Hindenburg's plan must predominate. Falkenhayn took both to the German Emperor and advised the adoption of Conrad's without naming the author. William II agreed. Hindenburg was relegated to a subsidiary operation and Falkenhayn came over to run the main business himself. One can imagine the fury of the Hindenburg clique, who were beginning to think they owned the Eastern Front.

As it was, more German divisions had to be brought in. Yet another German army, the Eleventh, was formed under Mackensen, with the expert Colonel Hans von Seeckt as chief of staff and mentor. It consisted of eight German and three Austrian divisions. This was becoming a favorite organization with the Germans, who thought they got the utmost out of the Austrians by its means. The Austro-Hungarian troops fought well, anyhow on the offensive, under higher German command, but the relations of the Central Power allies worsened. The senior Austrian officers found

---

* This paraphernalia for a road journey may sound odd to the present generation. Covered cars did exist and were commonly used by generals in the west. For a long drive at very high speed, however, many preferred an open car. In dry weather the narrow mudguards afforded little protection against dust.
† Kuhl, I, 257.

the majority of the German commanders and staff officers arrogant and dictatorial. On the left stood the smaller Austrian Fourth Army, commanded by the Archduke Joseph Ferdinand. There was plenty of shell and the concentration of guns was heavy for that date. The Central Powers had concentrated superiority of strength, despite the 35 per cent Russian superiority on the whole front.

After a four hours' bombardment on May 2 the Germans and Austrians strode forward between Gorlice and Tarnow on a twenty-eight-mile front. They found that Radko Dimitriev's Third Russian Army had abandoned its ill-constructed trenches. The second position was stormed next day. Then, as Conrad had foretold, the defense began to collapse. Not only the Third Russian Army but also the Eighth, Brusilov's, began a precipitate retreat. Guns and transport were abandoned in masses. Prisoners, often delighted to be taken, were rounded up by scores of thousands. Reinforcements melted like lead in a foundry. A junior British officer, Captain Neilsen, wrote of the Third Army, to which he was attached, on May 19:

> Their losses have been colossal. They confessed to over 100,000 on the 16th, but I think they have lost more. *And on June 6:* This army is now a harmless mob.... We are very short of ammunition and guns. All realize the futility of sending men against the enemy, they with their artillery and we with ours.*

This was rout, sanguinary rout. It looked as though it could never be halted. It was not for a long time, but it did begin to slow down, and wherever this happened the Russians began to fight again. Dimitriev having been got rid of, their Third Army was behaving better under a new commander named Lesh. The Russians had made frequent counterattacks, and the unmetaled roads delayed the assailants as much as the human opposition. By July 1 the front had passed beyond Lemberg; on the thirtieth Archduke Joseph's cavalry clattered into Lublin. On August 5 Warsaw, the Polish capital, was abandoned by the Russians as the result of Austrian thrusts from the south and Hindenburg's participation from the Narev. On the whole front the forces of the Central Powers was tramping forward now. They dragged up their big howitzers—some

* Knox, I, 284, 287.

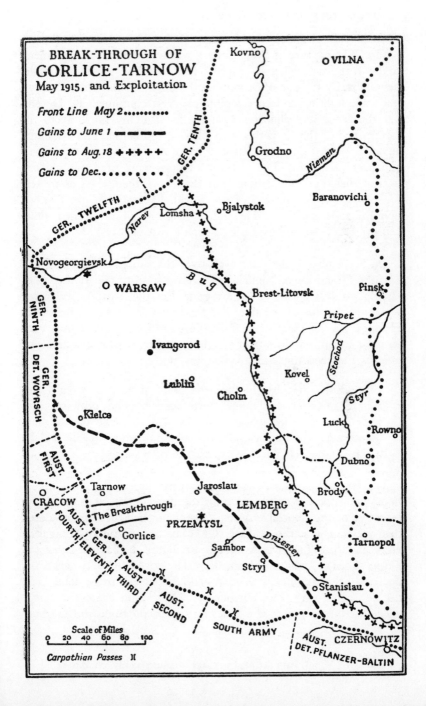

BREAK-THROUGH OF
GORLICE-TARNOW
May 1915, and Exploitation

Front Line May 2 ∙∙∙∙∙∙∙∙∙∙∙
Gains to June 1 ▬ ▬ ▬ ▬
Gains to Aug. 18 + + + + +
Gains to Dec. ∙ ∙ ∙ ∙ ∙ ∙ ∙

Kovno

○ VILNA

GER. TENTH

GER. TWELFTH

Narev

Lomsha ○   ○ Bjalystok

Grodno

Niemen

Baranovichi

Novogeorgievsk

GER. NINTH

○ WARSAW

Bug

Brest-Litovsk

Pinsk

Pripet

GER. DET. WOYRSCH

● Ivangorod

Stochod

Kovel ○

Lublin

Cholm

Styr

○ Kielce

Luck

Rowno

AUST. FIRST

Dubno

Tarnow

Jaroslau

LEMBERG

Brody

CRACOW ○

AUST. FOURTH

The Breakthrough

PRZEMYSL

Tarnopol

GER. ELEVENTH

○ Gorlice

Sambor

Dniester

AUST. THIRD

Stryj

AUST. SECOND

Stanislau

SOUTH ARMY

AUST. DET. PFLANZER-BALTIN

CZERNOWITZ

Scale of Miles
0   20   40   60   80   100

Carpathian Passes)(

16-inch—and pounded the fortress of Novogeorgievsk into surrender. The capture of Brest-Litovsk was world news for a moment, to be forgotten when its captors had marched a hundred miles beyond it. By the end of September the offensive was virtually over, but some fighting and considerable progress continued. By December the front was almost a straight line running north from the eastern end of the Carpathians to Riga on the Baltic. The maximum advance was 300 miles; the Russians had lost over 300,000 in prisoners and over 3,000 guns. The victorious troops were tired out and had outrun their communications, but they bore themselves as makers of history and felt on top of the world. Excusably might General von François exclaim: "The military history of no former times can produce a second example of such a feat of arms!" *

Yet it was not Cannae, not the end.

On September 8 the Tsar took over the supreme command and sent the Grand Duke Nicholas as viceroy to Caucasia. It was a last attempt to save Russia and the régime. But the situation called for a giant at the side of the ruler and the breed did not exist in Russia. He took for his chief of staff Alexiev, far from a giant, not very strong-minded, no more than a highly competent strategist and staff officer. This was not enough. Brusilov writes:

> I consider that, had he been the Chief of Staff of a real Commander-in-Chief, he would have been beyond criticism. But with a commander whose mind he had to make up for him, whose every action he had to guide, and whose feeble will he had to strengthen, Alexiev was not the right man.†

The fatigue of the troops and the overtaxing of the communications were not the only factors in the decision to close down the offensive of the Central Powers. Falkenhayn had indeed considered this question as early as June. On May 4 the Austro-Hungarian commander in chief, the Archduke Frederick, had learned that the Triple Alliance, which had not been denounced by Italy when she declared her neutrality, was at an end.‡ What was to be done? The decision taken may seem obvious to wisdom after the event, but it needed a fine nerve at the time. It was to continue the Gorlice-

* Kuhl, I, 226.
† Brusilov, p. 171.
‡ Schwarte, V, 101. Italy declared war, against Austria only, on May 23.

Tarnow offensive as though nothing were amiss and leave two corps, with *Landsturm* and garrison troops, facing the whole Italian Army. Conrad was displeased, but not because he was scared; he was burning to strike Italy. Clearly, the Italian theater would soon have to be strengthened. Then there was the Western Front. On the eve of the French offensive in Champagne, Falkenhayn had prudently ordered Hindenburg to dispatch a corps to France and refused his half-mutinous plea to keep it "for ten days or a fortnight." It arrived just in time and its influence was decisive.

The most important consideration was, however, the campaign in Gallipoli, an account of which follows. Week by week, Falkenhayn studied the reports from that theater. While the Turks held out—and they were doing well—he could afford to go deeper into Russia. The reports, however, grew uglier, above all regarding the ammunition supply. That he could not remedy while Serbia sat victorious on the Constantinople railway. He had postponed his schemes against her in favor of the offensive against Russia. Now the time had come to pump fresh blood into Turkey. So a stream of German and Austrian troops moved back through Hungary to the Danube and the Save. With them went Mackensen and his bear-leaders Seeckt and Hentsch. The Hindenburg clique, who wanted the job, raged and jibed—Mackensen would have to be rechristened "Prince Eugene," said Hoffmann. But it was not really Mackensen, a figurehead, of whom they were jealous. Their gall rose because the real performers, Seeckt and Hentsch, had been preferred to Ludendorff and Hoffmann—and as Falkenhayn's protégés. How they hated that man! These moves brought quietude to the Eastern Front.

Chapter III

THE FATAL HELLESPONT

No episode of the war is more poignant than the effort to force the Dardanelles. As pure tragedy it may not equal the Somme, yet the tragedy of missed chances, the might-have-been, often strikes the imagination even more forcibly than a human holocaust. In the former aspect the Dardanelles surpassed the Somme, while in the latter, with its half million British, French, and Turkish casualties, it is a holocaust second only to that of the French carnage. And, whatever the final effects of the Somme, one is hard put to it to say what could have been made of it, except the attrition which it produced. The thought of what might have been made of the Dardanelles still tortures the romantic. Listen to one who is essentially romantic, though a brilliant military historian: "It was the most imaginative conception of the war, and its potentialities were almost beyond reckoning. It might even have been regarded, as Rupert Brooke had hoped, as a turning point in history." *

January 2, 1915, was the beginning. On that day a telegram from the British ambassador in Petrograd † reached London with a plea from the Grand Duke Nicholas that a demonstration against the Turks should be arranged to induce them to withdraw troops from the Caucasus. Only a demonstration, no matter where, and not for the purpose of reopening the Black Sea, as most people think! But the eyes of Lord Kitchener turned to the Dardanelles. He did not aspire to be the savior of Russia, but he did realize that she had taken a terrible battering and needed all possible support. By a supreme irony, the following days saw the overwhelming defeat of the Turks

* Moorehead, p. 364.
† The name of the capital had been given a Russian form as a patriotic gesture.

at Sarikamis and the end to their threat in Caucasia, whereupon the Grand Duke withdrew his request.*

The prospect was not alluring. The Gallipoli peninsula was hilly, rocky, almost trackless but for one road along the eastern flank. The heights dominated the Straits, which varied in breadth from four and a half miles to under a mile. Guns ashore would find ships easy targets. The most dangerous point was the Narrows, fourteen miles in, where Leander, and Byron, had swum across—one for a girl, the other because the first had done it.

> The winds are high, and Helle's tide
> Rolls darkly heaving to the main;
> And Night's descending shadows hide
> That field with blood bedew'd in vain.

Byron's "field with blood bedew'd" was the plain of Troy, but nearer the scene of his exploit lay a bloodier battlefield of the future.

There was a credit side. If a fleet passed through, Constantinople—probably, though not certainly, all Turkey—would lie at the mercy of the attackers. Greek islands were available as advanced bases and anchorages. At first it looked as though further aid would come from Greece. Her great prime minister, Venizelos, was ready to participate. Russian anxiety lest Venizelos should claim Constantinople canceled the project.

British views were strangely divided. Fisher, the First Sea Lord—whose master, Winston Churchill, was the soul of the enterprise in the War Council—chopped and changed. If he had any consistent view it was that the Straits could not be forced without the aid of the army. Kitchener, all-powerful Secretary of State for War, with tremendous prestige, was more favorable. Yet he would not take forces from France, and but for a single division in England, the last of those made up of regular troops from overseas, there were only raw, untrained troops available. And General Sir Ian Hamilton, the man appointed to command the Anglo-French expeditionary force on the way—what is to be said of him?

First, the most absurd misinterpretation is that of Hamilton as a dilettante. He was a finished professional, a musketry expert among other things. At the same time he had intellectual and imaginative gifts of a high order. An ideal combination, one might suppose.

* Larcher, p. 91. He suggests that the Russians did not seem eager for the British to reach the Bosporus.

Perhaps, but there was also a touch of unsteadiness of purpose, of inconsequence, somewhere at the back of that interesting mind. The conventional spirits who distrusted him because he wrote elegant prose, and less distinguished verse, were criticizing him for the wrong reasons, but he was in fact not wholly dependable as a soldier. His outlook on the venture naturally varied in enthusiasm according to the resources promised—and they too changed often—but it varied too easily.

But Hamilton is not yet on the scene. For a moment it looked as if he and his army would not be needed at this stage. Having no troops on the spot, but a large fleet at his disposal, including eighteen battleships or battle cruisers from the most modern to very ancient, the naval commander, Vice-Admiral Carden, tried to do the job with naval forces alone. He started on February 19, 1915, and continued with breaks until March 18. The start was encouraging. The forts near the entry to the Dardanelles were so effectively pounded that from February 26 marines and bluejackets were able to land, blow up guns, and walk about as though they owned the place. Then followed an unfavorable period, in which the mine sweepers' crews, of enlisted fishermen, were cowed by the Turkish fire and had to be replaced by naval volunteers. By mid-March, however, all was ready for the attack on the Narrows. This was to be the great day.

It was carried out under a new commander, Vice-Admiral de Robeck, because Carden had broken down under the strain. The batteries at the Narrows fell silent beneath the terrific fire, which included that of the 15-inch guns of the *Queen Elizabeth*. Then came disaster. In succession, the old battleships *Bouvet* (French) and the *Irresistible* and *Ocean* were sunk, on a new mine field which should have been discovered. The fine battle cruiser *Inflexible* looked as if it would share this fate, but reached Tenedos Island. The French *Gaulois* also limped there and the *Suffren*, though not mined, was put out of action. De Robeck's staff officer, the dashing Commodore Keyes, believed to the day of his death, thirty years later, that the enemy was beaten. Recent evidence shows that the enemy thought so too.* But not all Keyes' pleading could induce de Robeck to risk another purely naval effort, or Hamilton to advise it, after the virtual loss of six capital ships.

Meanwhile, after consideration so brief and hasty that it would

* Aspinall-Oglander, *Gallipoli*, I, 105.

make the hair of modern planners stand on end—though, whether for good or ill, they could not have matched the speed—the land troops had sailed. They had been allotted no definite role pending news of the fate of the naval attack. Maps were rare and incorrect; intelligence about the Turkish army was poor and about the peninsula almost nonexistent. Such planning as there was fell to Hamilton on the spot, and at least he and his staff showed remarkable activity and energy.

The force available to clear the way for the fleet consisted of the regular Twenty-ninth Division, the Anzac Corps of two divisions, the Royal Naval Division (the basis of which was the group of brigades sent to Antwerp the previous year), and one French division. The main task was naturally allotted to the Twenty-ninth, which was to land on beaches at Cape Helles, the toe of the peninsula, and if possible secure the dominating height of Achi Baba, five miles inland, on the first day, April 25. The Australians and New Zealanders were to land on the west coast north of Gaba Tepe, just north of the Narrows and where the peninsula itself is only four and a half miles in breadth, and to straddle it. The French were to make a false landing at Kum Kale, on the Asiatic shore, a plausible threat of a major operation on that side. The Royal Naval Division was to demonstrate against the narrow northern neck of the peninsula at Bulair, which on the map looked the most suitable place for a landing, but had been ruled out owing to the strength of its fortifications. These two last-named divisions were afterward to be transferred to Cape Helles.

The Turkish commander was Liman von Sanders, chief of the German military mission. He had six divisions, one more than Hamilton. He posted two on the Asiatic side, one at Helles, two at or north of Bulair, and one, his reserve, concentrated near Maidos, in the Narrows. Thus was the stage set. And, whatever be the verdict on the naval attack, the mere mention of which still makes some critics foam at the mouth, it had certainly given Liman warning. On Hamilton's side was at least the knowledge of what defenses he had to face; these had been well photographed for that date, by aircraft of the Royal Naval Air Service, the only ones available.

A feeling of astonishment and distress is evoked even now as we contemplate the landings. At Helles one was repulsed altogether with frightful loss by Turkish riflemen who quitted their trenches under the naval bombardment and returned when it was done. The slaughter in the sallyports of the *River Clyde*, a collier run aground on the eastern flank of the cape to serve as a landing ship, was appalling. In many boats every man was hit. Two other landing forces, unopposed or nearly so, lay on their objectives and enjoyed the scenery. They did not go to help their comrades because they knew nothing about them. The plan had for reasons of security been kept too secret. Troops sufficient to overcome all the Turkish forces at the toe of the peninsula were thus unemployed. At one point a panic led to a withdrawal. Still, after dark small footholds were gained.

The Anzac landing began with a calamity. The troops were set ashore a mile too far north, facing precipitous cliffs. They climbed and scrambled forward at random, getting in a mile or so where they found fair going, but often checked just above the beach. Here there was no panic, but there was something dangerously near it, a heavy drift to the rear. Again after dark real progress took place.

The British commander in chief was in the flagship. With wireless communication to the beaches he would have been well placed, but as things were he learned little of what went on. Would it have been helpful if he had? Perhaps not, for Ian Hamilton was obsessed by the doctrine that subordinates given their tasks should not be interfered with in performing them. Up to a point this doctrine is sound, but he made a fetish of it. The effects will be seen again.

His opponent, Liman, mounted his horse, and—*risum teneatis amici?*—galloped the wrong way, to Bulair, where the demonstration took him in completely. A bombardment of the outer Bosporus forts by the Russian Black Sea Fleet may have increased his interest in the northern neck of Gallipoli, especially as he knew that the Russians had a corps at Odessa prepared to intervene.* He spent the night at Bulair. He had first ordered his division at Gallipoli to follow him. On learning of the pressure farther south he did at least send five battalions down to the Narrows by boat. On the morning of April 26 he sent the rest of the two divisions at Bulair down toward the real battlefield.

The man who saved the day was the young commander of the reserve division, an evil-tempered, profligate soldier of native genius,

* Allen, p. 287. Fine inter-Allied cooperation at last, it may be thought. Unhappily it was mostly politics: if Constantinople were occupied Russian troops must be there. At least as a demonstration Russian moves were useful and caused anxiety to the Turks.

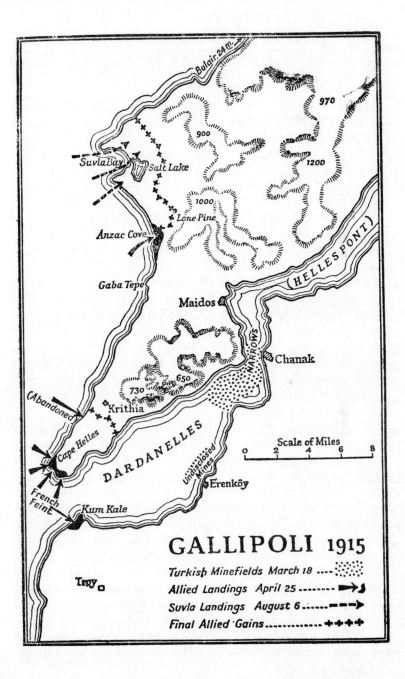

Bulair 24 m.

970

900

1200

Suvla Bay

Salt Lake

1000

Lone Pine

Anzac Cove

Gaba Tepe

Maidos

(HELLESPONT)

NARROWS

Chanak

730

650

Krithia

(Abandoned

Cape Helles

DARDANELLES

Undisclosed Mines

Erenköy

French Feint

Kum Kale

Scale of Miles

0   2   4   6   8

Troy

GALLIPOLI 1915

Turkish Minefields March 18 ....

Allied Landings April 25 ....

Suvla Landings August 6 ....

Final Allied Gains.............

Mustapha Kemal. He accompanied the single battalion he was authorized to send against the Anzacs, drew in without authorization the whole division, and held the heights. If ever one man turned the tide of battle it was he.

Horrors and heroism on both sides, together with events outside the theater of war, can now only be mentioned till the next crisis is reached, and even that must be more briefly narrated. At home Fisher, after an outburst of temper, resigned his position as First Sea Lord on May 15. On May 26 a coalition government was formed and Churchill was removed from the Admiralty. It was a bad omen for Gallipoli.

On the peninsula a berserk mass attack by the Turks was routed with a loss of 10,000 men on May 18. On the twenty-second a conference between representatives of the foes was held in a dugout to arrange a truce to succor wounded Turks still alive, and to bury the dead. It was interrupted, in the tradition of Gallipoli, a mingling of rough humor with death, suffering and misery, by an Australian soldier poking his head round the doorflap and demanding: "Have any of you bastards got my kettle?" * Those within, who included the Anzac corps commander (Lieutenant General Birdwood), Hamilton's chief of staff (Major General Braithwaite), and Mustapha Kemal, could only deny knowledge of the utensil. The truce took place on the twenty-fourth, and the grisly work was done with as much seemliness as possible.

At sea British submarines, creeping under the mine fields in the Straits, sailed into the Sea of Marmara and even the Bosporus to play havoc with Turkish shipping. Among their victims was a liner carrying 6,000 troops, sunk with all hands. The British never realized how great was their effect, but they did appreciate the loss of three more old battleships, two sunk by German submarines and one by a Turkish destroyer. It made an end of the security that the naval forces had so far enjoyed. The effect was virtually to deprive the army of the support of naval guns.

A series of local offensives led to an advance of about three and a half miles at Helles, but also straight to the cemeteries. It was now a matter of trench-to-trench attacks, as in France. Meanwhile the troops grew weary and sickened in great numbers with dysentery, till by July a thousand were evacuated every week. Their food was mainly canned meat—the fat melted to oil in the heat—biscuit,

* Moorehead. p. 185.

tea, and jam. The resources of military caterers more or less stopped there when fresh meat and vegetables could not be had and bread could not be baked.

Then followed an unexpected reversal of fortune. The new British government backed the campaign determinedly. The former War Council became "the Dardanelles Committee," as though for Britain at war the Straits were all that counted. It was nearly the case. The Mediterranean Expeditionary Force was given priority over France in ammunition. It had already grown from five to eight divisions; now five more were promised, bringing it up to thirteen, two of them French. De Robeck got 14-inch gun monitors for bombardment, more naval aircraft, and armored landing barges. The Turks had now sixteen smaller divisions.

This time the main attack was to be made at Anzac, and supported by a new landing, by a corps of two divisions, in Suvla Bay, a little to the north. The two forces were to join hands and together advance to the Narrows, thus cutting off by far the greater proportion of the Turkish army. It would meanwhile be attacked by the Helles Corps. The plan was a good one. The chances of surprise at Suvla were excellent. If that were secured it seemed certain that speed and daring would see the Allies through.

The start was fixed for August 6. At Helles the guns would open at 2.30 P.M., an Anzac diversion at 5.30, the main Anzac assault at 9.30, and the Suvla landing immediately afterward. The Helles attack can be dismissed in a few words. It was essentially a holding operation and it held the Turks in their places. Actually it did more, straining and scaring them so much that there was talk of abandoning the position. Liman fiercely stopped that faint-hearted nonsense— and the front held.

At Anzac the diversionary attack at Lone Pine led to hand-to-hand fighting of bitter intensity. Historians and journalists often use the words "hand-to-hand" loosely: here they were literally true. The fortunes at Anzac were mixed. All attacks fell behind the program, as might indeed have been expected in a night advance over such ground. Some failed altogether. After reorganization of the columns the corps tried again on August 8 with limited success. Next day a few hundred British and Gurkhas made a ferocious attack on the Turks holding the crest of the mountains, swept them off it after more genuine hand-to-hand fighting, looked down into the Straits below, saw Turkish reinforcements being ferried over from the Asiatic side and cars speeding along the road, started, unsupported though they were, to run down the far slope toward Maidos. Then--they were crushed by half a dozen heavy shells, and all was slaughter and confusion. They believed that the fire came from British monitors, but this the Navy denied. However, the Turks were off the heights at last.

The Suvla affair started perfectly. The leading troops were put ashore without resistance to speak of. The build-up was not interfered with. Yet there was a fantastic lack of any sense of urgency from the corps command downward. At a time when there were in fact 1,500 Turks to hold up two divisions the generals talked of landing artillery to bombard the enemy's defenses. The Turks actually did everything possible to help by botching the movement of reinforcements. The British did not know either of these facts. Of course not, but they might have found them out. Two vices of the original landing were reproduced: the troops did not know enough about what they had to do, and Hamilton intervened too late. Some of the scenes, troops making tea, bathing in the sea, lying in the sun, were reminiscent rather of an August bank holiday than of one of the most vital military operations of modern times. Another feature was also re-created: Mustapha Kemal, placed by Liman in command of the northern flank at Anzac and the whole Suvla defenses, again played the part of a great fighting man. One Turkish charge drove back the British at Suvla; another, a tremendous affair with fearful loss on both sides, recovered the Anzac heights.

Frantic efforts were made by those who still believed in the campaign to have another offensive mounted. When General Sir Charles Monro, sent out from France to report, advocated evacuation, there was an outburst of revulsion and a determination to resist such ignominy, extending to Lord Kitchener, who had raised the question earlier. Yet after he himself had visited the peninsula, he cabled, on November 22, his recommendation that Anzac and Suvla should be evacuated and Helles retained for the time being. So it was arranged.

Hamilton and his staff officer Braithwaite were ordered home. Monro was placed in over-all command of the Gallipoli peninsula and Salonika, from which a new campaign was developing. Birdword, formerly the Anzac corps commander, was placed in direct command on the peninsula, to carry out the evacuation. Some forecasts put the casualty list for the withdrawal as high as 30 or

40 per cent, mostly prisoners. The staff work was good this time. The troops were gradually thinned out. The last rear guards were taken off in the small hours of December 20. Despite last-moment destruction of stores, a vast amount, including very valuable food, was left to the Turks. But not a man was lost in the withdrawal.

That was all very well, but what about Helles? It was quickly decided to evacuate this holding also, but the chances of repeating the success did not look to be one in fifty. Then came a marvelous slice of luck. Liman did the obvious thing, marched reinforcements down to Helles and on January 8, 1916, put in an assault after a heavy bombardment. The Turks surprisingly flinched and then fled in face of the British fire. By this time 19,000 men had been taken off. Next night the Navy embarked the remaining 16,000 in one lift, in the midst of a dangerous storm. Against all expectation, not a man was left behind. The wry satisfaction with which the British greet alleviations of the calamities brought upon themselves by their own follies turned this success into something like a victory.

Every step in the campaign has been endlessly debated. Let us stick to the main points. The peninsula—and the passage of the Dardanelles—could have been secured. Either the first or the second landing would have served had the chances been taken. These having been lost, the decision to withdraw was correct. Otherwise, the effects of winter weather on the ramshackle landing facilities, coupled with German support of Turkey over a direct railway to Constantinople, might have led to a fearful disaster.

The failure was due partly to the rawness of the majority of the troops; mainly to errors in command. These were few but overwhelming. They were hardly worse than Anzio, but mattered more. The Turks, with less scope for major mistakes, made fewer.

The fighting quality of both sides was out of the ordinary, even if that of the allies, assailing a readily defensible objective in inferior numbers, must be accounted the higher. Ordinary bravery withstands smashing bombardments and will charge under withering fire. To maintain the ability to do this in the conditions under which British, French, Australians, New Zealanders, Indians, Turks, and a handful of Germans lived on the Gallipoli peninsula is a far different thing. Men who have looked since at the tiny ledges, a few yards away from Turkish trenches, from which companies never moved in daylight, have held their breath and marveled.

The sublimity of the tragedy may have encouraged attempts to make certainty out of what is properly conjectural. If the Dardanelles had been opened, so would the Bosporus, and the vast merchant fleets immobilized within would have been set free. Russia would not have suffered such a defeat as she did at German hands. But to go on to declare that Russia would have been saved from revolution and the world from communism is speculation. All that can be said is that Gallipoli held out greater promise than any other "sideshow." The men of Gallipoli *might* have changed the fate of the world.

Falkenhayn and Conrad had decided that, to keep their partner Turkey in the war, the Constantinople railway must be cleared of the enemy. This meant putting Serbia out of the war. Ever since the great Serbian victory over the Austrians the Allied foreign ministers, Grey, Delcassé, and Sazonov, had foreseen something of this kind. They could do nothing to keep the Germans and Austrians from mounting a new offensive, but they tried to fetter their feet by bringing in Bulgaria as an ally or at worst inducing her to remain neutral. It was a question of who could bribe highest in terms of Serbian territory, but Grey and his colleagues were at a disadvantage because they had to obtain Serbia's assent to every offer, and that was not easy to get. Serbia could never bring herself to trust the king of Bulgaria, popularly known to Britain as "Foxy Ferdinand," or any of his subjects, from highest to lowest. The Allied Powers did induce Serbia to offer a great deal, but not enough for Bulgaria's maw. On September 6, 1915, a military convention for the overthrow of Serbia was signed at Pless by Conrad, Falkenhayn, and the Bulgarian Colonel Gančev. Serbia was placed in a hopeless position because Bulgaria lay along her eastern flank and within a hand's reach of her only north-south railway, along the valley of the Varder.

Two armies, one German and one Austrian, assembled on the Save and Danube. Colonel Hentsch, of Mackensen's Army Group staff, carried out with great ability the extremely difficult administrative preparations. German propaganda has asserted that his timidity lost the Battle of the Marne, yet here, a year afterward, he was accounted one of the best German staff officers. The German army commander was General von Gallwitz, the Austrian, General Koevess, two good choices. A vast concentration of artillery prepared the passage of the rivers. Nothing was to go wrong this time.

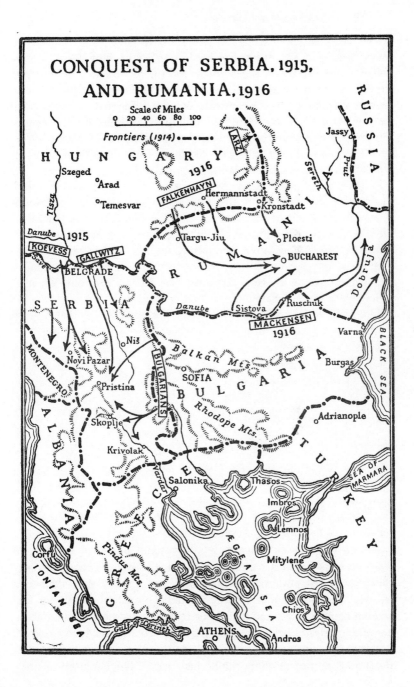

CONQUEST OF SERBIA, 1915,
AND RUMANIA, 1916

Scale of Miles

0   20 40 60 80 100

Frontiers (1914) •—•—•—•

H U N G A R Y

Szeged

○ Arad

○ Temesvar

ARZ

1916

FALKENHAYN

Hermannstadt

Kronstadt

Danube 1915

KOEVESS

GALLWITZ

BELGRADE

Targu-Jiu

○ Ploesti

○ BUCHAREST

R U M A N I A

Jassy

RUSSIA

Seret

Prut

S E R B I A

Danube

Sistova

Ruschuk

MACKENSEN

1916

Varna

Dobruja

BLACK SEA

Niš

Balkan Mts.

MONTENEGRO

Novi Pazar

Pristina

BULGARIANS

SOFIA

B U L G A R I A

Burgas

Skoplje

Rhodope Mts.

Adrianople

Krivolak

T U R K E Y

A L B A N I A

Vardar

Salonika

G R E E C E

Thasos

SEA OF MARMARA

Imbros

Lemnos

Corfu

Pindus Mts.

AEGEAN SEA

Mitylene

IONIAN SEA

Chios

Gulf of Corinth

ATHENS

Andros

The Germans and Austrians would have given the Serbians a heavy beating in any event, but could not have routed them. It was Bulgaria's role to smash the Serbians by a flank attack. The Austro-German offensive began on October 7; the Bulgarian blow from the east was struck on the eleventh, one Bulgarian army attacking in the direction of Nish, the other aiming at Skoplje, on the upper Vardar. Gallantly as the Serbians fought, they were swept away by the overwhelming strength of their foes. Yet Putnik twice avoided the encirclement planned by Falkenhayn.

Bulgaria's mobilization had warned the Entente Powers of what was coming. Serbia had no direct access to the sea. The only route by which aid might be sent was through the Greek port of Salonika. The Greek prime minister, Venizelos, agreed that French and British troops should move through, though he said he would have to make a formal protest. Before leaving the Mediterranean, Hamilton had to part with two divisions, one British and one French, which were sent to Salonika.

The affair was bedeviled by international politics. France found a job for General Sarrail, who had been dismissed by Joffre but had strong left-wing political backing. In Greece King Constantine, whose queen was the German Kaiser's sister, and Venizelos, a supporter of the Franco-British cause, were on bad terms. On October 5, a few hours before the first British and French troops landed at Salonika, Venizelos resigned and the invitation to intervene in Serbia's favor was canceled. After some hesitation the British decided not to turn back now that troops were already ashore. The Greeks made no resistance, but the attitude of officers was unfriendly. However, General Sarrail disregarded this dangerous background and pushed north along the road and railway up the Vardar valley. The British division went only as far as the Greek-Bulgarian frontier—because the British government forbade a further advance.

Britain, like a timid bather, would not go in above her knees. She was engaged in a campaign for which only a section of her government felt enthusiasm and which her general staff detested; had put her troops under a French general suspected of playing for his own hand, and yet had half deserted him when he was in trouble; was acting from a base (Salonika) threatened by potentially hostile Greek forces, with easily cut communications; and had little belief in the goal, that of rescuing the Serbian army. The infirmity of purpose and confusion of mind of the coalition government were discreditable.

The Serbians could not be reached. Sarrail, now with three French divisions, was blocked by the Bulgarians in superior strength about Krivolak, forty miles up the Vardar from the frontier. He made a brilliant retreat, covering every move and beating off assaults in which the Bulgarians surged forward as though possessed of a spell to deflect bullets. If so, it did not work. The British division was, however, roughly handled near the frontier. The Bulgarians were expected to enter Greece, but Falkenhayn, for political reasons and the state of his communications, persuaded them to halt on the frontier.

What should have been done now? Perhaps the wisest course for the British and French would have been to reembark forthwith, as the British general staff desired. However, as the French were infuriated by the proposal, Britain gave way and stayed. Reembarkation would have been somewhat dangerous, since secrecy was unattainable. This was not uninhabited country like the Gallipoli peninsula, and the base port was a city of 200,000 souls. Moreover, Greece was neutral. The German consul's agents had stood on the quay counting troops and boxes of shell as they were landed. In December the four enemy consuls were arrested and deported.

It had been another triumph for Falkenhayn and for the Entente a miserable start to a new campaign. It unleashed derisive comments on British and French military capacity all over the world, though in fact political ineptitude was the more responsible. Then, when the two allies started to create a heavily wired "entrenched camp" just north of Salonika, German humorists split their sides with laughter. Prisoners of war, they said, were confined in barbed-wire cages when first captured, but history afforded no precedent for an army going into a cage made by itself and shutting the door. (The defenses were, of course, a precaution against a hurried forced reembarkation being necessary after all.) The best to be said was that Sarrail had greatly aided what was left of the Serbian armies to retreat through Albania. This march was a terrible tragedy also. Thousands died of cold and hunger in the mountains. So wasted were survivors that, after Allied ships had borne them to the Greek island of Corfu, cases occurred of French nurses lifting full-sized men single-handed from their hospital cots and carrying them in their arms.

The final stroke was dealt by Koevess, with Austrian troops only. By January 25, 1916, he forced the Montenegrin army of 36,000 men to lay down its arms. He then pushed on into Albania, drove back a weak Italian force, and halted on the Vojusa near the southern frontier. These were useful strategic gains on the Adriatic coast.

Chapter IV

SACRO EGOISMO PER L'ITALIA

ITALY came into the war as the ally of France, the United Kingdom, and Russia by a devious path. In face of Austria she moved from alliance to neutrality and from neutrality to hostilities. Her chief motive was her desire for Austrian territory, the Trentino—the southern Tirol, largely inhabited by people of Italian stock—and Istria, including the port of Trieste. This was a predatory aim, even if dignified by national sentiment. Before denouncing the Triple Alliance and declaring war on Austria-Hungary, one of her partners in it, Italy approached that partner and tried to get what she wanted, or as much of it as might be, by implicit threats of war in the event of refusal. The Austro-Hungarian government, regarding the claims as preposterous, turned them down, despite some German pressure in favor of compromise. Italy then went to the Entente Powers and drove a very hard bargain before she would join them as a belligerent ally. The enthusiasm afterward professed by the Italian government for the ideals of the Entente thus makes odd reading today. At the time it did not ring so hollow because the arrangements made were kept secret. To say that this was the whole story—something like blackmail demanded from Austria and then favors offered to the Entente if the tender were high enough—would be false as well as ungracious. Enthusiasm for Britain and France was genuine and widespread in Italy. The two motives were intertwined: popular sympathy for the Entente aided the government in its policy, while the feature of that policy concerning the return to the motherland of folk of Italian origin appealed to patriotic irredentists. The prime minister, Antonio Salandra, coined a most appropriate phrase when he described Italy's policy as "*sacro egoismo*."

The original treaty of alliance with Germany and Austria signed in 1882 had been directed against France. It was prolonged and somewhat extended in scope on three occasions before the outbreak of war in 1914. In 1902 the Italian government got from France the pledge of a free hand in Tripoli, with the consequence that the two countries came to a secret agreement by which each promised to remain neutral in a war in which the other was attacked. So France, the only power actually named in the original treaty, was removed from its purview.*

The German general staff was never enthusiastic about the treaty with Italy. The Austrian, by Conrad's day, was of the same opinion. Italian governments have sometimes been given to so overembroidering a Machiavellian policy that their pretenses, instead of hiding their real intentions, make them easier to divine. Now the Italians repeatedly brought up the question of sending forces to the upper Rhine should Germany find herself at war with France. The "cover plan" was further built up when they suggested the violation of Swiss territory so that their contingent might be railed direct to its front instead of by the roundabout route through the Brenner Pass. This was overdoing it. The Germans rejected the proposal and remained skeptical about Italian aid.

Still, it might come off, and General von Moltke saw no reason why he should not make preparations for it, since no harm would be done if they turned out to be unproductive. Early in 1914 staff talks took place in Berlin at which timetables were drawn up for the movement of three Italian corps to the Rhine. All the while, however, Moltke and Conrad thought Italy was more likely to join the Entente, but that the most likely case of all was that a victorious German invasion of France would keep Italy neutral. All doubts ended when on August 3 Italy proclaimed her neutrality on the ground that Austria's action against Serbia, taken without consulting her, was a violation of one of the clauses of the treaty.

The diplomacy by which Italy's path to war was guided does not belong to military history. On April 26, 1915, a secret treaty, known as the Pact of London, was signed by Sir Edward Grey and the ambassadors of Italy, Russia, and France.† Italy pledged herself to pursue the war with her three new allies against all their enemies—she did not in fact declare war on Germany until August 27, 1916.

* Edmonds, *Military Operations, Italy*, p. 1.
† The English text was first published in 1920 as a parliamentary paper.

She was promised the Trentino, Cisalpine Tirol, Istria with Trieste, Dalmatia, a footing in Albania at Valona, and the Dodecanese, which she had seized from Turkey in a recent war. If Turkey were partitioned, Italy would be reserved a share in the southern part of Asia Minor, and if German colonies were annexed by Britain or France, Italy would have a right to territorial compensations.

The situation of Italy was favorable in so far as Austria-Hungary was deeply engaged, but in no other way. She had not begun to replace the war material and stores consumed in the Libyan war with Turkey until after her neutrality had been proclaimed in August, 1914, and then she found herself short of funds and factories for a rush job. Strategically she was worse off still. Almost the whole of her long frontier with Austria was covered by dense Alpine and pre-Alpine chains. Everywhere the Austrians looked down upon their new foes. From Feltre to the head of the Adriatic an almost square salient jutted out northward for some fifty miles, so that the Italians had to face east and west as well as north. Even the most promising sector for an offensive, in the east, where the Isonzo ran southward just inside the Austrian frontier, was grim and forbidding. Though the land beyond the river sloped only gently westward, it was broken by irregular ridges and valleys and the plateaus of the Bainsizza, the Selva di Ternova, and the Carso formed "enormous natural fortresses," the Carso "a howling wilderness of stones sharp as knives." *

When Italy declared war on May 23, 1915, she had about 875,000 troops with the colors and thirty-six infantry divisions. On that day she was faced by about 100,000 Austrian troops. However, the offensive of Gorlice-Tarnow had won such a magnificent success that another three divisions were already on their way and some eight more followed early in June. The Italian chief of the general staff— King Victor Emmanuel II being the nominal commander in chief— was General Luigi Cadorna, an artillery man aged sixty-five. The Austrian army group commander on the Italian front was the Archduke Eugen. To command the Isonzo front, clearly the most important, the competent Slav, Borojević von Bojna, was sent from Galicia.

The fighting of the year 1915 was confined to Italian offensives. Conrad would have been delighted to strike at the enemy, but with the Serbian offensive on his hands in addition to the main campaign against Russia, even this sanguine man realized that that was out of the question. The operations can be described in few words because

* Edmonds, *Military Operations, Italy*, p. 11.

the four Italian threats were all made in roughly the same place and
carried out in a similar way. Where they did differ was in intensity,
owing mainly to reinforcement in artillery on both sides. Throughout, the immediate objectives were "the howling wilderness" of the
Carso and the town of Gorizia; the more distant objective was
Trieste. The offensives were even given a single name by the Italians
and distinguished only by numbers: First, Second, Third, and Fourth
Battles of the Isonzo. The fighting was grisly owing to the rocky
nature of the country; the burst of high-explosive shell sent deadly
fragments of stone flying in all directions, so that the proportion of
killed to wounded was exceptionally high.

The First Battle lasted from June 23 to July 7. The attack was
carried out by the Third and Second armies commanded respectively, by the Duke of Aosta and Lieutenant General Frugoni, with
a numerical superiority of about two to one. Cadorna then called a
halt, but only for eleven days, while he brought up more heavy
artillery but also gave the Austrian command time to reinforce
Borojević's Fifth Army by two divisions. The Second Battle, from
July 18 to August 3, was bloodier but equally unfruitful. This time
Cadorna was compelled to stop because of shortage of ammunition.
His losses amounted to just on 60,000 against Austrian casualties of
nearly 45,000. Only a few outpost positions had been won, and
Austrian maps show no change in the main front line.

The Third Battle did not take place until the autumn. During this
interval Cadorna filled his depleted ranks, carried out training, and
brought up heavy guns from fortresses. By mid-October he had
1,200 guns on the scene as against 212 in the First Battle of the Isonzo.
This time he aimed once more at Gorizia, in the center, but started
with attacks on the wings: on the right against the Carso, on the left
against Plavo, on the Isonzo and facing the Bainsizza. Twenty-five
Italian divisions faced fourteen Austrian.

The Third Battle started on October 18, 1915, and lasted until
November 4th. As in the case of the so-called First and Second, the
Third and Fourth were in reality one and the same battle, and would
have been so recorded by the British and French. The Fourth lasted
from November 10 to December 2, twenty-three days. The total result was three dents in the Austrian front, two on the right and one
at Plava. The Italian infantry often displayed great bravery in the
assault, but the artillery support was defective, the organization

weak, and the task a cruel one. The losses were frightful, 117,000 in the two battles. The Austrians did not come off lightly with upward of 72,000.

All that Italy had achieved between late June and early December was to draw a dozen Austrian divisions to the frontier. This had in no way hampered the exploitation by the Central Powers of their brilliant victory at Gorlice-Tarnow. It had not interfered with the *Niederschlag* of Serbia. For Italy herself it had failed to gain any strategic advantage or even a tactical one. Meanwhile she had lost on all parts of the front a quarter of a million men. Why did Cadorna persist in attacking in this region? The first answer is that the only alternative for an offensive was at the other end of the front in the Trentino and that, despite better communications, he considered this less promising. An advance through the Trentino led nowhere, or only into the tangled mountain masses of the Tirol, and, beyond the Adige and the Drave, lay the mightier chain of the high Alps. From Trieste the Danubian plain might be attainable through the famous "Laibach gap." *

He would certainly have met with a hot reception if he had got there in the latter half of 1915, though if the Russian advance had continued through the Carpathians it would have been nearly all up with Austria. Second, Cadorna expected the Austrians to be further reinforced and that German forces would eventually appear. He felt he could not sit still and allow the enemy to mount an offensive at his leisure.

Borojević and his troops had shown skill and determination in holding their strong position. The defense had been carried out behind the Isonzo, except for a wide bridgehead at Gorizia. Austria had borne the burden stoutly. She had been given no appreciable help by Germany. The so-called Alpine Corps of good Bavarian mountain troops but only a division in strength, had been sent to the Dolomites but with orders not to cross the Italian frontier. Falkenhayn was pleased that Italy had not declared war on Germany, and did not intend that Germany should declare war on her until it suited him. It was perhaps natural that he should not want to get mixed up in the Italian war while he was engaged in the campaign against Serbia. Yet his attitude did not make for cordiality between the allies. The Emperor Francis Joseph, having had himself briefed on the situation by Conrad a month before Italy went to war, remarked in his pithy

* Today Ljubljana.

way: *"Die ganze Politik Deutschlands ist keine glückliche und loyale."* *

Conrad was determined to strike Italy as soon as he possibly could. Falkenhayn, now that he thought he had crippled the Russians sufficiently, was determined to launch an offensive on the Western Front. In 1916 these two extremely able soldiers, who had cooperated with such outstanding success in 1915, were to turn their backs to each other and go their own ways, not to the profit of their respective states or that of their own military careers.

* Regele, p. 377. ("Germany's whole policy is far from auspicious and loyal.")

Chapter V

THE WAR AT SEA, 1915

WHAT were Britain's aims in the war at sea? Were they the correct aims? These questions were debated even during the war, and much more keenly after it. The British man in the street was not a highly instructed naval strategist or tactician, but he knew the subject better than the man in any foreign street. When the war was over the conduct of Jellicoe in the Battle of Jutland, for example, was discussed hotly and with bad temper. And the issues hung on technical matters such as whether his method of forming line ahead was sufficiently aggressive.

Even before the war naval strategy had been the subject of controversy. Sir John (later Lord) Fisher, a former professional head of the Admiralty who was brought back by Churchill at the beginning of the war, inspired the "blue-water school," a name which indicates its beliefs. It scoffed at the notion of invasion and was jealous of any attention paid to the army. A more extreme body of opinion, wittily nicknamed the "ultramarine school," asserted stridently that the first duty of the navy was to seek out and destroy the enemy's fleet. Not at all, said Sir Julian Corbett, a well-known writer respected by Mahan. The navy's primary object, he said, was to keep open the sea routes in the most economical way. His opponents called his doctrine that of the "bolt from the blue" or the "blue funk" school.

In fact, the alternatives before the Royal Navy, and in principle any navy, were not so simple. If Corbett suggested—and he sometimes seemed dangerously near doing so—that it hardly mattered whether the hostile fleet were destroyed so long as the sea routes were kept open, or that no risks should be taken in an effort to destroy it, he was wrong. "There is no complete and perfect substitute for victory. Just as dead men tell no tales, destroyed fleets can no longer take advantage of an unexpected opportunity." * And, at the other extreme, what folly it would have been for the Grand Fleet to try to seek out and destroy the High Seas Fleet if the latter took refuge in the Baltic, blocking the narrow entrances with submarines, mines, and coast artillery! No, it was a matter of balancing risks and chances, of seeking and creating opportunities. There was certainly a difference between the attitudes of Jellicoe and Beatty, and the latter was by temperament and conviction bolder than his chief; but they were much nearer to each other than their champions who waged a paper war.

Similar considerations had to be taken into account by the Germans, and among them controversy, though kept secret at the time, was sharp. On the one side stood the ardent minister of marine, who was also the creator of the modern German navy, Grand Admiral von Tirpitz; on the other the admiralty staff and the two first commanders of the High Seas Fleet. Tirpitz shouted for greater boldness. He virtually accused his opponents of cowardice. The High Seas Fleet was from one point of view more at liberty to take risks than the Grand Fleet and from another less so. Valuable as it was to Germany, her fate did not completely depend upon the High Seas Fleet, whereas that not only of Britain but of her allies depended on the Grand Fleet. Churchill, while highly critical of Jellicoe's leadership at Jutland as overcautious, was honest enough to admit that he was the only man in the world who at that time could have lost the war in an afternoon. On the other hand, the High Seas Fleet was almost always the weaker and at some periods very much so. The Germans' best hope was that a bit of luck with destroyers, U-boats, or mines would hit the Grand Fleet so hard as to bring about equality. Otherwise the desires of the two sides were not dissimilar. They wanted to meet outside the mine fields in the open water of the North Sea and trust to maneuver, gunfire, torpedoes, and to some extent submarines, for the advantage. And both were suspicious of traps. The Germans were the more cautious because the defense of the Baltic, where their secondary fleet was supporting their land forces against the Russians, was a feature of their strategy and because Admiral von Ingenohl, commanding the High Seas Fleet, was timid.

* Falls, *Ordeal by Battle*, p. 140.

In January, 1915, the situation with regards to the most modern battleships was very unfavorable to Britain, whereas in battle cruisers it was most satisfactory. Owing to loss, damage, and normal docking the Grand Fleet could send out only eighteen dreadnoughts against the German seventeen. In battle cruisers Beatty had five, against four German, of which only three really counted as such. The fourth, the *Blücher*, was out of her class, a heavy cruiser carrying 8-inch guns as compared with the 12-inch of the splendid *Derfflinger* and the 11-inch of the *Seydlitz* and *Moltke*. The *Von der Tann* was under repair after a collision. The *Lion*, *Tiger*, and *Princess Royal* carried 13.5-inch guns, the *New Zealand* and *Indomitable* 12-inch. Nevertheless Ingenohl, willing to wound and yet afraid to strike, kept his battleships in harbor and ordered out his battle-cruiser squadron, with light cruisers and a strong destroyer screen, to drive the British fishing fleet and the patrol away from the Dogger Bank. The British admiralty was aware that there was to be a sortie on the night of January 23, and of its approximate strength. It divined that the German force would come at least as far as the Dogger Bank. And so that night, as the Germans left Wilhelmshaven, the British put to sea from their various harbors, that of the battle cruisers being now Rosyth. It was an intricate operation made the more difficult because wireless silence was enjoined unless the dispatch of a vital message were called for. But the Grand Fleet knew its job by now. Barring a change of mind on the part of the German commander, the opposing forces were certain to meet.

And meet they did. Just after 7 A.M., as dawn was breaking, the British light cruiser *Arethusa* engaged the German light cruiser *Kolberg* west of the Dogger and hit her so hard that she turned away and disappeared. Beatty altered course toward the gun flashes. Shortly afterward the German battle cruisers were seen. Immediately they received the *Kolberg*'s warning they had concentrated and begun a flight for home.

Now began a tremendous chase. Beatty knew his leading ships just had the legs of the enemy, but he could catch them only by an overlap. A stern chase in the enemy's wake was barred by the danger of floating mines tossed out by the fleeing light cruisers and destroyers. The speed of Beatty's flagship, the *Lion*, rose to 26 knots, but the *Indomitable*, whose trial speed had never passed 25, was keeping up. "Well steamed *Indomitable*!" signalled the Admiral, and demanded further efforts from his own engine-room. The *Lion*'s speed rose to 27, then to 28. It was magnificent.

Fire was opened at the vast range of 20,000 yards and before it had been reduced to 15,000 the *Blücher* was being constantly hit and was soon in flames. Though the *Indomitable* was still out of range, Beatty had four battle cruisers to engage the four German ships. The sound principle that when possible no hostile ship should be left to fire undisturbed was, however, not being carried out. Owing to an error, the *Derfflinger* was not being fired at. Her gunnery was first class and she repeatedly hit the *Lion*, on which two other ships were also firing. The flagship was having a very bad time. On the German side the *Blücher* was nearly done for and the *Seydlitz*, flying the flag of Admiral Hipper, was getting a severe pounding. The German tactic of firing at the van—that is, the *Lion*—was a relic of the old days of sail and short ranges, theoretically incorrect now. And yet how right the enemy was, in fact, to bombard the pursuing flagship!

Just before 11 A.M. the *Lion*'s speed dropped to 15 knots and the others passed her. Her wireless was silenced and she had only two signal halyards left. As he fell out of action Beatty's signals were misread because the flags were blown end on to the other ships. And so a chance was lost which even today makes old sea dogs grind their teeth. By an incredible misunderstanding of Beatty's meaning—and his spirit—his subordinate diverted the whole attack to the *Blücher*, which was finished anyhow. She fought on with magnificent gallantry. Only when she was completely out of control and unable to defend herself did she strike. Shortly afterward she turned turtle and sank. Meanwhile the other three German battle cruisers continued their flight untouched.

By the time Beatty had come up in a destroyer further pursuit was useless. The action of the Dogger Bank was over. Beatty's luck was cruel. He had done all that mortal man could. A great chase victory seemed to be in his hands. He had good cause to feel he had been let down. Looking back one feels that he was almost certain to have got at least the damaged *Seydlitz* as well as the *Blücher*. One must not, however, forget a weakness in the British battle cruisers which was to be demonstrated all too clearly later on. German casualties were high; British were trifling, and in the *Lion*, badly injured though she was, the loss was only eleven men wounded.

This action has been given space beyond its physical, though not its moral, importance. Sympathy has been expressed for Beatty, and it is deserved. Yet one last question must be asked. Supposing that Nelson and his captains had been transported through the years to this squadron, what would have happened when damage to the *Lion* removed her from the pursuit, with the admiral on board? Surely the answer must be that his subordinates, the "band of brothers" who at the Battle of the Nile had done the right thing on their own initiative, but within the frame of his tactical doctrine which they knew by heart, would have done the right thing here. They would, in fact, have left the *Blücher* to be torpedoed and have continued the pursuit of the *Seydlitz, Derfflinger,* and *Moltke.* Beatty fell short of the Nelson standard because he had not made of his captains such a band of brothers and impregnated them with his ideas.

On the German side Ingenohl was promptly dismissed. His successor, Admiral Hugo von Pohl, was, however, a disastrous figure, and 1915, so happy for the German army, was a miserable year for the navy. Under him naval morale dropped. Among his immediate juniors something like a revolt broke out. One, Captain von Trotha, said openly that the corps of officers was disgusted. Another, Captain von Levetzow, becoming Pohl's chief of staff in early January, 1916, bearded him in his cabin and told him that the leadership of the fleet was no longer trusted. Two days later the unhappy admiral had to be removed to a hospital ship. His successor, Admiral Scheer, significantly summoned Captain von Trotha to be his chief of staff and Captain von Levetzow to be chief operations officer.* The High Seas Fleet had got a good commander in chief after just a year and a half, but a great deal of moral damage had been done in that time. On February 23 Admiral von Pohl died.

One of the reasons why the bolder spirits in the German navy had urged activity and enterprise was that Britain was heavily committed in the Mediterranean. The malcontents argued correctly that the situation of the High Seas Fleet was not likely to be as favorable again, so that the time to bring on a battle if possible was now or never. The strain came chiefly from the effort to force the Dardanelles, but not wholly. The watch on the Austrian fleet in the Adriatic also proved troublesome. On April 26, 1915, the French cruiser *Gantheaume* was sunk by an Austrian submarine in the Straits of Otranto, less than one-third of her crew being saved. It was then

* *Krieg zur See: Krieg in der Nordsee,* IV, 392.

decided that the regular blockade patrol must be left to French and British destroyers. The almost inevitable consequences followed this relaxation. Austrian submarines began to appear off the Greek island of Corfu. And on May 6 an Austrian light cruiser was seen and chased in the Ionian Sea, between Cephalonia and the Italian Calabrian coast, some 125 miles outside the Straits of Otranto. This was unpleasant from the Entente's point of view when dense and lightly escorted traffic was passing to and from the Levant. Italy's entry into the war in May, 1915, might have been expected to make the control of Mediterranean waters easier, but it did not. Britain had to reinforce the Italian fleet for problematic situations in the mind of its command which did not in fact take place.

In one of the two nearly land-locked seas, the Baltic, the Russians left the initiative to the enemy and their surface fleet remained in the Gulf of Finland. They had not yet put into service two dreadnoughts building at the outbreak of war, though these must have been nearly ready by the end of the year. The German fleet, though consisting only of seven cruisers and a handful of destroyers and submarines, dominated the Baltic. Russian caution was in part due to anxiety lest the Baltic Fleet of Grand Admiral Prince Henry of Prussia should suddenly be reinforced through the Kiel Canal.

In the Black Sea the position was the reverse. The Russians dominated it, partly because their superiority in strength was greater than in the Baltic and the Turkish naval forces were indifferent, partly because Admiral Eberhart was more enterprising than his Baltic colleague. The Russian Black Sea Fleet included two modern pre-dreadnought battleships, and one of the two dreadnoughts building was completed before the end of 1915. Admiral Eberhart had two anxieties: first, a shortage of coal, a stock enough for emergencies but which had to be husbanded; second, the speed of the *Goeben*, which might do a great deal of damage in a tip-and-run raid, and then escape pursuit. The Baltic Fleet was a great asset to the land army, and the relations between Eberhart and Yudenich ensured that it was used to the best effect when he needed its support.

Before the end of 1914 Britain had swept virtually all German surface warships off the trade routes. Simultaneously, however, the threat of German submarines and large-scale mining in home waters was growing heavier. In reply Britain multiplied her squadrons of trawlers and drifters, manned chiefly by deep-sea fishermen. The

U-boats were becoming more enterprising and dangerous, but during the first quarter of 1915 they could not be called a major menace. A system of regulating supplies to neutrals on the basis of peacetime importations was tentatively expanded, but it looked as though serious trouble with these countries was at hand, and especially with the United States, that which mattered most of all. Then, on February 4, 1915, the Germans gave notice of a submarine blockade:

"All the waters surrounding Great Britain and Ireland, including the whole of the English Channel, are hereby declared a war zone. ... Every enemy merchant ship found within this war zone will be destroyed without it being always possible to avoid danger to the crews and passengers. ... It is impossible to avoid attacks being made on neutral vessels in mistake for those of the enemy."

The United States thereupon warned Germany that she would hold her responsible for the loss of American ships or lives. The first neutral to suffer, however, was Norway. On February 19, the day after the "war zone" notice came into force, one of her ships was sunk without warning. On May 1 an American tanker, the *Gulflight,* was torpedoed. She was towed into Scilly, but her master lost his life. The *Lusitania,* with many American passengers, was sunk on May 7, with results in England mentioned later. On August 19 four Americans were drowned when the combined passenger and freight ship *Arabic* was sunk off the coast of Ireland. By this time the government and people of the United States were deeply angered. What appeared to the Germans as their "threatening attitude" scared Bethmann-Hollweg and perturbed the Emperor. The chancellor's advice was that the unrestricted campaign should be abandoned. The fierce old Tirpitz fought him tooth and nail because he believed that Germany had no hope of victory without the "sink at sight" policy. He seemed for a moment to have won, but a day later the Emperor threw his promise to him overboard. On September 1 the German government informed the United States government that its demand for the limitation of submarine warfare had been accepted. The effect was a temporary slackening of all U-boat activities.

One reason, however, why the Emperor had yielded in face of the "threatening attitude" of the United States was that Germany had not as yet boats enough to make the policy effective. Though heavy British troop movements to France were taking place as the Territorial divisions matured, all the transports had got through safely. In the four weeks ending on March 31 the total movement of British ships amounted to over 6,000 in and out and the losses to 21. In the Straits of Dover the British admiralty had brought into play an inspiring countermeasure. Before the middle of February, seventeen miles of "indicator nets" had been laid across by flotillas of drifters. These nets were made of wire and sustained by small buoys or glass balls. Each was detachable when a submarine ran into it, so that the submarine should be enveloped by it. A buoy moving along the surface would then indicate its presence. Some trouble occurred with the nets and the buoys proved unreliable, but the glass balls were excellent. After the war many an English or French bather would find one on the beach and learn vaguely that "it had something to do with the submarine war." The new measures brought a quick and triumphant success, though its architects did not realize its extent for some time. On April 10 the German admiralty issued an order that U-boats should no longer pass southward through the Straits of Dover; the attacks on British transports were to continue, but the U-boats were to sail to their various rendezvous round the north coast of Scotland. This was a heavy handicap for them.

Yet their numbers were growing and their captains and crews were gaining experience. By August the figures for the losses wore an uglier look. They were 42 British ships, double the number sunk in March. On top of this seven were sunk by mines, chiefly in the western approaches—and this meant that the mine laying also was the work of U-boats. The total gross tonnage lost was 148,000. In September it dropped to roughly 100,000, proof that the relaxation of German measures against neutral shipping benefited belligerent Britain also. In the last three months of the year 1915 the Germans concentrated their efforts in the Mediterranean. Seventy British ships were sunk in this period as against 96 in the previous three months, though as the average size in the Mediterranean was rather greater than in the North Sea and the Channel the tonnage was proportionately rather higher. And, though Britain was coming off better, her French and Italian allies were being far harder hit. They lost 100,000 tons in the three months, October, November, and December.

Arming merchant ships was an obvious precaution, but those who called the British admiralty a lunatic asylum when a freighter was caught unarmed had no notion of the complexity of the problem. Holland would not let any armed merchantman into her ports and as late as September, 1915, the United States authorities held up a

British merchantman until she had put her gun ashore.* Then, in the case of neutrals, did it give the Germans a better right, or a more plausible excuse, to sink a ship if she mounted a gun? Did it help if the gun were mounted right aft, so that it was clearly intended only for defense when in flight from an attacker? Another measure of defense adopted by Britain was the fitting out of decoys, known as "Q" ships, which posed as merchantmen but carried hidden guns. Their bag of U-boats was not a large one, but they exercised a certain moral effect.

The magnificent British submarine fleet naturally found fewer targets. Some of its finest and most deadly work was done in the Gallipoli campaign. A few boats also entered the Baltic. Here they went hungry to start with, but, even so, perturbed the German commander in chief in those waters. In a message to his fleet Grand Admiral Prince Henry of Prussia wrote: "I consider the destruction of a Russian submarine will be a great success, but I regard the destruction of a British submarine as being at least as valuable as that of a Russian armored cruiser." † In the autumn the profits became material as well as moral. The first German merchantman was disposed of in October, and between then and the end of the year three German cruisers were sunk. Less spectacular but enormously effective was the work of the submarines in the North Sea. Day after day, night after night, in constant and deadly peril from mines, torpedoes, depth charges, and bombs from airships and airplanes, they nosed their way to the mouths of the Jade, the Weser, and the Elbe. They were an influence unheard and almost unseen but never ceasing to be felt. They were a threat always present in the mind of every German captain. They were the antennae of the Grand Fleet hovering in its Scottish bases. They haunted poor Admiral von Pohl and perhaps hastened his death.

* Fayle, II, 206.
† Corbett, *Naval Operations*, II, 186.

Chapter VI

THE TURKISH OUTER THEATERS
AND GERMAN EAST AFRICA

BRITAIN, now with France as junior partner, instead of
senior as in the west, fought Turkey for the Dardanelles from
February throughout the year 1915. During this year the Entente
Powers engaged the Turks in three other campaigns. In Caucasia
the Russians found that their crushing winter victory, though it
had virtually destroyed the Turkish forces on the spot, was not
decisive and that more hard fighting had to be faced. In Egypt the
British defended the Suez Canal against a Turkish offensive. In
Mesopotamia the British advance begun in 1914 became more adventurous. The Caucasian and Mesopotamian campaigns overlapped,
since a small Russian force entered northern Persia and moved
toward the frontier of Mesopotamia, within which a British force
was then locked up in Kut-el-Amara, on the Tigris.

The presence of Russian and British forces in these outer theaters
of war was undoubtedly necessary. For Russia, indeed, Caucasia
was hardly an outer theater. She faced the risk of invasion. This
was the third war within just over sixty years in which a secondary
campaign in Caucasia was fought to accompany a major campaign
in Europe. The first was the Crimean War, the second the Russo-
Turkish War of 1877. In the First World War Turkey was to start
with not heavily committed outside Caucasia and could deploy
very strong forces there. Russia had no option but to engage her
with all means that could be mustered. These means were reduced
by the dispatch of Caucasian troops to the main Eastern Front.

For Britain the Suez Canal was vital as a waterway. Apart from

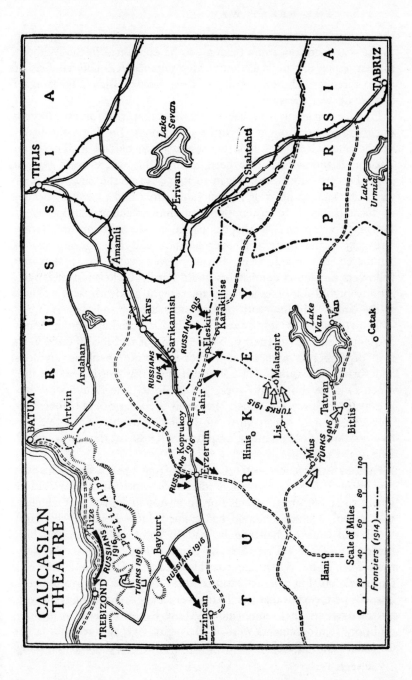

CAUCASIAN THEATRE

TABRIZ

Lake Urmia

P E R S I A

Shahtahti

Lake Sevan

TIFLIS

Erivan

Amamli

Kars

Sarikamish

RUSSIANS 1915

Eleskirt

Karakilise

Malazgirt

Lake Van

Van

Catak

BATUM

Artvin

Ardahan

RUSSIANS 1914

Koprukoy

Tahir

RUSSIANS 1916

Erzerum

Lis

TURKS 1915

Tatvan

Bitlis

T U R K E Y

Rize

TREBIZOND

Pontic Alps

RUSSIANS 1916

Bayburt

TURKS 1916

RUSSIANS 1916

Erzincan

Hinis

Mus

TURKS 1916

Hani

Scale of Miles

0   20   40   60   80   100

Frontiers (1914)

the passage of troopships, quantities of food and fodder, growing as the war went on, came through to be consumed in the Mediterranean, especially in Macedonia. Mesopotamia was entered first of all to safeguard the oil installations on Abadan Island. Here again were wise war measures.

Equally sagacious was the conclusion that the forces carrying out these missions ought to gain a little room. To sit on the banks of the Suez Canal was not the best way to defend it. To sit on Abadan Island would have been absurd. But where were you to stop? Directly the British began to move across the Sinai desert or the vast swampy plain of Mesopotamia they had to collect hordes of local laborers, to say nothing of noncombatant Europeans or Indians. By the end of the campaign in Mesopotamia the ration strength of the force was over 400,000 and the fighting troops numbered not much over 100,000. Even with all these camp followers the actual combatants could hardly be kept on their feet. At any period ten times as many men might go down with sickness as the enemy laid low with bullets and shells.

The trouncing which Enver Pasha had suffered at Russian hands had not slackened his energy. Now he used it to back efficient German professionals who set about reconstituting shattered divisions and forming new ones. The Turkish staff was bustled about and, much as it was bored by work, had to do it. The results were impressive, anyhow on paper. Between February and November Turkish strength rose from forty divisions (500,000 men) to fifty-two divisions (800,000 men), despite heavy losses at the Dardanelles.* This was the zenith.

Russian intelligence on the Caucasian front proved bad. This was not unusual, but one would hardly have expected it in a theater where the commander was as fine an all-round soldier as Yudenich, with a staff which he himself had trained. He was left in the dark. Until mid-June he believed he had in front of him in the hills northwest of Lake Van three or at most four divisions. Actually there were eight. When therefore his lieutenant Oganovski launched an attack on July 10, to capture these hills, he was prodding a hornet's nest, except that the Turks were sluggish hornets. However, by the sixteenth their commander, Abdul Kerim Pasha, was moving up heavy reinforcements west of Malazgirt, twenty-five miles north of Lake Van. Turkish counterattacks were beginning. Fighting

* Allen, p. 289.

grew hotter and hotter. The odds against the Russians were three to one, but Oganovski's far from quick eye took in only gradually the trouble he had brought upon himself. He fell back to Malazgirt, but too late. The Turks, their blood up and the vision of a great victory shining before them, pounced upon him. Round the town they had a fivefold superiority. Oganovski had not even kept his superior properly informed, and only when Yudenich sent a staff officer to Malazgirt, on July 22, did he learn how bad things were. The battle was then already lost. By the end of the month Oganovski's corps was streaming northward, its spirit broken and its transport lost.

The victory was a tonic to Constantinople, at a moment when the pressure on the Gallipoli peninsula was intense. Need it be said that Enver's dreams of a great pan-Turanian offensive returned? He ordered Abdul Kerim to pursue the enemy and drive him over his frontier. But Abdul Kerim could not march without securing his long communications, and the task devoured a large proportion of his force. It was big enough to thrash Oganovski's depleted and dispirited corps, but what if fresh Russian forces appeared on the scene? Despite Enver's exhortations, Abdul Kerim went forward with circumspection.

The reaction of Yudenich was typical. He assured the alarmed viceroy in Tiflis that all was well. He did not reinforce the unhappy Oganovski or communicate his plan to him. He would have to discard him anyhow, but not in the middle of a confused and critical operation. He was mounting an independent counteroffensive and had for this purpose scraped together a force of 22,000 horse and foot round Tahir, on the left flank of the Turkish advance northward from Malazgirt through Karakilise.* When Yudenich decided that the Turks had advanced deeply enough into the trap, this force, under General Baratov, was to sweep round its rear and cut its retreat.

These affairs seldom come off quite as planned. In this case the very slackness of the Turks was to their advantage. Their columns, which should have been closed up, were straggling over some twenty miles and consequently were not fully enveloped. However, Abdul Kerim had to make off as best he could. Baratov's Cossacks caught a number of guns and large quantities of stores blocked in the streets of Karakilise. Six thousand prisoners were taken by the Rus-

* Karakilise means "Black Church." The name is today Karakose.

sians and the killed and wounded are said to have numbered 10,000. The success was welcome to Russia in the black phase in which Poland was lost. Yet Yudenich had not the strength to exploit his victory.

The rest of the year was fairly quiet. On September 24 the Grand Duke Nicholas, after resigning his post as commander in chief, arrived in Tiflis. He came, however, as viceroy of Caucasia and left the conduct of operations to Yudenich, merely giving him an occasional directive and vetting his plans. Yet the grand duke was responsible for one well-inspired move, the dispatch of a force into north Persia, where the German military attaché was engaged in a plan of a type classic in German semipolitical strategy, the setting up of a pro-German splinter government in Hamadan. The result was a bloodless Russian victory. With limited strength in a secondary theater of war, while his country was suffering heavy defeat in the main one, Yudenich had done well in the year 1915.

Though Egypt was nominally a Turkish province, its links with Turkey were slight; though the chief British official was called modestly "consul general," he was in fact the ultimate authority; and though the Sudan was nominally held jointly by the United Kingdom and Egypt, the former undertook its administration and defense. On December 19 the Khedive, an extreme pro-Turk then living—and agitating—in Constantinople six weeks after Turkey's entry into the war, was deposed. His uncle, Prince Hussein Kamel Pasha, was raised to the throne with the title of sultan.

The Germans had sent to Syria one of their ablest staff officers, Colonel Baron Kress von Kressenstein, who stirred the Turks into laying on with great energy an expedition against the Suez Canal. It was a formidable undertaking. No opposition was likely in the Sinai peninsula, but it was practically waterless desert, with no roads but camel tracks. Even the austere and frugal Turks did not see how they could send over more than three weak divisions, some 20,000 men. This was no compliment to the British because there were four strong, though green, divisions and other troops in Egypt. The Turkish aim was opportunist; at best to start an Egyptian revolt and take the country; at worst to destroy a section of the canal. Kress sent only a small detachment along the easiest route, which followed the coast, in fear of interruption from the sea, and marched through the heart of Sinai. The Turks dragged German-pattern pontoons with them over this sandy route. From every

point of view it was a great feat. On the canal they had to face not
only the garrison but British and French warships moored in it
and in the lakes through which it passes.

As the enemy approached on the evening of February 2, 1915,
a dust storm began. All night the Indian sentries, their faces screened
in their puggrees and the breeches of their rifles wrapped in rags,
peered unavailingly into the murk. The assault was launched in the
small hours of the third between Lake Timsah and the Great Bitter
lake. Three boatloads actually crossed the canal, but all these men
were either killed or captured. The main body, pounded by the
ships' guns, never succeeded in closing, and its retreat was not
long delayed. Sir John Maxwell, commanding the Force in Egypt,
could undertake no serious pursuit for lack of desert transport. The
expedition was a fiasco and yet created respect for the Turks.

During the rest of the year Egypt was stripped of troops but
became a dumping ground for all that the Gallipoli forces left
behind them. At one time this included 52,000 horses and mules.
Trouble now shifted to the western desert, which was to be the
scene of much more vital battles in the war of a generation later.
Turkish propaganda and German money had whipped into hostility
the nomadic head of a powerful Mohammedan community, the
Senusi. He proved unexpectedly formidable because he had a
clever young Turkish colonel, a Baghdadi Arab named Ja'far Pasha
el Askeri, to train and command his levies. Enough troops remained
in Egypt to deal with him, but the problem was mobility rather than
numbers, and mobility involved the mustering of large camel convoys. After several relatively hard-fought actions, interspersed
with months of long and trying marches and fruitless pursuits, the
Dorset Yeomanry practically ended the campaign with a brilliant
charge (the Action of Agagiya, February 26, 1916) in which Ja'far
was wounded and taken. Never again did the Senusi's adherents
stand up to a British attack.

From December, 1915, the Gallipoli forces, weakened in numbers
and in health, poured back to Egypt, where thousands of their
wounded and sick in hospital could join them as they recovered.
The evacuation of the peninsula at once raised the question of how
far this easing of pressure would further Turkish designs on Egypt.
All agreed that invasion would be practicable only in winter, when
the water supply in Sinai would be most plentiful. Estimates of the
strength of the invading forces were, however, at this time unac-

countably and even ridiculously high both in Egypt and at the War Office. There was talk of two or three hundred thousand men marching across Sinai. This failed to take into account not merely the difficulties of supply but even the total Turkish strength south of the Taurus. When the practical Sir William Robertson reached the War Office as chief of the imperial general staff he cut the estimate to 100,000, which about represented Turkish hopes.

Meanwhile fresh troops were actually sent out from home to help hold Egypt against an imaginary danger. A system of defense was constructed east of the canal. General Sir Archibald Murray was appointed to command the forces on and behind the canal, still known as the Mediterranean Expeditionary Force but shortly renamed Egyptian Expeditionary Force. Maxwell remained in command of the small Force in Egypt. Before the withdrawal from Gallipoli the War Office had established an organization in Egypt called the Levant Base, to serve Gallipoli and other theaters of war, and had put its commander directly under the quartermaster general (for supplies) and the adjutant general (for troops) at home. There were thus for a time three independent military authorities in Egypt, a grotesque arrangement. A ribald and blasphemous wag was moved to write an "Athanasian Creed," destined for almost world-wide fame, on the Egyptian Expeditionary Force, the Force in Egypt, and the Levant Base:

"The first incompetent, the second incompetent, and the third incompetent.
And yet there are not three incompetents: but one incompetent."

In Mesopotamia the occupation of Qurna, at the junction of the Tigris and Euphrates, has been recorded.* Reinforcements were sent from India, so that by March the force consisted of two divisions and a cavalry brigade under the command of General Sir J. E. Nixon. He took his instructions from the commander in chief in India, who directed him to make a further advance, to Amara on the Tigris, seventy miles above Qurna as the crow flies—nearly twice as far as the river runs—and Nasiriya on the Euphrates. It was the insidious policy of another step forward. Before it could be taken, a minor Turkish offensive had to be beaten off and Major

* See p. 98.

MESOPOTAMIA

Scale of Miles
0   25   50   75   100

Little Zab

Sharqat
28/10/18
Mosul 27 mls.
Kirkuk
7/5/18

Tikrit

Kanaqin

HAMADAN

Samarra
24/4/17

Baquba

Kermanshah

PERSIA

Ramadi
29/9/17

BAGHDAD
Ctesiphon
Aziziya
21/9/17

Pusht-i-Kuh

Musayib

Kerbela   Hilleh

Sannaiyat
Sheikh Sa'ad
Ali el Gharbi
Kut
al Amara   28/9/15

Ali Sharqi

Shatt-el-Hai

Amara
3/6/15

Tigris

Ahwaz

Karun

D e s e r t

E u p h r a t e s

Nasiriya

Qurna
9/12/14

3/3/15

25/7/15

Pipe Line

Karun

BASRA
25/11/14

Shatt-al-Arab   Fao

Abadan I.

Tigris   Hanna
Sannaiyat
Sheikh Sa'ad
Kut
Dujaila Redoubt

The Kut Position

KUWAIT

Bubyan I.

PERSIAN GULF

General Gorringe was sent with a column up the Karun River to drive the Turks out of Ahwaz. He chased them away from the neighborhood of the oil fields, which were not further threatened throughout the war. At the end of May, Major General Townshend moved up the Tigris and took Amara. In late June, Gorringe moved against Nasiriya and after a month's campaign in grilling heat took that too.

Next Nixon suggested that he would be more comfortable if he held Kut-al-Amara, another ninety miles up river by air line—and this time over twice as far round the bends. Once more he was told to go ahead. It must be realized that the Baghdad-Basra railway did not then exist and that there were no roads. In summer the flat ground was so hard-baked that movement was easy, though large numbers of pack animals were needed; in winter huge areas were regularly flooded. The main transport avenues were the two great rivers, the Tigris being better than the Euphrates. The journeys of the steam launches were doubled by the windings of the rivers and they chugged upstream with their cargoes at a miserably slow rate. In any case they were, to begin with, short in numbers and extra craft had to be brought over long distances. This strain on the communications coincided with a shortage of doctors and a grave muddle over medical equipment and stores. When heavy fighting began the sufferings of both sick and wounded became atrocious and the matter became a scandal which shocked and angered the people of Britain.

Using both land and water transport, Townshend reached Kut on September 28 with his own Sixth Indian Division and a cavalry brigade. On the outskirts of the town he fought a brisk and brief battle with a Turkish force of about the same strength and gave it a good hammering.

No one had said much so far about the possibility of taking Baghdad, but the famous city beckoned to the imagination. Townshend certainly had it in mind when he pushed straight on to Aziziya, halfway from Kut. At this point, however, a fall in the depth of the Tigris halted him. If Baghdad could not be taken with a rush while the Turks were off balance, it would have to be done deliberately, bearing in mind that the Turks might bring considerable reinforcements from Caucasia. Nixon forbade Townshend, who was inclined to be a showman, to advance beyond Aziziya. Then Whitehall began to buzz with excitement. Strategically, the importance of Baghdad was not high, but the government saw a chance of refurbishing its prestige, which had declined owing to the now inevitable failure of the Gallipoli enterprise, by a showy success against Turkey elsewhere. When the general staff demanded reinforcements it was given the two Indian divisions in France, though these could not reach the scene for over two months. On October 23 the Cabinet concocted the following telegram which it authorized to be sent to the viceroy of India: "Nixon may march on Baghdad if he is satisfied that the force he has available is sufficient for the operation." Here was a neat formula which conveyed the Cabinet's wishes but put the responsibility for failure on Nixon.

Time slipped by and opportunities receded while Townshend's force was being stocked at Aziziya. He did not march until November 11, with a strange transport assortment of river launches, mules, camels, and even asses. Turkish reinforcements arrived just as he was about to attack at Ctesiphon on the twenty-first. Every time the force had met the Turks in this theater up to date they had beaten them handsomely, but the Indian troops, Townshend declares, "had their tails down" because they found themselves so far from the sea. When the Turk has had time to dig in to his liking he is a formidable defender. The attack broke down after a good start. The loss was crippling, nearly 4,600 out of a total of 14,000. As usual it was the infantry which bore the brunt: the thirteen Indian and three British battalions, already weak, must have lost on the average nearly 50 per cent. Having sent back the wounded, Townshend began his retreat on November 25. He fell back to Kut, which he decided to hold in view of the exhaustion of his troops. He estimated that his food supply would last two months and expected to be relieved within that time.

The Turks followed and began the investment of the town on December 7. Kut stands in a loop of the Tigris and the situation of Townshend in 1915 has been compared to that of General Benjamin Butler in 1864 in the Bermuda Hundred, lying in a loop of the James River, "bottled with the cork in." * The British and Indian governments had walked into this trouble. They had gratuitously accepted the risk for the sake of a military benefit of minor importance, but still more in the hope of providing the Mohammedan world with a sweetener to take the taste of Gallipoli out of its mouth. Meanwhile the expedition sent by the Grand

* Edmonds, *Short History*, p. 384.

Duke Nicholas into Persia under the orders of General Baratov had reached Hamadan, but it was a small lightly armed force—and 230 miles away. More significant was the arrival at Baghdad of one very old soldier, aged seventy-two, Field Marshal von der Goltz, whose knowledge of Turkey went back to the eighties. His reputation as a writer had spread over the military world, and the British duly marked his coming. It was likely to make the relief of Kut a difficult operation.

The only one of the African colonial campaigns which has not already been recorded up to its conclusion is that in East Africa. This campaign, essentially a chase of the elusive German commander Lieutenant Colonel von Lettow, was in the year 1915 mostly marking time. The fighting took on the character of raiding. British, Belgians in the Congo, and Germans enlisted more native troops. Control of all the lakes was secured, in the case of Lake Tanganyika by two motorboats, sent by sea to the Cape and thence overland through the Congo. The German light cruiser *Königsberg*, which had taken refuge in the Rufiji River the year before and forced her way so high up that she could not be reached by the guns of normal warships, was destroyed in July. The delay in making an end of her was due to the fact that two monitors with 6-inch guns had to be brought to the scene. With the aid of air observation they made short work of her. Think of the effort needed to account for this one little raider! She had done a lot of damage before being driven up the river and it was thought she might come out again unless either destroyed or blockaded for the duration of the war. The crew's life was a miserable one. They were assailed by intense and humid heat and tortured by insatiable insect pests.

Unless she won the war in the main theaters, Germany had no hope from the first of saving any of her colonies, but at least they had plenty of nuisance value. One way or another, they occupied most of the military effort of the Union of South Africa, so that only a single infantry brigade—though a grand one—ever represented it outside the African continent.

Chapter VII

HOW THEY FARED AT HOME

LITTLE room can be found for the life of the nations at war. It seems opportune, however, to open a few loopholes bearing on it and to risk the reproach that the glimpses are so slight as to be hardly worth while. Naturally, the effects of the war differed widely from one country to another, but there were also similarities throughout. Every belligerent state imposed heavy controls. Trade, even where it flourished, was conducted under difficulties and at sea in face of deadly danger. Rationing of food was nearly universal. All countries suffered from shortages somewhere. Monetary inflation pressed harshly on those with fixed incomes, including small *rentiers* in retirement, widows, and working men and women unable to keep pace by collective bargaining. On the other hand, capitalists in essential industries made fortunes and organized labor won rich rewards. Farmers naturally did well and at worst rarely went hungry. The diversion of industry to the purposes of war lowered the general standard of comfort and filched from many even what they had looked on as the necessities of life.

Increasing shabbiness was depressing. It was seen far and wide. Buildings went unpainted, often unrepaired. Rolling stock on the railways suffered from decay and rough treatment by troops. Winter journeys in unheated compartments with broken windowpanes were an ordeal. Roads were neglected—in 1917 a British general might drive fast and smoothly through the desert of last year's Somme battlefield and then, on leave, find himself shaken in every bone on the London-Brighton road. Not only the amenities of life but all the arts and every form of culture fell into eclipse. Socially, one of the unhappiest features was the severance of populations overrun by the enemy from their own people—in the case of Belgium and Serbia the complete or nearly complete occupation of the country. In many cases this involved the separation of families, women and children left behind when the men fell back with retreating armies. Even in the victorious countries the effects were felt after the war and not only in the obvious ways in family life but in a curious resentment felt by the temporary exiles against their compatriots who had been privileged to live under the rule of their own governments.

In a few great cities, capitals especially, a febrile gaiety appeared. The night haunts gave the military provost services much trouble and even anxiety. The theater was popular, but the taste was largely for light reviews and "leg shows." Even in London, Paris, Berlin, Vienna, and St. Petersburg, the vast majority of the population lived sober and rather dreary lives, but a section, which included many men in uniform, drank, reveled, danced, and wenched.

Britain, like other belligerents, started by temporarily closing the London Stock Exchange and, also like others, had recourse to paper money. (The gold in circulation proved a great asset, and most of it crossed the Atlantic.) Trade dropped and unemployment rose, but in both respects recovery was swift, in trade by mid-September.

Morally, but for a section of Nationalist Ireland—and Unionist Ireland, where no strike occurred throughout the war, was fervid in loyalty and zeal—the nation was united. People in general met the war without chauvinism but with hearty enthusiasm. The early defeats and the retreat from the French frontier came as a shock, but the victory of the Marne, though far from a full compensation for what had gone before, raised spirits again. A remarkable and amiable feature of the early phase was the good temper of the country.

It lost some of its fineness in the unhappy year 1915. The government's conduct of the war came under fire. The use by the Germans of poison gas at Ypres caused a wave of anger, even hatred. This rose to fury in some quarters when, on May 7, 1915, the liner *Lusitania* was sunk without warning by a German submarine with the loss of well over half the 2,000 passengers and crew. London mobs attacked and in some cases burned bakers' shops, baking being very much a German trade in the capital. The headmaster of Eton made a plea for less hatred and hounding of luckless people of German origin, and was savagely abused for his pains. Passing mention may be made of the degrading absurdity of dachshunds being stoned by boys.

The more intelligent were touched by a chill. It seemed that the French and British were stuck fast in the west, whereas the Germans could do much what they liked in the east. All realized that the results of the offensives in Champagne and Artois had fallen far short of expectations. The first half of 1916 brought no relief A brief but fierce revolt by Irish extremists or patriots—it all depends on the point of view—upset and astounded everyone, assailed a few tender consciences, and worried the prudent who thought of its effects in the United States. The Battle of Jutland, in which the Grand Fleet suffered more heavily than its adversary but confirmed British command of the sea, was pessimistically presented to the public. The strain of Verdun on the French caused anxiety. Then came the Battle of the Somme. The first reaction was encouragement and pride in the new armies. But casualty lists then began to appear. They were appalling. The casualties for the first day, not exactly known while the war lasted, were 57,240, of whom nearly 20,000 were killed or died of wounds. Britain had never dreamed of such slaughter in battle. The country was shocked and staggered, but it remained cool and determined.

Thereafter the mood fluctuated with the fortunes of the fight. The entry of the United States into the war in April 1917, was recognized as an enormous reinforcement. The slow motion and heavy loss of the Ypres battles and the drubbing of the Italians at Caporetto caused a numbing of spirits rather than nervousness, and the defeats of the first half of 1918 even more anger than anxiety. On the other hand, the first Allied counterstroke, on the Marne in July, 1918, did not create high optimism because most people had come to feel that we should need two million Americans in battle before we achieved victory. In fact, the Germans were reeling in August. Meanwhile, the lighter side of war was not eclipsed. Londoners who could went to *The Bing Boys*; the others saw Charlie Chaplin on the screen. Dancing became a rage. On Armstice Day London went crazy, but even then the provinces remained composed.

Britain lost her best blood and her treasure, but fewer hardships fell upon her than on the belligerents of continental Europe. She was not invaded. Food rationing did not start until late. Restaurant meals were not restricted till November, 1916. Still, meat and sugar both became short in supply and those who thought ration cards entitled them to meat were shocked in 1918 when their butchers opened perhaps three days a week and sold out in an hour. There were a fair number of deaths, not formally of starvation but from the inadequacy of the nourishment available to support unwonted exertion, such as that of an elderly businessman going to work on a bicycle because he could get no fuel for his car. And though Britain was less shattered by the tremendous influenza epidemic of 1918 than most other lands, deaths in London rose to 750 a week in October, and many died before a doctor had time to cross their doorsteps.

The plight of France was worse. Half of her coal fields and the iron ore of Briey and Longwy had fallen into the clutches of Germany, together with a big proportion of her industrial manpower. On the other hand, the country was nearly self-sufficing in food production. A touching and memorable sight was that of the peasants working in the fields within a mile or so of the front line, hardly raising their heads when a shell burst in the next field. Occupied France suffered gravely, the children particularly from shortage of milk. Fighting France suffered heavy hardship, but was better off than most belligerents.

France faced an assault undreamt of by Britain, a defeatist campaign against her spiritual vitals. A series of treason trials disclosed a horrifying state of affairs. They involved a former Prime Minister (Caillaux) and a former Minister of the Interior (Malvy), both sentenced to imprisonment. The first had supported the organ of defeatism, Le Bonnet Rouge, for services rendered during the trial of Madame Caillaux; the second had subsidized this treasonable rag, which had thus received money from both French and German governments. A hideous traitor, Bolo, was supplied with funds from Germany to corrupt the daily press, but a large proportion stuck to his fingers; one journal only accepted his aid—and it ratted. People of the older generation in England still sometimes speak of "a Bolo," but the name has perhaps been confused with Bolshevist. The methods of the famous prosecutor Mornet were unconventional. When Bolo belittled him from the dock as an undistinguished lawyer he replied:

"It is as representative of the French Republic that I mean to get your head " *

* Adam, p. 25.

Another scoundrel, Pierre Lenoir, received 5 million francs—mostly when the franc was above its prewar value *vis-à-vis* the United States dollar—in worn and dirty notes seized by the Germans in captured French towns. The traitors were of all shades. Caillaux was of the palest hue. He did not regard himself as a traitor and it may be that we should not; but he conveyed in Italy the impression that France was at her last gasp in 1916. The vilest may have been Almeyreda, who had lived by blackmail for keeping names and comment out of "scandal sheets" and who offered himself for hire to Germany. He was found strangled in his cell.

German money flowed in all directions and not all its channels can be identified even now. Its effects were serious, though they left untouched the great majority of the French people. There were also fanatics of defeatism who did not need bribing. When the Germans launched their offensive in March, 1918, four French cavalry divisions, which would have been very useful, were in the interior, watching for revolutionary outbreaks in industrial areas.

Germany was a land in which vast grain crops were extracted from very light soils with the aid of chemical manures. This was a vulnerable situation because of the lack of some of the most important manures, especially when Britain declared that shipments to neutrals were contraband if the goods were likely to go to Germany, and thus closed a huge hole in the blockade.* The case was much the same with fodder for animals. The Germans were compelled to mortgage their future by diverting fodder to human consumption. The third winter of the war, significantly known as "the turnip winter," was gray and grim. Moreover, this use of the turnip and particularly of the swede (rutabaga) had to be paid for. It reduced the winter cattle feed available and proportionately decreased the next year's supply of milk and butter. The blockade was a deadly weapon, though the German excuse that it was the main factor in the victory of the western Allies is a myth. In the latter part of the war some relief was obtained through the booty secured by the army, above all in the Ukraine.

The well-disciplined people of Germany stood up to the burden

* Sullivan, p. 95. He states that between November, 1913, and November, 1914, exports from New York to Denmark were multiplied above twelve times. In some cases neutrals needed larger imports for their own use, but not on this scale or anything like it.

and sorrows of war very well. A second myth created by propagandists is that the army was let down by the nation. In fact, the nation, hungry, wretchedly clad, its cuts and wounds bandaged with paper, its hands washed with a soap substitute resembling the abrasives then used to scrub sculleries, its coffee made from roasted acorns, its motor trucks shod with iron—the nation held out till the army was thoroughly beaten. The German nation was tough. Yet tough nations who endure long—as Teutons can and do—hit the floor hard when they fall. The collapse of the German people, like that of the German army, was thorough.

The ills of Austria-Hungary were largely due to the weaknesses already mentioned. Independent Hungary, rich in foodstuffs by comparison with other sections, would not share out fairly. Bohemia, whose Czech troops started going over to the Russians in formed bodies before the war had lasted a year,* was disaffected and uncooperative throughout. The efficiency of Germany in expedients was lacking in her ally. Austria produced no Walther Rathenau, the genius in war organization and especially in ersatz who carried out such extraordinary feats of "making do" for Germany.

The peoples could not be held together. Even the Emperor Francis Joseph, strong and vital despite his age—he was born in 1830—was unequal to the task. His successor's chief aim was to make peace. After the old man had gone there was no national leadership worth the name. There was not even anyone to induce Germany to hand over more than a very small proportion of the grain that came in as spoils of war, and the Viennese had the chagrin of seeing the trains carrying it to Germany pass through their city.

The fate of the dual monarchy was a strange one. Thanks to Germany's having taken over more than half the weight of the campaigns against Russia, to substantial if brief German aid in Italy, and to the superiority of the *Kaiserliche und Königliche* troops to the Italians, Austria-Hungary reached the last phase of the war in a situation satisfactory on paper. Three of her enemies, Russia, Serbia and Rumania, had been utterly defeated and her armies stood on the soil of the fourth, Italy. Yet she was exhausted, sick of the war, hopelessly disunited. The defeats suffered by Germany from August, 1918, onward created dismay amounting almost to panic in the minds of her rulers. In a matter of a couple of days her forces in Italy collapsed in face of the final offensive of the

* Kuhl, I, 377.

western Allies, and the rickety but respectable and on the whole beneficent political structure immediately fell to pieces.

The tribulations of Russia were the most tragic of all. The weaknesses which hampered her were at least as great as those of Austria, but of a different sort. The racial problem was a little less acute, though Poland, Finland, the other Baltic provinces, the Ukraine, and (in Transcaucasia) Georgia, Armenia, and Azerbaijan declared their independence after the army had been routed. On the other hand, neither organization nor communications were up to the Austrian standard and industry was less well developed.

The early defeats had mainly a military significance. The bulk of the land lost and partly devastated was Polish, and the Russians were unmoved by the frightful sufferings of the Poles, who for their part often disliked the Russians more than the Germans. Later on Russia got her share of the misery, and it was a heavy one. Civilians driven from their homes by the advancing enemy had to cover great distances. Nothing approaching the standard of the refugee camps opened in France, rough and austere though these were, was produced in Russia. The cold of the winter of 1916 was savage. We know that the death roll from exposure, disease, and hunger was enormous, though the figures have not survived. The army, which had to be fed at all costs, transported the greater part of its meat from Siberia in the least economical way, live cattle on the railways. The trains could have carried far more in dead meat if refrigerating plants had been available and many times as much if can-making and can-filling plants near the pastures had not been so rare; in which case it would also have been possible to alleviate to a greater extent the distress of the refugees and the population of the towns.

The United States did not become a belligerent until April, 1917. Her food problems were not serious. The energies of the wartime food administrator, Herbert Hoover—chosen because of his success in organizing the distribution of food in Belgium—were directed to obtaining more food for the allies of the United States. In his time they received about thrice what had gone to their countries in peace. The United States had become one of the chief arsenals of Britain, France, and Russia before becoming a belligerent. Here there is a resemblance between the two world wars; the difference is that she did much more for her own forces in the second than in the first, both fought under a Democratic administration, in each case with a remarkable President.

In 1914 the average American felt no such interest as the average Britain in affairs outside his own country. He had, however, an interest, mainly humanitarian, in Europe and was inclined to sympathize with the British outlook. The German invasion of Belgium shocked and angered him. Regarding the policy of the United States, there was a certain cleavage between East and West, the former regarding the possibility of intervention with less distaste than the latter. Yet the overwhelming volume of opinion was in favor of keeping out of the war.

In this intention the country was given a strong lead by its President, Woodrow Wilson. He bade it be "impartial in thought as well as action." It is to be doubted whether he was impartial in his secret heart, but this humane and imaginative man for long continued to look on himself as a predestined peacemaker. He secured his second term in 1916 largely as the leader who would keep the United States neutral.

Wilson's position was strengthened by the naval policy of Britain. She added goods, including copper, rubber, gasoline and later cotton, to the contraband list; she declared cargoes contraband even if shipped to neutrals, where there was a probability that the goods would be passed on to Germany; she brought American and other neutral shipping into her ports for search, on the plea that the submarine menace made this too dangerous at sea. The United States protested frequently, but did not go beyond that. Britain's excuse that these measures were essential to her very existence prevailed in fact, though rejected in theory. Still, it is fair to say that until Germany introduced unrestricted submarine warfare the Americans had more to complain of from Britain than from her, and there is no knowing what would have happened if Germany had refrained from this measure. What fools the Germans proved themselves, for all their skill in war!

Anti-interventionist sentiment was very strong. One proof of its strength is the swift postwar reaction to isolation. Seventeen years after the war—and only four years before the next began— an able writer, Walter Millis, could call Theodore Roosevelt—or at least his words—"faintly treasonable" because he was always a champion of Britain and early became an advocate of intervention. The United States ambassador to Britain, Walter H. Page, comes

off even worse—"singularly treasonable" and "distinctly treasonable." * Page was undoubtedly rash and more deeply influenced by
the English atmosphere than an ambassador ought to have been. Yet
no one can doubt that he was a staunch patriot. He also possessed
the imagination to see farther into the future than his American
contemporaries. Soon after his arrival and over eight months before
the war he put this question to Wilson: "Now what are you going
to do with the leadership of the world presently when it clearly falls
into our hands?" †

A more important writer than Millis, this time an Englishman,
has put the case against intervention on a lofty level, where it
comes close to Wilson's. Major General J. F. C. Fuller quotes the
President as saying to a reporter, the day before he delivered his
war message to Congress, that so long as the United States kept
out there was a "preponderance of neutrality," but that "if we
joined the Allies the world would be off the peace basis and on to
a war basis. It would mean that we should lose our heads along
with the rest and stop weighing right and wrong." Wilson contended, until the Germans cut away the ground from under his
feet, that the existence of a liberal-minded power, uncommitted to
either side, would be of vast benefit to the world. Fuller agrees
with him and sees the entry of the United States as a tragedy. But
for it, he says, the war would have ended in a deadlock which both
sides would have realized and "a negotiated peace would have been
agreed, with the United States as referee, before Lenin could have
got into the saddle." ‡

This conception is not without nobility, but it will not stand
examination. Assuming that a negotiated peace would have been
desirable—an assumption which will not be accepted by all—it is
not certain that it would have come about. It is not certain that the
western allies could have avoided defeat. Besides, people do not
think on these lines; few of them are seers, and most who are prove
wrong. We can see that western Germany, the main part of a
country which suffered catastrophic defeat in the Second World
War, is better off than Britain, the only nation which fought Germany from the beginning of that war to its end. Yet this result was
outside experience and could not have been foreseen. No courageous

* Millis, *Road to War*, pp. 125, 131, 423.
† Hendrick, I, 144.
‡ Fuller, *The Decisive Battles*, III, 270.

nation could have acted on the principle; perhaps the national leader who came nearest to leading his people along that path was Pétain, in 1940.

The people of the United States and even the government argued the case on simpler lines. The reasoning was sometimes confused. Early in 1916 Senator William J. Stone, Chairman of the Foreign Relations Committee, wrote to the President about "preparedness," a current doctrine which covered both ideals and military strength:

"I have heard some talk to the effect . . . that after all, it may be possible that the program of preparedness, so called, has some relation to such a situation as we are now called upon to meet." *

In other words, the United States, to the writer's astonishment, was doing what she professed to be doing. It reads like irony but was, in fact, naïveté.

The steps by which the nation approached the war must be described later. The man who led it up them was the President, who had been the champion of peace and won his second term of office in 1916 on the platform of "no war." He certainly did not rush matters or move in front of public opinion. He tried every variation from impartiality in thought and deed to armed neutrality in face of Germany. The anti-interventionists, headed by William Jennings Bryan after he had left the Cabinet, fought on, but it was a losing battle. When the United States became a belligerent it was less nearly unanimous than Britain two and a half years earlier, but the great decision was accepted and even urged by the vast majority.

* Millis, *Arms and Men,* p. 218.

Book Three—1916

Chapter I

CLAMOR OF DRUMFIRE

THE war which had flashed and flamed spasmodically was becoming a steadily burning furnace: fierce, sinister in temper, devouring. It had opened with battles between professional armies, and behind them immediate reserves and reinforcements who had for the most part undergone military training in time of peace. By the end of the year 1915 the belligerent nations were calling heavily on their total manpower, the whole body of their male youth—with large numbers nearer middle age. They had adapted their industries to the production of arms and equipment. They were buying from the neutrals to fill gaps and financing the transactions with loans. They were mortgaging their future to provide the means of victory because, in the bitterness prevailing, they could not face a future without victory. Any hint of compromise was regarded as treason. Doubters of various grades of pessimism were to be found, but probably only in the Austro-Hungarian Empire and to a lesser degree in France had their opinions any significance as yet. The voices of those who were vocal were drowned in the unceasing din of the guns.

Signs had already appeared, and were to be confirmed, that the war would become to an ever greater extent a war of material. Evidence of the tendency appeared above all in the increase of medium and heavy artillery and of shell (including gas shell) for artillery of all natures, and in the appearance of short-range trench artillery. Other forms were mining and the provision of roads, railways, bridging, piped water supply, buried telephone cable, shell-proof shelter, ever-extending entrenchment. In fact, it was more than material warfare; it was siege warfare, but on a scale such as the ages in which this was predominant had not known. Though only on the Western Front and in Italy had there been no intervening phases of open warfare, other fronts were likewise influenced by the new conditions.

How was the offensive to break the deadlock? National leaders, strategists, and tacticians were seeking to solve that problem. Many commentators have told us and go on telling us insistently that the generalship of this war was narrow-minded and mediocre. There is little evidence to support such an opinion. Generals from the Western Front who got fresh chances elsewhere—Falkenhayn in Rumania, Allenby in Palestine, Franchet d'Esperey in Greece, Serbia, and Bulgaria—maneuvered fast and brilliantly. The wiseacres conclude that they were bad, hidebound, mudbound generals in the west and became good, creative, fertile generals in changed scenes. Is it likely? No, it was the circumstances of the Western Front that shackled them.

Western Front strategy was obviously limited in possibilities. The way would have to be prepared for its exercise by tactics—that is, by fighting and breaking the deadlock. Both sides did apply themselves unceasingly to tactical study, but without making great progress. It may be said that the German tacticians were more inventive and flexible than either the French or the British, but not until 1918 were their achievements notably better, and then there were special circumstances which need not be discussed at this stage. It was British brains that were producing the best deadlock-breaker, the tank, though this was, to start with, misused.

France, Britain, and Germany all regarded the Western Front as the principal front, where the war must be won or lost. Germany was as convinced of this as the two Entente Powers, and, if she had turned east in 1915, it had been because the Russians had to be held and so buffeted that they would not interfere with her plans in the west. Surely, however, it may be said, if the Western Front was unbreakable, it would pay to go round and find a back door. This alternative was hardly prominent as yet because the French and British allies still hoped to break through and now at the outset of 1916 believed that they had for the first time amassed strength enough for the job. People had, however, begun to think of the alternative, and next year Mr. Lloyd George, then Prime Minister, was to advocate it.

The attempt to force the Dardanelles had been a well-inspired venture and probably should have been more strongly supported. Now that it had failed the choice was narrow. The Baltic had been considered and found impossible in the circumstances of modern war. Italy and Macedonia were not promising for an offensive, though Italy had the advantage that the French railway communications with it were good, nearly as good as the German. But what of British command of the sea? It must be confessed that this was not the most efficient means for the opening or expansion of a major European front. The German railway system was better—and not subject to submarine attack.

When at the end of 1914 Falkenhayn had to reinforce the Eastern Front rapidly he sent for General Groener, chief of the field railways, and asked how much he could handle. Groener replied that he could send from France four corps (eight divisions and corps troops) simultaneously, each on a double-track railway, in four and a half days. He could later repeat the process. Sea transport could not approach this speed. Broadly speaking, wherever French or British forces were sent in Europe they might expect to be met by German reinforcements from the first. The troops of the Entente could of course move farther, on to the outer periphery of the war, but their effect in Palestine and Mesopotamia did not justify the expenditure of men, money, and material. The Mesopotamian campaign was, in fact, not a contribution to winning the war so much as a contribution to its dreary and bloody prolongation. Macedonia was the best alternative theater. Some good French opinion—including that of Franchet d'Esperey, who knew the country and had a wide strategic vision—saw great possibilities in it from the first, but the communications in Serbia were atrocious and impossible to develop to any great effect. Thus a victory on the Greek frontier might have no morrow. It is true that a brilliant Allied victory was won here in the end, but Bulgarian war-weariness and the obviously approaching collapse of Germany on the Western Front were big factors in this belated success.

Those who condemn and deride the policy of the "westerners" pick out scraps of evidence which suit them, avoid those which do not, and add a few dubious assumptions. In particular, they omit one vital consideration: that, though the risks of a crushing defeat on the Western Front may have been less than elsewhere, the effects of such a defeat would be far more deadly than anywhere else. If one side committed itself too deeply on some other front it might give its adversary an opportunity to win a great victory in the west. This consideration applied more to France and Britain than to Germany because, except from Italy, they could not bring back their troops as fast. And if the stronger side did not attack on the Western Front it played into the hands of the weaker, which asked nothing better than that it should be left in peace during the phase of weakness.

Nor is it reasonable to attribute the delay of the Entente in winning a decisive victory or the narrow margin by which it avoided decisive defeat in 1918 to the conditions of the Western Front alone. Lack of coordination was also a factor. One man, General Joffre, did a great deal to coordinate the Allies, more than all their governments put together. He was often balked, but his achievement was considerable. On the other hand, the efforts of Britain, the expanding partner in the Entente, were ill coordinated internally, and this was undoubtedly the cause of great loss and waste.

Britain's situation was unique. At Christmas, 1915, when her army in France was still slender, Falkenhayn wrote in a memorandum to the Kaiser that the British Empire was the "arch enemy . . . the soul of resistance." Britain abolished the voluntary system of enlistment in January, 1916. She thenceforth adopted the continental-pattern mass conscript army, something which had never before occurred in her history. Yet at the same time she fulfilled her traditional and immemorial role, her role in half a dozen wars, by maintaining the biggest navy in the world and keeping the seas for her allies. On top of all this she was building a large air force, which was also to become the greatest in the world.

This achievement excites admiration and wonderment. And yet how tragically did she weaken it by lack of coordinated effort! Departments—the War Office, the Admiralty, the India Office, which was running the campaign in Mesopotamia—went their own ways. Their aims often conflicted, but the compensative machinery to remedy this state of affairs was inadequate on the political side and practically nonexistent on the military. Decisions were made sometimes too hastily, before the facts were clear; sometimes so slowly that the occasion had passed before they were reached. Misunderstandings were not cleared up. Even if it be presumed that a partial "eastern" strategy was correct, Britain chose the wrong theaters for her greatest effort in this field. Palestine and Mesopotamia paid dividends, of course, but not adequate ones.

On top of these handicaps Britain suffered from others which were unavoidable in view of the initial weakness of her army. First, she could not deploy her full strength until the year 1917. And, since this was the year of the two successive Russian revolutions, the initiative then passed to the Central Powers. Secondly, owing to this initial weakness, British commanders in chief in the west were deprived of a due share in forging strategy and had to make it conform to the sometimes unreasonable demands of their allies.

The new British commander in chief, General Sir Douglas Haig, was a Scot of ancient lineage, a cavalryman, aged fifty-four, but several years younger in appearance and impressively handsome. His prewar record was very good and he had been one of Haldane's instruments in the reorganization of the army. He was dedicated to the profession of arms. He was always respected by all ranks, but could not be called either a popular or an inspiring leader. He lacked the gifts needed for such roles in a large force. He was constantly out and about, seeing as much of his troops as he could, often combining business with exercise by sending his horses up the day before a visit and then riding for some hours round headquarters, billets, and camps. Yet he was so stiff or shy, so little given to speech and so inarticulate when he spoke, that these opportunities, though valuable in other ways, did not bring him closer to his men. On paper he was lucid and thorough.

He gave, in short, the impression of a strong, well-intentioned, but somewhat conventional man. Of late another Haig has been revealed in his diaries, less pleasant perhaps, but more interesting. The Calvinistic streak, the careful comments on the sermons preached by his chaplain, are not unexpected. What is surprising is the delicate malice of his sketches of visitors, the amusing but uncomfortably bitter wit, the flow of criticism, the animosities in some cases, for example toward Mr. Lloyd George and General Sir Henry Wilson, amounting almost to detestation. Haig was a complex character.

He was a man with a will of steel, cool-headed, and morally courageous. As a strategist he was good. Few serious students of his career would describe him as a notable tactician, except in defense, where he was admirable as corps commander and commander in chief alike. Most of the best ideas in infantry tactics were originated by the Germans, and then were sometimes misunderstood when they came to the knowledge of the British general staff. As might be supposed, Haig's tactical contributions were practical and down-to-earth, not, as he might have put it, the pretentious fancy stuff produced by those overintellectual Frenchmen and bespectacled plodding Germans.

Haig sent his army into a series of battles in which it suffered shocking loss and achieved virtually only one form of success, that of grinding down the Germans, spiritually as well as physically. He somehow held it together when it almost dissolved under the weight and fury of the German offensives. Hardly was it patched up than he set it going again—forward. He laid on it a burden heavier than that borne by any other national contingent in the Hundred Days of victory. He took more prisoners than the French and Americans combined. And he came through on Armistice Day with the best army then existing in the world.

At the beginning of 1916 the plans of both sides in the west were offensive. Falkenhayn's must come first because it was the first to be put into operation. No precedent can be found for this remarkable conception. Falkenhayn began by postulating that Britain was the "arch enemy." He did not, however, see his way to attacking her directly: an invasion was out of the question and major operations in Mesopotamia were almost equally so; attack on Salonika could at best occupy Entente troops. He was complimentary in deciding that he would rather not attack the British forces in France while he was so deeply committed on the Eastern Front—it was an astounding compliment since at that time only thirty-five British (two of them Canadian) divisions had reached the Western Front. For a full-scale offensive against the British thirty divisions would be needed and could not be found. As he could not knock out Britain he would attack an ally.*

Conrad wanted him to join in attacking the Italians, but he replied that he could not ask the German people to give their blood except for a direct interest.† No, he would attack France because he believed that her powers of resistance and the will of her people were weakening. He would attack some renowned site, the loss of which would bring down with a run French prestige

* Falkenhayn, p. 209.
† Regele, p. 384.

and courage. After a glance at Belfort, he chose Verdun, famous as a fortress, not only for the reasons given above but because its capture would strengthen the German front. He would do the work in a new way: steady pressure; limited objectives on a narrow front; the heaviest artillery concentrations ever made. He would draw the French army in mercilessly. He would bleed France white.

A little earlier Joffre held an international conference at Chantilly, on December 6, 1915. He came to an agreement with the representatives of Britain, Russia, and Italy, that all four allies should launch offensives with the greatest possible strength as soon as a common effort could be organized. These attacks must either coincide or be delivered at dates so close that the enemy would be unable to meet them in turn by the transfer of reserves. During the period of preparation wearing-down operations should be undertaken.

On December 29 Joffre summoned Haig for more detailed business. He proposed a vast offensive by their combined forces on a front of sixty miles astride the Somme. He also suggested a number of preliminary attacks by both, but Haig preferred not to make more than one bite at the cherry and Joffre did not press this project. Haig was not being captious—he never was that, though sometimes obstinate. Indeed, it may well be that he ought to have resisted the Frenchman's choice of ground. He would rather have attacked in Flanders, where he might hope to roll up the enemy's seaward flank and drive him off the Belgian coast. The offensive proposed by Joffre had no strategic possibilities. However, as had happened in 1915 when Sir John French was commander in chief and was to happen again in 1917, British views gave way to French in the interests of the alliance. Haig also agreed to relieve the French Tenth Army which had since the summer been sandwiched between his own First and Third Armies.*

The Emperor of Russia had decided to attack on an even greater scale than his allies in the west, but his armies had had so hard a time of it and stood in so great need of reorganization that he did not consider he could carry out preliminary attacks or undertake his main operation until well on into the summer. In Italy, Cadorna intended to go hammering on in the Isonzo country, which always obsessed his imagination.

At sea Admiral Jellicoe could not "seek out and destroy" the

* See p. 113.

enemy. He could hope for a victory only if the enemy would oblige him by coming out. He felt confident that the new commander of the High Seas Fleet, Admiral Scheer, would make sorties. At the same time he was convinced that his opponent would do everything in his power to lead him into traps, in particular pounce on his battle cruisers, launch torpedo attacks, use Zeppelins and airplanes to drop bombs, and sow the British path with mines, while avoiding if he could a full fleet battle against superior strength. Jellicoe considered that he would have to act with prudence because a slip, a bend of fortune in favor of the enemy, or even accidents might gravely diminish the strength of the Grand Fleet.

The British commander in chief was correct in his appreciation. Scheer believed that unrestricted submarine warfare was the only certain road to victory. He would have liked to introduce it at once, but the opposition of the Emperor and the Chancellor could not at this stage be overcome. Meanwhile he would make the best of the increasing number of U-boats at his disposal and reinforce them with surface raiders. On fleet actions in the North Sea his directive ran precisely on the lines of Jellicoe's appreciation:

"The present disproportion of the forces forbids us to seek a decisive battle against the British forces when united. Our conduct of operations must therefore tend to prevent this decisive battle being imposed upon us by the enemy.... We can attack in various ways, perhaps even with superior force, with at least the advantage of being always the aggressor.

"The means at our disposal are: war against merchant ships by U-boats and raiders, mines, air attacks, and greater activity of surface ships."

Thus Jellicoe and Scheer were at one in positive ideas and in reservations. The Briton wanted the enemy to come out; the German wanted to "entice" the enemy out. Yet neither was disposed to gamble. Scheer was a bolder, abler, and more dangerous commander than either of his two predecessors, but he agreed with them in the principle that decisive battle with the British forces when united was to be avoided. Jellicoe's attitude was what it had been all along, but he was impressed by the fact that the submarine menace, and in the North Sea still more the mine menace, had grown since the beginning of the war. Both had reason for caution, but Scheer the greater incentive to boldness. He could lose a valuable asset, which the Germans hoped to have in their pockets when they sat down to a peace conference. He could not lose the war.

Every portent and signpost pointed to a mighty and terrible struggle in the year 1916. On all sides there was stark determination to achieve victory at all costs. So numerous were the combatants, so heavily had they been armed by the growth of warlike industry, that, whether or not the deadlock was broken, the losses and all the miseries of war were certain to increase. In fact it proved to be a year of killing.

Chapter II

THE HELL OF VERDUN

THE Hell of Verdun" is an apt, if hackneyed, title. It was used by both sides. The five months' battle incised on the combatants' mind an ineradicable impression, which spread out through the world at large. Verdun was assuredly one of the most hellish of conflicts and is still one of the most famous of the war. The true fighting front extended hardly more than fifteen miles, from Damloup to Avocourt, and the fury of the struggle was generally much more narrowly confined. It was during the first fortnight limited to the right (or east) bank of the Meuse, and not until the end of of the seventh week did the Germans launch a major offensive on both banks at once. This compression of power and concentration of artillery on narrow sectors made them veritable hells. "We were unceasingly rocked, as if by an earthquake," writes a defender of Hill 304, who was buried and dug out by his comrades thrice that day, May 3.* For sheer horror no battle surpasses Verdun. Few equal it.

Verdun was a very ancient fortress. After the Franco-German War of 1870 it was still accounted valuable in blocking the valley of the Meuse, but useless as merely a fortified town. Verdun was therefore surrounded by a circle of forts on the fashionable pattern, to keep hostile artillery at a safe distance from the citadel. By 1885 ranges had increased, so a new chain of forts was built farther out, four miles from the town or more. Since then ranges and hitting power had increased still further, and though the outer forts had in the interval been strengthened by concrete and steel, their role

* Palat, X, 351.

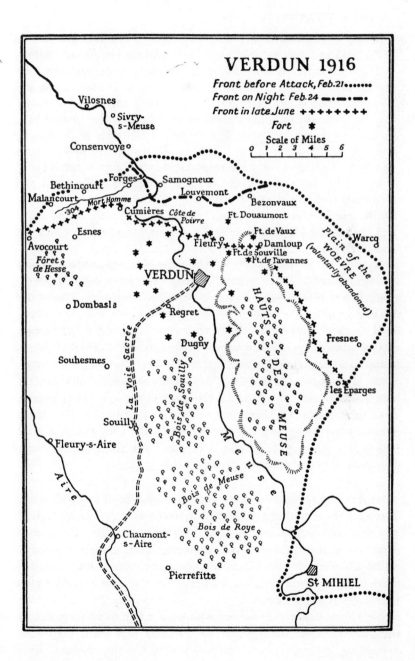

VERDUN 1916

Front before Attack, Feb. 21 ●●●●●●●
Front on Night Feb. 24 ━ ● ━ ● ━ ●
Front in late June ✛✛✛✛✛✛✛
Fort ✱

Scale of Miles
0 1 2 3 4 5 6

Vilosnes

Sivry-
s-Meuse

Consenvoye

Bethincourt   Forges   Samogneux

Malancourt   Louvemont
          Mort Homme
          .304   Cumières   Côte de   Bezonvaux
Esnes   Poivre   Ft. Douaumont

Avocourt   Ft. de Vaux   Warcq
Fôret   Fleury ✱ Damloup
de Hesse   Ft. de Souville
                              Ft. de Tavannes

VERDUN   Plain of the
                                            WOEVRE
                                            (voluntarily abandoned)

Dombasle

          Regret

Souhesmes   Dugny   Fresnes

                                            les Eparges

Souilly

Fleury-s-Aire   Bois de Souilly

Aire

                    Bois de Meuse

          Chaumont-   Bois de Roye
          s-Aire

          Pierrefitte   St MIHIEL

La Voie Sacrée

Meuse

HAUTS-DE-MEUSE

appeared so diminished that their artillery was removed for service in the field and they were allowed to deteriorate because of neglect.

They had indeed been underrated. Even in their present state they proved useful as buttresses to the field works, as shelters, command posts, munition stores, and means of providing hot food for troops. Had not their organization been permitted to lapse they would have played an even greater part. The French commander in chief came under heavy criticism in the Chamber of Deputies on this account and for unreadiness in other respects. He was lucky to escape as easily as he did. But for bad weather the assault would have been launched nine days earlier and would have caught him unprepared, without readily available reserves, though some signs suggesting an offensive had been noted a month earlier. When the test came Joffre was not found wanting.

Verdun lay in the middle of the base of a semicircular salient facing northeast. The Meuse ran through the town roughly northward but in bold curves. It was here an inconsiderable stream, but its bed lay in a deep gorge in the plateau. This was agricultural land, worked from small villages, with very few isolated farmhouses. Astride the Meuse the plateau was broken by slight hills and ridges, rising to a maximum of 1,000 feet or so. Many woods, some large, some little copses, gave variety to a commonplace scene. On the east side of the salient lay the flat clay plain of the Woëvre. The main battlefield astride the Meuse was a mixture of chalk and clay, which when stirred up in wet weather turned to the consistency of glue and in dry gave off dense clouds of dust. The front line lay some three miles beyond the outer forts.

The German Crown Prince, commanding the Fifth Army, wanted to attack on both sides of the river, but Falkenhayn had picked the battlefield as requiring a minimum of troops and therefore confined the operation to the right bank to start with. Six divisions were to attack on a frontage of only six miles, which was, however, speedily to be widened. The two French divisions on which the assault fell held between them over eight miles. The German superiority in artillery was still greater.

The bombardment began on February 21. It was very violent and punctuated by the frightful explosions of 305-mm. and 420-mm. howitzers. In many places the trenches of the first position were obliterated. Some gas shell and a great deal of lachrymatory was mingled with the high explosive. Nevertheless, the assault launched at 5 P.M. was disappointing. Two divisions actually fell back to their starting line during the night. Yet the Germans gained a footing in the foremost trenches and annihilated one French regiment, which lost 1,800 men out of 2,000. French reserves were on the move, but only one division was close at hand. The French command awaited the morrow with deep anxiety.

This proved justified. By February 24 the Germans had progressed all along their front to a maximum depth of three and a half miles. The second position had been captured. Worse still for the French, unsteadiness had appeared in a battalion of North African *tirailleurs*, who could not face the drumfire north of Louvemont in the center of the front. That day the commander of the central army group (G.A.C.), General de Langle de Cary, decided to abandon the plain of the Woëvre, which had not been attacked.

Blacker still was February 25, a day as ignominious for the French as it was brilliant for the Germans. An unnecessary withdrawal occurred near the left flank, accompanied by indiscipline and even panic, though, as always happened in this battle, when some troops cleared out, others blocked the enemy before he could break through. Most unhappy of all was the loss of Fort Douaumont, left ungarrisoned and taken by a single German company. The news set the German army, all Germany indeed, huzzaing. To the French army and France it came as a sickening shock.

At midnight General Pétain, summoned the day before by Joffre, took over command astride the Meuse. He could not have arrived at an uglier moment, to fight a battle that seemed to be lost already. Yet heavy reinforcements were on their way. The new leader was in himself no mean reinforcement. Calm and methodical, he set about bringing order out of chaos. One of his deepest anxieties was for his communications. The main artery was the narrow secondary road from Bar-le-Duc, forty miles south. Would it hold? Thanks to widening, incessant work, and first-class organization, it held. One driver in the early days is said to have sat for over fifty hours at his wheel. For hours together trucks passed at the rate of one every five seconds. The road became known as "la Voie Sacrée."

From now on the reinforced French began to resist in good earnest. Their artillery hammered on every fold in the ground that sheltered or might shelter German troops. Pretty good progress was made on the twenty-sixth, but by the twenty-eighth "the German attack on Verdun was virtually brought to a halt." * It was a deep disappointment. One cause was the flanking fire of the French artillery from the left bank. To drive back these guns Falkenhayn ordered an extension of the attack west of the Meuse.

It was launched on March 6, a dark, cold day, with occasional snow showers. The Germans forced their way in hard fighting across the Forges, a tributary of the Meuse. By the eighth they gouged out a holding two and a half miles deep and captured the second line on a frontage of over four miles. A tremendous struggle followed for the dominating hill, prophetically named le Mort Homme. The assailants struggled up on to the northern peak, but the French clung like leeches to the southern half. The bad weather rather favored them, since the German aircraft had hitherto held the mastery, and at the start by the combination of attack in the air and shelling of airfields the French were practically driven out of the skies. Now both air fleets were often grounded, a bigger handicap to attackers than to defenders. In April the Crown Prince's task became stiffer still. The French now equaled their foes in strength on the ground and in the air. They constantly counterattacked, though they succeeded only in limiting the advance. The left-bank attack failed in its main purpose: it did not stop the French flanking fire.

Meanwhile the fighting had begun to take the form of trench warfare to a greater extent than in the first phase. The effect was even more terrible. The landscape assumed a lunar aspect, an unending succession of shell craters, some immense. The woodlands were reduced to a debris of tangled, shattered boughs amid stumps. Here and there rotting bodies of men and horses protruded from the churned and tortured soil. As the weather grew warmer the stench of carrion became more disgusting. Troops left long in this inferno appeared to age. Their eyes sank in their heads; their features became drawn.

The transformation of the battle is illustrated by a remarkable incident. On April 10 and 11 the Germans launched heavy attacks south of Douaumont, partly on the large Bois de la Caillette. The assault was shot to fragments by machine guns and the survivors were flung out of their scanty gains by a counterattack carried out by a hundred men. So sharp was the failure that the corps com-

* Weltkrieg, X, 115.

mander, General von Mudra, was relieved and replaced by General von Lochow.*

On his side Pétain had removed several commanders who could not stand the strain. He had, however, benefited by the arrival of two first-class lieutenants. Robert Nivelle had come in at the head of a corps and Charles Mangin with his fine Fifth Division. At the end of April, Pétain took over command of the G.A.C. and Nivelle succeeded him in command of the Second Army. Mangin was later promoted to the command of a corps. These two men were to be closely associated on this battlefield and others, but their fates were to be very different. They became the soul of the defense of Verdun.

In the final phase the German advance slowed down still further, but nevertheless on the right bank won some important successes. Early in June the Fort de Vaux, southeast of Douaumont, was, writes the German chief of the general staff, "captured by our brave troops after long and—even for the Verdun battle—extraordinarily stubborn fighting." † Since the arrival of Pétain the forts had been furnished with permanent garrisons and Vaux was held by 300 men under Commandant Raynal. It seemed impregnable and continued to resist after the Germans had surrounded it. Nivelle had left himself with insufficient reserves, and his weak relief effort failed. The final scenes almost defy description. Access to the latrines was cut by fallen masonry. The fort became abominably filthy. German troops who pushed up close to it declared that the stench emanating from holes and cracks in the wall sickened them. Raynal and his men held on till beaten by a want that none could resist: the water gave out. On June 7 the Fort de Vaux was surrendered. Raynal was received and congratulated by the Crown Prince in person.

On the left bank the Germans were resigning themselves to deadlock. They still hoped to decide the issue on the right, or rather the Crown Prince's resolute chief of staff, General Schmidt von Knobelsdorf, got his way to make the attempt. The object was to capture the inner forts of Souville and Tavannes. On June 21 the German artillery used for the first time "greencross" gas shell, filled with a deadly type of phosgene. The effect was overwhelming in silencing French batteries, but the success was not up to expectations. Though thousands of Frenchmen were prostrated or reeled rearward, the defense was never smashed. However, the village of Fleury was lost

* Weltkrieg, X, 146.
† Falkenhayn, p. 239.

and the Germans came within striking distance of Fort Souville.

This was the final crisis. Before it was weathered it worked heavily on the mind of the army group commander, General Pétain. He was a masterly soldier, but he lacked the tonic of optimism which heartens the greatest commanders. If Souville and Tavannes fell it did not look as though Verdun could hold. In any case much of the artillery on the right bank was likely to be pinned down and lost. Pétain prepared in secrecy—the angry Nivelle being the only subordinate to share the unwelcome project—a plan of voluntary withdrawal. Joffre knew of it and did not object to a study. But he in-formed Pétain on June 26 that the artillery preparation for the Battle of the Somme had begun and that the right bank of the Meuse *must* be held; he himself would answer for the consequences if there were a loss of material. The deputy chief of the general staff, on taking to him for approval the telegraphic message in this sense, called attention to the weight of the responsibilities he was assuming. "*J'en ai pris bien d'autres,*" said Joffre calmly.* They soon passed him by; for the guns on the Somme compelled Falkenhayn to let the battle peter out.

Some differences of opinion had arisen between Joffre and Pétain. Pétain's method was to relieve divisions as quickly as possible. Up to the end of June sixty-five divisions had passed through the fire of Verdun, whereas the strength of the Second Army did not exceed an average of twenty-four. Joffre had already been compelled to cut down the French contribution to the Somme offensive. He was determined that it should not be canceled altogether. The Germans used only forty-seven divisions up to August so that the average division endured "the hell of Verdun" considerably longer. The losses did not fall far short of the French: 281,000 to 315,000, or slightly less than seven Germans to eight Frenchmen.†

The German tactics at Verdun were often brilliant. Daring and shrewdly led reconnaissance parties would start in darkness and probe the defensive front for weak places. If they found the French alert and active, the attack would often be postponed and further artillery preparation undertaken. The ground and the loops of the Meuse suited tactics of envelopment, which were carried out with skill and

* Palat, X, 434.

† Edmonds, *Short History*, p. 159. Several French estimates of French losses are much higher, but obviously include the sick. Except in an unhealthy climate or intense cold the sick almost all recover, and quickly, however hellish the battle.

boldness. In no other battle of the war on a similar terrain and against such strong defenses was so much use made of scanty tactical opportunities. The hasty counterattacks of the French offered less scope for maneuver. It was in defense pure and simple—traditionally their weakest feature—that they most excelled, though there were some glaring exceptions. Their artillery was, as usual, well handled. Had the monster howitzers been permitted to do their deadly work without interruption, Verdun's fate would have been that of Namur and Antwerp, but they were harried and in many cases destroyed by the French long 155-mm. guns.

The Germans partly succeeded in their aims and came near to doing so completely. Could the attack have been launched, as intended, on February 12, when it would have had a superiority of five to one in infantry, it might have reached the inner forts at an early stage. However, the commander who opens a great offensive in February in northwest Europe cannot plead bad weather as an excuse for failure. Few German historians regard Verdun as a victory, whereas most French do so. This is not a conclusive argument, because French propaganda about Verdun was so effective as to influence even trained historians, but it should count. Certainly the battle aroused the more pride in the French nation, despite the shocking losses.

French lapses in morale have been noted, and more could have been. Captured Germain mail revealed some poor morale also, though this evidence may be deceptive because intelligence officers pick out the letters of the weaklings and the frantic. Yet all in all, few modern instances of valor and endurance excel that of the opposing forces at Verdun. Nations that breed such men are vital. Yet, if they fight many such battles, they will be partly reduced to breeding from the milksops, the indispensable young men kept at home, and the invalids. The next generation will be not only smaller in numbers but less vital.

By the autumn the French found themselves strong enough to hit back at Verdun, though only on a limited scale. On October 24 Nivelle's Second Army launched an attack conducted by Mangin, with only three and a half divisions, but making up for shortage of infantry by the weight and superb handling of the bombardment. The forts of Douaumont and Vaux were recaptured, so that the venture was a moral as well as a tactical success. Mangin took 6,700 prisoners and the German losses in killed and wounded were very high. The French then had to lie low and save up their ammunition, but on December 15 Mangin attacked once more, on a wider front. Four of the five German divisions involved were fatigued, one having only just been transferred from the Somme front. This offensive was even more successful than the last and resulted in the capture of Bezonvaux and the Côte de Poivre. The maximum depth gained by the two was three and three-quarter miles. Over 11,000 prisoners and 115 guns were taken. And whereas the German losses in their prolonged offensive had been substantially lower than the French, about seven to eight, in the two brief French thrusts they were 55,500 to 47,000, over eight to seven. Another feature of the French effort was the strength, dash, and skill of the air force, which ruled the skies and in liaison with the artillery hammered that of the enemy unmercifully.

Before the second attack Nivelle had passed on to another task, but he directed the operations and they made him illustrious. He was the man of the moment. We shall shortly see where his reputation carried him.

Chapter III

THE SOMME—BATTLE OF ATTRITION

HOW near a thing was the French defense of Verdun is shown by the appeals of Pétain to Joffre and the demands of Joffre to Haig that the offensive of the Somme should be hastened. Neither hesitated to say that Verdun must be "relieved."

While the long preparations for the battle were in train Britain had to face two unpleasant distractions. The more important was a series of airship raids on the home country. The moral effects were not fully known at the time because the material effects were so slight. The British people in this war had not contemplated air bombing and did not in all cases take it well. On February 10, 1916, a panic broke out on a rumor that a Zeppelin had appeared over the eastcoast wateringplace of Scarborough. Two government factories in Gloucester, 180 miles away, closed down. The falling off in production and the indignation of public opinion induced the government to form ten home-defense squadrons of the Royal Flying Corps.

To anticipate a little, the first Zeppelin to be shot down was the victim of Lieutenant Leefe Robinson on September 3. He was awarded the Victoria Cross. On October 2, Lieutenant W. J. Tempest shot down a different type of airship, a Schutte-Lanz, captained by Commander Mathys, the greatest airship captain of the war. Airship raids afterward tailed off, but weather was as important a factor as defenses in their defeat.

The "Easter Week" rebellion in Ireland—almost entirely in Dublin —took the authorities by surprise, and for a short time the capital was largely in the hands of the rebels. Then troops under General Sir John Maxwell, the former commander in Egypt, closed in remorselesly and extinguished the revolt. Fifteen leaders were executed. The power and influence of the moderate nationalists led by John Redmond, already on the wane, now disappeared. They passed to the extreme and militant organization known as Sinn Fein ("Ourselves alone!"). However, no further grave trouble appeared until after the war, when the British army had been demobilized and the units consisted for the most part of immature youths. The Military Service Acts of early 1916 did not include Ireland, and, though two years later conscription was legally extended to the country, it was never applied. In consequence most of the Irish battalions of the new armies eventually disappeared.

The French army had been so mangled at Verdun that its effort on the Somme could be only a shadow of what Joffre had originally intended. The main battlefield was now to be British and north of the river. Here the country was one of sharply cut ridge and valley, dotted with villages in which practically the whole population was or had been concentrated, to make the most of a scanty water supply. The development of water supply on the British side of the line was one of the heaviest items in the preparation. Despite precautions, an artillery or supply unit would sometimes descend with its animals on a commune and promptly drink the wells dry, to the anger and discomfort of the villagers. The mere work of accommodating the waiting host was enormous. "A temporary satellite city had to be improvised." * Vast quantities of ammunition, supplies, bridging and other engineer stores, and road metal were amassed. Telephone cable was buried as deep as five feet.

A number of minor German attacks took place before the opening of the Battle of the Somme. Two, both on the British front, may be mentioned as designed in part to interrupt the preparations. On May 21 the Germans, by an excellently organized attack, recovered the crest of Vimy Ridge. It was an unpleasant affair for the British because the ground had been won at such heavy cost by the French, who had handed it over only in March. However, Haig resigned himself to its loss rather than start a flare-up which might have had an unfortunate effect on his main effort. On June 2 the enemy took Mount Sorrel, two and a half miles east-southeast of Ypres. This time Haig ordered the Canadian Corps to recover the high ground which counted, and this was done eleven days later.

By now all was nearly ready for the great venture. From Mari-

* Edmonds, *Short History*, p. 179.

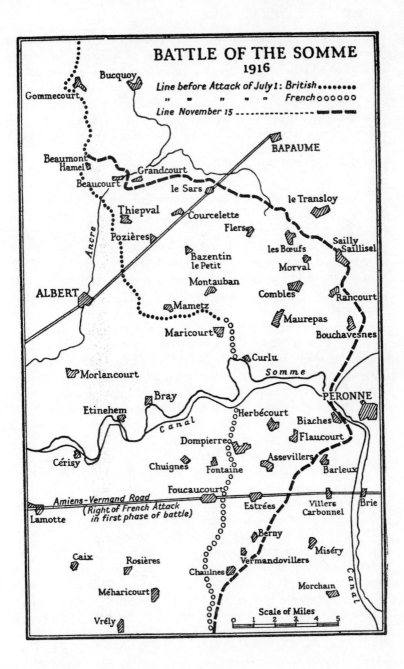

BATTLE OF THE SOMME
1916

Line before Attack of July 1: British ••••••••
     "   "   "   "   French ooooo
Line November 15 ---------------

Gommecourt

Bucquoy

BAPAUME

Beaumont
Hamel

Grandcourt

Beaucourt

le Sars

le Transloy

Thiepval

Courcelette

Flers

Pozières

Sailly
Saillisel

les Bœufs

Bazentin
le Petit

Morval

Montauban

Combles

ALBERT

Rancourt

Mametz

Maurepas

Maricourt

Bouchavesnes

Curlu

Somme

Morlancourt

Bray

PERONNE

Etinehem

Herbécourt

Canal

Biaches

Dompierre

Flaucourt

Cérisy

Chuignes

Fontaine

Asseviiers

Barleux

Foucaucourt

Amiens–Vermand Road
*(Right of French Attack
in first phase of battle)*

Estrées

Villers
Carbonnel

Brie

Lamotte

Berny

Caix

Miséry

Rosières

Vermandovillers

Chaulnes

Canal

Méharicourt

Morchain

Vrély

Scale of Miles

0   1   2   3   4   5

court north of the Somme, to Gommecourt, a front of eighteen miles round the curves, stood five corps of General Sir Henry Rawlinson's Fourth Army and the right-hand corps of General Sir Edmund Allenby's Third, eighteen divisions, of which fourteen were to attack in first line. The frontages of divisions were rather wider than those of the Germans on the first day at Verdun, though the defenses there had not been nearly as strong. The gravest British weakness was the shortage of medium and heavy guns and howitzers, production of which was still far short of its peak, and—scarcely yet realized—the very bad quality of the shell.

Of the fourteen first-line divisions eleven came either from Kitchener's new armies or the Territorial force, two legions of amateurs about to engage a first-class army still leavened with professional, peace-trained soldiers. Here stood the flower of Britain, drawn from all classes of the community but on the average the best of all. Though the first universal service act was nearly six months old, these men were volunteers with hardly a conscript in their ranks. In some cases they had enlisted in groups of friends, so that here and there platoons were made up of men most of whom had known each other in civil life, bands of brothers. In such a case we talk in billets or dugouts might be of streets, of football fields, even of lanes and farmhouses, at home. They were in high spirits and inspired by high hopes. They were ready to give their lives. The French could muster only five divisions in first line astride the Somme. On the whole front of attack the German Second Army of General Fritz von Below had six divisions in line, with five more fairly close at hand. There were three, in places four, lines of defense, to an average of five miles deep. The fortifications were very strong. The Germans, incomparably the hardest workers of any of the belligerent armies, had dug in the chalk excellent trenches and excavated numerous deep dugouts, proof against anything but a direct hit by an 8-inch shell.

The objectives drawn on the maps mean little—nearly all attackers in war lean to optimism in chalking maps with red, blue, green, and yellow lines. Haig hoped for a deep penetration at an early stage. A cavalryman himself, he looked forward to exploiting success with his arm, and held the very large force of three British and two Indian cavalry divisions standing by. On the other hand, his subordinate, Rawlinson, whom he considered his best army commander, was inclined from the first to think that the battle would be one of attrition and that limited attacks supported by the full weight of the artillery, with pauses to allow it to move forward, would pay best. For the first day an advance of just over two miles at the maximum was planned.

The preliminary bombardment began on June 24. It was to have lasted five days, but had to be extended for two more because the assault, which should have taken place on the twenty-ninth, was postponed owing to bad weather until July 1. Hour after hour the guns roared. The German garrison had a sorry time of it. "*Das mörderische Feuer,*" as the official account calls it, not only destroyed the wire in front of the first position, blew in many lengths of trench, and put a number of guns out of action, but often made it impossible to send up food and water at night. Thus hunger and thirst were added to nervous strain. The casualties are said to have been "considerable," * but so were those of the British, especially among the men engaged in thickening the bombardment with trench-mortar fire.

July 1 was a warm, sunny day, but the acceleration of fire before 7.30 A.M., the hour of the assault, raised clouds of smoke and dust to overhang the battlefield. Including the supply services, over half a million troops were assembled west of the front of attack, of whom well nigh 100,000 advanced at this hour. They were overweighted with small-arms ammunition, grenades, and rations, while large numbers carried picks or shovels for entrenchment, so that they could move only at a steady walk. The distance they had to cover varied with the breadth and the features of no man's land. For example, on the front of the Thirty-sixth Division south of the Ancre a sunken road crossed it parallel to the German front, and the leading troops formed up here without heavy loss. In the same division we may observe a demeanor typical that day. The officer commanding the Ninth Royal Inniskilling Fusiliers wrote:

"I stood on the parapet between the two centre exits to wish them luck.... They got going without delay; no fuss, no shouting, no running, everything solid and thorough—just like the men themselves. Here and there a boy would wave his hand to me as I shouted good luck to them through my megaphone. And all had a cheery face. Most were carrying loads. Fancy advancing against heavy fire with a big roll of barbed wire on your shoulders!" †

* Weltkrieg, X, 345.
† Falls, *History of the 36th (Ulster) Division*, p. 52. Owing to the very heavy losses among commanding officers in the battles of 1915 strict orders were issued

As the Allied artillery lifted, the stout-hearted Germans ran up the dugout steps and soon the rattle of machine guns was heard amid the thunder of field and heavy artillery. How well we got to know the sound of that gun, a little slower than our own and with, it always seemed, a slight stutter in its burst of fire! Into this storm marched the infantry.

South of the Somme the French gained a brilliant and complete success. Some British historians have ungraciously asserted that this was because the Germans did not expect them to attack at all after their losses at Verdun, but it is clear from German accounts that such was not the case. Their tremendous superiority in heavy artillery, which resulted in the pulverizing of large sections of the German defenses, had something to do with it, but they merit the credit due to speed, dash, and tactical brains. As on many occasions in this battle, their formations were less rigid than those of the British and proved less easy targets. The single French corps north of the Somme also did well, as did Sir Walter Congreve's Thirteenth Corps next to it, capturing Montauban and smashing a German counter-attack to fragments. In the orders of this corps the sentence appears: "The field artillery barrage will creep back by short lifts." This is the first mention of the "creeping" or "rolling" barrage, which shortly afterward became a matter of standard practice, though constantly developed. The main object was to keep the defenders' heads down till the last moment. Only in the Thirteenth Corps was it used on July 1. The next corps farther north had a partial success at Mametz.

This was all. On nearly half the Allied front and three-quarters of the British there was at most temporary progress. The rest of the story is complete and bloody defeat. Heroic deeds were performed all along the battlefield, but heroism was not enough. The resistance was very stout. The German artillery was crippled, so that the defense fell largely upon the machine guns, and it was the machine gunners, perhaps only a hundred teams and guns doing the real work, who kept the front from breaking in pieces. The British losses were 57,470, of whom 19,240 were killed or died of wounds. The

that they should not go forward with their men into the enemy's trenches. These orders were strongly resented. Later the rule was that either the commanding officer or the second in command, and a certain number of other officers and men, were kept out so that battalions should not be crippled by losses; but the man in command was not confined in his actions.

German losses were much lighter, though still heavy. One division immediately south of the Somme, relieved next day, suffered a loss of 5,148; another, facing the British right and French left, relieved on July 4, a loss of 4,187.*

Haig must have been bitterly disappointed that night, but he was not yet aware of the terrible total of his losses. On discovering them and the vast expenditure of ammunition on July 1, he decided to confine the offensive for the present to his right, where he had success to exploit. He placed General Sir Hubert Gough in command of a new army, later numbered the Fifth, astride the Ancre.

How was one to cross the fire-beaten ground and get to close quarters with the enemy? Rawlinson showed imagination and daring in his solution. After fierce local fighting bringing only small gains, he launched an attack, four divisions abreast in darkness in the early hours of July 14. The objective was the Bazentin Ridge, on the forward slope of which ran the German second position. The ground was fairly open, but the risk of troops swerving off their true line of advance or of being caught by daylight without cover were scaring, so much so that the French left would not take part. Careful leadership brought it off. Some 6,000 yards of the second position were captured, without undue loss. The Germans hurried forward three divisions, all their available reserve at the moment, to plug the breach. Six days later the French Twentieth Corps captured a strong intermediate position between Maurepas and the Somme.

German reinforcements were now coming in fast, particularly artillery units and extra guns to replace those captured or destroyed. The number of corps and divisions engaged became too great for one army headquarters to control. Below's command was therefore limited to the north side of the Somme and Germany's best general utility man, General von Gallwitz—he had within the past twelve months held commands in Russia, in the Balkans, and at Verdun—took over south of the river. He was also given command of both armies as a group.

The success of July 14 had re-created hopes in many British minds. The carnage that bought so little, the deadening influence of a war of attrition, were not, it seemed, inevitable. If the fortunes of the next big thrust, farther north along the ridge by Pozières, were to be as fair as those of the last the chances of such a happy development would look good.

* Edmonds, *Short History*, p. 182. *Weltkrieg*, X, Anlage 3.

No, it could not be done. Rawlinson's effort on July 23 was a failure. The sole success, and a fine one, was on Gough's front, the capture of Pozières itself by the two Australian divisions of the First Anzac Corps. The corps, commanded by a British officer whom the Australians were happy to serve under, Lieutenant General Sir William Birdwood, had just arrived from Egypt. Elsewhere it was all death, taking, losing, and retaking the remnants of woods or pulverized villages. Haig had gone over to *la guerre d'usure*, the warfare of attrition. What is more, he had adopted it more completely than Joffre, who had been a disciple of attrition when Haig was hoping for a break-through and a wheel northeast. Foch, commanding the G.A.N., did not use the word attrition, but he at no time looked forward to a break-through. When the French front was cut down he was deeply disappointed and did not see the value of the offensive, except to ease pressure on Verdun.* Nearly all his interventions had for their purpose the broadening of attacks to the utmost. He often failed to get his way.

So it went on, Haig imperturbable and nursing the hope that by mid-September the German resistance would be so reduced that a powerful assault might lead to a break-through. August was the month of attrition at its height: continuous, heart-breaking milling at close quarters, minute gains at best, each ending with groups of crumpled corpses strewn about the objectives. The battle was becoming as hideous as Verdun, with the one exception that Verdun was fought in generally bad weather and the Somme in weather generally good, though Verdun ran into summer and the Somme into November. Divisions in which the tattered ranks of the infantry had been filled up again were appearing a second time. The German defense was becoming more and more one of tiny groups of men crouching in shell holes. It proved effective, though it seared the nerves and exhausted the bodies of those who carried it out.

In the skies the battle was going well for the French and British. The French Nieuport scout, made available to the British, and then the Spad, also of French design, won the mastery of the air. The German Fokker's great days were over. The original makeshift British anti-aircraft guns—cavalry 13-pounders mounted on car chassis—were being replaced by 18-pounders bored out to 3-inch, excellent guns of their time. Yet for upward of three months anti-aircraft artillery was needed only to a limited extent by the Allies.

* Falls, *Marshal Foch*, p. 10.

Their policy was offensive: the object of their fighters was to allow artillery-contact, reconnaissance, and photographic aircraft to live over the enemy's lines. The Germans were driven to fight almost entirely on the defensive and suffered in consequence great losses in artillery. But by October the Halberstadt and Albatros had redressed the balance and the German air force was going in for contact work in a big way. All in all, however, 1916 was a good year for the R.F.C. and the French air force. Their infantry owed much to them.

The losses incurred at Verdun and on the Somme, criticism of the conduct of both battles, a great Russian success, and the declaration of war by Rumania had weakened Falkenhayn's position. The Emperor, who liked and trusted him, defended him firmly. However, the pressure for a change grew when Hindenburg's staff, inspired by Hoffmann, induced their chief to take part in it—and aim at the succession. They goaded him into threatening his own resignation if his rival were not removed. This would have been a moral shock for all Germany, which regarded the old man as a hero-god, Wotan in human form. After a painful struggle William II gave way: Falkenhayn was dismissed on August 29. He was succeeded by Hindenburg, with Ludendorff as first quartermaster general.*

Falkenhayn did not pass into obscurity and will make further appearances, but this was the end of his power as virtual German commander in chief and the guiding spirit of the German-Austrian-Turkish-Bulgarian alliance. It may well be that new blood was called for. There may have been greater strategists in the First World War, though he was superlatively good at his best, but there is no more interesting or remarkable figure. No other of anything approaching his position held the doctrine that "a good peace" rather than decisive and overwhelming victory should be the goal. It is true that this doctrine was not based on the virtue or the profundity of the philosopher who argues that excessive force must always be an evil and the bane of him who uses it as well as of him who is subjected to it. Falkenhayn advocated unrestricted submarine war. Had he been 25 per cent stronger he would probably have fought for a military triumph rather than "a favorable draw." And yet perhaps he had an inkling of the subtler and more disputable theory too. He writes in his typically aloof, deadpan third person: "He felt no regret that the burden which had been laid on his shoulders two long years before,

* The title in the German army had no administrative significance. It stood for assistant chief of the general staff.

at the most critical moment of the war, should be taken off ... he believed that he was no longer in a position to do useful service to the Fatherland in his present office.

"But it was only with great anxiety that he contemplated the certainty that a change in that office, under the circumstances, must inevitably mean a change of system in the conduct of the war." *

He did not deign to add, nor did he need to: "It is you I mean, General Ludendorff."

When the new regime took over, Falkenhayn and O.H.L. had been installed for about a fortnight at Pless, which he had quitted at the beginning of the Battle of Verdun. His reason for the move was that the situation on the Eastern Front appeared worse than that on the Western—hardly a compliment to the Anglo-French effort. Hindenburg reached Cambrai on September 16. On the very day of his arrival he issued orders for the construction of a vast new line of defense which would greatly shorten the front and serve for a voluntary withdrawal in case of need—and this *was* a compliment to Joffre, Foch, and Haig. Meanwhile he had scored a political victory: unified command for Germany over the whole alliance. Conrad was infuriated. Hindenburg, he wrote, was "simply a popular cover-name for Ludendorff," and while Falkenhayn had sought only German ascendancy in the alliance, Ludendorff sought "the submission of our monarchy to German leadership"; he was said to have asserted that "Germany's victory spoils must be Austria." †

The Hindenburg-Ludendorff combination did not alter the situation on the Somme. In fact September, particularly the latter half, was for the British the best month of the year. On the fourth the French Tenth Army under General Micheler entered the battle on the French right, and the fighting front was extended to some twelve miles south of the Somme. On both banks and on the whole British front to the Ancre the Allies bashed their way forward in fierce and bloody fighting and weather which had turned wet. Then the British took a short breath before the great coordinated assault that Haig had prepared. He attacked on September 15 on a ten-mile front from Combles to the Ancre valley beyond Thiepval, with twelve divisions, including the fine Canadian Corps, engaged for the first time in this battle, and the equally fine New Zealand Division. They were faced by six and a half German divisions. This time Haig put in

* Falkenhayn, p. 291.
† Regele, p. 284.

—where they did not break down or even fail to start—thirty-six armored tracked vehicles, "males" mounting 6-pounder guns, "females" machine guns, which in messages about their progress from workshop to railhead had been described as "tanks." That day a page in the annals of warfare was turned.

The first entry recorded promise rather than performance; indeed the results of the fighting made it painfully clear that no breakthrough would come that autumn. Yet the moral effect—three-quarters of the value of the tank, at all events in that war—was striking. As new army troops of the Forty-first Division swarmed, cheering wildly, in the wake of the single tank which passed through the village of Flers, it did look as though the British had got a battle winner. Haig thought so, and five days later sent home a request for a thousand tanks. Yet the advance, though good, was not sensational; on that and the following days the depth extended to an average of a mile and a half and a good deal more in the center at Flers. Though the fifteenth was fine, the ground was sticky from past rains, and further wet days gradually bogged the offensive. The German view is that the defense was "virtually broken" on that day, but the latest batch of divisions formed on Falkenhayn's initiative and others more or less recovered from the effects of Verdun had provided reinforcements to solidify the front. Micheler's Tenth Army scored a success, but the capture of Berny and Vermandovillers, five and eight miles, respectively, south of the Somme, had little effect on the main battle.

Haig has been bitterly reproached for having used his tanks, divulged their existence, and exhausted their strategic surprise value at a moment when he had only a handful, forty-nine in all, available. All the parents and early leaders of the new force were agreed that it should be used in mass. Haig was wrong. Yet, while the criticism of experts like Major General J. F. C. Fuller as a staff officer in tanks and Captain Liddell Hart as a student of war is sound, most of the attacks on Haig have come from those without either knowledge or imagination. This was to be the great blow of the autumn offensive. Haig based high hopes on it, and the German evidence just mentioned shows that they were not ill founded. In any case, how long should he have waited? Six months? Well, just six months later he mustered forty-eight tanks for the Battle of Arras. It might not have been possible to keep the secret so long. Haig made a mistake, but it was, *at the time*, excusable. Some experts even hold that he was justified by the experience gained.

Haig may no longer have counted on a break-through, but he had no intention of relaxing the pressure. In fact, he hoped to extend the attack far north of the Ancre again. The next attack, on September 25, had results similar to the last. The chief British prizes, if such they can be called, were the villages of Morval and Les Boeufs. Thiepval, now with hardly a stone standing on another but with many deep cellars in the chalk intact, was stormed on the twenty-seventh. It had been held with wonderful tenacity. The British had come to regard it as a site accursed, and few so small can have spirted forth death to so many.

The weather had now completely broken and the battlefield became a wilderness of mud. The mud of the Somme is notorious, but rather less so than that of Ypres next year. The connoisseurs, survivors of both battles, are not all agreed that Ypres should prevail. Ypres the more holding, but the Somme the more slippery, is one verdict. Men were frequently so deeply bogged that it took an hour or more to dig them out. In these circumstances Haig's plan to capture the high ground south of the Ancre known as the Transloy Ridges and those on the north bank could be effected only by a succession of small attacks with limited objectives and at high cost.

At the instance of Joffre the attack was continued after even Haig would have closed it down for the winter. And then, as late as November 13, Gough won a battle which Ludendorff has called "a particularly heavy blow" to the Germans. The ground had dried a little; Gough had concentrated exceptional weight of artillery; and he had driven a mine shaft under a strong point in the German trenches. On the dark morning of November 13, in dank, clinging fog, seven divisions went forward to the assault astride the Ancre, two south of the river. The mine destroyed a considerable number of the defenders and its neighborhood. On the left two divisions failed, but the other five advanced three-quarters of a mile and upward, capturing the field fortress of Beaumont-Hamel. Twelve hundred prisoners were taken out of this place alone. The troops were astounded by what they found: underground refuges, some two stories deep, fitted with bunks, tables, and chairs and lit by electricity; stocks of canned meat, sardines, cigars, and thousands of bottles of beer. Next day Beaucourt, in the Ancre valley, was stormed and more ground was gained south of the river on the eighteenth. But a blizzard that day and rain the next brought the offensive to an end. The Battle of the Somme was over.

There have been disputes about the casualty figures, the critics of Haig and Joffre striving to make the most of them. Those given by the British official historian are: British, 419,654 and French, 194,451, a total for the western Allies of 614,105; German 650,000. The German total is an estimate, whereas the British and French figures are as precise as research could make them. British divisions engaged number fifty-five (including four Canadian, four Australian, and one New Zealand), French twenty, and German ninety-five. A considerable number of these had a second spell and a few came in three times.

The French fought finely on the Somme, but after the first short phase it was largely a British battle. From the British point of view this battle was fought in the wrong place—where there were no strategic objectives—and at the wrong time—before sufficient resources had been gathered. The lack of heavy artillery on and before July 1 was the main factor in the failures of that day. The British started with one heavy or medium gun or howitzer per fifty-seven yards, as against the French scale of one to twenty. On the British front the deep dugouts were nearly all intact after the bombardment, whereas on the French a considerable number had been destroyed. Defective ammunition—"dud" shells which did not explode—added to the trouble. It would be absurd to argue that there would have been a break-through, perhaps even that the battle would have been a satisfactory one but for these handicaps, but it would certainly have been more successful. This was an offensive on a front undisturbed for nearly two years, on which the defenders had worked like beavers, very different from the half-dug trenches at Verdun, a legacy of slackness and overconfidence.

The British tactics were in the main clumsy, lacking the skill shown by the Germans at Verdun—the evidence of study and German comparisons between British and French troops point to the same conclusions here. The British army was, as pointed out, largely an amateur force and its tactical instructors were too stiff and conventional. Yet for determination and devotion the army that fought on the Somme has never been surpassed. Many Germans, foremost among them Ludendorff, have borne witness to the weight of the blows delivered on the Somme and their effects upon the defending German forces. One consequence was to be the retreat to the Hindenburg Line, another the peace proposals of December, though here the summer victory of Brusilov in Russia played its part. In view of the later achievements of the German army the claims of Joffre and Haig to have worn it down have been derided, but they are supported by admissions from the German side. The loss in officers and underofficers was particularly damaging.

Only high hearts, splendid courage, and the enormous endurance of the flower of the nations of the British Empire engaged could have won the results attained. Only wonderful powers of resistance by the Germans could have limited them to what they were.

Chapter IV

JUTLAND: THE UNRESOLVED BATTLE

THE Briton looking back on the Battle of Jutland still asks, as the more intelligent Briton asked them: "Was this the spirit of Nelson?" It may well be—and the writer of these lines is of that view—that the commander in chief of the Grand Fleet at Jutland needed more of the spirit of Nelson. Yet the problem is not simple. Should the weaker fleet be almost certain to run for it on meeting greatly superior strength, then the stronger fleet must hasten and take risks if it is to bring on a decisive battle. The risks of 1916 were of a kind unknown to Nelson: torpedoes fired from destroyers and submarines, mine fields, loose mines thrown into the water in retreat. These were the means by which Admiral Scheer, the commander of the weaker fleet, hoped to bring the opposing forces to equality or near it. They were formidable, and much more so to the stronger fleet during a running engagement in pursuit than in a pitched battle. In this case the commander of the stronger fleet, Admiral Sir John Jellicoe, deeply conscious of its importance to his country, was beset by anxiety lest he should lose half of it to underwater weapons "before the guns opened fire at all." * Once we know what was in the minds of the Admirals events become more rational.

It has been shown that Scheer's intention was to entice the British into a trap. With this aim he carried out two sorties, one on March 6, the other on April 24 and 25. In the second he bombarded East Anglian towns, Lowestoft heavily. No contact between the main forces occurred, but they did not miss each other by much.

Scheer was eager to try again, but waited for the repair of the *Seydlitz*, which had limped home from the last sortie holed by a

* Churchill, *World Crisis*, 1916-1918, I, 115.

British mine. He believed, rightly, that while he was scheming to trap Jellicoe the British commander in chief had plans for trapping him. Scheer's bait was Hipper, dispatched with the battle cruisers, a light-cruiser squadron, and destroyers to show himself off the Norwegian coast, while Scheer followed with the main fleet, keeping out of sight of the Danish shore. Hipper was to reach his destination— so as to be reported from Norway—before nightfall on May 31. He did not get there. The Germans used their radio imprudently and the British Admiralty, in possession of their code, warned Jellicoe in good time. The British fleets from Scapa, Cromarty, and Rosyth put to sea between 9.30 and 10.15 P.M. on May 30 with the precision acquired by long experience, sailing on a course converging upon that of the enemy.

British superiority in strength had vastly increased since the Battle of the Dogger Bank. Of the opposing reconnaissance forces, Beatty's fleet included six battle cruisers and a battle squadron of four magnificent "superdreadnoughts" against Hipper's five battle cruisers. In all the British had twenty-eight dreadnoughts and nine battle cruisers against sixteen German dreadnoughts and five battle cruisers. In cruisers the disparity was still greater. Only in torpedo strength were the opposing fleets nearly equal.

Midnight, May 30/31, marks a memorable point in naval annals. On the day then beginning the only great naval battle of the war was to be fought. Nothing approaching the power of the opposing fleets had ever before been involved in a clash. Not only was the Battle of Jutland—*die Schlacht vor dem Skagerrak*, as the Germans call it— without a successor in that war; it has never had a successor in European waters, and, if any prophecy about warfare is safe, we may say that it never will. It was the last great naval battle in which air forces virtually did not count. Curiously enough, no submarines took part in the battle either, though they did take part in the operations, and the British might have suffered loss from those sent out by the Germans to waylay their fleets near their harbors. Omitting submarines, therefore, it is estimated that 250 vessels were present, sixty-four mounting guns from 11-inch to 15-inch and that twenty-five admirals flew their flags. The two fleets sailing through the misty night to their encounter constituted at that moment "the culminating manifestation of naval force in the history of the world." *

The advanced forces discovered one another about 2.20 P.M.

* Churchill, *World Crisis*, 1916-1918, I, 120.

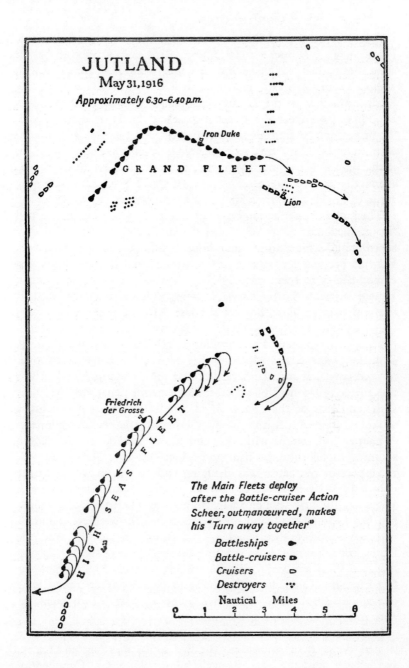

JUTLAND

May 31, 1916

Approximately 6.30-6.40 p.m.

Iron Duke

G R A N D   F L E E T

Lion

Friedrich der Grosse

H I G H   S E A S   F L E E T

*The Main Fleets deploy
after the Battle-cruiser Action
Scheer, outmanœuvred, makes
his "Turn away together"*

Battleships	
Battle-cruisers	
Cruisers	
Destroyers	

Nautical   Miles

0   1   2   3   4   5   6

through the contact of their scouts, in approximately latitude 55.48, longitude 5.24. Hipper turned to lure Beatty toward Scheer's battle-ships. Beatty had just changed course northward in accordance with Jellicoe's initial orders to close the battle fleet if he had not by now made contact with the enemy. He quickly turned south again to cut Hipper off from the swept channel at the Horn Reefs. Evan-Thomas, commanding his battle squadron, did not turn for another eight minutes. This tragedy has created unresolved controversy: was it that smoke hid signal flags from him, and did he actually, as the Admiralty asserted, receive a wireless signal ten minutes before he turned? The day was now fine, with a light breeze.

The battle-cruiser action began at 3.48 P.M., when Hipper opened fire at the great range of 16,500 yards. The foes converged at a sharp angle, which made range-finding difficult, but before 4 P.M. fire had become accurate. The Germans scored the more hits and caused Beatty to veer away slightly. Then the *Von der Tann* landed a close salvo on the *Indefatigable*, which blew up and capsized. It was a shattering blow, but not the last. After a brief easing of the fury owing to lengthening range, it narrowed again. Then the deadly process was repeated. The *Derfflinger*, celebrated for her gunnery, sank the *Queen Mary*. Much ink has been spilt inconclusively over these disasters. It may be hazarded that the *Indefatigable*'s loss was due to the ignition of powder bags in a turret penetrated by three shells and that of the *Queen Mary* to the closeness of successive salvos, a wonderful feature of the German battle cruisers' gunnery.

Hipper had fought with skill and nerve. Backed by the superb shooting of his ships, he had won a local victory. Now, however, the aspect of the battle was changing and he was in worse danger than before. Even before the last hit on the *Queen Mary* at about 4.23 P.M., the first 15-inch shells from Evan-Thomas's battle squad-ron had begun to fall, and they were extremely accurate. Hipper's van was seriously threatened by the British destroyers. And the British battle cruisers were shooting better than ever. Beatty, having lost two ships and with his own flaming beneath him, said to his flag captain: "Chatfield, there seems to be something wrong with our bloody ships today. Turn two points to port." Two points to port was two points nearer the enemy.

Gallant, and successful, as he had shown himself, Hipper now turned away to the southeast. His flag signal was hoisted at 4.27, and eleven minutes later Beatty's admirable scout, Commodore

Goodenough in the *Southampton*, reported that the German main body was approaching. Beatty swung northwest, then north, to meet Jellicoe. Soon the firing died down for want of targets. The Grand Fleet was approaching in six columns with Rear Admiral Hood's battle-cruiser squadron (three battle cruisers and two light cruisers) to the east. At 5 P.M. Hipper also turned north again. Scheer was already in action, and as Evan-Thomas turned to follow Beatty he came under terrific fire both from the German battle cruisers and the leading battleships. His squadron received many hits but was saved by the 13-inch armor and good maneuvering. In this phase of confused fighting the *Lutzow*, Hipper's flagship, received crippling wounds. Toward the end of the melee, as the Grand Fleet closed, the armored cruiser *Defence* was sunk and her sister ship the *Warrior* so badly damaged that she sank next day.

Now was the time for Jellicoe to intervene and win the battle. At 6.15 P.M., having waited to get a "fix" on the High Seas Fleet, he hurriedly deployed his columns into line ahead. But he deployed to port, that is, away from the enemy, a maneuver which his critics have never forgiven. It was the safer course against torpedo attack, but it sacrificed the chance of catching Scheer by surprise. It also risked collisions with Beatty's ships which, in order to take their station in the van, had to pass across the battleships as they deployed. Almost miraculously good seamanship avoided disaster. But disaster of another kind was to come. A salvo from the *Derfflinger*—again the *Derfflinger*!—sank the *Invincible*, the battle cruiser in which Sturdee's flag had been carried in the Battle of the Falklands eighteen months earlier and which now carried Hood's. She took down with her the admiral and virtually all hands.

Meanwhile Scheer, advancing in a northeasterly direction, had sighted Hood's squadron and mistaken it for Jellicoe's leading battleships, which were actually some four sea miles to the northwest. Scheer therefore believed that he was headed off and would be enveloped if he maintained his present course. This was to a certain extent true; Scheer's situation was not as bad as he supposed, because, whereas he believed for the moment that he saw battleships ahead, they were really battle cruisers; but his plight was serious enough. He decided to turn away from the enemy.

The normal method by which ships sailing in line ahead turned on to another course was in succession, each turning as nearly as possible at the same point, as though passing round a buoy. The danger of this maneuver when in contact with the enemy was that each ship as it reached the turning point would come under terrific fire from a number of hostile ships. The alternative was a "turn away together," all ships turning simultaneously in their tracks so that the original van became the rear on the new course. It demanded superlative seamanship, and even with that might lead to confusion and accidents. Scheer, however, foreseeing that his outnumbered and outgunned fleet might run into a hornets' nest from which only drastic action could save it, had kept this maneuver constantly in mind, and practiced it. Moreover, in order to be ready to use it as safely as possible, he had established a distance greater than normal between his battleships. At 6.35 P.M. he gave the order for the "turn away together" to starboard.

The High Seas Fleet received a number of hits but speedily disappeared from Jellicoe's view in the gathering evening mist. He did not follow: in fact he turned away. If it was fear of torpedo attack, the German destroyers showed little initiative and only four torpedoes were fired—at Beatty, not Jellicoe's battleships. As for mines, he could have closed in some five miles without entering the German wake, and mines could be nowhere else. Luck might have brought a submarine or two to the area, but a submarine force could attack the Grand Fleet only by lying in wait for it. Here there was no question of that because Beatty had lured the Germans into this part of the North Sea. On the German side the *Lutzow* was now low in the water and useless. Hipper took to a destroyer and handed over command to Captain Hartog of the *Derfflinger* until such time as he could rehoist his flag. He did so in the Moltke, but not till after dark. The *Lutzow* had finally to be sunk.

Now came an extraordinary development in an amazing battle. Scheer suddenly reappeared with his battleships, steering nearly east. He afterward declared that he had turned to engage the British again, but it is not unchivalrous to suggest that he may have hoped to pass across their rear and end the risk of being cut off from home. What actually happened was that he ran straight into Jellicoe, steaming south with divisions in echelon.

Bedlam broke loose. As the German ships emerged one by one from the mist, heavy fire was opened upon them. The battleship *St. Vincent* fired twenty salvos. This is regarded as the main action of the battle. It was not so in vital damage inflicted. No capital ship was sunk in that brief storm of fire. Still, Scheer could not face it.

Disaster of some kind must follow if he held on. Once more the battle cruisers were bearing the brunt, but the leading battleships were being hit too. At 7.17 P.M. Scheer for the second time made a simultaneous turn away, leaving the unfortunate battle cruisers under Hartog to fight a rear-guard action. They were hammered with fire. Both the *Derfflinger* and the *Seydlitz* burst into flames. The *Von der Tann* was hit, but she was in the line only to make the enemy spread his fire, for she could not herself fire a gun.

Scheer was saved from the terrible fate overhanging him. Once again, true to theory and to form, at sight of the German smoke screen and the advancing destroyer flotilla, Jellicoe turned away. The range widened and for the second time the High Seas Fleet disappeared from Jellicoe's view.

But not from Beatty's in the *Lion*. He could see it still. And at 7.45 he sent a signal which deserves immortality: "Submit that the van of the battleships follows me. We can then cut off the enemy's fleet." No subordinate could have given his superior franker—or better—advice. Perhaps one might add, more reproachful. A quarter of an hour later Jellicoe issued an order to his Second Battle Squadron in the sense of Beatty's signal. Its commander neither increased speed nor, though he did not know where the *Lion* was, asked for her position. Contact was not regained.

Jellicoe was still between Scheer and the German harbors, but in his own view his power was largely nullified by darkness. He sailed quietly south by east in night cruising order, three columns a mile apart. Again the Admiralty handed him a fine chance. It had decoded Scheer's order and now signaled Jellicoe that Scheer was making for the Horn Reefs channel. Jellicoe took no action on the report and sailed on. At almost the moment he read it, 11.30 P.M., Scheer crashed into the light forces astern of the Grand Fleet, turned briefly away, then came at them again. A chaotic, tumultuous affray followed, with several collisions—one between hostile ships— and sinkings. These included the cruiser *Black Prince*, which strayed amidst the German fleet and was put down in four minutes. The German pre-dreadnought battleship *Pommern* was cut in two. Scheer got through at last, but Jellicoe could still have caught him, and pursuit of the *Seydlitz*, the *Derfflinger*, and the battleship *Markgraf* (with one engine killed)—these at least would have been, in a simile that would have come home to Beatty, like hunted three-legged foxes. Jellicoe decided that, owing to the difficulty of collecting his destroyers, it was "undesirable for the battle fleet to close the Horn Reef," though he had intended to do so in daylight. He turned northward at 2.30 A.M. on June 1.

Nothing that followed is of importance. The battle was over; the series of chances which Jellicoe had won or which had been put into his hands had been lost one after another. It now remained only to go home. The respective losses were: British—three battle cruisers, three cruisers, eight destroyers; German—one battleship, one battle cruiser, four light cruisers, five destroyers. The serious part of the British loss was due to structural defects in the battle cruisers. British casualties numbered 6,784; German 3,039. It should be noted that the *Pommern* was an old battleship and that Jellicoe had not brought out a single pre-dreadnought.

The battle had been fought with the purest heroism and most splendid self-sacrifice on both sides, though on both a few destroyer commanders had failed in initiative. ¡The Royal Marines still keep bright the name of Major F. J. W. Harvey, V.C. The *Lion*'s midship turret, which he commanded, was hit by a shell which killed all within but himself and his sergeant, wrecked the turret, and started a fire. Harvey lost both his legs. Twenty minutes later the cartridge in the breech of an up-cocked gun slid out into the flames and ignited other charges. The flash passed down the trunk and killed all the handling parties below. But the magazine doors were shut. The dying Harvey had found strength to order through the speaking tube: "Close magazine doors and flood magazines." Beatty did not know then how closely destruction had breathed upon his flagship. This is but one case of many. The bravery of Jutland was collective.

Of the two commanders in chief, Jellicoe proved himself the more skillful and retained control the more thoroughly; Scheer, clumsy by comparison, except in his two battle turns, was the more adventurous and determined. The Briton made little positive use of his overwhelmingly greater strength. He fought to make a German victory impossible rather than to make a British victory certain, and though both sides claimed the victory there was no real victor. The battleships of the main British fleet took only a secondary part in the fighting. The casualties in the British battleships numbered 197, but of these 190 were suffered by Evan-Thomas's four ships in the squadron under Beatty's orders and seven in those of the main fleet. Beatty showed himself a gallant and determined leader, undaunted by shocking losses. The scale of this narrative has not afforded room to reveal the ability of Evan-Thomas. Yet the man of the battle was Hipper, fine in seamanship, dexterous in maneuver, plucky, persistent, and the handler of an instrument owing its proficiency to his fostering care. His chief of staff was a certain Captain Raeder.

The Battle of Jutland made no change in the strategic situation. British predominance remained as great as ever. A smashing British victory would have given Britain more freedom of action. Several expert commentators have assumed that it would have permitted a British fleet to penetrate the Baltic.* This, like the arguments about the Gallipoli campaign, is speculation, but the consequences of such a penetration would have been immensely favorable. The moral effects on both sides hardly need discussion.

Scheer came out again on the night of August 18 to carry out a scheme based on a raid on Sunderland long in his mind: Hipper was sent ahead with three battleships and his two effective battle cruisers to carry out the bombardment and serve as a bait, Scheer following in support.† No fewer than twenty-four submarines entered the North Sea in advance and eight airships came out as scouts. Once again Scheer gave himself away by his radio messages and so early that the British could leave their harbors simultaneously. The German submarines scored a fine success by sinking two British light cruisers, and though the battleship *Westfalen* was torpedoed by a British submarine she managed to get back to her base. Otherwise the expedition was turned into a fiasco by a false report from an airship which deceived Scheer, so that he retreated without making a contact. Jellicoe, convinced that he was being led into a submarine ambush, returned home.

He had always expected this to happen; now he could say that he was right. The effect was to make him more cautious than ever. He decided that "the fleet ought not to operate" south of latitude 55.30 N. or east of longitude 4 E." ‡ The latitude was approximately that of Alnwick, in Northumberland; the longitude well west of the waters in which the Battle of Jutland had been fought. Scheer's ideas were moving on similar lines and his theories were confirmed

* Frost, p. 528.

† The *Seydlitz* was ready for sea in mid-September; the *Derfflinger* in mid-October. How much more profitable it is to send a cripple to the bottom than to maim her, however terribly!

‡ Newbolt, *Naval Operations*, IX, 48.

218 THE GREAT WAR

when two of his battleships were hit by a British submarine off the
Horn Reefs in November. Long before this he had begun to abandon
hope of being able to afford the risk of meeting the Grand Fleet.
He turned his energies to persuading the Emperor and Bethmann-
Hollweg to permit an unrestricted submarine campaign. With both
admirals in this frame of mind fleet battles became unlikely.

Even while precluded from using "sink-at-sight" methods, the
German U-boats, now numbering seventy-four, had a profitable
year. In the first two months the effects of the Emperor's action
in calling off the local unrestricted form of war in September, 1915,
were still felt.* In March, 1916, however, British losses rose to
twenty-six ships of 99,000 tons and in April to forty-three ships (six
sunk by mines) of 140,000 tons, the worst month since August, 1915.
Then came a drop: 64,000 tons in May, 37,000 in June, 82,000 in
July, and 43,000 in August. However, those of Britain's allies leapt
up to 83,000 in August. The concentration on U-boat warfare which
followed the Battle of Jutland was showing. The figures for September were: Britain 105,000, Allies 45,000, neutrals 76,000 (Norwegian
43,000). The one encouraging feature of these depressing statistics
was success in resistance, which demanded a high spirit in masters
and crews. Out of ninety ships carrying guns which were attacked
during September, nineteen were sunk; without means and will to
resist a high proportion of the remaining seventy-one would assuredly have shared their fate. But worse still was to come in
October, when Britain lost 176,000 tons (highest ever), her allies
74,000, and neutrals 102,000 (highest ever). And 176,000 precisely
was the average for the last two months of the year.† It seemed a
terrible total at the time. How small it was to appear by comparison
with that of the early months of 1917!

At the end of November Jellicoe hauled down his flag in the
Iron Duke, to become First Sea Lord. His appointment to the Admiralty was due largely to the growth of the U-boat menace,
especially in the western approaches and the Mediterranean. He
was expected to bring administrative abilities to the task such as
no other could equal. His successor in command of the Grand Fleet
was Admiral Sir David Beatty.

The loss of one British ship has been left unrecorded. On June 5

* See p. 153.
† Fayle, II, 250, 268, 271, 331, 302, 358.

the cruiser *Hampshire*, which had served at Jutland, took aboard Field Marshal Lord Kitchener, bound for Russia on a mission at the invitation of the Emperor. Owing to a gale she sailed west of the Orkneys and her escorting destroyers had to turn back. That evening she struck a mine, one of those laid by German submarines on the night of May 28, before the Jutland sortie. She sank quickly with almost all hands, including the Secretary of State. Kitchener had lost power and—in the inner circle only—prestige. His office, which he had magnified immensely, had been reduced even below statutory limits. The politicians had ceased to tremble in his presence, and, with the exception of Mr. Asquith, the Prime Minister, distrusted him. The burden of the war lay heavy on him and affected his self-confidence. Kitchener undoubtedly made many mistakes and caused disappointment by his lack of clarity in explaining his ideas. And yet there is a good cause for regarding him as the greatest Englishman of the war. What he had accomplished in making Britain an armed community was immense, and in the realm of the spirit his contribution to his country was no less splendid. Churchill, who was often opposed to him, hoped that, when future generations surveyed his achievements as strategist, administrator, and leader, they would also remember "the comfort his character and personality gave to his countrymen in their hours of hardest trial." * He was an inspiration to the people never fully replaced.

* Churchill, *World Crisis 1916-1918*, I, 35.

Chapter V

BRUSILOV'S IMMORTAL DAYS

THE Emperor Nicholas II was a weak man. As commander in chief of the Russian armies he could not even fulfill the easiest task of an absolute monarch in war, that of arousing enthusiasm when he reviewed his troops. They had in them a deep store of enthusiasm, but he did not know how to tap it. Yet his loyalty as an ally was a quality which should stand to his credit when his melancholy reign and tragic end are reviewed. He had every intention of fulfilling his pledge to Joffre by setting on foot a big offensive in June, 1916. Earlier than that his chief of the general staff, Alexiev, did not believe it possible to strike with good prospects of success. The reorganization after the disasters of 1915 went a long way during the winter and spring. The ranks were filled; the troops were well fed, well clothed, and generally in good heart; there were rifles and cartridges for all, even if of several types; machine guns were more numerous; field artillery ammunition was adequate. The worst remaining shortages were in heavy artillery, though here too some improvement appeared, and in aircraft.

In February the north-south front established after the defeats and retreats of the previous year was held by three vast groups of armies: Kuropatkin—the defeated commander in the Japanese war —from the Gulf of Riga to Dunaburg; Evert thence to south of the Pripet marshes; Ivanov thence to the Rumanian frontier. Immediately after the opening of the German offensive Joffre appealed to the Emperor to launch a diversionary attack. It was a situation in which a commander like Haig, thinking of his own plans and determined not to sacrifice his troops by sending them forward unready, might have refused. The Emperor not only accepted but opened the offensive as early as March 18.

It was a big thing too, though to have thrown in the same force on a narrower front would probably have been preferable. The inner flanks of Kuropatkin's and Evert's groups were to attack on a front of ninety miles. The whole of this front was not to be assailed simultaneously, but in sections, with the main weight on either side of Lake Naroch, which has given its name to the battle. Numerically, the Russian superiority was great, about five to two, but as on the Somme, though on a simpler pattern, the Germans had strongly fortified their front. The ground had of course been frozen to the consistency of rock, but on March 18, though the ice on the lake and the rivers remained unbroken, up to a foot of water overlay it. This was not good weather for an offensive.

The tragic story can be shortly told. The artillery preparation troubled the defense far less than when most ineffective on the Somme. The troops of the armies of Scholz and Hutier were fully on the alert. One after another of the disjointed Russian attacks rushed into their fire and broke down completely with heavy slaughter. What penetration was made could be measured in hundreds of yards, and it was sooner or later recovered. German losses were about 20,000; Russian 110,000 including 10,000 prisoners. Like previous winter battles in Russia, this was marked by exceptional suffering. There must be still a few veterans with limbs maimed by frostbite in this campaign.

The next cry for aid came to the Tsar from Italy in May. The Italians were being driven back by the Austrians and could claim that among their foes were divisions transferred from Russia. The fate of Verdun still hung on a thread. The Russian command had previously decided that the main offensive of the year should be launched in the center, but now, since Evert was not ready, it demanded of the new commander of the southwest front, Brusilov, whether he could help. He said yes. He was that kind of man, and Nicholas II had done few better services to the Russian army than in appointing him to succeed the hesitant Ivanov. Brusilov had already demanded that he should take part in the offensive and had been given a free hand, but told to expect no reinforcements. Having watched the mounting of earlier offensives, he realized that the laborious preparations gave them away. He therefore ordered his army commanders to get to work at some twenty points and disposed his reserves so that they afforded no clue to his intentions. He realized that this dispersion would weaken his blows, but he was ready to pay that price for surprise. His main attacks were to be made in two sectors, on his right opposite Lutsk and on his left in the valleys of the Dniester and the Prut. One attraction of the latter was that success would impress Rumania, still neutral, but apparently edging toward the cause of the Entente.* When on May 24 the call came to attack alone he was nearly ready to do so on these lines. His four armies, from south to north Ninth, Seventh, Eleventh, and Eighth, were faced by five: the Austrian Seventh and the Austro-German (German-commanded) South Army; the Austrian Second and First in Böhm-Ermolli's army group; the Austrian Fourth and two independent corps in Linsingen's army group, Linsingen being a German officer but coming under the Austrian supreme command. On paper the Russians had only a slight superiority, about forty against thirty-eight divisions, but the Russian were much the bigger.†

The bombardment opened on June 4. That day infantry attacks penetrated to any depth at two points only, but on the morrow the full weight of the offensive changed the situation drastically. Time after time, when the enemy made a slight penetration such as was inevitable here and there, the Austrian troops to either flank, though hardly attacked or not attacked at all, made off rearward. The eager and impetuous Russians seized their chances. They tore a yawning breach in the Austrian Fourth Army. Some Austrian divisions disappeared. Enormous losses, coupled with "the moral collapse of the troops" made any further stand impossible.‡ By June 6 the Fourth Army was in disorderly retreat. In the south much the same thing happened to the Seventh Army. The multinational amalgam was splitting up. The Archduke Joseph's good regiments in the Fourth Army had melted in the furnace and his numerous Ruthenian regiments had stopped fighting. The South Army and the Austrian Second had hardly been attacked.

* Brusilov, pp. 235-241.

† Three-quarters of the Russian divisions had sixteen battalions; the rest twelve. The Austrian had twelve; nearly all the German only nine. To form new divisions the Germans had withdrawn one regiment (three battalions) from existing divisions, and this process was nearly complete. In the French army it was only beginning. The British did not reduce their twelve-battalion divisions to nine battalions until early 1918. In comparing strengths by counting divisions this factor must be taken into account.

‡ *Weltkrieg*, X. 452.

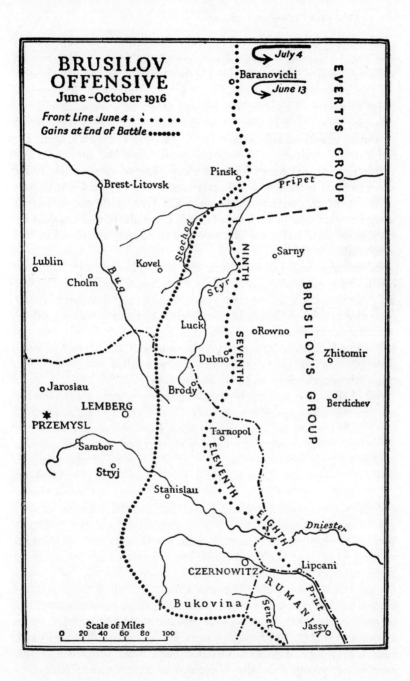

BRUSILOV OFFENSIVE
June–October 1916

Front Line June 4 · · · · · ·
Gains at End of Battle · · · · · ·

July 4

June 13

EVERT'S GROUP

Baranovichi

Pinsk

Pripet

Brest-Litovsk

Stochod

Sarny

Lublin

Kovel

Styr

Cholm

Bug

NINTH

Luck

Rowno

Zhitomir

Dubno

SEVENTH

Jaroslau

Brody

BRUSILOV'S GROUP

LEMBERG

Berdichev

PRZEMYSL

Tarnopol

Sambor

ELEVENTH

Stryj

Stanislau

EIGHTH

Dniester

Lipcani

CZERNOWITZ

Prut

RUMANIA

Bukovina

Sereth

Jassy

Scale of Miles

0   20   40   60   80   100

By June 9 Brusilov had taken over 70,000 prisoners. Yet now, in the Russian Empire's greatest victory of the war, old weaknesses were reappearing. First, Brusilov learned that a promised offensive on the Western Front commanded by Evert must be postponed. Next he was told by Alexiev that the attack as planned could not take place and that a smaller action at Baranovichi, eighty miles north of Pinsk, would be substituted for it. He was deeply enraged. He felt that he was being left virtually on his own and that the value of his victory was being frittered away. The truth was that Evert was scared of launching a full-scale attack on a purely German part of the front, thoroughly on the alert. On June 13 he put in a small attack at Baranovichi with two Guards divisions. It was smashed by the German fire and these fine troops were largely sacrificed to bad leadership.

Falkenhayn and Conrad from the rear, Hindenburg from the north, were providing such aid as they could, but so far it was only scraps. Lack of reserves, ammunition, and transport rather than any serious stiffening in the defense brought Brusilov's offensive practically to a stop by mid-June. He was determined that the halt should only be temporary. His southern thrust had already penetrated nearly thirty miles, the northern fifty, and twenty-five miles beyond the Styr at Lutsk to the Stokhod.

While Brusilov was taking breath Linsingen struck back at the northern Russian salient on June 16. The Germans had compelled Conrad to remove the Archduke Joseph from the command of the Austrian Fourth Army and he had been replaced by the Hungarian General Terszyanski; but the main motive power of the counteroffensive was in the assault group of General von der Marwitz, which had three good and well-rested German divisions. Some ground was recovered south of Kovel, but the result was in general a sad disappointment. The maximum gain after four days' fighting was up to eight or nine miles, which would have looked splendid at Verdun or later on the Somme, but did not count for much in these vast spaces in which troops were always thin on the ground by comparison with the Western Front. In other ways it confirmed the lessons of Verdun, which were to be further confirmed on the Somme, that counterstrokes against an enemy engaged in an all-out and successful offensive can rarely be expected to win more than a very limited success. Often enough those projected cannot even be set going. Falkenhayn decided to send German reinforce-

ments all the way to Pflanzer-Baltin's front on the extreme right
to provide the stiffening for a big counteroffensive, but one after
another they had to be diverted on the way to other even more
pressing tasks.

On the other hand, the next Russian effort, a renewed offensive
north of Baranovichi in greater strength than the last proved a
fiasco. Advancing on July 3, as usual in dense masses, the Russians
were mowed down by the fire of the German and Austrian defenders of Prince Leopold of Bavaria's group of armies.* Against
the German corps involved they failed completely; in the Austrian
corps also attacked they made a hardly appreciable dent. It was a
grievous reverse and left Brusilov still on his own.

At least Alexiev was sending him as reinforcements troops whom
Evert and Kuropatkin were too frightened to use against the Germans and greater numbers than Germany and Austria had drawn
from the Western Front, Italy, and the Balkans. Brusilov pressed on
again. After strokes here and there with mixed fortunes, mostly in
his favor, he renewed the offensive on the whole front on July 28.
He now won further successes which would have crowned with
laurels the heads of many leaders but did not seem great in the
light of what he had already done. Again shortage of ammunition—
or means to get it to his batteries—checked him. Yet with unconquerable spirit and unbending will he drove his armies forward yet
again on August 7. This time, despite the arrival in the south of
more German divisions, he did well, pressing up the slopes of the
Carpathians and overrunning the whole of the Bukovina. By now,
however, the enemy's reinforcements were beginning to give some
cohesion to the front and the Russian commander could no longer
maintain the momentum of his attack. North of the Pripet nothing
had been done to help him and, except for the two attacks at
Baranovichi, nothing had been attempted. He made one last effort in
September in support of Rumania, now in the war, but fatigue, losses,
and the strain on his communications had sapped his offensive
power and he could accomplish little more. In October the Brusilov
offensive came to a dead stop. Brusilov's armies had captured upward of 400,000 prisoners and upward of 500 guns.

At an early stage in the fighting the Germans had set about the
task of securing a single command—their own of course—over the

* An Austrian corps had been placed in this group as some compensation for
the German troops sent to the Austrian front south of the Pripet.

whole Eastern Front. Falkenhayn afterward thought that the agitation was part of a plot to make Hindenburg chief of the general staff in his place, which as we have seen was done. At all events the struggle was long and hot. Austria's pride was offended, and Conrad leaped forward to defend it. The two emperors were dragged in. The Germans and Austrians belabored each other in speech and writing as heartily as the Russians belabored them physically. Finally Francis Joseph, fearing that his dominions might break apart, perhaps even that Hungary might seek a separate peace, yielded to the German arguments. At last agreement was reached in a German victory, though not quite complete because it failed to secure the whole front.

On July 30 Hindenburg's command was extended southward 225 miles beyond the Pripet to just south of Tarnopol. As a sop to the Austrians the rest of the front southward to the Rumanian frontier was entrusted to a group of armies under the independent command of the Archduke Carl, the heir to the throne. It was hoped that loyalty to the house of Hapsburg would be strengthened thereby and influence the army favorably. The Archduke, however, had to take as staff officer, preceptor, and Hindenburg's agent, General von Seeckt. Thus Hindenburg acquired practical control throughout. He held it for a fortnight only before succeeding Falkenhayn as chief of the general staff and taking Ludendorff with him to the Western Front. His place on the Eastern was taken by Prince Leopold of Bavaria as supreme commander east (*Oberbefehlshaber Ost*), with Max Hoffmann as chief of staff—and again as the man who counted. As Hoffmann said of the chief who treated him with extraordinary kindness and trust, Prince Leopold was "certainly much cleverer than ———" (a good guess is that he wrote "Hindenburg" and that a prudent editor struck out the name) but he was "scarcely the star performer" and not to be considered "responsible." *

Brusilov is the only commander of the First World War after whom a great victory has been named. It is universally known to this day as "the Brusilov offensive." The title is well deserved. Hardly another instance can be found where one man by greatness of soul and determination made a brilliant victory so largely his own. He always believed that if he had been supported by the two other commanders of army groups, Evert and Kuropatkin, a decisive vic-

* Hoffmann, *War Diaries*, I, 155, 191.

tory—decisive for the fate of the whole war—would have been gained. We cannot be sure. North of the Pripet the Russians had to reckon not only with the defensive power of German troops and their great strength in artillery, but with their superior technical means for the purpose of fortification. However hard the Austrians had worked—and they had done a lot of digging—they could not have produced defenses equal to those of the Germans. Yet it can hardly be denied that to make no serious attempt to back Brusilov's victory was folly as well as failure of courage on the part of the Russian command.

The campaign shook both Russians and Austrians. It probably contributed to the fate of the Russian army in the following year. Yet for the Austro-Hungarian Empire it was a dreadful calamity. The prestige of the imperial forces had sunk. Conrad's apologists may argue, as he did, that infiltration by the Germans was harmful in some respects and helped to lower Austrian self-confidence and loyalty, but there was no alternative now. Signs of deadly decay, flaws fatal to any army, had appeared. In late July an Austrian division in the First Army lost 12,000 men, most prisoners of war— all its infantry strength and more—but only two guns.* What did this mean? It meant that the divisional artillery had galloped away and left the infantry in the lurch. "Batteries in wild flight" and similar phrases are used in German and even Austrian accounts. Now in all sound armies the artillery tradition is one of stoutness of heart and self-sacrifice in defeat and retreat. Time and time again breaking fronts have been re-formed by such courage on the part of the artillery; in many a battle artillery officers have rallied discouraged infantrymen drifting back through the gun lines and led them forward again. Deeds of this kind are found in the long and fine record of the Austrian artillery. Where this spirit ceases to exist no army can face a hostile offensive with the hope of victory.

The entry of Rumania into the war resembled that of Italy and Bulgaria in being the result of a deal in land which only victory could confirm. Rumania had refused to join the Central Powers in 1914 on the plea that her treaty with Austria did not apply to the state of affairs. She thought the matter over for two years, and then came in on the side of the Entente. She missed a golden

* *Weltkrieg*, X, 541.

opportunity by haggling. Had she made up her mind two months sooner, the case of the Central Powers would indeed have been desperate; in fact, it would seem that there must have been a collapse somewhere, probably in southeast Europe, just possibly on the Somme. As it was, Rumania waited till the fighting on the Russian front was nearing its end. On August 17 she concluded a treaty with the United Kingdom and France. On the twenty-seventh she declared war on Germany and Austria.

Her chief prize was to be Transylvania, the fine country west of the Carpathians, but she was also promised the Banat farther south and the southern Dobruja, the last-named being Bulgarian territory. Her army numbered some 500,000 men, in twenty-three divisions, of which thirteen were either reserve or improvised formations. It was rather poorly officered—too many of a dandified, idle, patent-leather-booted type still to be found in several armies—only fairly well armed, but with its ranks full of strong peasant soldiers, good enough material if it had been better handled. Alexiev had given the command sound advice: to stand fast in the passes of the Transylvanian Alps, which were easily defensible, and take the offensive through the Dobruja, between the Danube and the Black Sea coast. But the Rumanian government had its eyes fixed on Transylvania and was determined to secure that territory first. Two armies were, therefore, concentrated along the Transylvanian Alps, one at right angles to them along the southern Carpathians, where it was in loose touch with Brusilov's Russians, and only one in the south.

It was there that the enemy got in his first blow. A motley force —German, Bulgarian (the largest), and Turkish, had been assembled under Mackensen on the Bulgarian frontier between the sea and the Danube and on the south bank on the great river. On September 2 the right wing invaded the Dobruja and drove back the Rumanians. Despite considerable Russian reinforcements it continued to progress northward all through the month. The disillusioned Rumanians, who must have wished that they had listened to Russian advice, had to hurry forces south. Meanwhile in the north they had debouched through the mountain passes into the promised land of Transylvania against slight resistance from the mostly second-grade Austrian troops on the spot. Hurrahs went up from the Entente countries and their sympathizers.

By the early days of September four German divisions were moving east through Hungary by train. The Rumanian advance after coming through the passes became so slow that two armies, the German Ninth (three German and two Austrian divisions) and Austrian First (one German and four Austrian divisions) could be formed and concentrated less than forty miles from the crests of the Carpathians and Transylvanian Alps. The commander of the Ninth Army was the discarded chief of the general staff, Erich von Falkenhayn. He was naturally very much on his mettle in his new role and, it proved, in dazzling form. He wasted no time. He fell upon the Rumanians, first at Hermannstadt on September 30, then at Kronstadt,* on October 8, defeated them and drove them back. They succeeded, however, in avoiding his attempts to cut them off from the passes and once in the mountains fortified themselves and stood firm. Then Falkenhayn probed one pass after another and by marching and countermarching bewildered the defense. Finally he decided to stake all on forcing the Vulkan Pass. Now replacing clever and delicate maneuver by brute force, he crashed through by November 26. Another victory, this time in the southern foothills at Targu-Jiu, opened the way into the Rumanian plain. The defense in the other passes having been turned, the Rumanian command decided to abandon them. Simultaneously Mackensen forced a passage of the Danube above Sistova. The two invaders raced each other for Bucharest. Falkenhayn, now reinforced by four more German divisions, won this contest. He entered the Rumanian capital on December 5, and another column took the valuable oil fields of Ploesti next day.

Long before this the weather had broken. Rain poured down in sheets, causing rivers and streams to overflow and create morasses, turning the wretched roads to quagmires. The Rumanians had destroyed nearly every bridge. Falkenhayn continued to struggle northeastward, his troops on short rations and without winter clothing. Though Ludendorff provided none of that, Falkenhayn records bitterly, he sent a flood of telegrams, "as superfluous as they were distasteful." In the last days of the year the Rumanians halted and stood fast on the lower Sereth. By this time the Russians had taken over the northern frontier of the Dobruja and much of the front running thence to the Carpathians. The forces of the Central Powers had shot their bolt and could do no more. Quiet fell upon the front.

* The present-day Rumanian names are Sibiu for Hermannstadt and Brasov for Kronstadt.

The Rumanians had lost 310,000 men, of whom nearly half were prisoners of war.

Instead of acquiring Transylvania, for which she had entered the war, Rumania had lost all her existing territory except the northern province of Moldavia. A temporary capital was established at Jassy. This corner of the kingdom was maintained largely on Russian bounty. One of Brusilov's best subordinates, Saharhov, commanded the Russian forces directly and the Rumanian through their own general staff. The combined greed and imprudence—not an unusual combination—of the Rumanian government had brought untold miseries upon the people, but its quiet determination to fight on in what national territory remained to it was not without dignity.

The year had been an unhappy one for Germany and disastrous for her Austrian junior partner. They had both in some measure themselves to blame, since Conrad and Falkenhayn had clearly underestimated the power of recuperation of the Russian army. They might, however, have taken some comfort from the fact that the year had ended better than had semed possible in the east and without a British break-through on the Somme. This result was in part due to the errors and clumsiness of their enemies. It was still more largely due to the excellent and well-run railways of Germany which enabled forces to be swung between the Eastern and Western Fronts with extraordinary speed and to the engineering skill and clever handling of transport which brought them quickly from railheads to firing line. Most of all it was due to the coolness, steadiness, and dour resistance of the German troops, in Russia often of the older classes, *Landwehr* and even *Landsturm*. German historians talk of Austrian panics and are coy about their own. Panics occurred in the German ranks in Russia. But the general standard of courage, fortitude, and self-confidence was high. The commanders who had such troops to rely on in days of adversity were fortunate. It was almost impossible to ask or expect of them more than they were ready to give and capable of giving.

Chapter VI

THE LONG CAMPAIGNING SEASON IN ITALY

T HE Italians, like the Russians, launched an early offensive in the year 1916, but whereas the latter was an emergency and diversionary operation to relieve pressure on Verdun, Cadorna's effort in Italy was carried out in accordance with the agreement at Chantilly. Joffre hoped for no more than a minor operation early in the year, but this proved a slight effort indeed. The Austrians seem to have sized it up in advance and to have felt no anxiety about it. As already mentioned, Conrad had begged Falkenhayn to co-operate with him in inflicting a decisive defeat upon Italy; Falkenhayn had refused, in the main because he was pinched for resources with which to undertake his offensive against Verdun. He had also rejected Conrad's proposal that German troops should relieve nine Austrian divisions in Russia so that the latter could be sent to the Tirol to strengthen the forces there facing the Italians. He considered that Italy was geographically too deep to be overwhelmed by any concentration that the Central Powers could muster. "Even if the blow succeeds," he wrote to Conrad, "it will not be fatal to Italy. Rome will not necessarily be compelled to make peace because her army has suffered a heavy defeat in the extreme northeast of the country. She certainly cannot make peace against the wishes of the Entente, on whom she is absolutely dependent for money, food and coal." *

Conrad was therefore left to his own resources, but determined to persevere in his plan. His detestation of Italy was always apt to

* Falkenhayn, pp. 194-199.

influence his otherwise good judgment. And he withdrew some fine divisions from the Eastern Front to reinforce the Archduke Eugen's army group in the Tirol, according to Falkenhayn saying nothing about the transfer and even trying to conceal it. But he could not strike yet. More than almost anywhere else in Europe, active operations from the Tirol were dependent on the weather.

Cadorna was attacking on the Isonzo—that goes almost without saying. There he could defy the weather to a greater extent than could Conrad in the mountains, but he nevertheless found it trying. On the high ground snow was falling, on the lower rain, with fog hanging about, when the Italian bombardment opened on March 11. On the third day the assault began. Three little lodgements were made "at the same old three places," as the Austrians remarked, two facing the Carso and the other at Plava. On the fifteenth the action ended. A British critic calls it "a gesture of cooperation with the allies." * The Austrians, less complimentary still, suggest that the name "Fifth Battle of the Isonzo" was applied to the affair to give the impression that there had been "a serious battle." The losses on both sides were small, but those of the Austrians cannot have been much more than half those of the Italians.

Meanwhile Conrad had been concentrating his big striking force in the Adige valley. This, and the deployment in the southern Trentino, were immense tasks, with Trent a bottleneck from which only a single broad-gauge railway ran southward. When it was done the weather proved unfriendly. Never, said the impatient Conrad, had snow fallen so late in the Trentino. The offensive had to be postponed until May 15.

Conrad had established the Archduke Eugen as army group commander, with the most brilliant Austrian soldier of his seniority, Major General Alfred Krauss, as chief of staff. He had mustered two armies, the Eleventh (Dankl: eight divisions) and the Third (Koevess: seven divisions). The Italians had got wind of the concentration and had six divisions on the spot under the First Army, with two more under short notice to move. Yet if Cadorna was not surprised in place or time, he was in the third element, that of weight. The Austrian army, at home in mountain war and with old scores to pay, attacked with dash and skill. The two foremost Italian positions were quickly overrun; thousands of prisoners were taken; and by the fifth day the advance had penetrated up to five miles,

* Edmonds, *Military Operations, Italy,* p. 15.

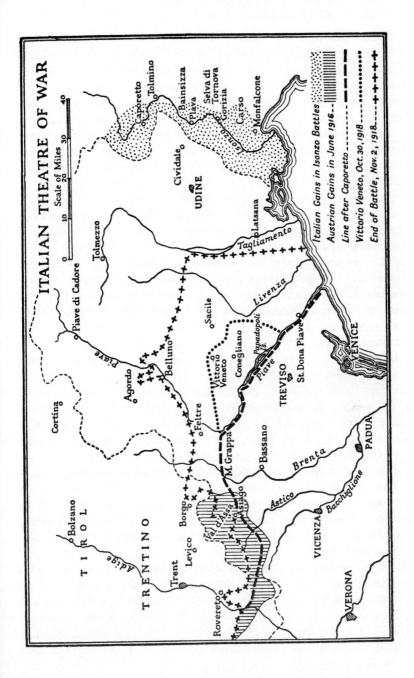

ITALIAN THEATRE OF WAR

Scale of Miles
0   10   20   30   40

Italian Gains in Isonzo Battles
Austrian Gains in June 1916
Line after Caporetto
Vittorio Veneto, Oct. 30, 1918
End of Battle, Nov. 2, 1918

Caporetto
Tolmino
Bainsizza
Plava
Selva di
Tornova
Gorizia
Carso
Monfalcone

Cividale
UDINE

Latsana

Tolmezzo

Tagliamento

Piave di Cadore

Livenza

Cortina

Sacile

Belluno

Papadopoli Is.

Agordo

Vittorio Veneto

Conegliano

Piave

VENICE

Feltre

TREVISO

St. Dona Piave

Bolzano

T I R O L

M. Grappa

Borgo
Asiago

Bassano

Brenta

PADUA

Trent
Levico

Astico

Bacchiglione

VICENZA

Adige

Rovereto

VERONA

T R E N T I N O

Piave

in places through the third position. Not the speed attained in Russia, but very much better than that of Verdun and the Somme.

But the Austrians had attacked on a wide front for their numbers, and as they fanned out it increased to some forty miles. Their dispositions were faulty, the Eleventh Army having assaulted on the whole front, with the Third behind it to exploit success. This looked pretty on paper, but it was in fact clumsy—the Germans always gave a front from the start to every army engaged, however narrow.* Now the Austrians, at an unfavorable moment, had to divide the front between the two headquarters. The advance began to slow down somewhat and hang back on the wings. Still, it looked splendid. Falkenhayn, who had fought against the venture, sent a telegram of the warmest congratulations and Conrad answered with equal friendliness.

By the beginning of June, Cadorna had thrown in all his available reserves. The advance slackened further. By June 10 it virtually stopped. The maximum progress was twelve miles. This was good progress, but the Austrians had not debouched from the mountains, though on the Asiago plateau, at the headwaters of the Astico, they had come near to so doing, and the Brusilov offensive had begun on June 4. We have seen what happened there. There was nothing for it but to stop the operation. Whether it could have been restarted with the aid of reinforcements is a matter of guesswork. There were no reinforcements. And on June 16 Cadorna launched a powerful counteroffensive. The Austrians rightly evaded the blow by slipping back and abandoning a fairly large proportion of their gains. There could be no doubt that a victory had been won, yet Conrad was disappointed. Some 45,000 prisoners, 300 guns, masses of food and stores—the booty was immense, but the strategic situation had not been seriously altered. The effort made to mount the offensive had gravely compromised the front in Russia and enabled Cadorna to turn once more to the Isonzo with better prospects than ever before.

The one strategic advantage of the Italians was that, fighting on interior lines, they could move troops far more speedily than the Austrians from one flank to the other. Cadorna was able to attack on the Isonzo by August 6. This time his two armies, the Third and Second, had twenty-two divisions against the nine of the Austrian Fifth Army. In medium and heavy artillery his superiority was four-

* Kuhl, I, 430.

fold. His aim was much more modest than that of Conrad had been: the Isonzo at Gorizia. The weight of the assault was beyond what the Austrians could bear. By the third day the Italians crossed the river and secured Gorizia. Cadorna scented a bigger success than he had counted on to start with. The second phase was, however, not equally favorable, though a footing on the Carso was secured. By now Austrian reinforcements were arriving, though in small numbers, and the defense became master of the situation, a state of affairs already familiar in this war.

If Cadorna had gambled—and he had vast resources by comparison with those of the enemy—it is possible that he would have achieved the elusive break-through. He was no gambler. He went back on his intention to capture the Austrian bridgehead at Tolmino, fifteen miles east-northeast of Gorizia, and brought the offensive to an end. He had lost over 50,000 men against an Austrian loss of over 40,000. His winnings were a bridgehead at Gorizia, a foothold on the Carso, and progress three miles deep on a front of fifteen miles. The success does not appear striking and was dearly bought. Nevertheless, it had a considerable effect. The enormous loss of the Italian army in the Austrian Trentino offensive, about 286,000, had shocked the country and led to the fall of the prime minister, Salandra. This battle had shaken the position of Cadorna as, curiously enough, it had that of his opponent, Conrad. Now at least the Italians had had a win and secured a jumping board which might prove useful in the future. The Sixth Battle of the Isonzo stimulated Italian morale.

Alas for Cadorna's hopes! He could not jump from the jumping board. In three further actions, each of three days, grandiloquently named the Seventh, Eighth, and Ninth Battles of the Isonzo, though all one battle with excessive pauses for breath, little was accomplished. In mid-September the aim was to work up the Carso, but only a little ground was won, despite a colossal bombardment. A renewed attack on October 10 achieved a little further progress. The last push on November 1 was undertaken to enlarge the Gorizia bridgehead and again advance on the Carso. It likewise failed to pay off. The campaigning season was now over; the troops were completely exhausted; and the results were a scanty return for all the blood and material expended. The best that can be said from the Italian point of view for these autumn operations is that they stretched to the utmost the powers of resistance of the Austrians and inflicted on them serious loss; lower, it is true, than those of the attackers but which the defenders, with their commitments in Russia and Rumania, could less well afford. The casualty figures were: Italian 75,000, Austrian 63,000, including over 20,000 prisoners.

It is curious that when the tactics of attrition in the First World War are discussed and those who practiced them are, as is often the case, condemned, Cadorna's name seldom or never comes up. Yet he was the out-and-out attritionist of the war and one who always suffered more from attrition than his foe. It cannot be denied, however, that he was a capable organizer or that his switch from the Trentino to the Isonzo this summer was well carried out.

Conrad's offensive in May was the first he had launched in this theater. Had the Germans participated and launched with the Austrians a simultaneous offensive on the Isonzo a smashing victory would doubtless have been won, but Falkenhayn's commitment at Verdun and the calls of the Russian front made this impossible, to the deep regret of Conrad, the Archduke Eugen, and General Krauss. He, as well as General von Kuhl, a capable soldier and historian, believed that a great Austro-German offensive in Italy would have been preferable to engaging the available reserves against Verdun.* He may have been right, but there is point in Falkenhayn's reasoning about the defensive depth of Italy.

The troops on both sides had shown valor and fortitude. Trenches and tunnels in the rock afforded good protection against bombardment, but the exertion of constructing them was enormous. The life was miserable, especially for the Austrians, who were less well fed than the Italians. The high plateaus such as the Carso and the Asiago made the most dismal surroundings, whitish rubble powdered with yellow picric acid, bitterly cold in winter, naked and unshaded under a blazing sun, whose heat they reflected in summer. And warm weather brought myriads of flies, as on the Gallipoli peninsula. It may be all this was no worse than the mud, but at least from the muddy battlefields of France fairly good billets and primitive comforts were not far off. There were few comforts near the Asiago plateau.

* Krauss, *Die Ursachen unserer Niederlage,* pp 183, 187. Kuhl, I, 432.

Chapter VII

MACEDONIA AND EGYPT

AN unrealistic light falls upon the international force based on Salonika at this period and imparts to it a ludicrous appearance. A writer of fiction who introduced the political and military complications would be reproached with disregard for plausibility. Britain had sent a strong force to a new theater of war, but not to fight if it could be helped. She remained opposed to any offensive action. However, she felt she could not refuse Joffre's demand to ease the pressure on Verdun, though in point of fact the battle was not affected by action in Macedonia. The obvious first step was to move the Entente forces out of the barbed-wire cage known as the Entrenched Camp and push them up toward the frontier.

There was no great risk in doing so when the advance was undertaken in April. By May, when it had approached the frontier on a narrow front astride the Vardar,* only one German division remained. On the other hand, General Sarrail, the Entente commander in chief, had now five British and four French divisions at his disposal and was being reinforced by six Serbian divisions. After medical treatment and rest at Corfu, famous as a health resort, these troops reached Salonika by sea in April and May, and were rearmed and reequipped by the French. The veteran Voivode Putnik had been incapacitated by the strain and suffering of the retreat to the Adriatic and his place as chief of staff to Crown

* Still the Vardar in Yugoslavia, but the Axios in Greece. The river was known as the Vardar throughout its length in the First World War. It must be remembered that Macedonia, including Salonika itself, had become Greek only in 1913, as the result of victory in the Balkan Wars.

Prince Alexander was taken by General Bojović. British and French officers, observing the ineradicable lines of semistarvation on the faces of many Serbian soldiers, could not believe that they had recovered physically or spiritually from their harsh experiences. This judgment underestimated their toughness. In a typical Balkan terrain they were fine troops and inspired by a passionate longing to recover their country.

The advance toward the frontier began in April at the speed of a snail. The British in particular were handicapped by shortage of the pack transport required, for which mules had so far arrived only on a small scale. The Greek covering forces accepted the situation, in some cases even shared the guard on bridges. The government proved less friendly. On May 26 the Bulgarians occupied Fort Rupel, in the Struma* valley seven miles inside the Greek frontier. It became clear that they had informed Athens in advance, though the French accusation that the fort had been occupied with Greek "connivance" was an exaggeration. General Sarrail demanded stringent measures. Earlier in May Lieutenant General Sir Bryan Mahon had been replaced in command of the British force by the younger and stiffer Lieutenant General G. F. Milne, who was expected to take a stronger line in opposing arrogant action by Sarrail against the Greeks; but he now had to support French demands that a nonparty "business" government should take office and that the army should be demobilized. Athens yielded, but the corps holding the Bulgarian frontier east of the Struma, in a region which Sarrail did not intend to occupy, remained at war strength.

Sarrail now told Milne that he had definite orders to carry out an offensive to "impress" Rumania, still hanging in the wind. The British government promptly ordered Milne to limit his aid to demonstrations. However, the Bulgarians intervened in the farce. The ill-advised action of Sarrail in obtaining the demobilization of the Greek army had emboldened them. Hitherto, except at Rupel, they had merely pushed observation posts over the frontier because they feared that an invasion would bring in the Greek army on the side of the Entente.† The demobilization gave them a freer hand. On August 17, three days before Sarrail's offensive was

* Now the Strymon.
† *Weltkrieg*, X, 597.

due to start, they suddenly swept forward in two heavy columns against the ends of the Allied front.

On the eastern flank the French cavalry was driven over the Struma, but the British Sixteenth Corps on the right (southwestern) bank blew up the bridges and prevented the enemy from crossing the river. On the western flank, however, the Serbians were taken by surprise, lost Florina, and were pushed back to Lake Ostrova. News of "a great Bulgarian victory" was flashed round the world. It indeed impressed Rumania, but not as intended. Pessimists at Salonika said: "Now you see we were right about the state of the Serbian army." They were not. The Serbians quickly recovered their balance. Ten days after the beginning of the Bulgarian advance Rumania declared war on Austria-Hungary.

As scenery the northern frontier, separating Greece from Bulgaria in the eastern half and Serbia in the western, was magnificent. To the military eye, however, the panorama was forbidding. The frontier had been deliberately traced along crests. West of the Struma valley these rose to some 4,000 feet, and the southern side, overhanging a flat plain, was like a wall. West of the Vardar the highest peaks exceeded 8,000 feet, tailing off into the celebrated "Monastir Gap" between the large lakes of Ostrovo and Prespa. Through this opening the Bulgarians had invaded Greece and it was the most promising place for what had now become a counteroffensive. Sarrail's Serbian troops were ready for action and he had been further reinforced by an Italian division and a Russian brigade.

The attack began on September 12. It was hastily mounted and many people took a glum view of its prospects, but it started with a fine Serbian success west of Lake Ostrovo. A fierce and bloody struggle followed for the twin peaks of the Kaimakčalan—the right peak 8,284 feet high. The Serbians clawed their way up, were driven down, and stormed the heights again on September 30. The loss of this buttress and observation post, combined with French pressure in the Monastir plain, caused a rapid Bulgarian withdrawal to the bend of the Crna. On their own soil the Serbians were animated to a tremendous effort. They fought their way across the wide river, though they got only a precarious hold on the north bank.

Thereafter the advance became slower, but the fighting no less ferocious. Blow after blow was struck by the Serbians, each success being followed by a Bulgarian withdrawal. By November the snow came and was driven almost horizontally by howling winds. The troops, poorly supplied, suffered grievously, and losses from sickness were added to heavy battle casualties. Yet the pressure was kept up. The Bulgarians were fought nearly to a finish. Dreading a collapse, the Germans formed two improvised divisions with battalions from as far away as France. And they too had to give ground. On November 19 French and Serbian cavalry entered Monastir. The advance had exceeded twenty-five miles, but the troops could do no more. The Bulgarians had all but cracked, and would have but for Germain aid. It was a wonderful achievement in such country and latterly in vile weather, but it was dearly paid for. The casualty list was about 50,000 including 5,000 suffered by the British in subsidiary operations. Milne had stretched his instructions as far as they would go and carried out many small attacks, mostly successful, just east of the Vardar and in the Struma valley. The Bulgarian and German casualties were probably about 60,000, including 8,000 prisoners. Unhappily, the well-timed Bulgarian advance on the flanks had delayed the start and the Rumanian front was never seriously affected by the Battle of Monastir.

The political background of the battle was preposterous. On August 24 the Bulgarians advanced to Kavalla, thirty miles east of the British front on the Struma. Here a Greek corps surrendered and was carried off to Germany for internment. The Entente fleets staged a dramatic naval demonstration off Salamis. In September the Greek government made a conditional offer to enter the war as an ally of the Entente powers. Before a reply had been concocted, the Liberal and pro-Entente leader Venizelos appeared at Salonika and set himself at the head of a "provisional government" already formed by his adherents. Next day, October 10, the French admiral announced that he would demand the surrender of the Greek fleet, and the British government could not stop him. In this hateful atmosphere the answer to the Greek note was sour: the adhesion of Greece was not wanted unless she declared war on Bulgaria at once. Next the French admiral demanded the handing over of arms to compensate for those taken by the Bulgarians. On being refused, he landed sailors at Piraeus, was fired on, and suffered heavy loss. The French government, which had egged him on, now professed to treat him as a semilunatic and recalled him; but the Entente imposed a blockade, which brought the Greek government to heel. All Greek troops in Thessaly, behind the Allied front, were withdrawn to the Peloponnesus.

The King of Greece and his followers had been by turns arrogant and shifty. The French had behaved like bullies. The British had been the shabbiest of the three, because they knew that what they did was shabby. They protested against French action and then countenanced it with token forces, in the seizure of the fleet, the landing, and the expulsion of the Greek troops from Thessaly. Lieutenant General Milne and Rear Admiral Hayes-Sadler had to carry out distasteful tasks.

Under the influence of their exaggerated estimate of the strength in which Turkish forces could cross the Sinai peninsula the British began the year 1916 toiling on the defenses of the Suez Canal. It was an enormous task, involving water supply, metaled roadways in the sand, floating bridges on the Canal, railway extensions, and of course entrenchment and wiring on a very big scale. Like the Entrenched Camp at Salonika it never served any useful purpose and had less justification than the former because the danger was slighter.

Already two signs had appeared that the spectacle of a quarter of a million Turks marching over Sinai to the conquest of Egypt was a mirage. Troops were under orders to leave Egypt and the commander in chief, General Sir Archibald Murray, was proposing to move out into Sinai, where he considered it would be easier and cheaper to defend the Canal. Between mid-February and late June, of fourteen divisions either in the country at the beginning of the year or formed in it,* nine went to France and one to Mesopotamia. This left Murray with only four Territorial divisions, a remarkable change. He was, however, fortunate enough to be allowed to keep a large force of mounted troops of high quality, the Australian and New Zealand Mounted Division and a number of brigades and regiments of British Yeomanry, some of them still engaged in the little war against the Senusi.

While the Canal defenses were still unfinished, Murray pushed out into Sinai. He was laying a railway east of the Canal and had to cover it by fairly strong forces. These started with a minor disaster. A Turkish force attacked the Yeomanry detachments in two oases lying twenty-five and thirty-two miles east of the Canal

* Two Australian divisions and one New Zealand were formed in Egypt. Mention has been made of their participation in the Battle of the Somme in the autumn.

and destroyed over three squadrons. The only other result, how-ever, was to delay the progress of the railway for a few days.

Murray had come to the conclusion that the best line on which to defend the Suez Canal was that between El Arish and Kossaima, because all the tracks which might be used by a raiding or attacking Turkish force passed through one or the other. The two places were about a hundred miles east of the Canal and near the Palestine frontier. Though he had talked airily of 250,000 Turks crossing Sinai with great rapidity, his own advance was to be a plodding one, tied to a railway and a pipeline. Slow but sure! He had first-class military and civil engineers and Egyptian fellaheen provided willing, cheerful, but timid labor. The railway did do away with the need for a road. An astonishingly effective one for light motor vehicles and men afoot was improvised by pegging down wire netting in the sand. The scenes of labor were picturesque. Where the pipeline was to run beside the railway, pipes were rolled out one by one from a slow-moving train by singing Egyptians enjoying a new game. Ahead ranged mounted troops, their horses subsisting unhappily on brackish well water.

At the moment when the desert blazed in the full heat of summer the irrepressible German Kress von Kressenstein advanced once again with a considerable Turkish force, some 15,000 strong. This time he had the support of German machine-gun companies and artillery partly manned by Germans. The venture was nearly as daring as the last and more difficult, because the advance to the Suez Canal had been made in the cool of winter and when the water supply in Sinai was at its maximum. This time the advance was directed against the railhead at Romani, five miles northwest of the Qatiya oasis. The likelihood of success was small because the British could bring up much greater strength, provided they could supply enough water. The original strength about Romani was about the same as that of the Turks.

The Turks attacked before dawn on August 4, and with high gallantry. To the connoisseur of tactics Romani is an artistic and sparkling battle. Murray's left lay on the shore and was covered by the big Bardia Lagoon. He assumed that the Turks must rely on turning his open right flank. He prepared a false flank—a tactical device modish before the war in Britain—hiding the extension in the dunes and holding a mounted reserve ready to take the attacker himself in flank. This came off, but there was some bungling and a delay in striking the decisive blow. As a consequence the main body of the Turks got away. The enemy was, however, smartly defeated, losing between five and six thousand men as against a little over 1,100 British casualties. The retreat was skillful and the Turks showed extraordinary endurance in heat and a shortage of water which hampered and at times prostrated the men and horses of the pursuers.

Apart from keeping open the Suez Canal and the Red Sea, British policy had the object of nullifying the Turkish attempt to raise the Mohammedan world against the Entente by the proclamation of *Jihad*, a holy war. Support of an Arab revolt in the Hejaz was the most promising measure. Such a revolt in fact began on June 5, 1916, near Medina, and on the ninth the Arabs overpowered the small Turkish summer garrison of the holy city of Mecca, chiefly with the aid of Egyptian mountain batteries sent from the Sudan. Taif, seventy miles to the southeast and the summer station of the main Turkish force, surrendered with 3,000 men in September. After this the Turks generally had the better of it and little more was accomplished that year.

By December the Egyptian Expeditionary Force was nearing its goal after a year of what the Book of Deuteronomy calls "walking through this great wilderness." On the twenty-third it struck at the Turkish outpost camp at Magdhaba, twenty-five miles southeast of El Arish, with the Australian and New Zealand mounted division and a newly formed brigade of camelry. After hard fighting it enveloped the Turkish redoubts and swallowed the whole garrison but for a mere handful who contrived to escape. It was now in the center of the line on which Murray had proposed to base the defense of the Suez Canal and Egypt itself: Kossaima to El Arish.

It had come a long way at great financial cost—including piping from the United States and rails from the Egyptian State Railways —to defend the Canal. Even now, however, it seemed unlikely that a halt would be called. The pressure for a further advance was political, and unless its nature is realized and borne in mind the picture of the Palestine campaign will not appear in perspective. The new Prime Minister, Mr. Lloyd George, had been for a short time Secretary of State for War in succession to Lord Kitchener. Like many another, he was appalled by the slaughter on the Somme. He, and less wholeheartedly the War Cabinet in general, believed that Turkey might be eliminated from the war by an overwhelming success in Palestine obtained at relatively small cost in human life. He was growing doubtful about another "side show," Salonika, on account of the sinkings by German submarines, whereas a very high proportion of supplies to Egypt came from India, Australia, and New Zealand.

The C.I.G.S., General Sir William Robertson, was a Westerner. He had tried unavailingly to withdraw the British troops from Macedonia. He preferred Palestine to that because he had a hold on the British force and had no Sarrail to deal with, but he hesitated to send more troops there and Murray told him he needed two more divisions if he were to cross the frontier. At the same time Robertson did not want to balk the Prime Minister and agreed that a success in southern Palestine would be valuable. These divergent aims led a strong and clear-minded man into a somewhat weak and vague policy. He ended the year by informing Murray that "notwithstanding the instructions recently sent you to the effect that you should make your maximum effort during the winter, your primary mission remains unchanged, that is to say, it is the defense of Egypt." * "Defense of Egypt" was becoming, as "defense of the Mesopotamian oil fields" had become, an ambiguous phrase.

* MacMunn and Falls, *Egypt and Palestine,* I, 260.

Chapter VIII

CAUCASUS—PERSIA—MESOPOTAMIA—
EAST AFRICA

W HAT would Turkey do with the troops released by the evacuation of the Gallipoli peninsula? Some would fight in European theaters, but the majority would almost certainly move east. And so, although Asia Minor was not a major theater of the war, it caused the Russians a lot of anxiety at the opening of 1916. By the reckoning of Yudenich, however, these Gallipoli divisions could not begin to appear before the end of March. He must therefore strike first to put out of joint the destined Turkish offensive. Climate and terrain did not encourage operations in January, but he had hardy troops. He had also provided for them short fur coats, trousers lined with cotton wool, felt boots for marching in snow and resting in bivouac, thick shirts, warm gloves, and fur caps.* He made his plans and preparations and only then went to Tiflis to win the approval of his master, the Grand Duke Nicholas. This was typical of their relations.

Yudenich's scheme was typical of himself. On this front, with barely enough troops to hold a fortified position, the Turks were committed to a cordon system of defense. Yudenich adopted the ideal solution for hill and mountain warfare: a feint attack, a secret concentration—though small and chiefly in artillery, the arm in which he was strongest—astride a good road, in this case that from Kars to Erzurum, and a break-through. He took the Turks by surprise and in mid-January won a fine victory at Koprukoy. However, he failed to envelop the enemy as he had hoped and Abdul Kerim re-

* Allen, p. 327.

treated in haste to Erzurum with a loss of 25,000, in many cases from frostbite. The miseries of the previous winter once again afflicted the unhappy Turkish troops. In February the Russians stormed the ring fortress of Erzurum, a wonderful feat for a field army without siege artillery. They did it by a swift break-through between the forts which rendered them useless. The conditions may be illustrated by the fate of a battalion of Don Cossack infantry, every man of which was frozen to death in a blizzard.

Simultaneously Yudenich launched a small offensive along the coast of the Black Sea. Here one sharp-cut valley after another ran down to the cliffs, affording a succession of defensive positions. Normally an advance would have been step by step, and perhaps the half dozen or so Russian battalions could have made none. But this was a combined operation with warships of the Black Sea Fleet, including an old battleship, taking in enfilade Turkish troops in the valleys. Another feature was a landing in rear of the defense from small shallow-draught Black Sea cargo boats. The naval bombardment had a shattering effect on the Turkish troops on whom it fell. The defense broke down and the worst military vice of Turkish soldiers, desertion in great numbers, came into play. The result was that Yudenich's subordinate Lyakov, reinforced by two brigades in transports from Novorossisk, entered the port of Trebizond on April 18. It was another fine success because this was the best roadstead—though that was not saying much—along the northern shore of Anatolia, with a good road to Erzurum, and so invaluable from the point of view of supplies.

Now the irrepressible Enver Pasha, who returned to Constantinople on March 8 after a tour of inspection in Syria, reappears in his old form. As usual, his plan to restore the situation was grandiose. The Turkish Third Army under a new commander, Vehip Pasha, was to engage the Russians from the Black Sea to the Kara-su, or western Euphrates. A new Second Army, under Ahmet Izzet Pasha, now being formed mainly from forces previously engaged at Gallipoli, was to advance before the end of March on Bitlis, at the southwest corner of Lake Van, to outflank the main Russian forces and threaten their rear. On paper the project had points in its favor, though even on paper the weakness of the Turkish communications should have been apparent. In practice it was the plan of "an incorrigible amateur." * Divisions railed to Ankara had a month's march at fifteen

* Allen, p. 376.

miles a day before they came within striking distance of the Russians. The scheme also rested on the assumption that the Russians would sit still, unwarrantable where a man like Yudenich had to be dealt with.

No flamboyance entered into his thinking. He had no intention of launching a great strategic offensive of the type in Enver's restless and inconstant mind. Though he was a favorite of the *Stavka* (the Emperor's headquarters), he was well aware that Caucasia was for it a secondary theater. His indispensable task was to prevent the Turks from renewing their offensive against Transcaucasia, but he did not mean to adopt the defensive pure and simple. A successful limited offensive against useful objectives would be profitable. And if wider horizons were opened up by the defeats which he constantly inflicted on the Turks, he was not the man to let opportunities slip.

Vehib struck first. Without waiting for the reinforcements strung out over the wretched road and rail communications, he launched an attack west of Erzurum on May 29. He won a certain amount of success, but then the offensive petered out. In June Enver became worried about Trebizond, where the Russians had opened up a new sea route by which they had already received reinforcements. Needless to say, he ordered Vehib to retake the port, without bothering to make sure that he had the means. Vehib did as he was told and his troops supported him well by a splendid march coastward across the range known as the Pontic Alps. The necessary strength to dislodge the Russians from Trebizond was, however, lacking. Once again only a limited success was achieved.

Yudenich had taken more time to ready his forces, but he had wasted none of it. His main blow was to be struck at Bayburt, the apex of a triangle the base of which ran from Erzurum to Erzincan. As before, he preferred in this country to split the enemy's front rather than to turn his flank. He launched the offensive on July 2.

At first the Turks resisted strongly and when driven out of one position stood again doggedly on the next, but once the Russians had made a deep cut their pressure on the raw edges thus laid open forced the enemy into a retreat which at some points became hasty and disordered. The battle developed into a major Russian victory, crowned on July 25 by the capture of the important road center—and very ancient and beautiful little city *—of Erzincan. The Cossack cavalry

* The description no longer applies. Erzincan was almost entirely destroyed in the earthquake of 1939 and has been built anew.

rode on for another twenty miles spreading panic in the Turkish rear. Yudenich had put the Turkish Third Army out of action. Nothing more was to be expected of it this year. To the 17,000 casualties and the same number of prisoners of war in Russian hands were added swarms of deserters living on the country. Divisions fell to a strength of three to four thousand. It was a brilliant success and far from costly.

Meanwhile, however, the Turkish right-wing army, the Second, was at last getting ready to launch the offensive which Enver had optimistically hoped to begin four months earlier. It did not get going until August 2, by which time Yudenich had already beaten the Turkish Third Army and was ready to send south troops which had taken part in this victory. The one place where the Second Army gained a striking success was on its extreme right. Here Mustapha Kemal, wearing the laurels won at Gallipoli, was now in command of a corps. His troops captured Mus and Bitlis. In the wild semidesert country between the two branches of the Euphrates the Turks achieved nothing and lost again any little ground they had won. And yet this was largely a "Gallipoli army" the ranks half-filled with recruits but with a kernel of victorious experience, proud and high-spirited. It was well beaten, but not routed like the Third Army. And there were few desertions, for good reason. This area was inhabited by impecunious Kurds who would have stripped deserters to the skin, if indeed they did not take that too. Both sides went early into winter quarters after a very hard campaigning season.

The achievements of Yudenich and his troops, who were largely drawn from Caucasian stocks, was remarkable. He won his battles not only because he attacked in the right place or because his men were always ready for a crack at their secular foes, the Turks. He won because he was a great organizer, a *rara avis* in Russian military history. His troops were mostly rustics, not yearning for amenities which they had never known and ready to put up with hardships so long as they were not left to freeze in winter and were tolerably well fed all the year round. Yudenich and his staff looked after them, as is proved by the fact that throughout the whole period during which the army of the Caucasus fought in a theater which might have proved a death trap its health was excellent.* It did suffer heavily during this winter, but far less than the Turks.

The doings in Persia had more importance than those of 1915.

* Larcher, p. 409.

In the account of that year it was mentioned that the Grand Duke had sent a force into Persia to counter German interference. The commander was Baratov, who had gained renown under Yudenich at the Battle of Karakilise. The British pleaded for a diversion from this force in aid of the unhappy Townshend, bottled up in Kut. The Russians were annoyed. Baratov's numbers looked respectable on paper, but he had only four battalions of infantry. What could he do? And anyhow, why was Townshend not a bit more active? However, every appeal made to Russia by her allies in this war was answered when humanly possible and sometimes when this could hardly be said. So Baratov moved in April, not on Kut—that was out of the question owing to the strength of the besiegers—but on Baghdad. Before he made serious contact with the enemy the British force in Kut capitulated. This was on April 28. Von der Goltz did not live to see his triumph, though long enough to know that it was coming. He died on the nineteenth of cholera.

Next Enver decided on a "pan-Turanian" invasion of Persia. Pan-Turanianism had begun in vague and mystic propaganda for the reunion of the Turks with kindred peoples and had been taken up by the Young Turks after the revolution of 1908. They were often lax Moslems and skeptics, in other cases Jews, so were not interested in the pan-Islamic doctrine which had previously appealed to Turkish emotions. But the idea behind the invasion of Persia was in the main an attempt to exercise propaganda, through Afghanistan, on India and Asiatic Russia. It was thus a moral offensive and may have been worthwhile, though the two divisions devoted to it left the Turkish forces in Mesopotamia weak and gave the British an opportunity to recover from the disaster at Kut.

Before the Turks set out, Baratov crossed the frontier and clashed with them at Kanaqin. This was sheer impudence on his part, but the Turks were so lethargic that he was not made to pay a heavy price for it. He was driven back to Hamadan and in August driven out of that town. But, having been reinforced in the interval, he managed to make a firm stand in the Sultan Pass. Enver's scheme, supported by his German staff officers, had not succeeded in establishing Turkish or German influence in Persia.

In January, on the arrival in Mesopotamia of the Third and Seventh Indian Divisions from France, Alymer made his first attempt to relieve Kut. He pushed the Turks out of their advanced position but on January 21 failed to storm their main line. Aylmer should perhaps now have awaited the arrival of the British Thirteenth Division, from Gallipoli via Egypt, but already anxiety was being felt about the food supply in Kut. He therefore attacked again at dawn on March 8, to fail once more. Lieutenant General Gorringe now took over from him and put the Thirteenth Division in to storm the main Turkish lines on April 5. Hope leapt up again when he succeeded. Unhappily, penetration to Kut involved forcing the passage of a defile, a mile-wide corridor between the Tigris and a marsh. This failed, and the attempt to run supply ships to Kut met the same fate. As already stated, Townshend surrendered to Halil on April 29. The siege had lasted since December 7, 1915, that is, five lunar months, whereas it had originally been estimated that the food would suffice for two only. A certain amount more was found in barns and cellars.

The strength of the force captured, including sick and wounded in hospital but excluding followers, numbering a third as many again, was just over 10,000. This was a trifling number by comparison with the hauls made in successful European sieges—e.g., 85,000 men at Novogeorgievsk—but it was for Britain a damaging and discouraging reverse, above all since it came so soon after the defeat on the Gallipoli peninsula. Yet curiously enough, its effects in the Middle East proved relatively small.

On the death of old von der Goltz command of the Turkish Sixth Army passed to Enver's young uncle, Halil Pasha, who proved a determined leader. Halil received Townshend with elaborate courtesy, and the captive British general was treated almost as a guest for the rest of the war. The fate of his troops was very different. They marched off in fierce heat and driven along remorselessly. Men who fell out from exhaustion were flogged with the whips carried by the mounted escort. Many died by the way. The death rate remained high after they had reached their camps, so wretched was the ration. The excuse was that the Turkish population got no more to eat. Townshend's conduct was later strongly criticized. It may be that he could in no case have done anything for his troops, but it would have been more seemly to accept no favors, such as permission to go shooting, from his captors.

In August Lientenant General F. S. Maude succeeded General Lake, who had himself six months earlier succeeded the original commander in Mesopotamia, General Sir John Nixon. Maude was an enterprising man and a good tactician, but he had to stand still for the time being. The chief of the imperial general staff, Robertson, warned him against getting involved in operations such as had hitherto drained British resources; the general staff was contemplating withdrawal to Amara, which Townshend had reached in June, 1915, and possibly a complete withdrawal from the theater of war.

Maude was not best pleased to be told that he had taken over a purely defensive force, likely to carry out another withdrawal. (He had commanded the Thirteenth Division at Gallipoli and had been the last member of it to leave the beach.) He now benefited by a slice of luck. General Sir Charles Monro, who had recommended the abandonment of Gallipoli, paid a visit to Mesopotamia on his way out to take up the appointment of commander in chief in India. Naturally, Maude poured out his woes to his important visitor, an invaluable supporter in a forward policy because India provided so big a proportion of the resources. Monro was convinced. It was the old story, two British authorities working against each other.* In this case the Indian command prevailed over the War Office. The War Cabinet agreed to a renewed advance by Maude. The best the War Office could do was to take over command of the campaign hitherto exercised from India. Maude now had at his disposal five divisions, four in two corps on the Tigris and the fifth on the Euphrates. With cavalry, reserves, and lines-of-communication troops, the ration strength was 340,000, but only 166,000 fighting troops, 107,000 of them Indian and the remainder British. Turkish fighting strength was estimated to be about 42,000, half on the Tigris, the rest on the Euphrates or in reserve at Baghdad. Even this was an exaggeration, according to Turkish accounts. The Sixth Army was melting fast, like all the others, and reinforcements were always less numerous than casualties in battle or from sickness. Turkey may feel that Britain paid her a high compliment in the great superiority of numbers she saw fit to bring against her in this theater as well as later in Palestine.

Maude began his advance on December 13, one corps on either bank of the Tigris. The task of that on the left (northern) bank of the river was to create a diversion. South of the bend in which Kut lay the other corps crossed the big tributary of the Tigris, the Shatt el Hai, without meeting as much opposition as expected. Then

* See pp. 97-98.

heavy rain held up the British. However, in this country, though rain brought inundation, the ground dried quickly after it ceased. By February 4, 1917, the Turks had been forced to abandon all holdings on the south bank. On the seventeenth Maude launched his diversionary attack at Sannaiyat, fourteen miles below Kut, and by this and a later operation succeeded in attracting the attention of Halil as desired. Meanwhile the Turkish troops, completely out-gunned, had been enduring a hammering so heavy and persistent that Maude was at a loss to understand how they went on facing it. On the twenty-third he played his best trump, forcing a passage of the river in a big bend six miles above, that is west, of Kut. The troops ferried across to form a bridgehead had ferocious fighting and the assembling of the pontoon bridge began under point-blank fire from the enemy. At last sufficient room was cleared and by 4:30 p.m. the 295-yard bridge was open to traffic.*

The effect upon the Turks was strikingly similar to that of the victories of Yudenich and those of Allenby in Palestine which were still to come. The askers, nearly all Anatolians, had shown astonishing grit and endurance under almost ceaseless bombardment. Then, on a sudden, when they could stand no more, they became palsied and prostrated. The whole force fled upriver. The last stage of the pursuit was carried out by the Royal Flying Corps, which bombed the retreating Turks, and by the navy's flotilla of little gunboats, which created a panic by short-range fire. The Sixth Army was put out of action by Maude as the Second had been earlier by Yudenich.

It has been shown that the year 1915 was uneventful in German East Africa. Matters were very different in 1916. In early spring the considerable forces of the Union of South Africa which had been freed by the conquest of German South-West Africa the previous summer were concentrated near Mombasa under the command of General Smuts, for whom Britain felt great respect because he had proved so formidable a foe in the South African War. He set afoot one of those elaborate enveloping movements which so often promise more on paper than they provide on the ground. He had not far short of 20,000 in fighting strength, 13,000 white, the remainder Indians and Africans, not counting the Belgians in the Congo, who were prepared to cooperate with him and in practice accept his orders, or a small mainly native force in Nyasaland. The Germans had ex-

* Moberly, III, 170.

panded their original force of fifteen companies fourfold. They had now reached their maximum strength of over 3,500 Europeans and 12,000 askaris.

Smuts with the main force was to advance due southward; the Belgians under General Tombeur, with a small British column, were to move between Lake Victoria and Lake Tanganyika in a southeasterly direction on Tabora; Brigadier General Northey's Nyasaland force, striking off from the northern end of the lake of the same name, was to move northeast. Finally, it was hoped that a Portuguese column—Portugal entered the war on the side of the Entente in March of this year—would advance northward from Portuguese East Africa; but this last part of the program was not satisfactory.

Smuts handled the main force capably. He moved in several columns, feeling for his elusive foe in the bush, always endeavoring to envelop or even to surround him. It was, however, an almost hopeless task. The size of the country in relation to the number of troops, the heat and sickness which hampered those of European stock and indeed the Indians also, the weight of the transport needed to keep white men on the march at all, put outstanding advantages into the hands of Smuts's opponent, Colonel von Lettow-Vorbeck. And he was the man to make use of them. His own askaris were lightly equipped and their needs were trifling by comparison with those of whites. His Germans were either officers and subofficers or colonists, in either case acclimatized and knowing how to look after themselves, besides being provided with several porters apiece for their food, equipment, and drugs.

Lettow dodged, swerved, and twisted. He himself was never brought to decisive action, though some of his lieutenants were. The campaign of envelopment became in fact a plodding advance by Smuts, dropping sick men by thousands. The Ninth South African Infantry was 1,135 strong on February 14 and 116 on October 25, with very small battle casualties.*

However, maneuver as he might, Lettow always had to retreat in the long run. By July, Smuts reached the important Central Railway, from Dar-es-Salaam to Ujiji, and established control over it, but the bulk of the enemy's forces slipped through between him and Northey. The Belgians also reached the railway at Tabora on September 19 and took over the section of the line west of it. The

* Hordern, p. 521.

northern and by far the larger part of the colony was thus cleared of the enemy. Lettow's force and others commanded by General Wahle and Major Kraut had been much diminished in strength by constant hurrying, but they were still capable of giving trouble in plenty.

In January, 1917, Smuts left to represent South Africa at the Imperial Defense Conference. The general belief at the time was that he had all but finished his job. This was very far from being the case and it was probably well for his reputation that he was able to quit the scene after an undoubted success measured by the extent of the territory from which he had expelled the Germans and their askaris. Tactically he had made no serious mistakes. The great mistake was that of his predecessors: not realizing much more quickly the inevitable consequences of fighting a white man's war in an unhealthy black man's country. And this mistake must be attributed very largely to slackness in the preliminary study of the climate and the prevalence of malaria, dysentery, pneumonia, and a number of purely tropical diseases. The obvious answer was the expansion of native forces.

The whole aspect of the campaign was now about to change. The war in a black man's country was henceforth to be fought mainly by black men. It is to the credit of Smuts that, though he expected to finish the campaign in from six to nine months, immediately after his arrival he began expanding the King's African Rifles. By the end of the year he had thirteen battalions formed or forming, and the final strength was twenty-two. He also received a West African brigade from Nigeria. The bulk of the white South African troops, or their survivors, and all the Indian troops were withdrawn. Thus a force suited to the country was obtained, though so late that a number of battalions of the King's African Rifles proved inferior to the veteran units in the German service.

Despite the handicaps under which the British fought, the achievement of Lettow deserves undying fame. He was cut off from home. He could entertain no hope of a decisive victory. His aim was purely to keep the British on the stretch as much as possible for as long as possible and to make them expend the largest possible resources in men, in shipping, and in supplies. By this yardstick he was successful. No one who studies the campaign can doubt that a high proportion of his success was due to his personal qualities: skill, speed of thought, determination, and inspiring leadership. He was one of the greatest masters of the art of bush warfare

Book Four—1917

Chapter I

PEACE MOOTED—THE WAR GOES ON—THE UNITED STATES A COMBATANT

THE year 1917 bears the marks of two prodigious occurrences: the Russian Revolution and the entry of the United States of America into the war. The first was the greatest event of modern times, one which has changed the character of the world. It has already proved itself as far-reaching and *revolutionary* as the French Revolution. Some would put it higher and argue that the ideas behind the second revolution were further removed from those then prevailing than were those of the first. The action of the United States in entering the war, though less important, was still immensely so. The political effects of neither can find a place in this narrative since they belong not to the war but to the post-war world. The military consequences were momentous. In some degree they balanced one another. One giant left the arena and another came in almost simultaneously, in the same cause. The departing combatant was, it is true, a giant armed and the incoming a giant barely half-armed; but the newcomer had vast potentialities, vast resources, and unweakened energy.

The elimination of Russia gave Germany her first and only chance of redeeming the loss of the Battle of the Marne in 1914 by winning the war on land. Simultaneously her U-boats gave her a chance of winning it at sea. The appearance of the United States as a belligerent was a powerful factor in the defeat of Germany in the first element and a considerable one in the second. Estimates of the weight of this factor differ, but one feature cannot be disputed by any sane person with a passable knowledge of the period: the entry of the United States into the war was an immense moral stimulus to weary nations and weary fighters.

Another feature of this year is that, for the first time, peace proposals appeared in the open. They were put out by belligerents—the governments of the Central Powers; by a neutral at that time—the government of the United States; and by the Vatican. The German supreme command believed itself doomed to defeat "if the war lasted"; * the only way to win was by unrestricted submarine warfare, which the chief of the naval staff, Admiral von Holtzendorff, told his colleagues would make Britain sue for peace before the harvest, "even taking into account a break with America." †

The Imperial Chancellor still withstood this measure, backed by the Emperor. Bethmann-Hollweg demanded that peace proposals should be sent out. He could count on support from the Emperor Carl, who had succeeded to the Austrian throne on the death of Francis Joseph on November 21, 1916. The soldiers and sailors did not object; if, as was likely, the proposals were turned down, Germany would claim greater justification for an unrestricted submarine campaign. So it was arranged. The fall of Bucharest on December 6, 1916, provided a success which made it look as though the move were made from strength. The notes were presented on the twelfth. They declared boldly that Germany and her allies were resisting ceaseless attacks, but justified in hoping for fresh successes; nevertheless, though prepared to fight to the end, they desired "to stem the flow of blood," and they believed their proposals would serve as a basis for an enduring peace. Not a word was said about these proposals.

And no wonder! They included the cession of all or part of the Belgian Congo to Germany; her retention of the Briey-Longwy basin in France; establishment of German "influence" in Belgium or retention of Liège in default of this; "improvement" of the Austrian frontier with Italy; partition of Montenegro between Austria and Albania; rectification of the frontier with Rumania; enlargement of the Austrian Empire and of Bulgaria at the expense of Serbia; further "examination" of the Dardanelles question.‡ It looks as though the notes were issued partly in hope that if the United

* Ludendorff, I, 307.
† *Weltkrieg*, XI, 481.
‡ *Österreich-Ungarns Letzter Krieg*, V, 719.

States, under a President passionately devoted to peace, could be induced to take part in a peace conference, it would never be drawn into the war on the side of the Entente. All this was kept secret, but for a brief, vague, and deliberately misleading outline sent to Colonel House for President Wilson by the German ambassador.*

These identical notes were presented and published at a moment when President Wilson was drafting and redrafting one of his own, a call to the warring nations to state their peace terms. The German move had prejudiced his prospects, but he did not abandon his intention. On December 18 he addressed circular notes to the American diplomatic representatives accredited to the belligerent governments. He said that he was not offering mediation; he was proposing that soundings should be taken to determine how near "the haven of peace," for which all mankind was longing, might lie.†
The governments of the Central Powers still did not venture to disclose their proposed terms, but they suggested a direct exchange of views between the belligerents.

The governments of the Entente Powers replied first to the notes of their enemies, which they did not consider to be sincere. They answered in brief that, since there could be no hope that reparation for wrongs inflicted would be made or that guarantees against future aggression would be given, they were unable to accept the invitation. On January 10, 1917, they replied more fully to President Wilson. They told him that their war aims included the restoration of Belgium, restitution for invasions, restitution of territories seized *in the past* by force or against the will of their inhabitants, the liberation of Italians, Slavs, Rumanians, and Czechoslovaks from foreign domination, and the expulsion of the Ottoman Empire fro Europe.

These terms had not the slightest chance of providing even a basis for discussion. For Germany they involved the return to France of Alsace-Lorraine; for the wretched Austria they meant the break-up of the Empire. The fulfillment after the war of the proposals affecting Austria has been generally condemned. It was an error to make them a feature of Allied policy. Even had the United Kingdom and France not adopted this policy it seems almost certain that the Austrian Empire would have split in pieces. Yet

* *Foreign Relations of the U.S.*, 1917. Supp. I, p. 34.
† Scott, pp. 235-244.

the Entente need not have labeled itself as the first advocate of this disintegration.

On January 22 the President delivered to the Senate one of the noblest and most famous of his addresses, on the essentials of permanent peace. His plea for "peace without victory" was not tactful and was little appreciated in Britain. Yet, for all its merits, tact is not the supreme virtue. Had he said "peace without conquest" no criticism would have been heard, but the words would not have rung as clearly and grandly down the corridor of time. Shadows of the future League of Nations appeared. Most striking of all was the sentence on the role of the people of the United States as peace-makers:

"To take part in such a service will be the opportunity for which they have sought to prepare themselves by the very principles and purposes of their polity and the approved practices of their Government ever since the days when they set up a new nation in the high and honorable hope that it might in all that it was and did show mankind the way to liberty." *

Admirable indeed—but those who believed that the United States ought to keep out of the war must have recalled this passage sourly when the President led her in exactly ten weeks later.

The shift was due to the German decision to reintroduce unrestricted U-boat warfare on a bigger scale. This time a zone in which all vessels, neutral included, would be sunk at sight was to cover the United Kingdom, France, Italy, and the eastern Mediterranean. In Washington the German ambassador informed the Secretary of State, Mr. Robert Lansing, of this procedure on January 31, one day's notice. Holtzendorff and his ally Ludendorff had won. They had browbeaten the Chancellor into surrender and the Emperor had given way. The refusal of Britain and France to discuss the German proposal of negotiations influenced William II, but this does not automatically prove its good faith. Bethmann-Hollweg lasted only until July 13. He was succeeded as Chancellor by Dr. Michaelis, who gave way a couple of months later to Count Hertling, an ally of the militarists.

The United States would not go back on the pledge of nearly a year earlier that continuance of this type of warfare would lead to severance of relations with Germany. This was carried out on February 3, but it did not involve hostilities. On the same day

* *Foreign Relations of the U.S.*, 1917. Supp. I, p. 24.

Wilson told Congress that the United States "did not desire any hostile conflict with the Imperial German Government." * He clung to the hope that armed neutrality would suffice. Attacks on American ships and the anger of the country over the German proposal to Mexico of an alliance and the annexation of Texas, New Mexico, and Arizona made him abandon this policy. On April 2 he demanded from Congress a declaration that a state of war existed between the United States and Germany. President and country had moved full circle. Everyone is entitled to his own opinion as to whether they were right, and a British opinion may be prejudiced. This is given for what it is worth: the President, the Congress, and the American people were right.

Meanwhile, the Austrian Emperor was making behind the back of his German partner an attempt to negotiate a separate peace with France and Britain. His channel of communication with the president of the French Republic was his brother-in-law, Prince Sixte de Bourbon. Long negotiations came to nothing, mainly because no terms that Austria could accept would satisfy the claims of Italy. The Pope's plea for peace in August also fell on stony ground. In England one individual effort was notable because of the character and past political life of the man who made it. The Marquess of Lansdowne had been Foreign Secretary in the last Conservative Cabinet. He was one of the architects of the Entente. In November, 1917, he published in the *Daily Telegraph* a letter with the same significance as a memorandum which he had circulated to the Cabinet in 1916, casting doubt on the possibility of decisive victory and urging that peace proposals should be entertained. These appeals, like the public moves of the Central Powers, the United States, and the Pope, and the secret move of the Austrian Empire, had no effect. The war was to go on.

The ignorant assumed that the United States would be able to afford instant and mighty aid to her new partners in every field. The President's address made it clear to the thoughtful that this was not so. He spoke of cooperation in council and action, of loans, mobilization, and the full employment of the navy at once. The United States Navy was in fact a formidable fleet. The army was, however, only a skeleton and to put flesh upon it was going to be a long task, which would show no results at all for some time.

* *Foreign Relations of the U.S.*, Supp. I, p. 147.

However, in the early spring of 1917 Britain and France, while they looked forward eagerly to American aid in the land war, did not regard it as a matter of life and death, as was to be the case later. Both were about to launch great offensives, that of the British starting three days after the American proclamation of war against Germany. On the other hand, aid in the sea war was vital. The losses from submarine attack had become disastrous and horrifying. The statesmen and the naval staff officer in Whitehall, looking at the monthly totals of sinkings so carefully hidden from the public, could tell at a glance that they pointed to inability to fight on, starvation, and surrender. There was no arguing about it. It must come if this went on.

When Vice-Admiral W. S. Sims, U.S. Navy, reached London on April 9 for consultations with the British Admiralty, nothing was concealed from him and he was astounded by what he was told. Jellicoe, now First Lord of the Admiralty, said to him: "It is impossible to go on with the war if losses like these continue." Page, the American ambassador, told him they were facing "the defeat of Great Britain." * Obviously the first need was destroyers. Battleships were much less important owing to the predominance of the Entente navies in that type. Indeed Sims was shocked to hear that modern American dreadnoughts would be a positive burden owing to the shortage of oil fuel; if any capital ships were sent over they should be the older-fashioned coal-burners. That was in itself a staggering commentary on the plight of Britain.

Sims stayed in the country and set up a headquarters to control the naval detachments which would move to European bases as soon as plans had been worked out and would be put at the disposal of the British commanders on the spot. This was a generous policy on the part of the United States government. No evidence that it brought about the slightest friction from first to last is to be found. Meanwhile one action was taken immediately. On May 4 a squadron of six American destroyers arrived at the port of Queenstown, an excellent strategic point for protecting ships passing south about Ireland. The aid was slight, but an earnest of more to come which aroused enthusiasm and gratitude. By June 5 thirty-four "Yankee boats" were based on Queenstown and playing their part in the tough and exhausting Atlantic patrols.

* Sims, pp. 6-8.

Nothing of the kind could be done by the army. Not a single division existed, though the total numerical strength was considerable. The equipment shortage was far more serious. This extended even to rifles, and it was a piece of good fortune that the Lee-Enfield was being manufactured for the British. There were virtually no aircraft or pilots worthy of the name. General John J. Pershing, appointed commander in chief of the Expeditionary Force, was convinced that the regular army and the National Guard ought to have been raised to war strength in 1916. He was probably right, but the advantage would have been small unless the conversion of peace industry to war had been undertaken on a big scale. Soldiers have to be trained, but it takes far longer to arm and equip them when the machine tools have to be made before production can begin, even in a trickle. It is difficult to follow the workings of President Wilson's mind on this subject. Apparently it did not concentrate fully on those issues which made no spiritual appeal to him.

Pershing, like Sims, went to London, but two months afterward, arriving on June 10, and the first reinforcement of land forces was correspondingly later. In June a great convoy of eleven troopships and four supply ships, very heavily escorted, crossed the Atlantic unscathed. The first American troops to reach France landed at Saint-Nazaire on June 28. General Pershing did *not* say: "Lafayette, we are here!" on that or any other occasion, but someone else did.

Meanwhile a deadly calamity had struck the French army. A moral disease afflicted it, so grave that it seemed to make a decisive German victory certain. When Pershing reached Europe in June all was transformed. Between the plunge of the United States into war and his arrival the huge offensive on which the French had built unlimited hopes had proved an agonizing disappointment. Mutiny had swept through half the army. The best to be hoped for now was that, after a long period of nursing, during which it would be incapable of anything beyond occasional limited operations, its spirit could be restored. Even this was not certain, and if the Germans learned the truth and tested it by an attack there was no knowing whether the French would stand. Another peril had appeared on the lowering horizon. Revolution had broken out in Russia and the Emperor had abdicated. Though France and Britain hoped that the new republic would fight on and some optimists believed that the Russian forces would fight better than ever, the more prudent chalked a note of interrogation over their appraisements of the future on the Eastern Front.

When Pershing reached France he was immediately, on June 22, given a disquieting though still guarded report on the French army by Pétain, now commander in chief. He was told that within it and in the country generally morale was very low. In August, Pétain opened his heart further and disclosed that mutinies had occurred. The result was that Pershing found himself in a ring of French soldiers and statesmen, with the British less vocal but not silent, calling for American infantry. "Never mind the guns, never mind the transport. We'll provide them. Only bring your young soldiers over to fill our thin ranks. The fate of France and of the war is at stake." * That is a fair summary of the ceaseless appeal. The obstinate man stuck his toes in. He was going to build up an American army and lead it to victory. His infantry was not going to be used as French cannon fodder. He would not yield. Yet he was reasonable and open-minded. He did compromise on a big scale in 1918 by lending divisions to the French and a few to the British before he was ready to form an American army. The British were more modest and argued more cogently. Robertson told Pershing that his demands were not selfish and that in fact it was easier and required much less shipping to send men than material. On that point Pershing agreed; anyhow the American cupboard was so bare that he had little choice. Rifles and machine guns apart, the A.E.F. was armed virtually throughout by France and Britain. But all this was talk, not action, to start with. Only on October 31 did an American division enter the line.

There had been little method, or none, in the army's preparation before the United States came in, but once she was in, business was managed realistically and with forethought. Wilson was bold enough to adopt conscription ("the draft") from the first. Warned by British and French experience, the War Department earmarked a large proportion of regulars as trainers of the new forces. Orders were placed for arms and equipment on a vast scale, though not much of the output ever reached France. Pershing arranged that the American lines of communication should interfere as little as possible with those of the French and British. Biscay ports were to be the doorways to France. From them good railway communications ran, well east of the overworked focus of the Paris lines, to

* Pershing, *My Experiences in the World War*, pp. 77, 134.

Chaumont, which the commander in chief selected as his headquarters.

At the end of the year 1916 the B.E.F. had reached a strength of fifty-six divisions. By the time the full campaigning season began, about the end of March, it was expected to number sixty-five, including two Portuguese. Portugal had been at war with Germany since March, 1916, and the first Portuguese troops landed in early January, 1917. The heavy artillery would by the early spring have twice as many guns as at the opening of the Battle of the Somme. The Royal Flying Corps did not expand quite as fast as had been hoped, but there were fifty squadrons in the field by April. The B.E.F. was now so large and the demands of a war of material on manpower so heavy, that a number of substitutions were planned in this year and went on to the end. The most interesting reinforcement was Queen Mary's Army Auxiliary Corps, composed of women and officered by them. Over 10,000 served abroad, nearly all in France. In addition colored labor was enlisted in several countries, the greatest number coming from China, which provided 96,000 in the summer of 1918. Armies were becoming little worlds in themselves.

The French forces numbered at the beginning of the year 101 divisions and had nearly reached their maximum, though a couple more were to be formed. The heavy artillery was already so strong that no attempt had been made to expand it to the same extent as the British, but though the latter had caught up a little the French had still about twice as many heavy guns and howitzers in proportion to the number of divisions. The French were now producing their own tanks to their own designs.

Joffre and Haig had agreed upon their plans for 1917 by the previous November. Suddenly something happened which upset all calculations. Simmering parliamentary impatience with Joffre boiled up and the Prime Minister, Aristide Briand, was forced to make a change.

Joffre had become more than commander in chief in the zone of the armies. His title was "Commander in chief of the French Armies," French forces everywhere, including a French army in Macedonia. At Chantilly he had built up a system of control which included functions generally exercised by a war ministry. The deputies—there was less feeling on the subject outside the Chamber—

considered that his powers were excessive. They attacked him with
the bitterness characteristic of French politics because he denied
them access to the forces but hid their personal hatred under ac-
cusations of unpreparedness at Verdun and needless loss on the
Somme.

Briand's first intention was to bring Joffre to Paris, make him
the government's military adviser, and supplement rather than
supersede him by a soldier who would command the armies in France
and confine his energies to that.* The soldier chosen was Nivelle,
on his Verdun record and especially his recent victories. However,
the government came under renewed attack in the Chamber and
Briand found he could save it only by sacrificing Joffre altogether.
He accorded Nivelle direct liaison with the government and also
with the British and Belgian commands. Joffre was squeezed out.
President Poincaré revived in his favor the ancient dignity, long
in suspense, of Marshal of France, but for the rest of the war his
position was purely ornamental. The French and others were to
discover the value of that massive and seemingly uninspired figure
only after he was gone. Haig had taken the unusual step of
representing personally to Briand the danger of removing Joffre.

Whereas Joffre wanted Britain to take more and more of the
weight from France's weary shoulders, Nivelle intended to destroy
the main body of the German forces by French arms. He chose
for the decisive attack the Aisne front between Reims and Soissons,
where a force amounting to at least two-fifths of the French divisions and three-eighths to the heavy artillery would first break
through, then overcome all such German forces as were brought
into the breach, and finally push forward on to the enemy's main
communications. He was an artilleryman, and he believed he had
found the one formula for a genuine break-through: to overwhelm
the defenses with a terrific bombardment followed by an unusually
deep creeping barrage and capture in a single day the whole system
of defense including the line of the enemy's field batteries. With
surprise—a very important factor—and avoidance of the enemy's
strongest positions, this, he was convinced, could be done anywhere.†

All this was to be accomplished by the French alone. It was to
be the greatest battle in history, and the greatest victory. It was to
be talked of as long as war itself was discussed—as indeed is likely

---

* Falls, *Military Operations, France and Belgium 1917*, I, 26.
† Falls, *Military Operations, France and Belgium 1917*, I, 29.

to be the case. But there were two requirements. To make possible the concentration of the vast "mass of maneuver" necessary for the offensive, the British would have to relieve the French by extending their front southward from their present right on the Somme battlefield to the Amiens-Roye road, a distance of twenty miles in a straight line. Secondly, two major offensives must be carried out to hold the German reserves. The first would be the task of the British, striking out from Arras in the general direction of Cambrai; the second that of the French between the Oise and the Somme.

Nivelle visited Haig on December 20, 1916, to make his proposals. Haig at once agreed in principle. After some negotiation, becoming rather stiff on both sides, about various points, including the date by which the relief of the French was to be completed, the situation was fairly well cleared up. Haig would cooperate to the utmost of his power, but he made the reservation that if Nivelle's offensive did not go quite as well as he hoped, he, Haig, would be compelled to undertake in the summer an operation to clear the Belgian coast. He was being pressed to do this in order to put an end to the activities of U-boats based on Ostend and Zeebrugge. Doubts about the shining success were naturally unpleasing to Nivelle. But after all, why bother about the pettifogging proviso of an overcautious Scot when his own victory was going to drive the Germans, or what remained of them, back over the Rhine, and *ipso facto* off the Belgian coast? All seemed well, but Nivelle had shown himself rather arrogant, and the relations of the two men were not quite so cordial as at their first meeting.

Nivelle had, however, made a conquest elsewhere. Lloyd George, who had maneuvered his fellow Liberal, Asquith, out of office and become Prime Minister on December 7, 1916, believed the losses on the Somme to be due to the clumsiness of British generalship. He could not dismiss Haig because powerful colleagues would have revolted at the proposal. Nivelle spoke English and put his points well, whereas both Haig and Robertson were tongue-tied. Lloyd George caught fire from Nivelle and believed he was the man for the moment. He wanted to place Haig under the Frenchman's orders. But how? If the War Cabinet fully realized his intention there would be a storm. He must rush through a surprise. He proceeded to maneuver against Haig, the fighting arm of the government of which Lloyd George was the head. And his partner in the maneuver against his own countryman was a foreigner, Nivelle.

A crisis in transportation had occurred, and it was announced that an Anglo-French conference to deal with it would be held. This assembled at Calais on February 26, 1917. For Britain the members were Lloyd George, Haig, and Robertson; for France Briand, Lyautey (Minister of War), and Nivelle, with specialist advisers. Little was heard about transportation because that problem was now nearly solved and the conference was a fake. The British Prime Minister had informed Nivelle, through a junior French attaché in London, of what was proposed. At the conference he gave Nivelle his cue, asking him to "put on paper" the relations between the two commanders which he considered necessary. The meeting adjourned to allow the French representatives to do this. How they filled in their time is not recorded but the document had been drafted five days earlier and they had brought it with them.

The French proposal was that Nivelle should exercise authority over Haig in everything connected with the conduct of operations. A British chief of the general staff and the quartermaster general would live at the French G.Q.G., and this chief of the general staff would be the channel of communication with the British War Office. Haig was to be reduced practically to the role of a staff officer looking after discipline and promotions.

Robertson decided to resign if these proposals were accepted. Lloyd George agreed that they went too far. Eventually a new formula was produced. Haig was to conform to Nivelle's orders during the course of the operations, but was to have the right of appeal to his government and freedom in the methods and means employed. Such was the "Calais Agreement." Haig wrote on his copy: "Signed by me as a correct statement but not as approving the arrangement." Another conference had to be held in London before all was straightened out. It emphasized that British troops remained under the orders of their commander in chief and that Nivelle could communicate with the British army only through Haig.

So the worst had been avoided. Yet what had been done was dangerous enough in view of what was happening in French politics. The London Agreement was signed on March 13. By this time Briand's government was tottering and confidence in Nivelle and his plan was weakening. Next day General Lyautey was shouted down in the Chamber and he resigned. Three days later the government fell. Britain had placed her commander in chief, the greatest army she had ever put into the field, and the contingents of the dominions, under the command of a leader whose plans were distrusted in advance by his own government and subordinates. So ended one of the most unsavory episodes in British political-military relations.*

* Falls, *Military Operations, France and Belgium 1917*, I, 51-57, 536-539; Appendices, pp. 64, 68.

Chapter II

THE SPRING BATTLES IN THE WEST

HAIG began the year 1917 in the highest rank in the British army. In the last days of the old year King George V wrote to him in his boyish hand: "I have decided to appoint you a Field Marshal in my Army." This was, and was intended to appear, a gesture of confidence. A second but private gesture of support and encouragement came at a moment, early in March, when Haig was in a mood of anger and distress about the Calais Conference. "The King begs you to dismiss from your mind any idea of resignation. Such a course would be in His Majesty's opinion disastrous to his Army and to the hopes of success in the coming struggle." *

For the second time Haig was pledged to an offensive dictated by the French rather than that which he would have preferred, for the clearance of the Belgian coast. This time such an operation was more urgent than in 1916 because now the War Cabinet and Admiralty demanded it. He had, as already stated, warned Nivelle that he would insist on turning to Flanders unless the French offensive proved so overwhelmingly successful as to make this unnecessary; but he had also undertaken to extend his front considerably and must have expected a struggle to get the necessary troops relieved by the French in time for an offensive in the north if it was called for.

Nivelle did not consider the winter harassing operations on the Somme battlefield, which Haig had earlier promised Joffre to carry out, to be very important. If they delayed the relief of French troops down to the Amiens-Roye road it would be better to cut them out, he thought. He did not understand Haig or realize the bulldog

* Blake, pp. 188, 205.

streak in the man. The British commander in chief believed that the enemy was becoming exhausted. He was determined to maintain the pressure, costly though he knew it must be, so that the Germans should be given no chance for recovery before the spring offensive. If he could, he would fool them into the impression that the Battle of the Somme was starting again. He realized the state of the ground; he was well aware of the calls on his troops that such a program must entail. Yet he stuck to it, though he had to carry out the relief simultaneously and the roads in rear would be thronged with troops engaged in that and a little later with those moving to the Arras front for his big offensive. Resolution or obstinacy? The view on the other side may help to provide an answer. "The strain during the year had proved too great. The endurance of the troops had been weakened by long spells of defense under the powerful enemy artillery fire and their own losses. We were completely exhausted." And again: "We now urgently needed a rest. The Army had been fought to a standstill and was utterly worn out." The writer is Ludendorff.*

Since November 18, 1916, abominable weather had made Haig abandon offensive action. The Ancre valley was a muddy wilderness. In its midst little parties of infantrymen held sections of wet ditches called trenches or shell-hole posts accessible only in darkness. Reliefs lasted all night and troops staggered into their camps dead beat. The artillery horses became pack animals, and the wastage was high during the transport crisis, when the oats ration dropped to six pounds. Some improvement occurred in January, but the ground remained a morass.

The operations began on January 10, and no counterattack to recover the ground won east of Beaumont-Hamel took place. Frost set in about the middle of the month, disastrous for the future of thinly metaled supply roads but temporarily a benefit to operations. Most of the attacks were on a relatively small scale, but on February 17 three divisions were engaged astride the Ancre, where a sudden break in the weather limited the success, though it was still striking. The infantry fought confidently and bravely. All this was on the front of Gough's Fifth Army. Farther south Rawlinson's Fourth was relieving the French and was called on for demonstrations only, but some of these led to sharp fighting.

Meanwhile the British, at heavy cost to the R.F.C., had been slowly

* Falls, *Military Operations, France and Belgium 1917*, I, 39.

piecing together from air photographs perhaps the most famous defense line in the history of war since Mohammed, the Prophet of God, dug his trench in the seventh century. It was the *Siegfried-Stellung*, which they called the "Hindenburg Line." It hinged on the British front near Arras and ran through Saint-Quentin to Laffaux, six miles northeast of Soissons.* It was constructed in the first place as a precaution, but it presently became clear to Ludendorff that he must withdraw to it to save the troops from the terrible battering of Gough's artillery and the constant infantry assaults. He meant to stand on the defensive in any case in order to let the U-boat commanders show what they could do. Withdrawal involved giving up a lot of territory but shortened the front by twenty-five miles and saved thirteen divisions. The zone between the original front and the Hindenburg Line was made a desert. Towns and villages were destroyed. Even fruit trees were cut down or "ringed" so that they must die. Civilians were removed, but, in a few towns or villages left intact, children, their mothers, and old people were collected, useless mouths to be fed by France. Barbarities such as the smashing of mirrors and the searing of upholstered chairs with red-hot pokers were committed. The magnificent Château de Coucy was destroyed in case it should serve as an observation post. The army group commander, Crown Prince Rupprecht of Bavaria, was stopped from resigning in disgust only because this would look like a breach between Bavaria and the Empire.†

The blows dealt by the British Fifth Army were so severe that the Germans had to begin the retreat ahead of schedule. In order to finish work on the defenses they clung to villages west of the Hindenburg Line as outposts, until driven out of them in severe and bitter fighting. Otherwise they had little difficulty in keeping clear of the British and French pursuit. On the Fifth Army front they were all behind the wire of the Hindenburg Line by the end of March, though not farther south.

Meanwhile Allenby's Third Army and on its right Horne's First were preparing for the great offensive. The front was some fourteen miles long, the ground downland, unfenced and almost treeless. North of the trough of the river Scarpe, which split the battlefield, was the remarkable feature of Vimy Ridge, dropping abruptly to

* It actually ran a few miles farther east, but the Germans retired to it only up to Laffaux.
† Rupprecht, II, 116.

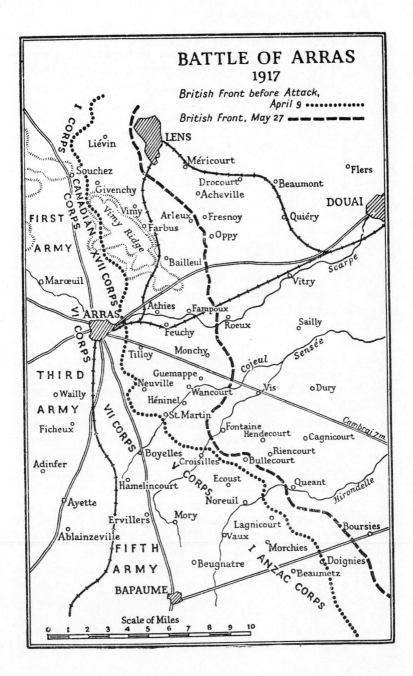

BATTLE OF ARRAS
1917

British Front before Attack,
April 9 ●●●●●●●●●●●●

British Front, May 27 ▬ ▬ ▬ ▬ ▬

I CORPS

Liévin

LENS

CANADIAN CORPS

Souchez

Méricourt

Givenchy

Drocourt

Flers

Beaumont

Acheville

DOUAI

Vimy

FIRST

Vimy Ridge

Arleux

Fresnoy

Quiéry

XVII CORPS

Farbus

Oppy

ARMY

Bailleul

Marœuil

Scarpe

Vitry

VI CORPS

Athies

Fampoux

ARRAS

Roeux

Sailly

Feuchy

Monchy

Tilloy

Cojeul

Sensée

THIRD

Guemappe

Neuville

Wancourt

Vis

Dury

Wailly

Héninel

ARMY

VII CORPS

St. Martin

Ficheux

Fontaine

Hendecourt

Cagnicourt

Cambrai 7m.

Adinfer

Boyelles

Riencourt

Croisilles

Bullecourt

Ayette

V CORPS

Ecoust

Queant

Hamelincourt

Hirondelle

Noreuil

Ervillers

Mory

Lagnicourt

Boursies

Ablainzeville

Vaux

Morchies

FIFTH

Beugnatre

I ANZAC CORPS

Doignies

Beaumetz

ARMY

BAPAUME

Scale of Miles

0 1 2 3 4 5 6 7 8 9 10

the Douai plain. Beneath the city of Arras were vast cellars and to the east of it vast caves, where hard chalk had been quarried for the rebuilding of the city in the seventeenth century. These provided accommodation for nearly 25,000 men. By tunnels from the underground barracks they could march up to the front in safety. Safety would have been complete but for the fact that the hinge of the German withdrawal was a short distance south of the city, and no time was left to prolong the tunnels to the new front. The withdrawal had the further disadvantage for the British that on the right flank they had to remake their plans and to attack far more powerful defenses than those previously facing them.

The Third Army's orders were to break the enemy's defenses from Croisilles to the junction with the First Army two and a half miles north of the Scarpe, and to advance on Cambrai, twenty-two miles southeast of Arras. The right wing of the First Army, the Canadian Corps, was to capture Vimy Ridge. The original attack was to be made by fourteen divisions, supported by the colossal weight of 2,817 pieces, up to 15-inch howitzers, forty-eight tanks, and about 450 aircraft. The Germans faced the attack with six divisions and a fraction of another and 1,014 guns. In the air they were markedly inferior, but possessed on the whole the better aircraft.

While the preliminary bombardment and air offensive were in progress the attack was postponed for one day at the request of Nivelle. It was launched on April 9, Easter Monday. The weather was not propitious. Squall after squall out of the southwest brought showers of rain, sleet, or snow. The troops were, however, in great heart. Their bearing had been an inspiration to Haig in his inspections. "I have myself a tremendous affection for these fine fellows who are ready to give their lives for the Old Country at any moment," he wrote to his wife four days after the battle had begun. "I feel quite sad at times when I see them march past me, knowing as I do how many must pay the full penalty before we can have peace." * This came from a man believed to be cold and unemotional.

On the right flank the assault was delayed till the afternoon because, owing to the German withdrawal, the troops were already on the first objective originally assigned to them and facing the Hindenburg Line itself. Here matters did not go as well as farther north. Astride the Scarpe the success was brilliant. Immediately north of the river Fergusson's Seventeenth Corps breached the German third line

* Blake, p. 217.

and took the village of Fampoux after an advance of three and a half miles, the longest in one day since trench warfare had buttoned up the front. In front of Vimy Ridge the four Canadian divisions had not so far to go—but they had to storm a very formidable position, and they did it. Vimy is a proud name in Canada to this day. Upward of 10,000 prisoners were captured. The two armies received splendid support from the R.F.C., but the tanks, though a few were invaluable, suffered all too many casualties from ditching and breakdown.

That night Allenby issued brief telegraphic orders for the capture of the remaining defenses and for the cavalry corps to be ready to go through. Things did not work out like that. Though the German troops were nearly fought to a finish and well over half their guns had been captured or knocked out, the British infantry now found itself facing trenches too far distant for the wire to have been cut, so that even one stout fellow behind a machine gun might hold up a brigade. Some useful progress was made, but the results were disappointing. Moreover, it was going to be stiffer from now on. The commander of the German Sixth Army, General von Falkenhausen, had made a grave mistake in holding his reserve divisions too far back, but they began to appear on this evening, and fresh artillery came into action—"a great arc of our batteries on a wide front behind our endangered positions. It was a most memorable and magnificent battle picture, lit by the evening sun," a grateful German remarks.*

April 11 was critical—and unhappy for the British. Allenby's picture of the situation was totally incorrect because bad weather prevented the R.F.C. from discovering the forward movement of the German reserves. He thought that he was "pursuing a beaten enemy and that risks must be freely taken." In fact, he was facing what was practically a new army. But though he did not realize that this situation had come, he saw that it might be coming. This, he thought, was the crucial day and if the enemy could not be kept on the move now the result might be stagnation. Actually the only worthwhile success south of the Scarpe was the capture of Monchy-le-Preux, perched on a knoll and a fine observation post. An attempt to put cavalry through at this point failed. On the First Army front the gains on the high ground were extended farther north on April 12, but thereafter the battle slowed to an inevitable pause. All the

* Falls, *Military Operations, France and Belgium 1917*, I, 275.

original divisions were exhausted and had to be replaced, though some returned for the next battle. The Germans were doing the same thing, but on their right flank they made a deep voluntary withdrawal from ground dominated by Vimy Ridge.

The second phase of the battle was brief, covering April 23 and 24. The Germans had sacked the chief of staff of the Sixth Army—their usual step when things went wrong—and replaced him by a brilliant tactician, Colonel von Lossberg. He had completely reorganized the tactics and established a system of defense in depth. The fighting was the fiercest so far; some officers who had been out since 1914 said the fiercest they had ever experienced. The British could muster only nineteen tanks; the German artillery was stronger than on the first day; and the infantry strength was the same on both sides. By sheer doggedness and superior grit the Third Army and the right of the First gained about a mile all along the front. German counterattacks were smashed. This was followed on March 28 and 29 by attempts to capture four fortress villages as a preliminary to a large-scale offensive on May 3. It went badly except at Arleux, captured by the Canadians.

Meanwhile activity had spread to Gough's Fifth Army on the right of the Third. On April 11 two Australian brigades got a lodgement in the Hindenburg Line at Bullecourt. Here the trenches bent eastward, so that a breach would have turned the flank of the Germans facing the Third Army. But no reinforcements were sent up and an artillery barrage was canceled because it was believed in rear that the troops had broken through into the open. One brigade was almost destroyed before the survivors were withdrawn. On April 15 four German divisions made a gigantic raid on two Australian near Lagnicourt. They broke in, but collapsed in rout when counterattacked. The German command believed their report that twenty-two Australian guns were destroyed by explosions in the bore, but in fact only five were thus treated.

Before the end of April Haig knew that something had gone very wrong with Nivelle's offensive. He decided to undertake the Flanders campaign. He had, however, prepared a general offensive on the present battlefield for May 3 in the hope that it would help to induce the French to go on fighting, and he let this proceed, but with strictly limited objectives. It was a ghastly failure, some thought the blackest day of the war. Nearly all the troops were bone-weary and gave way too readily when counterattacked by quite small bodies of the enemy. The only relieving feature was the capture of Fresnoy, on the Lille road, by the staunch Canadians.

Gough renewed the offensive at Bullecourt on the same day. Again he failed to break through, but this time the Australian and British troops refused to be driven out. Both sides fought like furies under tremendous bombardment concentrated on a strip of ground less than a mile and a half long. Savage combats lasted a fortnight. Up and down the Hindenburg Line swept parties of bombers in attack and counterattack. On May 6 the Germans put three divisions into a major counterstroke, to be routed after initial success. The final and fiercest fight was for Bullecourt itself, without which the footing could not be maintained. The ruins were at last secured and the struggle died down. The conditions were appalling, with unburied corpses littering the ground. Haig and Gough had at the end only two alternatives: to get Bullecourt or come out for the second time. Theoretically the latter might have been the wiser course, but it would have been a moral disaster.

The main battle petered out. Roeux was taken, lost, and recovered. Fresnoy was lost and not retaken. Between May 20 and 27 Snow's Seventh Corps captured the front trench of the Hindenburg Line by surprise attacks and bombing parties on a front of a mile and a half and the support line over a shorter distance. The fighting had been maintained, mostly with tired troops, to prevent the Germans from discovering that the battle was closing down.

Arras had a wonderful start. The blow dealt on April 9 was a triumph for British arms. None of the successes won later were comparable to it. The depth gained was about five miles on the greater part of the front. The British loss in killed, wounded, and missing was over 150,000. On the German side we have detailed figures for the Sixth Army, but not for the Second at Bullecourt. The two combined were certainly well over 100,000 and may have been not far short of the British. Over 20,000 prisoners were taken.

The conclusion must be that, though the British had made a considerable improvement in tactical skill since the Battle of the Somme, the infantry were better at a set piece than at improvising. The first day's attack was a set piece, and it went splendidly. The rest was mostly improvisation, and it never went as well. But errors and lost chances cannot all be chalked against the fighting troops. Staff work was too slow. Intermediate staffs fussed too long over orders. The

276 THE GREAT WAR

battalion commander is the man who *must* have his orders in time
if he is to succeed. Here in one or two cases the orders arrived *after*
zero hour. Delays, accidents, and friction are the commonplaces of
war, but they played too big a part here. On the German side nearly
every counterattack failed. The most striking feat was the reorganization of the system of defense amid the thunder of battle.

The German retreat to the Hindenburg Line had not affected
the front of Nivelle's main offensive between Reims and Soissons,
but it did prevent the G.A.N. from attacking halfway between that
front and the Arras battlefield. Two other factors were much more
serious. First, his plan was exposed to the enemy by captured documents. The Germans promptly interpolated another army in the
threatened front.* They transferred the vast labor force which had
worked on the Hindenburg Line to this front and constructed a
great new defensive position. The second trouble was that Nivelle's
army group commander between Reims and Soissons, Micheler, his
own special choice, became doubtful of the program and tried, unavailingly, to have it modified. Pétain, commanding the G.A.C. on
the secondary front, had disliked it from the first.

Monday, April 16, dawned. It was the day on which France was
to attempt one of the greatest feats in her great military history, one
that had come to be regarded as impossible in this war: end all by a
battle. The stakes were immense. *"L'heure est venue! Confiance!
Courage! Vive la France!"* was Nivelle's last message to his troops.
And indeed their courage was high as, in waves of "horizon blue,"
broken here and there by the khaki of colonial divisions, they
swarmed forward into the mist and battle smoke of that dull and
overcast morning, carrying the hopes of a nation.

If Nivelle could have stripped himself of illusion—but who is the
man that could in his place?—he would have realized within an hour
or two that the vitals had dropped out of his scheme. The German
artillery had been well and truly dealt with—though of course there

* One can go over the opposed strengths again and again, finding different
totals each time. If we include Nivelle's secondary front east of Reims and the
short inactive front covering the city, the figures are: French, fifty-two divisions (twenty-six in line, twenty-six in reserve); German, thirty-eight divisions
(twenty-one in line, seventeen in reserve on April 16. Within a few days one
French and three more German divisions arrived. The French had two Russian
brigades and six cavalry divisions.

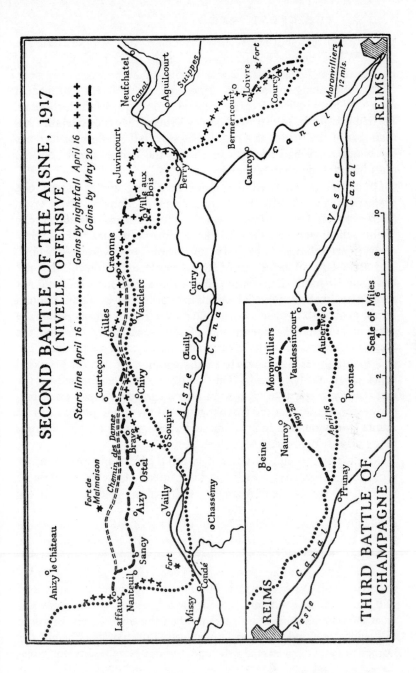

SECOND BATTLE OF THE AISNE, 1917
(NIVELLE OFFENSIVE)

Start line April 16 ·········· Gains by nightfall April 16 ++++
Gains by May 20 ▬·▬·▬

THIRD BATTLE OF CHAMPAGNE

Scale of Miles

was more in rear—but the accursed machine guns were clattering as usual. Whatever was happening—and details came in slowly out of the smoke-thickened mist—it was obvious that progress was slow. This was damning to prospects. Again and again Nivelle had made it clear that his whole conception depended on a quick break-through. He had not got it. In fact the first day's success was considerably less than that of the British at Arras. It also involved a holocaust of tanks for which there had been no parallel in the British attack. Nivelle must have felt death in his heart.

Of course he renewed the attack next day, and it gained one dramatic success. Under the heavy pressure of Mangin's Sixth Army from south and west simultaneously, the Germans abandoned the Vailly salient and fell back to the Hindenburg Line.* The withdrawal was voluntary but hasty, and many guns were left behind. The secondary offensive east of Reims was launched on this day and had a similar result: a maximum advance of a mile and a half and not a sign of a break-through. The gains of April 18 were slight. Though by the twentieth the French had taken over 20,000 prisoners and 147 guns and cleared the enemy out of the Aisne valley, though the German counterattacks were becoming feebler, the predominant impression on the assailants was bitter disappointment that the promised rupture had not been made. This impression was heightened by the fact that the medical services were overwhelmed by losses exceeding their estimates, so that the troops witnessed the tragic plight of great numbers of wounded lying about and awaiting evacuation. There is no sight more depressing to soldiers.

Nivelle now brought into line, between the Fifth and Sixth Armies, the Tenth (Duchêne) which had been intended for exploitation of victory. On the advice of Micheler he altered the goal. The offensive no longer aimed at a break-through; it was now a limited operation to obtain the whole of the Chemin des Dames ridge and disengage Reims. Even this was a mirage. Nivelle was now in the hands of the politicians, summoned from his command post when his presence was most needed, cross-questioned about every plan or even forbidden to carry it out. On April 29 Pétain was appointed chief of the general staff and "military adviser"—on the British pattern—to the government. Nivelle had one more success when the Sixth Army captured two and a half miles of the Hindenburg Line on the Chemin des Dames ridge. This was really the end, though Nivelle was not phys-

* See p. 270, footnote (*).

ically removed from his command until May 15. His successor was Pétain, the apostle of caution, who was succeeded as chief of the general staff by Foch. Besides Nivelle, his chief of staff, Pont, and two army commanders, Mangin and Mazel, were at different dates removed from their posts.

Neither French nor Germans ever kept their casualty lists as systematically or accurately as the British: Nivelle's return gave the losses up to April 25 only and put them at 96,125, including 15,589 killed, and this figure has been disputed, though it was accepted by the French Historical Service. Losses suffered by both sides during the whole course of the operations are estimated by a careful and well-informed British historian as: French 187,000; Germans, 163,000.* French politicians in their eagerness to discredit Nivelle circulated fantastically high figures for the losses. The soldier was given the impression that he had been defeated, whereas he had won a success greater than in many battles which had been proclaimed as smashing victories. The Germans, intensely relieved, proclaimed that their performance had been the most brilliant of the war. And out from their sewers crept the defeatists, some in German pay, to make their supreme effort. Undoubtedly it contributed to the trouble that followed, but some regiments involved had no contact with agents of treason.†

The French army cracked under the tensions to which it was exposed: disappointment, disillusion, losses, the weakness of the government, the confusion of the press, the campaign of the agitators, the flood of rumor, the Russian Revolution. The first mutinous incident occurred on April 29, not on the main front but on that of the Fourth Army in Champagne. While the offensive lasted, however, the malady did not become widespread; nor did it reach its height until ten days after the removal of Nivelle. Out of 119 acts officially described as "collective indiscipline"—a euphemism for mutiny—eighty occurred between May 25 and June 9. These acts were spread among fifty-four divisions, not counting the Russian troops, who became utterly demoralized. The new commander in chief, General Pétain, found the weapon entrusted to his charge by the nation bend-

---

* Edmonds, *Short History*, p. 221. If this is correct for the French, then the return to April 25 must be too low. The total from that date to the end of the battle on May 9 could not have been doubled.

† Pierrefeu, pp. 173-176.

ing in his hand. "The confidence of the Army in its chiefs, in the Government, and in itself was undermined." *

Mutinous acts included refusal to relieve other troops on the front, manifestations against the war, and some incendiarism. Men on leave behaved worst, which suggests that much of the infection came from the towns and railway stations. Leave parties beat up military police and railwaymen, uncoupled engines to prevent trains starting, waved red flags, and sang revolutionary songs. More than half the leave men returned drunk. It was not, however, mutiny of the most flagrant kind because attacks on officers were very rare.

Another mitigating feature was that news was practically never carried by deserters to the enemy, though some sensational reports eventually reached the Bavarian Crown Prince and seem to have been treated lightly.† Loyal troops were scraped together to hold the trenches and the artillery never wavered. Disaster might have followed if the Germans had realized the scope of the outbreak.

Courts-martial brought in over 23,000 verdicts of guilty, but only 432 death sentences were pronounced and only fifty-five men were shot. The commander in chief's personal work should always be remembered when his long and troubled record is reviewed. Having restored order, he strove to restore the spirit of the troops. He made many visits to units himself. He removed bad characters serving their sentences in the ranks, improved accommodation and conditions of travel, raised the standard of cooking. Above all he increased leave, so that the normal number absent at any one time was raised to 25 per cent, and might be increased to 50 per cent, when a division was withdrawn from the line. This policy was inevitable but it exercised a hampering effect on operations.

The recovery of the army was almost miraculous, but it was also slow. Whether or not it was complete is hard to say. The French forces appeared in 1918 to be inferior to the British in defense; even in attack, traditionally their strongest side, some divisions seemed to lack the drive of the British and Americans. Anyhow, in what immediately concerns us, the rest of the year 1917, the French were without doubt in a parlous situation. This was the cause of Pétain's appeals to Haig to keep the enemy engaged by every means in his

* Falls, *Military Operations, France and Belgium, 1917*, I, 503. The account of the mutinies in this official volume comes from the French official account, *Les Armées Françaises dans la Grande Guerre*, V, Chap. IV.

† Rupprecht, II, 212, 227, 230 (all in July).

power. It was the background to his confidences to Pershing and the early demands that American infantrymen should be drafted straight into their ranks. What Pétain said to Pershing has been recorded.* Haig was cautious on the subject, but he mentions that on June 16 Pétain had been "most frank" about the "indiscipline" which had occurred in the army, though he thought the situation already better, as was in fact the case. When Haig dined with Pétain in Paris in March, 1919, his host informed him that "the state of the French army was much worse than he had dared to tell me." On September 2, in the midst of the Battle of Ypres, at a moment when Lloyd George and some of his colleagues wanted to close down the offensive, Haig won the support of the majority for its continuance by stating that Pétain was still begging him to keep the Germans away from the French front.† It was because he did so that the German Crown Prince was not given the necessary troops to launch on the French front the offensive which was in his mind.

The French army had suffered a grievous moral blow, but it had avoided the complete disaster which overhung it in May, 1917. To aid the process of regeneration by Pétain, later on supported by the national regeneration brought by Georges Clemenceau as Prime Minister, France's British ally had to bear a heavy burden.

* See p. 262.
† Blake. pp. 244, 360; Edmonds, *Short History*, p. 249.

Chapter III

RUSSIA IN REVOLUTION

THE small and select circle of students of Russia in the
United Kingdom and France—hardly any were then to be found
in the United States—had been happily surprised that, after two
and a half years of war and of appalling loss and suffering, she
appeared unshaken politically. They knew how long was her record
of unrest and repression. Revolutionary aims had appeared in three
sections: the intelligentsia, the peasantry, and the proletariat of the
cities. The war with Japan had brought a serious explosion in 1905,
but defeat had been the detonator, not the charge. This was a com-
pound of several elements, the chief being the land hunger of the
peasants. In October grave naval mutinies broke out at Sevastopol
on the Black Sea and Kronstadt on the Gulf of Finland. Had the
army gone the same way, as for a moment looked likely, the effects
would have been terrific; but it was pacified. Next year the Russian
government took a step on the path to a more liberal system with
the creation of a form of legislative parliament, the Duma. It was a
short and perhaps timid step but promising. However, the Duma's
wings were soon clipped.

Nevertheless, things did move in the agrarian field, in education,
and in the public services generally up to the outbreak of war. That
brought widespread unity and freedom from party strife, which
might have lasted but for the heavy reverses suffered, the inefficiency
of the government, the disastrous influence of the Tsarina, enslaved
by the evil charlatan Rasputin—and one must add the Tsar's fatal
admixture of high-handedness and weakness. When the president
of the Duma warned him that revolution and anarchy might be on
the doorstep his comment was: "Again that fat-bellied Rodzianko

has written me a lot of nonsense, which I don't even bother to answer." *

On March 12, 1917, representatives of workers, soldiers, and both left-wing and moderate Socialists met in the Duma building and formed a council or "soviet," a term with which the world has become familiar. This is regarded as the day of revolution. It was that of the fraternization of the Petrograd garrison with the demonstrators in the street, the aim of nearly all revolutionaries. Between them the Duma and the soviet set up a provisional government, in which a Socialist named Alexander Kerensky became Minister of Justice. So far, though it was a revolution, it had taken a more or less bourgeois form. Yet it ended the monarchy. On the fifteenth the Emperor Nicholas abdicated and on the twentieth he was arrested.

The immediate effects were confusion, a drop in industrial output, and demoralization of the troops. The German government hesitated, partly because it was fettered on the Western Front, partly because it toyed with the hope of a deal with the revolution. Who can doubt in the light of later knowledge that, had the Central Powers struck in the midst of the disorganization, the forces already available would have sufficed to crush resistance? If so, Germany might have been able to switch nearly all her strength westward before American help arrived. In her agony and upheaval Russia made yet another contribution to the cause of the Entente, perhaps the greatest of all.

In May the soviet accepted an invitation to join a coalition cabinet. This time Kerensky became Minister of War and of the Navy, and his influence was decisive in what immediately followed. The Germans had sent into the country by stealth, like a plague microbe in a test tube, a certain Vladimir Ilyich Lenin. He headed the extreme or Bolshevik party and opposed the military offensive advocated by Kerensky. However, Lenin's time was not yet come. Kerensky had the majority. He appointed Brusilov commander in chief, and the offensive was launched on July 1.

It was powerful numerically. The troops had been chosen as the least intoxicated by the revolution, and the Siberian element was strong. The excellent plan was for the main blow to be struck against the South Army under Count Bothmer, near Brody, by two armies (thirty-one divisions) on a forty-mile front, and five days later Kornilov's Eighth Army (thirteen divisions) to attack the Austrians farther south along the Dniester and in the foothills of the Car-

* Mazour, p. 414.

pathians. The main northern attack came as no surprise to O.H.L. In fact, a few days before it began, Ludendorff telephoned to Hoffmann to ask whether it could be nullified by a counteroffensive. Yes, said Hoffmann without hesitation, provided four divisions came from the Western Front. He can hardly have believed his ears when told that they would come. They were the last troops in this war to be sent from west to east over Groener's well-organized railways.

Bothmer's army was composed of troops of three nations: four German divisions, three Austrian, and one Turkish in line. The Russians came at it in the old style, as though untouched by the revolution. They gained a promising success on the first day. But neither their burst of enthusiasm nor their discipline lasted. That weakness and the enemy's reserves took the steam out of the offensive, which ended with no further progress. The same thing happened against the little Second Austrian Army on the left, in Böhm-Ermolli's army group. But Kornilov's assault on July 5 from Stanislau in the direction of Halicz and Dolina was another matter altogether. Tersztyansky's Third Austrian Army was taken by surprise and its defense was overwhelmed by the weight of the Russian thrust. Here the advance exceeded twenty miles in the center of a front of about sixty. The situation was critical because the Russians were threatening the oil wells of Drohobycz. Once again, however, their chances were thrown away. They would advance no longer, and any slight effort they made was checked by German reserves. As Hoffmann put it later, if Russian morale had not been so bad the shave would have been still closer.*

It was touch and go whether the counteroffensive could be launched and only at the last moment could Hoffmann be sure that the Russian advance a little further south had been brought to a standstill near Halicz. He had summoned to prepare and control the bombardment an inconspicuous colonel on the retired list named Bruchmüller, whom he had employed in a successful minor operation in April. Later on this man was nicknamed *Durchbruch Müller* ("Break-through Miller") from the astounding effects of his bombardments and barrages. He was one of the greatest artillerymen of the war. The infantry assault began on July 19 in bad weather, which made the Galician clay holding. Bruchmüller's tremendous fire completed the demoralization of the Russians, so that a penetration of nearly ten miles was made on the first day. The attackers then

* Hoffmann, II, 177-180; Schwarte, V, 380-387.

wheeled half-right to roll up the front, and first the Southern Army, then the Austrian Third Army joined in, division by division. Resistance was trifling; the Russian troops were no longer fighting and were in many cases streaming toward their homes. The Russian gains in the Kerensky offensive were more than wiped out.

As already recorded, the Rumanians had been driven back in December, 1916, to the Russian frontier and a front covering their last province of Moldavia. The army had since been reorganized with the aid of a French military mission. On July 22, as a contribution to Kerensky's offensive, the Rumanian army and the Russian Fourth Army launched an attack between the fortress of Focsani on the Seret and the Carpathians, a front of some sixty miles. The Rumanians at least fought with spirit and won initial successes. However, on August 6 Mackensen counterattacked and drove them back. The Central Powers could not spare the troops needed for a decisive success, so both sides went to ground again.

In the north the front ran for about a hundred miles along the lower Dvina, but for the last thirty miles to the sea the Russians held a large bridgehead covering the city of Riga. It had long been looked on by the Germans as a menace, though one would have thought that by this time nothing could have made a Russian army menacing. However, Ludendorff suggested its capture. Hoffmann "naturally said yes," and, equally naturally, sent for Bruchmüller. Twice Ludendorff telephoned that he must have the divisions without which the offensive would have been impossible, and twice relented.* He hoped that a victory at Riga would appear to threaten Petrograd, though the capital was 300 miles away, and would thus unnerve the Russian government.

On September 1 Bruchmüller's massed batteries opened fire without registration, so as to secure surprise, but the five hours' bombardment did its job. Three divisions of General von Hutier's Eighth Army crossed the wide river by pontoon bridges and met no resistance to speak of. Again the Russian soldiers did not fight. However, they cleared out with such speed that only about 9,000 prisoners were left in German hands, a mere trifle by the standard of the moment. Riga was not much of a battle, but it has some interest as the last fought between the forces of the German and Russian governments in the First World War.

After the failure of Kerensky's offensive in July, Kornilov was

* Hoffmann, II, 183.

appointed commander in chief in place of Brusilov. The new man, brave and vigorous but rattle-brained, was expected to be a popular choice because he had commanded the Petrograd garrison and been the agent for the arrest of the Tsar. He became swollen-headed, perhaps aping the young Bonaparte, and in September attempted a *coup d'état*; but his troops refused to follow him and his plot broke down ignominiously. The Bolsheviks profited and the situation of Kerensky, Prime Minister since July, was undermined. Yet the Bolsheviks were not ready and several weeks passed in the harangues, counterharangues, and anarchy typical of the stage when a weak government is defending itself against fanatical foes on the eve of revolution.

It came in November. The government found itself helpless to resist because it had no backing but a few battalions, a handful of officer cadets, and—rather touchingly—a recently formed regiment of women. By November 7 all was over.* The Bolsheviks seized power with no more difficulty than Hutier had found in capturing the Riga bridgehead, and the last semblance of constitutional government ended without any exhibition of heroism. Kerensky was lucky to escape with his life.

On November 8 the "Provisional Workers' and Peasants' Government" was formed. At its head there was to be a Council of People's Commissars, which might be called a Cabinet. Lenin assumed the chief office of president or chairman, in effect Prime Minister; Leon Trotsky was given the charge of Foreign Affairs; and Joseph Stalin became Commissar of Affairs of the Nationalities. All opposition parties were outlawed, not merely because Russia was still in a state of war on the frontiers and threatened by civil war, but also because the Bolshevik party philosophy had no place for any of the trappings of democracy. Its conception of government was rule by a highly organized and highly privileged body, deliberately kept small and separated from the rest so that its zeal and purity should be maintained without tarnish.

In order to be free to impose its will on the country the Bolshevik government needed peace. There its views and those of the German government were similar. The sooner peace was signed, the earlier would the bulk of the German armies reach the Western Front for

* The title "October Revolution" is of course due to the fact that the old style calendar was still in force, so that ten days have to be subtracted, making November 7 October 28.

the decisive victory. It was all a matter of terms. A meeting was arranged at Brest-Litovsk and an armistice came into force on December 16 as a preparation for negotiations. Though the Foreign Ministers of the Central Powers arrived to take part in these, the master of the situation was Max Hoffmann. The Soviet delegation put forward the solution of peace without annexations. The answer it received was that it would be accepted on two conditions: first, the Entente Powers must agree to it also; second, it was not to apply to Poland or the Baltic states. The first proviso was reasonable from the point of view of Germany and Austria, since they were aware of their enemies' intention to dismember their empires. An ironical feature of the conference was the arrival of a youthful and ardent Ukrainian delegation to open separate negotiations with the Central Powers and obtain independence. Eager to feed their hungry people from this splendid granary, the Central Powers signed the so-called "bread peace" with the Ukraine on February 9, 1918.

Trotsky refused to accept the conditions of the Central Powers: autonomy for Poland, Finland, Estonia, Latvia, and the Ukraine, and the continued occupation of Russian territory. He tried every weapon from vituperation to bluff. The last took the form of a declaration for "no peace, no war." The Soviet government would simply withdraw from the war without making peace. He had chosen in Hoffmann an unpromising subject for a bluff. Trotsky was in fact playing into the hands of the opposition because Hoffmann welcomed an excuse to march into the Ukraine and organize the exploitation of its grain and flour. The Central Powers denounced the armistice on February 18 and moved forward. On March 3 the Bolsheviks had to sign a peace treaty stiffer than that originally projected in that Russia had to cede the region of Ardahan, Kars, and Batum to Turkey.

The Treaty of Brest-Litovsk was ratified on March 29, and, bereft of her ally, Rumania had to yield in May. The German and Austrian forces moved on to complete the occupation of the Ukraine. Hoffmann proposed to march on Moscow, which the Bolsheviks had made the capital, and was confident that he could do it, but he was overruled. Russia lay at the mercy of the Central Powers for the rest of the war. It was Foch and Haig who saved Bolshevik Russia.

In the War of the Spanish Succession ("Marlborough's Wars") a virtually unrelated war had taken place, the campaigns of Charles XII of Sweden against the Russians. The same thing occurred on a smaller scale in the First World War. Returning to his own country after the collapse of the Russian armies, a brilliant Swedo-Finnish soldier, General Mannerheim, was appointed by the new independent government of Finland to raise an army against the threatening Communist party, which was receiving arms and some active aid from the demoralized Russian troops. He began his campaign by gaining control of South Ostrobothnia—to ensure supplies from Sweden—in January, 1918. Ostensibly to support the Whites against the Reds, a German force landed at Hangö, seventy-five miles west of Helsinki, on April 4, Mannerheim did not want interference, but without this seasoned force, 9,000 strong, the civil war would probably have been long drawn out. With the aid of the reinforcement it was quickly ended. The Germans must, therefore, be considered benefactors to Finnish freedom.

In July, 1918, Czech troops which had fought in the Russian ranks were trying to make their way out of Russia via Siberia and the port of Vladivostok, which some had already reached. One body approached the town of Ekaterinburg, the Red Ural capital, where the imperial family was imprisoned. Fearing that the Emperor would be liberated the local soviet ordered his execution. The soldiers did their job thoroughly. They shot the Emperor, the Empress, their children, their doctor, three servants, and even the family's spaniel. Then they burned the bodies thoroughly so that no "holy relics" should be available to stir up reactionary sentiment. So passed Nicholas II. He was a notably ineffective ruler. One of his generals recalls watching him yawn throughout a vital conference. Yet he was honest, well-meaning, and extremely loyal to his allies. He is said to have died bravely.

The record must end there. The Russian Revolution was an event even more tremendous than the war in which it was born, but its ardors and miseries do not belong to the history of the war. From that point of view the results to be noted are: first, the elimination of a great partner in the Entente; second and consequently, the transfer of well over half the German strength in Russia and Rumania and of four Austrian divisions to the Western Front; third, grain and meat for the Central Powers from the Ukraine at a time when hunger was stalking the streets of their cities; fourth, a new lease of life to Turkey, who reoccupied her frontier with Russia and beat the Germans in the race for the oil of Baku.

Though the Russian armies won some great victories, defeat was more often their lot. Their achievement was none the less gigantic. The German divisions on the Eastern Front numbered 99 on May 1, 1917. At this date 141 German divisions stood on the Western Front as compared with 153 German, Austrian, and Turkish in Russia and facing Russians in Caucasia. If it is argued that Caucasia should be omitted as an outer theater—like Mesopotamia and Palestine, where the British were engaging the main Turkish strength—the dispositions of the Central Powers were: Western Front, 141 divisions (all German); Eastern Front, 141 divisions (99 German, 40 Austrian, 2 Turkish). Few, even of those who have studied this war, realize that Russia ever shouldered a burden as heavy as this. Had the Russian troops been better led and equipped, Germany must have cracked a year earlier than she did. Russia fought a great fight.

Chapter IV

THE CRISIS OF THE SUBMARINE WAR

THE German government's decision to introduce unrestricted submarine tactics changed the nature of the war at sea. Henceforth Germany staked all on strangling Britain and France, minimizing the strength of American intervention, cutting off and rendering helpless the British forces in Palestine and Mesopotamia and the Allied forces in Macedonia. Large resources were switched to the attack on commerce, not only directly to U-boats but by striking with surface warships against the Scandinavian trade and traffic in the English Channel and Mediterranean, as well as by a few vessels converted into raiders which undertook long cruises in distant seas. The German admiralty did not bank on destruction alone. It accounted fear an ally. It estimated that the U-boats would scare off the seas and confine to port two-fifths of the neutral shipping, and this was a fundamental factor in its calculation that the war would be won in five months. The first month of unrestricted war, February, 1917, was cheering. Forecasts came true. In the United States—February being the first of the two months of armed neutrality—American ships were "interning themselves." In British ports neutral skippers were refusing to sail.*

The peril was ghastly. It called for no speculation and little calculation. The statistics were all the more terrifying for their bald simplicity. If losses went on rising as they rose up to April—and what was to stop them?—the Central Powers would win the war. The fate overhanging the Entente was not fully known to the people at large. They realized that they were in grave danger, but its magnitude was hidden because the figures for losses were not re-

* Millis, *Road to War*, p. 400; Corbett, *Naval Operations*, IV, 355.

vealed and the sinkings of U-boats were overestimated. The strain was borne chiefly by the governments and the naval and military authorities.

We see now that the introduction of convoy acted like a spell. We know that it was urged by the Prime Minister, David Lloyd George; by the commander in chief, David Beatty; and by the American Admiral William Sowden Sims. We are apt to conclude that opposition to it and delay in putting it into force were due to pedantry and stupidity. Admiralty policy has since been stigmatized as "obstruction," and worse. In fact, the objections seemed cogent to many able men who were as eager to find a remedy as the three named. Putting too many eggs into one basket, or in other words presenting huge targets to the enemy, was the chief. Then, said the pessimists, the merchant service was not trained to keep station, so that straggling would be inevitable and would increase the risks. Convoys would have to sail at the rate of the slowest ship. The arrival of a mass of shipping all together would congest ports. The system would involve loss of time and waste of effort.

Yet surely these instructed minds should have formed a clearer picture of what actually happened. The allegedly fragile egg basket was in fact armored. The masters of the merchantmen, neutrals as well as British, French, and American, learned to keep station. British brains, with American professional advice, devised separate convoys for fast, medium, and slow ships. Convoys became so frequent and could be directed to so many ports that congestion was hardly increased. The delay, after the system was fully working, was mainly due to zigzagging to throw out the waiting U-boats, and that paid its way. And one other prophecy of the opponents of convoy, that it would demand as many ships in the escort as there were ships to be protected, proved utterly false. We are entitled to join in the condemnation of those who balked the convoy system, but it is cheap to rail at them. In many cases they were the men who later directed it so ably.

Draw a triangle with a base from Ushant, off Brest, to the Fastnet Lighthouse, off the southwestern toe of Ireland, and with Land's End at the apex. Roughly speaking, this narrow strip represents the main killing-ground of the U-boats, the graveyard of merchantmen, in the year 1917. The worst of the others were the North Sea—the Scandinavian trade being the heaviest sufferer— and the Mediterranean.

Before the introduction of the convoy system, the chief method of defense was patrolling by flotillas, including submarines, and by aircraft. To each of a series of "patrol areas" destroyers, patrol vessels, and small craft for mine sweeping and other tasks were allotted. Operations were coordinated by a department of the Admiralty, but commands were local. Outside coast areas the protection of trade routes was the task of the senior naval officers on the various stations. Mine barrages were established and the net laid by the British in the Channel was finally imitated by the French and Italians in the Straits of Otranto: "Submarine hunting," however, was the main feature of the system. It proved hopelessly impracticable. Where done at random, it might as well have been left undone. On information of the presence of a submarine it was worth trying, but time and time again the attacking forces reached the scene too late.

In British home waters—under which title the Admiralty included the Atlantic, the Arctic, and the Bay of Biscay because they were dealt with from home bases—the Germans employed, month after month, over 90 but under 100 U-boats. In August, 1917, the total reached 101, the only month in which the hundred was passed. Two-thirds and upward of these operated from German ports, the remainder, smaller boats, chiefly from Ostend and Zeebrugge. Their losses were trifling—ten for the first three months of unrestricted warfare, during which period they sank 844 ships of all nationalities. Their risks were less than those of fishermen in some waters.

The first convoy sailed from Gibraltar on May 10. It consisted of sixteen ships, comparatively lightly escorted till they were met by six destroyers from Devonport on the eighteenth. No submarine was encountered. To cut a long story short, by August a great system of Atlantic convoys had been established: fast (12½ knots) from Halifax to western British ports; medium (10 knots) from New York to both western and eastern ports; and slow (8 knots) from Hampton Roads and Sydney, Nova Scotia, to western and eastern ports alternately. In the same month it became necessary to institute west-bound Atlantic convoys, which shortage of escort vessels had precluded to begin with. Up to August the total sinkings of British, Allied, and neutral vessels in home waters by torpedo and mine since the start of unrestricted warfare were: February 212, March 297, April 335, May 230, June 230, July 201, August 148. They continued thus: September 141, October 118, November 103,

December 107, a total of 2,122. For these eleven months the losses in U-boats were 4, 4, 2, 5, 4, 6, 4, 10, 7, 8, 6. Of these 60 boats, six were sunk by seaplanes and one by the American Queenstown destroyers *Fanning* and *Nicholson*. Three were sunk by their own mines and two were interned in Dutch and Spanish ports.* The number engaged did not increase, but the building rate enormously exceeded the losses, whereas British and American shipbuilding failed to keep up with theirs. As late as September the British Admiralty considered that, though ruin had been avoided by a hair's breadth, the end might still be defeat unless losses could be further reduced. Concentration of shipping on the short North American route, withdrawal of the British merchant marine from purely foreign trade, and drastic cutting of imports were methods that could not be intensified. As for the Mediterranean, the losses for the eleven months were 844 ships, two-fifths of those in "home waters," and only two U-boats were sunk in 1917, both by the French, one of them by a French submarine. Another sinister effect was that the calls for escorts, cruisers, and even on occasion battleships as well as destroyers, were becoming serious. Beatty began to doubt the result of a battle if the High Seas Fleet came out in full strength, since he would have no time to concentrate his detached forces and had not yet been issued a new type of shell in which the defects revealed at Jutland were being remedied. The Grand Fleet was reinforced at the end of the year by five American battleships, commanded by Rear Admiral H. Rodman, and this force became the Sixth Battle Squadron.

To sum up, a victory had been gained, one in which nearly all the active and important work had been performed by Britain, but she was not yet certain of it. She had, however, good cause to feel encouraged.

Apart from the submarine war, the year was not highly eventful. In view of the attitude of the German and British admiralties and commanders in chief it was not likely to witness a repetition of the Battle of Jutland. Yet on one occasion at the end of the year the makings of a secondary action were present. The British had become concerned by the German minesweeping activities in the outer Heligoland Bight. These were generally covered by light cruisers and destroyers, with battleships sometimes held in support a hundred miles in rear, near Heligoland. Beatty ordered his succes-

* Newbolt, *Naval Operations*, V, 424-426.

sor in command of the battle cruisers, Admiral Sir W. C. Pakenham, with the First and Sixth Light Cruiser Squadrons, the First Cruiser Squadron and the First Battle Cruiser Squadron, to attempt to bring the German outpost forces to action. The date, November 17, was well chosen; Admiral von Reuter was engaged on a big sweeping enterprise and protecting his auxiliary craft with his light cruiser squadron. Two battleships were kept off Heligoland.

The effectiveness of the Germans' smoke screen was the main factor in saving their squadron, but the British staff work was deplorable. Information about the German mine fields was issued in different form to two admirals and a large danger area was not marked on the charts of two others, the commanders of the First and Sixth Light Cruiser Squadrons. Then the commander of the First Cruiser Squadron, Vice-Admiral C. L. Napier, for some reason never explained, ambled after the retreating Germans at 25 knots with his squadron capable of 30. Probably the most to be hoped for was the winging of one or two German light cruisers, which would then have been destroyed like the *Blücher* in the Dogger Bank action. Anyhow the chance was missed.

A few more events in home waters may be summarized. German destroyers raided the Channel on the nights of February 25, March 17, and April 21. The first action was a failure though they suffered no loss. The second was a fine success for its enterprising leader Commander Tillessen, who sank two British destroyers and a drifter. The third was a defeat, mainly due to the heroic action of one man. Commander E.R.G.R. Evans in the *Broke* put a torpedo into one destroyer at close quarters, passed round her, and rammed the second in the line. His own helpless destroyer escaped destruction almost miraculously. Evans, who was awarded the Victoria Cross, lived to become an admiral and was known all his life as "Evans of the *Broke*." Thereafter the Germans avoided the narrow waters for nine months.

Vice-Admiral Sir Reginald Bacon, commanding the Dover Patrol, bombarded the destroyer and U-boat bases of Zeebrugge in May, and Ostend in June. The results were fairly good, but such attacks had to be repeated if they were to have long effects, and he did not obtain all the necessary conditions for the rest of the year. On July 15 Commodore R. Y. Tyrwhitt, commanding the Harwich Force, caught six merchantmen off the Texel, drove ashore two which he then destroyed by fire, captured the remainder, and put a stop to an effort to revive German coastwise trade with Rotter-dam. The Germans, however, ended the year well with two highly successful raids on the Scandinavian convoy, on which they inflicted terrible loss. Henceforward Beatty attached a squadron of battle-ships as covering forces to these invaluable convoys. Earlier in the war this would have been considered a shocking heresy, but we now realized that commerce must be protected at any cost.

In the Mediterranean the first genuine convoys—five or six freighters with four trawlers—sailed between Malta and Alexandria at the end of May. The situation was gloomy. Britain had to depend largely on allies, and, though the French provided the strongest fleet and were easy to deal with, the Italians were singularly languid and apathetic, as well as obstinate. Nothing would induce them to patrol regularly the mobile barrage of trawlers and drift-nets which the British navy had established in the Straits of Otranto to con-fine the Austrian submarines and a few German to the Adriatic. Between July 24 and August 19 the so-called Italian "barrage forces," destroyers and small craft, never put to sea. The Japanese, on the other hand, were allies of high value. They kept their destroyers at sea for a greater proportion of their time than the British and at least 25 per cent greater than the French and Italians. They were immensely proud of being allotted most of the work of escorting troop transports, and their efficiency matched their enthusi-asm. Though a few transports were torpedoed, this was the one kind of Mediterranean traffic that could be called satisfactory. The American contribution was relatively small and did not begin until August, but without the five gunboats and three revenue cutters based on Gibraltar, through-Mediterranean convoys could not have been organized.

Convoy was less successful in the Mediterranean than outside it. As elsewhere, the greatest loss was suffered in April, so that it certainly brought about an improvement; but there was no re-semblance to the regular drop in losses which occurred in British home waters. In fact, the tonnage sunk in the month of December was the second highest for the whole year. It thus closed without bringing the uplifting of heart which convoy had already achieved in the Atlantic and off the British coasts.

This brief account has shown that the danger, while even fiercer, was not as widely extended as in the later world war, in conditions which are today more familiar. Submarines could cross the Atlantic;

in fact long-range boats operated off the American coast in 1917 with little hindrance to start with though with no great success, and were active off the Azores. They could not, however, exercise the sustained threat of the Second World War in mid-Atlantic, which was the result of far superior endurance, greater speed, larger numbers (a maximum of 196 in the fourth year of the Second World War as against 140 in that of the First), the use of submarine oil tankers or "milch-cows," and better communications. That fearful ordeal at least the hard-pressed commerce defenders of the earlier war were spared.

In the Mediterranean the Central Powers looked at first sight to be at a disadvantage. The maximum number of submarines based on Constantinople was 4. All the rest, Austrian and German, rising from 24 in February to 34 in December, operated from the Austrian naval port of Pola, at the head of the Adriatic, and had to pass the Otranto barrage twice in each cruise. In fact, however, Pola served the Central Powers well. Apart from the slack Italian defense of the barrage, the Straits of Otranto were very deep, deeper than the whole area of the North Sea, so that the U-boats found little difficulty in ducking the barrage.

No naval battle was fought in the Mediterranean throughout the war, but a spirited naval action occurred on May 15. The Austrian commander was Captain Miklos Horthy, destined for future fame as Hungarian dictator. He came out with three light cruisers to raid the Otranto drifters, while two destroyers simultaneously attacked Italian transports at Valona on the Albanian coast. The raid was a remarkable success. The drifter-line was smashed and fourteen of the craft were sunk. The British crews fought their single 57-mm. popguns with supreme heroism. Skipper Joseph Watt of the *Gowan Lea*, his craft riddled by a cruiser and summoned to surrender, called for three cheers, put on full speed, and rushed at his enemy. When their gun was hit its crew thought of nothing but getting it back into action again. For some reason the Austrian cruiser passed on without sinking the *Gowan Lea*, and Skipper Watt lived to wear the Victoria Cross. At Valona the Austrians sank an Italian destroyer and two out of three transports. In a long running fight with Italian, British, and French ships, the British light cruiser *Dartmouth* was torpedoed by a submarine and was lucky to reach Brindisi, and a mine laid by the same U-boat sank a French destroyer. Horthy himself was badly wounded and his flagship would have been caught had not the Italian admiral turned back at sight of a heavy Austrian cruiser from Cattaro. It was a well-managed raid, but it was not repeated.

It need hardly be said that the Germans had to reshape their estimates—and with them their propaganda. Britain was to have been crippled and starved "before the harvest." The year ended with that objective very far from attainment and disquieting signs of diminishing success. This could not be concealed from the country. It was indeed proclaimed by the leader of the Catholic party, Matthias Erzberger, in the Reichstag. And Germany and Austria were far hungrier than Britain, in some places near starvation. British blockade was beating counterblockade.

Chapter V

THE MUD AND BLOOD OF THIRD YPRES

WHEN Sir Douglas Haig made up his mind to attack in Flanders he did not know that the French army was for the time being virtually down and out. When that fact came home to him he had to think again. He might now have to face practically the whole German force in instalments, with little French aid but for a small picked army which Pétain was putting under his command. On the other hand, he was certain that a big German offensive against the French would lead to a disaster. On the basis of optimistic intelligence reports, he magnified a deterioration in the German army into something more serious than it was in fact. Though his plans—like his temperament—were less venturesome than Nivelle's, he cherished the hope that "the fetters of trench warfare would be broken." * He would go on.

The campaign had been in his mind for eighteen months. Here he found strategic objectives missing in the battles of the Somme and Arras. To root out the hornets' nests of Ostend and Zeebrugge would of itself be a triumph. To drive the Germans off the Flemish coast would lay open a flank to further attacks. Unhappily, the terrain was unpromising. Inside the coast sand dunes ran a belt of reclaimed marsh six to eight miles wide and crisscrossed with drainage ditches like a spider's web. Farther inland the ground improved, but the subterranean water level was still high. East of Ypres ran a narrow ridge which dominated the plain. The southern end, known as the Messines Ridge, could be taken in a separate operation, and Haig decided to capture this first.

He has been reproached for making two bites of the cherry,

* Edmonds, *Short History*, p. 244.

but he could hardly have mustered enough heavy artillery to do it all in one.* He had made remarkable preparations against the Messines Ridge. British tunneling companies, risking every hour a miserable death in the bowels of the earth from countermining, had driven nineteen shafts into the ridge and packed the chambers at the ends with gigantic charges. The Battle of Messines did put the enemy on the alert, but it is not the case, as Sir Hubert Gough believed, that the famous German forts were built between the two attacks, though a very few may have been.†

The Messines bombardment began intermittently on May 21 and was intensified from June 2. Heavy and medium guns numbered 756, about one to 20 yards on a front of eight and a half miles, and guns of all natures 2,266. At 3.10 A.M. on June 7 the mines went up and a colossal barrage 700 yards deep crashed upon the defenses. A blinding flash, a shuddering of the ground, a thunderous explosion, dense black smoke clouds spreading far and wide, heralded the assault. A divisional commander watching from Kemmel Hill described the scene as a vision of hell.‡ The noise was distinctly heard in England.

In semidarkness, deepened by the smoke and a mantle of dust, nine divisions, including one Australian and the New Zealand, with three more in reserve, moved to the assault against five German divisions, with four in reserve. The defense was demoralized from the very start, and many forward companies were already destroyed. Only after the crest was reached did any fighting beyond isolated combats take place. The struggle then became stiff and continued for a week, but all counterattacks were smashed and all objectives taken. British losses, light in the first assault, were increased by overcrowding on the ridge. The fortress of the Messines Ridge had been captured by bringing up to date and vastly expanding the methods of siege warfare as practiced by Marlborough. It was the right way to take such a fortress, but not the way to win a war unless the success were ruthlessly exploited.

Haig had first to get the government's leave to pass on to the greater offensive on the Ypres front. In London he found the War Cabinet not unnaturally alarmed at the prospect of the B.E.F. taking on the whole German array single-handed. It talked of waiting for

* Gough, p. 139.
† Thurlow, p. 11.
‡ Falls, *History of the 36th (Ulster) Division*, p. 92.

the Americans. However, the First Sea Lord demanded an offensive. Jellicoe indeed alarmed Haig by what his visitor described as his pessimism. He said that if shipping losses continued on their present scale it would be impossible to maintain the war in 1918. Haig of course realized already that things were bad, but such language was new to him. "This was a bombshell," he confided to his diary on June 19.* The War Cabinet finally gave Haig permission to undertake the Ypres offensive, but with the proviso that if losses proved disproportionate to results it would consider launching an offensive in Italy. It could attempt nothing really big farther afield because shipping would not run to it, whereas France and Italy were connected by two double railways.

Haig's plan was ambitious. First he would capture the rest of the ridge. An advance along the coast, aided by a landing, would follow. Finally he would thrust toward the neutral Dutch frontier. The northern front up to the Belgian right flank had long been under the commander of the Second Army, the veteran Herbert Plumer, a steady, reliable, but not very enterprising man. Haig wanted more drive than Plumer was likely to give to the offensive. He therefore brought up from his right flank the commander of the Fifth Army and his staff and handed over the main business to him. Hubert Gough was forty-six, and it is doubtful whether—apart from royal princes, nursed by hand-picked staff officers—there was then another army commander as young. In their several ways both were good soldiers. The trouble was that Gough's different ideas demanded revision of arrangements already made by Plumer, and that this caused delay. It is true that the French army under Anthoine also fell behind its program—partly because, owing to Pétain's pledge after the mutinies, so many men were on leave. It might have been possible, however, to launch a modified first attack without French aid. As it was, there was an interval of six weeks—of magnificent summer weather—between the close of the Battle of Messines and the day the infantry went "over the bags" at Ypres. The interval was to be paid for.

Sitting on the ridge and overlooking the British front, the Germans realized at once that a new attack was coming. They moved up reinforcements, thinning their front opposite the French. For the cause of the Entente it was a blessing, but a bad job for the British and Anthoine's First French Army. The Germans had put into

* Blake, p. 240.

force the defensive system introduced in the Battle of Arras, with an outpost zone to cushion the shock, and behind it a deeper battle zone. They had sown the ground with little concrete forts, some containing several chambers and impervious to any shell up to a direct hit with an 8-inch. Their counterattack divisions were ready to strike in the dangerous period apt to occur when an attacker reached his objective but before he had consolidated it and repaired the confusion.

On July 11 the Allies opened an air offensive with 500 British and 200 French aircraft, and after very heavy fighting to the end of the month gained a limited mastery. The bombardment started on the eighteenth, but owing to postponements the infantry did not move until the thirty-first. Gough attacked with nine divisions, Plumer on his right and the French on his left acting more or less as flank guards. The German army group commander wrote that day in his diary that he felt undisturbed because the Germans had never faced an attack with reserves so strong or who knew their job so thoroughly. The assault nevertheless began well, but hard counterattacks robbed it of much of its gains, so that the maximum advance, on Gough's left flank and Anthoine's right, was about two miles. That evening heavy and persistent rain fell. It was heartbreaking. The ground absorbed the wet like a sponge but kept it close to the surface. The shell holes, already close together though not yet lip to lip as they were to be later, filled with mud and water. Urgent though it was to maintain the pressure, there was nothing for it but to await better weather. The rain lessened, but the ground dried only to a small degree. Worse still, the second phase, the Battle of Langemarck, postponed to August 16 and undertaken in dry weather, was on balance a grievous failure. Very little ground was won and that only in the centre. From August 15 onward the Canadian Corps fought a long and fierce diversionary action near Lens, which ended successfully. On the twentieth the French signalized their progress to recovery by a victorious blow delivered by the Second Army under General Guillaumat on the Verdun front. These limited actions, however, caused the Germans only temporary anxiety because they were quickly recognized for what they were.

Once more the offensive came under political review. Once more Haig obtained leave to continue, though a minority in the Cabinet would have preferred to shift the main British effort to Italy. Haig had now changed his mind about methods and leadership. He put the main job into the hands of Plumer, who took over from Gough the front facing the ridge where it widened into a plateau. Plumer decided on extreme deliberation. He would secure the ridge by three separate battles, with very limited objectives, colossal barrages, and divisional frontages narrowed to about a thousand yards, so that a large proportion of the infantry, sometimes two brigades out of the three, should be available to deal with the German counterattack divisions. Between the three bounds there were to be pauses for the forward movement of artillery. Meanwhile intelligent and devoted work by the Royal Engineers, pioneers, and carrying parties kept supplies moving. Plank roads were constructed and hundreds of miles of "duck-boards" were laid across the mire. The conditions were none the less taking on the aspect of a nightmare: casualty-clearing stations with helpless patients under shellfire by day and air bombing by night; horrible scenes in horse lines and on the tracks.

Then, astonishingly, a good phase followed. The ground remained in a fearful state, but it dried; in fact Plumer's first two battles, Menin Road Ridge and Polygon Wood, were won in dust clouds. The third, Broodseinde, was triumphant but fought in rain which began on October 3. The German command became rattled, first holding its counterattack divisions forward to intervene quicker, then drawing them back again because their losses from artillery fire were so disastrous. The concrete forts were stormed, though at terrible cost. The Second Army was well up on the ridge.

But what was to follow? It was autumn now and the weather seemed to have broken for good. "*Witterungsumschlag. Erfreulicherweise Regen, unser wirksamster Bundesgenosse,*" wrote Crown Prince Rupprecht in relief on October 12.* He had been finding his troops growing unreliable and was preparing a withdrawal. Haig still wanted to secure the untaken part of the ridge at Passchendaele for his winter line. When he consulted Plumer and Gough they said they would prefer to stop but were prepared to go on. And so it was decided. He had long ago abandoned hope of an offensive on the coast. The Germans had in fact taken his little bridgehead over the Yser on July 10.

These last phases have ever since molded opinion on Third Ypres.

* Rupprecht, II, 271. ("Break in the weather. Welcome rain, our strongest ally.")

Few talk of that just concluded or have ever heard of it. Even the name of the last of all, "Passchendaele," is generally but erroneously applied to the whole offensive. Grim it was indeed. The battlefield had now the appearance of the moon through a telescope. Several men were drowned in the water or smothered in the mud. The moral and physical strain tried men to the uttermost and carried many beyond breaking point. The Australians had played a magnificent part in Plumer's three bounds and continued to do so. The turn of the Canadians came at Passchendaele, with which their country will always connect them. The approach to the remains of the little town had to be made along two causeways between bogs and streams. The first attack on October 26 made small progress, but on November 6 Passchendaele was taken. On the tenth the footing on the ridge was broadened. Then Haig stopped the offensive. He had another all but ready to touch off.

British losses from July 31 to November 10 numbered about 240,000. This represented a terrible toll, though seven-twelfths of that of the Somme, which lasted three weeks longer. The French in Anthoine's small army, who behaved well throughout, lost only 8,525.* The losses of the Germans, who employed in the battle very many more divisions than the British and French combined, may be estimated at 260,000.

Just before the last phase in Flanders, on October 23, Pétain launched his second attack, with Maistre's Tenth Army. It was another brief operation, prepared with minute care and supported by an enormous artillery concentration. Its physical object was to secure a better position on the Chemin des Dames, where a ragged front, difficult and costly to hold, was the legacy of the Nivelle offensive. All went like clockwork, the perfect offensive. But the Battle of Malmaison was morally a follow-up to that of Verdun, nine weeks earlier. It was an experiment which the commander in chief trusted would prove to be a tonic.† From that point of view also it was successful. The advance which secured the fort of Malmaison and the failure of the only big counterattack on October 29 led to a German withdrawal on a wide front. About 12,000 prisoners were taken. Ludendorff for a moment expected another

---

* *Armées Françaises*, Tome V, Vol. II, p. 179. The casualties were 5.3 per cent of the troops engaged, as against 12.3 per cent at Malmaison (for which see below).

† Pierrefeu, p. 186. The chapter is headed "Trial Operations."

French offensive, but Pétain was feeling his way and was satisfied with what he had got.

It is idle to speculate on what would have happened if the precious fine weather had not been allowed to slip away in Flanders; all that can be said with confidence is that the results would have been better and the losses smaller. Haig could not have begun the offensive in the spring and at the same time have carried out his attack at Arras as demanded by Nivelle. It is doubtful whether he could have refused to undertake the Arras offensive. The War Cabinet would probably have forbidden him to do so. However, for reasons which have been given, he allowed a long time to elapse between the Messines and Ypres offensives.

The weather in August, and still more in late October and early November, is the chief factor in the horrible reputation which hangs about Third Ypres. The second is a belief that the offensive was mere blind bashing. This is not the case. Tactics were never more skillful. The gunners caught on to the German methods of counterattack and with the cooperation of the R.F.C. so plastered all hidden ground that on several occasions German divisions were either pinned down or were so depleted and exhausted when they got within striking distance that they failed utterly. In many cases the infantry tackled the forts—pillboxes, as they called them—with skill, working round them under cover of Lewis gunfire and then killing the defenders at close quarters with rifles and grenades. However, even with good tactics, the human body is lucky to prevail over ferroconcrete, and many brilliant attacks failed, with nothing to show but a few corpses sprawled about the strong points.

It is hoped that the foregoing brief account will make it clear that popular verdicts on this battle, and on the British commander in chief's conduct of it, are too much simplified. The subject is one calling for constant qualifications. This applies particularly to his decision to continue the battle after the weather had broken. Most of the hostile judgments have come from those ignorant of the atmosphere on the German side. At the start the Germans often outfought the British. Toward the end the British could count on winning if they could get to close quarters. And it was largely the churning of the ground into a morass by their own artillery that held them up.

Those who saw it will never forget that battlefield in the wet: as far as the eye could see a vision of brown mud and water, with a mixture of both spouting to extraordinary heights when heavy shells exploded in the ground; patient men trudging along the "duck-boards," bent a little forward by the loads on their backs; equally patient horses and mules plodding and slipping under the weight on their packsaddles. It called for nerve and endurance, which were not wanting.

Chapter VI

ITALY IN THE LIMELIGHT— MACEDONIA IN THE SHADE

L LOYD George failed to induce his colleagues to send a British army to Italy. However, the British and French did send in 1917 a useful contribution in heavy artillery (guns and personnel). They also made plans for powerful aid in emergency, the initiation of which goes to the credit of the unfortunate Nivelle. What the Italian commander in chief, Cadorna, feared was the appearance of a strong German force in aid of the Austrians. He was also nervous lest the Germans should violate Swiss territory in order to strike Italy on a broader front. In April, Nivelle sent Foch, then without a command, to Italy, while his staff officer, Weygand, visited Switzerland. Foch outlined arrangements for speedy support of the Italian armies in case of need. The details were then worked out by administrative officers.

The French railway authorities promised sixty-two trains a day, but only twenty-eight of these to run through to concentration areas in Italy. The rest would carry French and British troops to French frontier railway stations, and these contingents would have to march across the mountains to stations on the Italian side. No detail was omitted. Timetables, halts for meals, billeting, sanitation, port facilities for supplies, contribution to supplies by Italy, military and civil jurisdiction, even notice boards, were provided for. Elasticity was left for variations. It was a fine achievement of Franco-British-Italian staff work.*

Meanwhile Cadorna had realized that the Germans were not coming just yet. He had promised to take part in the Allied offen-

* Edmonds, *Military Operations, Italy,* pp. 27-31.

sive, but did not strike until May 12, when the battles of Arras and the Aisne were over. It goes without saying that he battered away at the Isonzo front, in the Tenth Battle. He assembled 38 divisions against 14 Austrian. This big battle lasted seventeen days. The Italians gained ground on both flanks, east of Monfalcone and Plava, but in neither case two miles. Ground on these rocky plateaus took a lot of winning. As usual, Italian losses were far heavier than Austrian, over two to one, roughly 157,000 to 75,000. In June, Cadorna suffered a minor catastrophe on the other flank, in the Trentino, losing all his gains to a counterattack.

The Trentino having failed him, for his next offensive on August 18 he returned to his old beat, in the Eleventh Battle of the Isonzo. This time his numerical superiority was not quite as great, but still nearly two to one. On the Carso the Duke of Aosta's Third Army was completely repulsed. North of Gorizia, however, the Second Army, with a new commander, Luigi Capello, gained the first substantial success since the Sixth Battle in August, 1916. The Austrians were driven back beyond their last prepared defenses on the Bainsizza. They would have had to retreat further had not Cadorna called a halt because he believed the Germans were now indeed coming. He had advanced up to five miles on a front of ten and given the Austrians a shaking. Again the Italian losses were huge, all but double those of the Austrians. A British gunner, Lieutenant Colonel C. N. Buzzard, commanding a heavy group, commented:

"The hours named were never adhered to. . . . Fire was lifted far too soon; infantry had no support in passing over four or five hundred yards. . . . The remarkable thing is that with such utter lack of cooperation between artillery and infantry the Italian infantry ever take any of their objectives. The artillery preparation is good; a large number of the infantry are quite heroic; but to advance behind a proper creeping barrage is unheard of." *

Conrad (created a field marshal in 1916) had proposed to Ludendorff an Austro-German offensive. He was all the keener for one because he did not believe that U-boat war would bring England to her knees. In February the Emperor Carl dismissed him, but appointed him to command an army group in Italy, on the Tirolean front. His successor was General Arz von Straussenburg, intelligent but not strong and under the Emperor's thumb. Alfred Krauss was considered but turned down, probably because Carl

* Edmonds, *Military Operations, Italy*, p. 36.

knew he could never be master with Krauss beside him. Ludendorff kept Conrad's plan in mind. After the victory at Riga in early September he sent an army headquarters (Fourteenth Army: General Otto von Below), seven divisions, an air force, and heavy artillery to Italy. Ludendorff and Arz decided to attack on the Isonzo because they lacked strength for an offensive of envelopment on both wings of the semicircular front, which, if successful, would have almost completely destroyed the Italian army. In fact, Conrad's front was skinned of resources and he, the *fons et origo* of the operation, could contribute only minor aid. Even on the main front the Central Powers mustered only 35 divisions against 41 Italian, including reserves in each case.

The original break-through was to be made by Below's Fourteenth German Army in the Julian Alps, across the upper Isonzo above Tolmino. The little town of Caporetto (Karfreit to the Austrians) has given its name to one of the most famous battles of the war. Below's army contained the seven German divisions and five Austrian. His right wing in the mountains was a crack corps of three Austrian divisions and one of German Jägers commanded by Alfred Krauss. It was originally intended as a flank guard, but its climbing and marching powers, plus its leadership, proved a vital asset.

At 2 A.M. on October 25 a great bombardment began.* The German used heavy mortars—and lent forty-eight to Krauss—to smash the Italian first position, and heavy artillery against the second and third. They also drenched the defense, particularly the batteries, with shell gas, against which the Italian gas masks gave little protection. The assault was launched in wretched weather, rainy and foggy, with in the mountains snow showers, one of which temporarily held up part of Krauss's attack. This was, however, only an incident in a brilliant day for Below's army, that which mattered most. One of his German divisions covered nearly fourteen miles, rolling up the Italian front.† After a tough struggle in the mountains Krauss's men found little further resistance. One battalion had forty-eight hours' marching with a first fierce fight and later little combats before it got a rest. The two Austrian armies farther south, especially the coast area, fared much less well, but the Italian front was completely breached by the twenty-fifth, and the two northern

---

* Mid-European time, used by both belligerents. Summer time had ended.
† *Österreich-Ungarns Letzter Krieg*, VI, 529.

corps took 30,000 prisoners. The Italian Second Army was smashed and in flight. Single units fought good rear-guard actions, but the mass collapsed. Aosta's Third Army on the right simply retreated, without being broken by the Austrian First and Second Isonzo Armies. To the north the Italian Fourth Army, left high and dry by the flight on its flank, swung back in desperate haste. In fact, the Austrians, and even to some extent the Germans, were baffled by their own success. They had practically no cavalry, only a handful of armored cars, and little motor transport for the exploitation. What might have happened had they been better furnished can only be guessed. Some Italian units in formed bodies marched past Krauss's troops into captivity, calling out, "*Evviva la Austria!*" and "*A Roma!*" * The first genuine attempt to stand, forty miles in rear of the original front, was made on the Tagliamento. It was a formidable obstacle and the final objective of the Austro-Germans. Ludendorff wanted his German divisions, but the opportunity was too good to be missed. On November 2 Krauss got troops over by a half-destroyed bridge—and back the Italians went again. The rout ended on the Piave, to reach which Krauss's men covered seventy miles as the crow flies. Attempts by small German and Austrian forces to cross achieved very limited success. Anyhow, Below had had enough and knew that Franco-British forces had arrived. The Central Powers claimed 275,000 prisoners, 2,500 guns, and a vast booty which included thousands of horses and big stocks of food, both very valuable to them at the moment.

The Italian catastrophe was due more to bad leadership than to bad soldiers, though pacifist and treasonous influences played their part. For the attackers Caporetto was a great feat of arms, especially for Below's Fourteenth Army, led with superb confidence. One of the corps commanders, Berrer, was killed in a truck, up with his leading troops. If a corps commander has to die in war, this is surely a happier way to do it than to walk into a chance shell. Yet, bold as was the strategy of the Central Powers, "hindsight" suggests that Conrad with another German division and two or three Austrian divisions, might have broken through to Vicenza and that then there would have hardly been an Italian army left when the British and French arrived. As it was, only Conrad's left took part in the pursuit.

The British and French came quickly, thanks to the good prep-

* Krauss: *Das Wunder von Karfreit*, p. 65.

310 THE GREAT WAR

arations. They numbered six French and five British divisions and army troops. By November 10, the day the Italians established themselves on the Piave, four French divisions were assembling at Brescia and Mantua. The last British division arrived on December 12. The commanders of these contingents, Plumer and Fayolle, were chosen for their seniority and prestige. The two chiefs of staff, Foch and Robertson, and the two prime ministers, Painlevé and Lloyd George, were already in the country, all, as it were, coming to hold Italy's hand. Foch found Orlando, the Italian prime minister who had taken over in the midst of the disaster, determined to resist but displaying his resolution in an odd way. Italy, he said, would fight on, even if it had to be in Sicily. "It is on the Piave that you must resist," said the smiling Foch.* The Italians had now a new commander, Armando Diaz, eleven years Cadorna's junior and livelier in every way. Foch while he remained, Plumer and Fayolle after he had gone, took the line with the Italians that the Franco-British troops had come as a reserve and expressed their pleasure that the Italians had held the Piave without Allied aid. However, on November 25, to show that Italy's allies had not come as mere onlookers, four divisions entered the line where the Piave emerged from the mountains. Soon all was quiet and the reorganization of the Italian army could proceed.

On November 5 a conference at Rapallo set up, at Lloyd George's suggestion, a Supreme War Council, to consist of the President of the United States and the prime ministers of the other allies or their representatives and permanent military members. Its duties were to lay down military policy and the allotment of troops to the various theaters. Lloyd George hoped that he had established the political control he desired, but he reckoned without the Germans.

In the Battle of Monastir, General Sarrail, now known as commander in chief of the Allied Armies of the East, had won sufficient success to encourage him to renew the offensive in the spring, and had been reinforced. He had nineteen divisions (six French, six British, six Serbian, and one Italian). The extra British division was sent to mark British fraternity and did not denote any sensible increase of optimism about the campaign. General Milne was less despondent than the War Office. He doubted whether the strength sufficed to give the Bulgarians a real beating, but thought they might

* Foch, *Mémoires*, II, xxxvi.

pack up their gear and go if they were sufficiently hard pressed.

Early in the year both British and French took heavy knocks from German bombers. The Germans worked to an admirable principle: to every side show, Macedonia, Palestine, and Mesopotamia, they sent a few first-class aircraft, which obtained enormous success because the French and British planes were generally poor. Here, by good luck, Vice-Admiral Sir Cecil Thursby, commanding Eastern Mediterranean, was able to send more modern naval aircraft from the Aegean Islands, which brought about a great improvement. The fierce conflict ended in May when the German bombers, needed elsewhere, disappeared from this front.

Milne was called on to make a strong diversion on the eve of the main offensive. He attacked west of Lake Dojran on the night of April 24. The ground was a jumble of hills divided by ravines and strongly entrenched by the Bulgarians, in fact, the "Grand Couronné" and its offshoots formed one of the half dozen strongest field fortresses of the war. The attack failed with severe loss. It is only fair to Sarrail to say that the objective was not dictated by him. He had suggested the Struma valley, but Milne preferred Dojran because the wide spaces of the valley called for more troops and by June gains would probably have to be abandoned owing to the activity of the anopheles mosquito, a worse foe than the Bulgar. Then Sarrail had to postpone his attack. When he decided to launch it on May 9 Milne had to repeat his diversion on the evening of the eighth. Its fate was similar to the former effort. Sarrail's offensive was a failure too owing to lack of concentration and the quality of German battalions in the Crna bend.

The whole front fell into a mood of angry depression. The Serbians did not hide their disgust. Most of the Russian units had "gone Bolshy." Sarrail's professional and moral stock had reached an all-time low. The armies were plagued by malaria. British opinion had hardened against Macedonia. The government decided to transfer to Palestine the recently arrived British division, and later a second. The international force was glum, sick, and inharmonious.

It was distracted by an influence other than malaria and Sarrail's military inconsistencies—by the local politics into which he entered with what appeared unseemly zest. The British naturally felt gratitude to Venizelos and his party, but they did not desire to overthrow by force the opposite party, including the crown, in a country where their own position was somewhat ambiguous. They dreaded the role of bully. On the other hand, France was the leading spirit in the theater of war; the command was French; it was France that had re-equipped the Serbians. This conflict between principle and loyalty to the alliance affected the government and its instruments on the spot: the minister in Athens and the chargé d'affaires when he was withdrawn; Lord Granville, British diplomatic agent with the provisional government of Venizelos at Salonika; and most of all Milne.

Sarrail blustered. He talked of sending an international force to drive the Greek royalist troops out of Thessaly, where he considered they menaced his rear, and of requesting the French navy to destroy the bridges over the Corinth Canal and that between Euboea and the mainland. To Milne this was dangerous nonsense, but he did send a brigade to Katerini as a precaution, a very different matter. The troops were received with black looks, which changed to smiles within two days. A deputation from the town came to request that two hundred young men should be allowed to enlist in the London Scottish. The brigade stayed there three months. Sporting officers discovered that there was excellent woodcock shooting, had guns sent out, and happily forgot the war.*

The solution was to compel the Greek government to withdraw its troops to the Peloponnesus, which it agreed to do. But a further series of differences and embroilments, including gross ill treatment of Venizelists, followed. Venizelos demanded the abdication of King Constantine, with the somewhat paradoxical but possibly sound argument that it was the only means of saving the dynasty. The French decided to do it and the British government, doubtfully and rather shamefacedly, agreed. The French rushed out a "High Commissioner" M. Charles Jonnart, who rushed the business through. The King was advised by his prime minister M. Zaimis to submit. He announced that "solicitous as ever of the interests of Greece" he would quit the country accompanied by the Crown Prince or Diadoch, whom France and Britain debarred from the succession. Constantine did not formally abdicate, doubtless hoping that one day he would return. He sailed on June 14 and his second son, Prince Alexander, ascended the throne. In justice to the French action it must be added that the British government genuinely believed King Constantine to be a pro-German; that his cabinets had undoubtedly received loans from Germany; and that a section of the royalist

---

* Falls, *Military Operations, Macedonia*, I, 226-229.

press had become critical of the activities of royalist extremists. Yet the German wireless comment was stinging, though impudent in view of the fate of Belgium: "For the first time the Entente has carried through with complete success a joint military action. This success has been won at the expense of an army which had previously been disarmed and a people who had been starved" (by naval blockade).*

Venizelos became prime minister once again. He hurried forward, with French and British aid, the organization of a remobilized Greek army, and divisions were sent north as they became ready. The strange spectacle was seen of national and revolutionary forces, who might have been at each other's throats in civil war, serving together. The Venizelist divisions bore territorial titles—Cretan, Seres, Archipelago—those of the regular army bore numerical titles. For a time they were separated, the Venizelist divisions serving on the right wing under Lieutenant General C. J. Briggs, commanding the British Sixteenth Corps, and the regular under French command. No signs of ill will between them were observed. Apart from combats and raids, the front remained quiet for the rest of the year.

The somber background to a spartan campaign was the chain of hospitals, which from mid-June—even though Milne abandoned the Struma valley and drew his forces back to the hills—began to fill up with malarial patients. During the war about 110 per cent of the British Salonika army were treated in hospital for this disease, which means that many suffered more than one bout. Not all went into hospital. One officer was wont to relate that when attacked he drank a bottle of whisky neat and that when he woke up the malaria was gone.

The gaudy background was the city of Salonika, its well-known White Tower Restaurant, its theater where the audience maintained a continuous uproar and officers climbed out of boxes to join the actors and especially the actresses on the stage, its bawdyhouses and drinking dens. Such as its amenities were, they were brought to an end in August by a vast and disastrous fire which left the greater part of it a shell and rendered thousands of civilians homeless. But, for the exertions of the troops and the Royal Navy, and the heaven-sent arrival just before of two modern British fire engines, nothing would have been left.

Elsewhere the troops found relaxations. The British, after their

* Forster, p. 129.

kind, played football. They played it even within range and sight of the enemy. The Bulgarians did not interfere, but threw over a warning shell if any drill began. The private soldier considered this a proper policy. Officers formed two packs of hounds, with contributions from English hunts, and again the Bulgarians must have collaborated, because hounds which entered their lines in the Struma valley almost invariably returned to kennel.

When Georges Clemenceau became French prime minister in November he quickly recalled General Sarrail. To succeed him in command of the Allied Armies of the Orient he sent General Guillaumat. The new man came like a breath of fresh air. He was firm and decisive, but affable and courteous. He proved an excellent organizer and in particular pushed on the equipment and training of the Greek regular forces. All who met him, including Milne and Prince Alexander of Serbia, liked and trusted him. It was sad that such relief should have been caused by the departure of a distinguished soldier, with a great record in 1914, and in this theater, the credit of his brilliant early advance into and retreat from Serbia, to say nothing of a considerable victory at Monastir in 1916. Sarrail had unhappily become so rash that, left unchecked, he might have started a civil war in Greece; arrogant, secretive, unaccountable, and personally inactive, spending nearly all his time in Salonika, unlike Milne, who spent half his time bumping over bad roads in his car to visit subordinates and troops. Clemenceau's decision was right and the sense of deliverance was natural.

Chapter VII

CAMBRAI—THE GREAT EXPERIMENT

THE tank, "a self-propelled bullet-proof landship," had never been used as its farsighted pioneers had intended. Their vision had been assault in mass, whereas British armor had been used in what they contemptuously described as "penny packets." One reason was that there had never been enough. In fact, though Britain had invented the weapon, the French had put in thrice as many in Nivelle's offensive as the British at Arras.* The tank was not primarily destructive. It was primarily demoralizing. The number of men killed or wounded by tanks in the course of the war was minute in proportion to the total. The moral effect was tremendous.

Two men recommended the Cambrai front as good tank country. The first was Brigadier General H. Elles, commanding the Tank Corps; the second Brigadier General H. H. Tudor, commanding a divisional artillery there. It was the gunner who made the bigger contribution. He suggested a surprise assault and, to ensure surprise, omission not only of the usual preliminary bombardment but even of registration, the range being found by survey and calculation. On this front the British were up against the Hindenburg Line, with its two systems, five hundred yards to over a mile apart and each consisting of front and support trenches, and its vast barbed-wire aprons, still unrusted and in sunlight giving off a blue sheen intimidating to behold. To cut enough lanes by artillery fire would have taken long and lost the chance of tactical surprise. That method was not needed. The tanks would flatten the wire. They would render further service: if they advanced with the infantry, it would not have to move as close to the rolling artillery barrage as had

* Falls, *Military Operations, France and Belgium 1917*, I, 494.

become the practice in order to keep hostile machine guns silent. Barrages had become highly accurate and infantry bold in approaching them. Better to have a few men hit by a British 18-pounder shooting short than a line mowed down like corn with a scythe by a German machine gun. "Mon, the barrage was that fine ye could ha' lighted your pipe at it!" a Highland soldier declared after a successful attack at Ypres. And a poet wrote, years after the war:

> Slowly we creep towards the curtain's hindmost fringe,
> So close that the shells swoop over our very shoulders—
> A turn of the head and they would catch your cheek!
> They are bursting now scarce fifty paces on.
> Sublime are the red fury,
> The swiftness and the weight of their descent.
>
> Away behind me come my hoplites, stooping
> Under their loads and to make room for the shells.*

A barrage which infantry could hug thus—allowing for the hyperbole—would be impossible with unregistered fire and uncalibrated guns. So let a ragged barrage move farther ahead and the tanks do part of its job. And the mass of extra artillery brought in need not fire a round before zero hour.

The weather favored the venture. It was fine but misty day after day. Trucks carrying stone for the thinly metaled roads and even light steam rollers could work close up to the front by daylight, and the Germans saw little or nothing of other preparations. On the debit side the victory of the Central Powers in Italy was most unhappy. The British had none too many troops to spare and they, like the French, had arranged to send six divisions to Italy if she were in trouble. Actually only five were sent, making eleven in all, but at Rapallo the Italians were demanding fifteen, and for some time Haig was in doubt as to what the final call would be.

In the end he assembled 19 divisions for the attack by General the Hon. Julian Byng's Third Army. Byng was allotted 324 fighting tanks, as against some 48 employed at Arras. Five cavalry divisions, three British and two Indian, stood ready for exploitation. The R.A.F. contingent was immensely strong, but flying conditions were too unfavorable for it to achieve much in the way of support. The Germans had only six divisions—only two on the frontage first to be

* Barnes, p. 26.

assaulted—and were outnumbered to about the same extent in artillery.

Byng's aim was to smash through the Hindenburg Line, seize crossings over the Saint-Quentin Canal, and capture the high spur of the downs on which stood Bourlon Wood; then he hoped to seize Cambrai, but mainly to confuse the enemy. The vital exploitation was to be northward to the canalized Sensée River, seven miles north of Bourlon Wood. The German line ran west-northwest, so that the British, arriving on the canal near Oisy-le-Verger, would be ten miles behind it, and would bring about a precipitate retreat and heavy loss in artillery, if not in prisoners. Two-thirds of the tanks were to be used against the Hindenburg position and the rest held in reserve to capture another strong defense system, some three miles in rear. This was a mistake and one of the few in the planning. When commanders are faced by a first objective as tough as the Hindenburg Line they are apt to devote too great a proportion of their resources to it. The calls on tanks were likely to be heavy further on and only a small proportion of the primitive and trouble-prone tanks of those days could be counted on to fight for both objectives. Half for the Hindenburg Line, half for exploitation, including the rear line, was the allotment that would have paid best.

Otherwise the conception was very fine. The British had invented a revolutionary weapon, ranking with novelties such as the breach-loader and the submarine; they had at last found ideal ground, an all-weather, unscarred tank battlefield which offered strategic results better than those on which they had fought to please the French command; and they had evolved fresh tactics to suit the first use of the new weapon in the predominant role. In the background, however, was a nagging doubt whether reserves would suffice for a long and hard-fought battle. Malmaison was doubtless to be the last major French activity of the campaigning season, so that the Cambrai offensive would benefit by no diversion, though Pétain had moved up a strong corps of cavalry and infantry to aid in exploiting success. German troops from Russia were arriving. One division was to fight at Cambrai.

The surprise came off. The German army group commander recorded the day before that Irish prisoners had talked of an attack in this region,* but no precautions were taken on the spot. The German troops believed a big attack must be preceded by a bom-

* Rupprecht, II, 290.

bardment lasting at least several hours, perhaps several days. What happened was that at 6.20 A.M. on November 20 nearly a thousand guns opened fire with a mighty roar and that immediately afterward the defenders saw a line of great engines and wave upon wave of infantry bearing down upon them. No wonder they wavered.

The trenches of the Hindenburg Line were unusually wide and formidable obstacles to tanks. These, however, carried on top vast bundles of brushwood and a device to tip them forward, so that the tanks could cross the trenches on them. A fair proportion were ditched, but at first practically none were put out of action by the enemy. There was no German barrage; indeed at many points practically no opposition of any kind. By evening the advance exceeded three miles; both Hindenburg systems had been breached. One calamitous episode, however, made a blot on the victory. On the right wing at Flesquières, a ruin perched on a hilltop through which the Hindenburg support system ran, a field battery knocked out the tanks one by one as they breasted the slope, and the infantry could not break through without their aid. Though this mishap was repaired early next morning, it had a serious effect on the timetable. The commanding ground of Bourlon Wood was not captured, and though the Saint-Quentin Canal was reached, it was too late to put the cavalry through. Had this been a summer battle, the shortcomings might perhaps have been remedied that evening, but soon after 4 P.M. darkness was gathering. One hundred and seventy-nine tanks were out of action, though only sixty-five by German fire.

Haig directed Byng to capture the Bourlon ridge on November 21. A spirited assault broke through the rear line at Cantaing. Another secured Fontaine, east of Bourloon Wood, but the wood was not taken. The impetus of the attack was beginning to run out. O.H.L. and Prince Rupprecht were hurrying reinforcements to the scene. Four divisions arrived on this day; seven more were on the move. Haig told Byng that, since he might be called on to send more troops to Italy, he would be unable to maintain a long-drawnout and costly battle. Next day Fontaine was lost, but on the twenty-third the whole of the 300-acre Bourlon Wood was taken after fierce fighting for which only sixteen tanks could be mustered. This was open warfare, the first that British troops had seen for a long time, but for the relatively small affairs in the pursuit to the Hindenburg Line early in the year. The wood was the center of the struggle. The Germans now had plenty of artillery and many

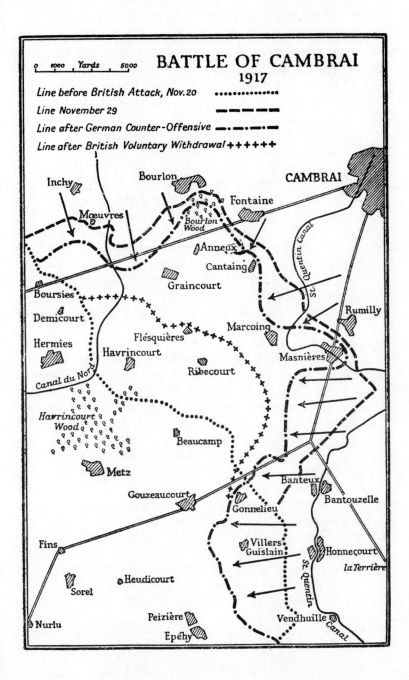

BATTLE OF CAMBRAI
1917

0 — 1000 — Yards — 5000

Line before British Attack, Nov.20 ••••••••••••••
Line November 29 ▬ ▬ ▬ ▬ ▬
Line after German Counter-Offensive ▬•▬•▬•▬•▬
Line after British Voluntary Withdrawal ++++++

Inchy
Bourlon
CAMBRAI
Mœuvres
Fontaine
Bourlon Wood
Anneux
Cantaing
Graincourt
Boursies
Rumilly
Demicourt
Marcoing
Hermies
Flésquières
Masnières
Havrincourt
Canal du Nord
Ribecourt
Havrincourt Wood
Beaucamp
Metz
Gouzeaucourt
Banteux
Bantouzelle
Gonnelieu
Fins
Villers Guislain
Honnecourt
la Terrière
Sorel
Heudicourt
St. Quentin
Peizière
Nurlu
Vendhuille
Epéhy
Canal

St. Quentin Canal

machine guns, cleverly and tenaciously used. The battle swayed to
and fro. In the attack on Bourlon Wood the village was penetrated
and lost. The Germans following up, got a footing in the northern
fringe of the wood but were then held. On the twenty-fourth they
secured half of it, but in the afternoon the British again entered the
village. The wood was a wonderful observation post, commanding
the battlefield. "The crown of battle, looming up above the combatants, was the great circular mass of the Bois de Bourlon." *

Ludendorff was in a state of nervous tension, talking on the
telephone about a thousand details. His nerves had well-nigh gone
once in Russia and were not to survive defeat in 1918. But he
boldly milked inactive fronts for reinforcements and his excellent
tactical eye was hardly required, since it was obvious what should
be done. The British Third Army, by reason of failure to advance
farther northward and its shortage of reserves, had got itself stuck
in a salient position, a bag some six miles deep and seven miles wide.
General von der Marwitz, commanding the German Second Army,
was ready to attack the salient on either flank and hoped not merely
to eliminate it but the force within it. Prince Rupprecht was extremely confident. He believed that for years no such opportunity
had been presented to inflict on the British at the least a stinging
Teilniederlage (partial overthrow). On the evening of November
27 orders were issued to the Second Army to launch the counteroffensive on the thirtieth: main assault against the southern flank
of the salient, so as to take the British not only in flank but—since they
were facing generally north—in rear also; secondary assault from
the north, west of Bourlon Wood; though no less than twenty divisions were available, more would be sent in the event of a great
success.

The arrival and assembly of the powerful hostile striking force
did not go unmarked by British observation posts. In particular
Lieutenant General Sir Thomas Snow, commanding the corps just
outside the battle on the right, sent urgent reports that the enemy
was massing in strength. For some unfathomable reason the staff of
the Third Army did not issue any special warnings; nor did it order
such tanks as had already been repaired or refitted in the workshops
to be sent forward again.

The Germans struck at 8.30 A.M. on the thirtieth after a heavy
night bombardment. The infantry came on in great style and in

* Falls, *History of the 36th (Ulster) Division*, p. 161.

accordance with its finest traditions. The local command on the southern flank boldly made use of the valleys for its thrusts, tactics which may expose columns to fire from higher ground but which have a deadly effect upon the defense if successful. By such methods and by the speed and enthusiasm imparted to the assault, the Germans broke in deeply, at one point nearly three miles. And they did not merely cause the right of the British salient on the new-won ground to cave in; they also captured the original British position farther south on a frontage of three miles. They penetrated here as far as Gouzeaucourt, two miles behind the front. Fortunately the Guards Division, having been relieved after heavy fighting and serious loss up at Bourlon, was still at hand. It threw the enemy out of Gouzeaucourt, but counterattacks to recover more ground failed.

On the north flank affairs were very different. Here the Germans, on breasting the ridge west of Bourlon Wood, had to move down a gentle slope, bare of cover and in full view of the defense. The British, on the other hand, were sheltered by the trenches they had captured or had dug new ones, so that the bombardment with high-explosive and gas did little harm. It was a remarkable spectacle, recalling the Battle of Mons, or even former wars rather than anything British troops had witnessed since 1914. The German infantry was as bold here as on the southern flank. It advanced in a series of "waves" or double lines, in places eight or even ten of them, and in rear small columns in artillery formation. But the British guns, firing on them frontally from the south and in enfilade from the west, shattered them and brought them to a speedy halt. The gunners were firing over open sights, jubilant and excited at finding such targets as they had never seen. When German batteries appeared, halted, and tried to unlimber, the horses were at once shot down and the men driven from the guns. The Germans did win a little ground, but most of that had been voluntarily abandoned. The general result was a sharp German reverse.

On the southern flank, where they had been victorious, the German effort was nearly spent. On the evening of November 30 Prince Rupprecht summed up the battle in a way characteristic of his common sense and honesty: "If the success is still not by a long way as great as was expected, it must nevertheless be accounted a sharp defeat of the enemy." * Next evening, no further success worth

* Rupprecht, II, 299.

mention having been reported, he concluded that the offensive was dead. Bitter fighting did continue, but it was on a small scale and on the familiar pattern, trench bickering with hand grenades. The last sparks of the battle were extinguished in an immense snow blizzard, still recalled by the survivors of those who experienced it.

Meanwhile Haig had concluded that he must yield some more of his gains because, as the result of his successful northern defense, the sack was now as deep as it was wide. He therefore ordered a withdrawal on his left and center to a front including Flesquières and a section of the Hindenburg Line. This was carried out with no trouble on the night of December 4. Gains on the northern flank were now not more than half as great again as the losses on the southern, which made the ringing of the church bells at home in celebration of the first victorious advance appear an act of folly. The casualties on both sides were similar, about 45,000; The British took 11,000 prisoners and the Germans 9,000.

On both sides errors had been made. The Bavarian Crown Prince considered that the assault on the southern flank had not been sufficiently concentrated against the vital objectives. He mentions too an incident, trifling on the face of it, which shows that the famous German staff machinery was not impeccable. At a conference before the counteroffensive Ludendorff spoke of the importance of taking the high ground about Flesquieres from the southeast and with a stroke of a charcoal pencil on the map showed how this should be done. Von der Marwitz remarked: "I will take good note of that curve." As a consequence, claims Rupprecht, the Second Army made its heaviest thrust too far north. If this were really so, the blame would fall on the army, since the orders, issued in good time, clearly indicated the direction of the main thrust.* In general, however, its achievement was splendid.

On the British side an official enquiry into the catastrophe of November 30 put the blame on the rawness and indifferent powers of resistance of the troops. The official British historian believes it to have been rather due to the inability of senior commanders to take their chances and points out that two of the three corps commanders concerned were later replaced.† It would seem that both factors counted. However this may be, the Battle of Cambrai was the type of the battle of the future and its influence on the Second World War was as great as that on the remainder of the First.

* Rupprecht, II, 297-300.
† Edmonds, *Short History*, p. 272.

Chapter VIII

THE OUTER THEATERS OF WAR

BY THE end of 1916 the Egyptian Expeditionary Force had reached the Palestine frontier. On January 9, 1917, it captured Rafah in an action brilliantly conducted by Lieutenant General Sir Philip Chetwode with mounted troops, largely Australians and New Zealanders. It netted practically the whole garrison of 2,000. Simultaneously Murray lost one of his four infantry divisions, sent to France. He was, however, strong in cavalry and mounted infantry, with two divisions made up of Australian, New Zealand, and British Yeomanry brigades. He now decided to capture the ancient city of Gaza, the gateway to Palestine. It was held by only seven Turkish battalions and five batteries, two of them Austrian and one German. The plan of Murray's subordinate, Lieutenant General Sir Charles Dobell, was pretty. The mounted troops would form a screen to hold off Turkish intervention from the east and southeast while the infantry took the place from the south. It had to be done quickly because communications were stretched and it was doubtful if 9,000 horses could be watered anywhere but in Gaza.

On March 26 the coup was nearly brought off. It might have been quite but for fog, accidents and misunderstandings. Intervention, under the vigorous leadership of Kress von Kressenstein, came promptly—for Turkish troops—but not in great strength. On the British side the cavalry was prematurely withdrawn to water just when it—not the infantry—had all but captured Gaza. The Turks were thus able to close in on the twenty-seventh and take the British infantry in enfilade with artillery. Dobell broke off the battle and withdrew to his original position. Murray cabled a misleading report which made Robertson suppose he had won a success, as a result of which he was informed, probably to his dismay, that his "immediate objective should be the defeat of the Turkish forces south of Jerusalem and the occupation of that town." He tried again to take Gaza on April 19. The situation was now changed because the Turks had dug themselves in along the Gaza-Beersheba road. The approach to their position was almost a glacis, and the British attack, gallantly as it was pressed, suffered a bloody repulse, with a loss of nearly 6,500 as against 2,000 on the Turkish side. This was too much for the War Cabinet and Robertson. Murray was recalled.

His successor, General Sir Edmund Allenby, who had commanded the Third Army at Arras, was a tall heavily built cavalryman, nicknamed "the Bull" by reason of his formidable appearance and still more formidable temper. He took over a discouraged force and raised its spirits in a matter of weeks. One might have expected the independent and critical Australians to find him too authoritarian and brusque, but they rejoiced in his strength. Like most new men he demanded reinforcements, and got them. Two divisions were sent from Salonika; another was formed from British and Indian units in the theater. Another had already been formed under Murray from yeomanry not remounted since the Gallipoli campaign. Allenby moved general headquarters from Cairo up to the front. Dobell had already been dismissed by Murray. Allenby formed two corps headquarters (Lieutenant Generals Sir E. S. Bulfin and Sir Philip Chetwode). He also formed a cavalry corps headquarters (the Desert Mounted Corps, commanded by the Australian Lieutenant General Sir H. G. Chauvel) and, having been sent two yeomanry brigades from Salonika, a new cavalry division, the Yeomanry Mounted Division. Seven infantry and three mounted divisions was a big army for a side show, especially as the Turks were in evil case. Their tinsel dictator had sacrificed vast numbers of them to his megalomania; Yudenich had pounded them in Caucasia; their finest remaining troops had been packed off to serve against Russia and Rumania; they had now, as we shall see, been routed in Mesopotamia; and, typically of Turkish troops, their askers had deserted by scores of thousands.

One last inflated scheme of Enver's collapsed. A large Turkish army of fourteen divisions, reinforced by a German force 6,000 strong, had been formed to retake Baghdad under the command of General von Falkenhayn. It was found that, though narrow-gauge railways had been cut through the Taurus and Amanus, it was out of the question to maintain such a force in Mesopotamia. At the same time the growth of British strength in southern Palestine had been noted. Troops of the new Seventh Army (Mustapha Kemal) therefore began moving into Palestine, but only one division was present and Falkenhayn himself had not reached the scene when the British attacked.

This was on October 31. Allenby's plan was to encircle and capture Beersheba and then roll up the Turkish front. It has been criticized because Beersheba lay twenty-five miles southeast of Gaza—actually farther south than east—which involved a long delay and gave the Turks a free hand to act as they thought best, and because, had they destroyed the wells of Beersheba, the great cavalry force would have been compelled to withdraw. However, though the Turks defended the wells stoutly, they had not sense enough to destroy them before they were driven out of Beersheba. Before the rolling up had been completed by Chetwode, Allenby modified his plan and ordered Bulfin to break through the Gaza defenses. Falkenhayn had already ordered the abandonment of the city, but the Turkish effort to stand north of it never looked as if it were succeeding. Allenby's maneuver had succeeded in driving the Turks, some units in panic, off the whole Gaza-Beersheba front, but, owing to errors and still more to lack of water, the cavalry failed to make hauls of prisoners as great as he had hoped for. He had, however, routed the Turks and captured a great proportion of their artillery and other material.

The British left wing now fought its way up the coast plain—"the Plain of the Philistines"—little troubled by such weak attacks as Falkenhayn could launch against its uncovered flank. On November 15 part of the force wheeled right-handed into the Judean Hills toward Jerusalem. Now came a phase of the hardest fighting of the campaign. Falkenhayn threw in stronger attacks, some of which were partially successful. Allenby found that the forces he had brought up would not suffice. Finally, after great efforts and considerable loss, he was able to mount an attack on Jerusalem, mainly from the west, with a secondary one from the south. It was completely successful, and on December 9 the chief of the municipality came out to announce that the Turks had gone and to hand over the keys of the city in the style of old wars.

Allenby made his entry into Jerusalem on the eleventh, on foot and without ostentation. He and his troops had met the demand of

Lloyd George, who had bidden him farewell with the words, "Jerusalem by Christmas." The capture of the Holy City and the conquest of southern Palestine did indeed arouse interest and satisfaction in Britain, and its moral value was greater than its material importance.

The Turks made a spirited attempt to recover Jerusalem by an attack with three divisions on December 26. The venture was nearly hopeless from the first, since Chetwode was on the alert and superior in strength to the attackers. The Turks were driven back with sharp losses. Next day Chetwode attacked in his turn and within four days had put a minimum of eight miles between the Turks and Jerusalem. The year ended in quietude with the British firmly established from north of Jerusalem to north of Jaffa, but incapable of a further advance until they had reestablished their communications.

Allenby had taken about 12,000 prisoners and 100 guns. His own losses up to the capture of Jerusalem were about 18,000 as against a Turkish loss of roughly 25,000. In view of the fact that he had odds of well over two to one in infantry in his favor and eight to one in cavalry, his achievement may not seem remarkable. In fact it was hard and costly work to turn Turkish troops out of defensive positions in this hilly, rocky, country. But perhaps the greatest feat was on the administrative side. Only two roads existed on which the motor trucks of those days could be used to any advantage. The bulk of the supplies and munitions were carried by camels, horses, mules, in the hills even donkeys. This was the kind of job the British army was good at.

Palestine was to some extent a political theater of war; Mesopotamia still more so. Britain and Russia had come to an agreement which reserved the zone Basra-Baghdad to the former. Oil and the possibility of raising cotton and increasing grain crops interested the government deeply. Britain's French allies watched the performance which followed with somewhat jaundiced eyes.* Sir Stanley Maude was now directed by the War Cabinet, which Sir William Robertson was helpless to restrain, to take Baghdad. The Turks were so weak and riddled with disease that it was mainly a question of supply. Maude had been furnished with great numbers of river craft, but not till March could he supply four divisions and the cavalry as far north as Baghdad. It must be realized that he had to hold a vast

* Larcher, pp. 341, 357.

country with a population of uncertain sentiments and temper and that his communications were very difficult to maintain. Even so, a ration strength of a quarter of a million as compared with a fighting strength of 120,000 is remarkable. In infantry the Turks assert that they were outnumbered by at least five to one, but their figures are always doubtful and have been proved in Palestine to be incorrect.* In combatant strength British superiority was probably two or three to one.

The advance began on March 5 along the north bank of the Tigris. The Turks made a stand on the Diyala, a tributary entering the Tigris ten miles below Baghdad. Maude promptly established a pontoon bridge across the Tigris under cover of a bombardment and passed his cavalry and part of one of his corps to the south bank. With this leverage he broke the Turkish front on the Diyala and on the morning of March 11 his troops entered Baghdad, abandoned by the Turks. He then pushed out columns to clear the Turks from the neighborhood of the city. He had taken 9,000 prisoners and had completely outmaneuvered the Turks as well as outnumbering them.

The Turkish commander Halil Pasha took up a position on the Tigris some sixty miles above Baghdad with the rags of his Sixth Army. He had been joined by a couple of new divisions each some 7,000 strong. Maude had some cause for anxiety when his agents reported the Turkish plan to recover Baghdad. He need not have worried for, as has been mentioned, the force destined for the operation was diverted to Palestine; but the War Office, not certain that this was so till well into the autumn, arranged to have him reinforced by two newly formed Indian divisions. He did not move again until the intense heat of summer was over. The miserable Turkish Sixth Army, perhaps only 30,000 strong, was now strung out over a vast front of some 250 miles, its right wing on the Euphrates at Ramadi, its left in the mountains on the Persian frontier, facing a lackadaisical though not yet wholly revolutionary Russian force, of which a detachment was in touch with Maude near Khanaqin.† The Turks offered no serious resistance when Maude attacked Ramadi, capturing most of the garrison. Early in November the British cavalry and an Indian infantry division were victorious in two engagements which led to a further advance of twenty miles to Tikrit.

* Falls, *Military Operations, Egypt and Palestine*, II, pt. 2, 453-454.
† Larcher, pp. 349, 351.

On November 18 Stanley Maude died suddenly of cholera in the house in Baghdad in which von der Goltz Pasha had died eighteen months earlier. It is no exaggeration to say that a wave of sorrow swept over Britain at the news. This Irish soldier who had replaced defeat and disgrace by victory was a hero to the people. Perhaps no other soldier aroused a comparable affection, though unlike several others, his name had been unknown outside the army until he received his first independent command. His successor was one of his corps commanders, General Sir W. R. Marshall. He began by driving the Turks out of Khanaqin at the beginning of December.

The R.F.C. had been prominent in all these operations. It brought in news of Turkish moves very quickly and often intervened by bombing the enemy. Both British and Germans were reinforced in the air during the year 1917, but the latter were never strong enough to do more than seize brief opportunities. The relations between British and German airmen and British (or Indian) and Turkish soldiers were very different. In the former there was a knightly, almost a comradely element. When the remarkable young German commander Captain Schultz returned to the theater of war with new aircraft the R.F.C. heard of it at once. To display simultaneously the excellence of its intelligence and its private admiration, it dropped the following message: "The British airmen send their compliments to Captain S. and are pleased to welcome him back to Mesopotamia. We shall be pleased to offer him a warm reception in the air. We enclose a tin of English cigarettes and will send him a Baghdad melon when they are in season. Au revoir."

This spirit was prevalent in the minor theaters of war, where the opposing air forces were small. It was displayed even more strikingly a few weeks earlier in Macedonia when Lieutenant von Eschwege shot down Lieutenant J. C. F. Owen and then defended him with all his power when the Bulgarians court-martialed their prisoner for setting fire to his aircraft.

Maude had indeed made a transformation in the scene. The old squalor had disappeared, though of course this improvement was based mainly on supplies from home. Now the troops in first line ate chilled meat in place of the eternal canned meat which they detested. Chicken farms provided fresh eggs; horticulture provided fresh vegetables. Air conditioning lay in the future, but electric fans were installed in the hospitals, and the buildings had glass windows. The health and spirit of the troops improved simultaneously. Yet the force was astonishingly inactive, not only in the hot season but through most of the cold. After securing Baghdad it sat on its gains, giving the Turks only an occasional push. Militarily, it was an absurd situation, since the Turks had been almost battered to pieces in the spring. But it was in fact a political rather than a military campaign. As this came home to him and he realized that the force was grotesquely strong, Robertson managed late in the year to get its best Indian division, the Seventh, transferred to Palestine, where it would at least find more useful occupation.

It has been recorded that General Smuts left East Africa in January, 1917, after having converted the force from one mainly white South African and Indian to one mainly native East African, with a West African brigade. His first successor was the inspector of the King's African Rifles, Major General A. R. Hoskins, but to please South African sentiment he was replaced in May by Major General van Deventer. The account of this campaign may now be wound up to the end of the war.

When the rains were over in July van Deventer staged a masterly offensive. At this time Lettow-Vorbeck's forces were in three bodies: he himself near Kilwa and a second force near Lindi, these two little places on the coast having been captured by naval forces; the third body under Lettow's chief lieutenant, Tafel, lay at Mahenge, 150 miles inland. The two coast forces contrived to break out, though much depleted, but Tafel was fairly caught and laid down his arms with 5,000 men. Lettow was not done with yet. Leaving his sick behind, he crossed the Ruvuma, marking the frontier with Portuguese East Africa, on November 25. He was by now very short of ammunition, but still hard to catch. Living on the country, hunted unavailingly by columns of British and Portuguese native troops, he kept going for nine months. Then he shed another third of sick askaris, doubled back north, passed round the head of Lake Nyasa, and entered Northern Rhodesia. He was hoping to cross the continent into Portuguese Angola. When, however, he heard of the armistice he surrendered on November 23, 1918.

His achievement will always be remembered with admiration, at least by his countrymen, but it was notable how impotent he became after Smuts had reorganized the British forces and van Deventer had brought his great experience to their handling. In this country no troops tied to wheeled transport could long maintain rapid movement. The porter with his load on his head was still essential away from the few roads. This logically pointed to the formation of a mainly indigenous force, with white officers and a proportion of white noncommissioned officers. Even had the roads been far more numerous and better in quality, white and Indian troops would always have suffered gravely from disease, with enormous wastage. The British did not realize this at first, and the reorganization took a considerable time when they did. But it paid hands down.

Book Five — 1918

Chapter I

LUDENDORFF TAKES THE STAGE

THE Treaty of Brest-Litovsk gave the Germans a wonderful chance to achieve victory on the Western Front by switching over forces now redundant on the Eastern. They decided early that if this opportunity were let slip they would be swamped by the Americans. Ludendorff held a staff conference on the subject before the Battle of Cambrai, on November 11, 1917. How far from his ken was the first anniversary, when German defeat was acknowledged by acceptance of dictated armistice terms!

No final decision about the locality of the offensive was then reached, but preparations were made at all points discussed. Finally it was arranged to make the British the victims and break through between the Scarpe and the Oise—to which they had been compelled, against Haig's wishes, to extend their flank—then wheel and roll up the front northward. The code name "Michael" was chosen for this operation. "Michael" would be followed by "George," in Flanders, once more against the British, who would by then have moved their reserves south. Of 194 divisions in the west by March 21—the total eventually reached 208—71 faced the 26 of Gough's and Byng's armies, the British right wing, and 2,500 heavy guns faced 976.

The British had been forced to imitate the Germans in reducing divisions from twelve to nine battalions. Even then divisions remained under strength, largely because Lloyd George insisted on keeping reserves at home to prevent Haig using them in another offensive. Unhappily the British tried to copy the Germans in another respect and misunderstood the pattern of the defense system of their enemy. They turned the foremost trenches into a "forward zone" to be lightly held, and the second line, two to three miles behind it, into a "battle zone," deepened by redoubts and machine-gun nests. There was to have been a "rear zone," but labor shortage reduced it to a single line and in some places the removal of a spit of turf to show where a trench should be dug. The misinterpretation of the German scheme lay in the fact that the Germans placed only one-third of the defending battalions in keeps, whereas the British locked up about two-thirds in them.*

Another point is that Haig allotted Gough on the right only twelve divisions on a 42-miles front and Byng on his left, fourteen divisions on a 28-mile front. The main reason for this distribution was that arrangements had been made with the French to support Gough, but it was an error, none the less.†

The German armies involved were the Seventeenth (Otto von Below) and Second (von der Marwitz) in Prince Rupprecht's army group and the Eighteenth (von Hutier) in the German Crown Prince's. Hutier had brought the artillery specialist Bruchmüller over from Russia, and his bombardment was the most shattering. Fire opened at 4.40 A.M. on March 21 and continued for five hours. Gas shell forced defenders to wear gas masks. Dense fog, thickest to the south, shrouded the battlefield, so that the British could see only a few yards ahead when the Germans assaulted. Parties passed round and enveloped the keeps, but the main body pressed straight forward. The defense was stout, but it was smothered. By night the Germans had everywhere overrun the forward zone; in places they had secured the battle zone or were fighting within it. The defending divisions were in most cases badly cut up. Signs pointed already to a British disaster. The Germans, by a combination of brute force and clever tactics, were heading for a great victory. Hutier, whose role was subsidiary, had scored the biggest success, which Ludendorff mistakenly exploited at the expense of the main thrust.

Gough committed the two divisions in G.H.Q. reserve behind him and in the afternoon Haig released the two behind Byng. Two cavalry divisions went to Gough's right. Haig also empowered Gough to pull back behind the Crozat Canal, linking the Oise and the Somme. In the air the British were not at a disadvantage and more than held their own in the fierce fighting which broke out when the fog lifted about 11 A.M.

* Wynne, p. 40.
† Edmonds, *Military Operation* , *France and Belgium, 1918*, I, 102.

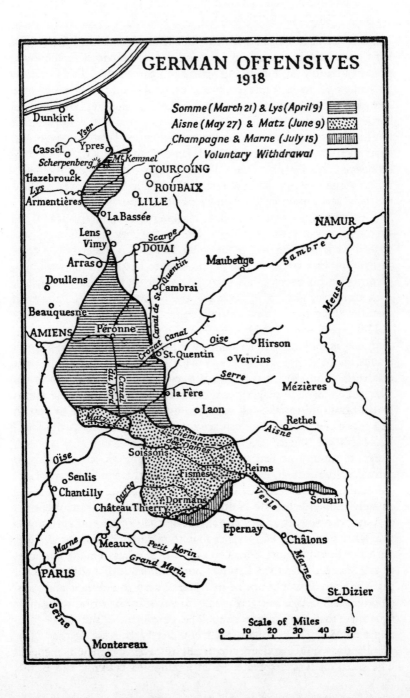

GERMAN OFFENSIVES
1918

Somme (March 21) & Lys (April 9)
Aisne (May 27) & Matz (June 9)
Champagne & Marne (July 15)
Voluntary Withdrawal

Dunkirk

Yser

Cassel
Ypres
Scherpenberg
Mt. Kemmel
TOURCOING
ROUBAIX
Hazebrouck
Lys
Armentières
LILLE

NAMUR

La Bassée

Lens
Vimy
Scarpe
DOUAI
Maubeuge
Sambre

Arras

Doullens
Cambrai

Meuse

Beauquesne

AMIENS
Péronne

Oise
Hirson
St. Quentin
Vervins

Canal du Nord
Crozat Canal
Canal de St. Quentin

Serre
la Fère
Mézières

Laon

Matz
Chemin des Dames
Aisne
Rethel

Soissons
Oise
Fismes
Reims

Senlis
Ourcq
Dormans
Vesle
Souain
Chantilly
Château Thierry

Epernay
Châlons

Marne
Meaux
Petit Morin

Grand Morin
Marne

PARIS

Seine
St. Dizier

Scale of Miles
0   10   20   30   40   50

Montereau

March 22 also opened with fog, but it cleared rather earlier. The R.F.C. was definitely on top now and did its best to help the hard-pressed infantry by low-flying attacks on the enemy. The Germans continued to make rapid progress, especially in the south, where the rest of the battle zone was lost. The Third Army still held its battle zone from the salient left by the Cambrai battle northward, but in fact it remained too long in this salient and was to pay for it. Individual acts of heroism in the defense were numberless, but they influenced the German tide only as a high patch of sand remains unsubmerged longer than the rest of the beach. On the twenty-third the Crozat Canal was lost; on the twenty-fourth the line of the Somme almost down to Péronne, marking here a German advance of fourteen miles in four days. On the twenty-fifth Gough was pushed back another four miles, while Byng, also under heavy pressure but on his own initiative, swung back to keep in touch with him, pivoting on his corps south of Arras, not as yet seriously attacked. An example of *Schrecklichkeit* was the bombardment of Paris with specially built guns of seventy-mile range.

The French were taking over Gough's right, but showed no signs of counterattacking; in fact their infantry was mostly coming up in trucks ahead of the artillery and with little ammunition but what was carried on the men. A gap between the Allies was appearing. The R.F.C. was displaying magnificent courage and self-sacrifice. It had been told to take "all risks," to fly "very low," and to "bomb and shoot everything they can see on the enemy's side of the line." It did all these things.

Pétain, though he had moved or was moving eleven divisions to the aid of the British, was doubtful whether this was the main German attack. He was right to think of his own front, but it was extremely unlikely that the Germans could mount two vast offensives at once. Worse still, it was clear to Haig that Pétain's intention was to fall back covering Paris rather than to maintain contact at all costs with the British armies. Pétain thought that it was Haig's intention to fall back covering the Channel ports. Ludendorff had prophesied that the French would not be in a great hurry to aid their allies and it looked as though he were going to prove right. It was urgently necessary that the defense should be coordinated. But how? The Supreme War Council had failed completely because neither Haig nor Pétain would hand over to it the reserves which it demanded. The situation was desperate. In an attempt to better it the British government sent out, on Haig's demand, the recently appointed Secretary of State for War, Lord Milner, and the C.I.G.S., Sir Henry Wilson, who had superseded Robertson in February.

The visit led on March 26 to the Doullens Conference, a milestone of the war. The President of the French Republic, Raymond Poincaré, took the chair. The others present were Clemenceau (Prime Minister since the previous November), Loucheur (Minister of Munitions), Foch, and Pétain; Milner, Haig, Wilson, Sir Herbert Lawrence (Haig's C.G.S.) and Montgomery (from the Supreme War Council). Haig had been on friendly terms with Pétain. He found most French generals too voluble, whereas this northerner was taciturn like himself and stuck to essentials. He had not been equally well disposed to Foch. Now they were opposite, in his estimation. He wrote in his diary: "Foch seemed sound and sensible, but Pétain had a terrible look. He had the appearance of a commander who was in a funk." *

Pétain remarked to Clemenceau that the Germans would beat the British "in the open field." † He spoke of the defense of the railway junction of Amiens. Foch struck in: "We must fight in front of Amiens. We must stop where we are now." Haig said: "If General Foch will give me his advice I will gladly follow it." Finally a formula was found and signed.

> General Foch is charged by the British and French Governments with the co-ordination of the action of the Allied Armies on the Western Front. He will make arrangements to this effect with the two Generals-in-Chief, who are invited to furnish him with the necessary information.

It may be added that his powers were increased on April 3, when another conference, at Beauvais, decided "to entrust to General Foch the strategic direction of military operations." In this case Pershing and General Tasker H. Bliss, American representative on the Supreme War Council, added their signatures to the document. On April 14 Foch was accorded the title of "Général-en-Chef des Armées Alliées en France."

So the united command in French hands, which Haig had resisted in the case of Nivelle and which had lapsed after the spring offensive of 1917, was established on Haig's initiative. It was a different sort of

---

* Blake, p. 298.
† Duff Cooper, II, 255.

command. In February, 1917, Haig had been placed under the orders of the French commander in chief. Now he was under a "supreme Allied commander" who bore responsibility to Britain as well as France. Foch regarded his appointment in this light.

Having issued orders to Pétain on the movement of reserves, he set out on a series of visits to the headquarters concerned. Pétain canceled the order of March 24 based on the defense of Paris and directed more divisions to Haig's support.

"Act 1, Scene 2" of the German offensive was named "Mars," an extension to Vimy Ridge, north of the Scarpe. It was astoundingly ambitious. Final objective Boulogne, seventy-two miles by road from Arras! * If this had gone as well as the attack of March 21 the war might have been nearly as good as won. Unluckily for the gambler Ludendorff, his nine divisions assaulting astride the Scarpe on March 28 struck four British as good as Britain could then show and of all the types in her army: regular, New Army, and Territorial.† The two south of the river had withdrawn to their battle zone, in general on orders, because the southernmost stood at the hinge of the original German attack and its right had been completely turned. The defenses north of the Scarpe were intact. All were well dug and wired. The Germans attacked with sparkling vigor and skill. They were fought to a finish and beaten by a defense at once elastic and resolute. Ludendorff stopped the attack that very night. "As the sun set behind rain clouds, there also vanished the hopes which O.H.L. had placed on the attack." ‡

The British achievement should be inscribed in gold letters on Britain's roll of honor. The defense of March 28 not only killed Ludendorff's plan to expand the battle but virtually ended the battle itself.

On the rest of the front, on which the southern face of the great bulge created by the offensive had been taken over by the French, things were beginning to go better. The most dangerous feature was the thrust toward Amiens, which caused acute anxiety before it was held. The offensive was closed down on April 5. The Germans were tired out and had outrun their artillery and to a great extent their

* Kuhl, II, 332.

† Right to left: Third Division [regular], Fifteenth (Scottish) Division [New Army], Fifty-sixth (First London) Division [Territorial], Fourth Division [regular].

‡ Edmonds, *Military Operations, France and Belgium, 1918*, I, 75.

transport. Their losses were enormous, and the British and French reinforcements were taking an ever increasing toll.

For Germany it had been a magnificent tactical victory, but not a strategic success to anything like the same extent. Ludendorff was one of the greatest tacticians of the war but little of a strategist. His view was that if one punched a big enough hole the rest would follow. This is often true, but he failed to make the most of the breach he had opened. He should have kept the thrust point north of the Saint-Quentin—Amiens road, but he was seduced into exploiting the easy initial success farther south. Still, he had done what nearly everyone had come to believe was impossible and had taken 90,000 prisoners. He had inflicted a loss of 240,000 (British 163,000, French 77,000) on his foes. But his own casualties were at least as great as, if not greater than, the sum of these totals. He had put a strain upon the German infantry, badly fed by comparison with that of the Entente, owing to the pressure of the blockade, which was to exercise a grave effect within the next few months. For the moment the British were in the worse case. Haig began the month of April with only a single division in reserve out of sixty (including two Portuguese). Sixteen had been or were being made up with drafts largely consisting of lads between eighteen and half and nineteen years of age. For three others reduced to remnants, drafts were not available. Foch had proved a splendid influence, but, on principle stingy with reserves, would not order French troops to take over the front farther north than the Amiens-Roye road. The French would not counterattack until their heavy artillery came up. They had not done so when the next German blow fell.

The British government, professedly on the advice of the C.I.G.S., General Sir Henry Wilson, ordered Haig to supersede Gough by Rawlinson and disregarded the commander in chief's protest. Gough had done all that man could. He was denied an investigation; "democracy demands its victims." * Rawlinson, then British military representative on the Supreme War Council, naturally changed the number of the Fifth Army to Fourth, because this had been his old command until its headquarters had been disbanded. Thus the ignorant believed that the Fifth Army had fled and disappeared.

By April 9 the German "battering train," including 137 heavy batteries, had been moved north to Flanders. The wastage and

* Duff Cooper, p. 267.

fatigue due to "Michael" were, however, so great that the program for "George" had to be cut; the reduction was marked by the change of the code name to "Georgette." The frontage of the offensive was now to be only twelve miles, from Armentières to the La Bassée Canal, but if all went well it was to be extended next day to just south of Ypres. The objective, or rather the general direction, was the rail center of Hazebrouck, but the Germans were prepared to exploit to the coast, which would mean the destruction of the greater part of the British army.

They had a marvelous slice of luck. Horne, pinched for troops, reluctantly postponed the relief of the tired and depressed Portuguese division in the center of the zone to be assaulted. It was to have come out on the night of the ninth. Instead it came out that morning, but without being relieved. The attack was on the pattern of that of March 21, preceded by a tremendous bombardment. On the right the German waves were shot to pieces by the troops of a rested, well-trained British division, but next door they drove the Portuguese in flight from the battlefield. Farther north they rolled back another British division, exhausted and shaken in March. The Scottish Highland division hurried forward to take the place of the Portuguese had been refitting and absorbing drafts, a process only half complete. The Seventh Gordon Highlanders had been to all intents and purposes destroyed. It had suffered a loss of 714 and had hardly a trained noncommissioned officer left. Its ranks were full of "boys." When it moved, the stores issued to it included only nine shovels.* Yet this division began by sharply checking the enemy's advance.

The Germans were disappointed by a maximum progress of little more than three and a half miles, but their success amply sufficed to induce them to stick to their plan of extending the battle north of Armentières against the right of the British Second Army on April 10. Again there was a March-pattern bombardment; again the British were hustled back. The situation was ugly, since Haig had virtually no further reserves. That evening Foch visited him and told him he was assembling a French relief force behind Amiens. Next day German progress was serious only in front of Hazebrouck and to Ludendorff "not satisfactory." Haig was, however, gravely concerned because he had so little room in front of this vital objective. He was a man not given to fighting with words. Now he resorted to them. His famous order of the day ended:

* Falls, *The Gordon Highlanders in the First World War*, pp. 185, 197.

"With our backs to the wall and believing in the justice of our cause each one must fight on to the end. The safety of our homes and the freedom of mankind alike depend upon the conduct of each one of us at this critical moment."

Attacks by the Royal Air Force * hampered German movements on the twelfth, and on that and the two following days the advance generally lagged, but on the sixteenth it secured Messines Ridge. Meanwhile Plumer had been put in command of the whole defense and in front of Ypres had withdrawn from dearly bought ground to the Steenbeck. On the seventeenth the Germans were held with bloody loss and their attack on the Belgians north of Ypres was utterly defeated. Foch had been moving French forces north but, true to principle, holding them back. By the twenty-first, however, he put into line the four divisions of the newly formed Détachement d'Armée du Nord (D.A.N.) to defend the Flanders heights and especially the commanding Mont Kemmel. Haig was still dissatisfied. From this period dates a chill in the relations of the two men, more on the Scotsman's side than the Frenchman's. It is probable that Foch sensed in the British, reduced to rags though most of their divisions now were and in some cases really unstable, a greater stubbornness than in the fresh French divisions. At all events he was completely honest. He had no thought of sacrificing British blood to save French. Soon he was to be reproached by Pétain for endangering the French front to save the British.

On April 24 the German command varied the program by reviving the offensive on the Somme battlefield and striking again at Amiens. Villers-Bretonneux was captured from the British and Moreuil from the French. Villers-Bretonneux—notable for the only considerable tank combat of the war, 13 German tanks and 13 British, seven of the latter light, being engaged—was recovered by Australian and British brigades. And though the Germans clung to some of the ground won here as well as to Moreuil the affair was on balance a bad failure.

In the north the Bavarian Crown Prince and the commanders of his Fourth and Sixth Armies, Generals Sixt von Armin and von Quast, were disappointed. The Belgians, who had not been engaged in a major battle since 1914, had "shattered" the attack launched against them. The anxiety of the German leaders was, however, not to be compared with that of Haig. His divisions were often ghosts. Time after time a hostile attack was followed by a flow rearward

* The creation of the Royal Air Force is described in Chap. IV.

of his weary young soldiers. There was no panic and the defense never broke down altogether. When resistance failed at one spot it warmed at another. This would have been consoling had there been more room, but as it was, every mile increased out of all normal proportion the prospect of utter disaster. And if the Flanders heights went——

Kemmel went on April 25, and the manner of its loss was disturbing. It had been successfully defended by worn-out British divisions; it was lost by relatively fresh French divisions. True, this was a tremendous blow with a colossal bombardment—per battery the most costly day of the entire war * for the British artillery—and an assault by seven fresh German divisions. Even so, there was no getting away from it, the defense was feeble. And next day, when a counterattack was arranged by the Allies, the British divisions advanced alone and the French did not move. This was ominous, even though that afternoon the French began to resist in earnest and the Germans made little more progress.

On April 27 and 28 there was a pause. Foch felt, however, that the Germans had not yet made their final effort. It was vital to prevent them from seizing the rest of the Flanders heights. He shifted reserves further north. He had not long to wait. In the small hours of the twenty-ninth another great bombardment began, changing to high explosive after two hours. The German Fourth Army attacked at 5.40 A.M., again with seven divisions. This time it met with a very different reception and a close and fierce fire fight developed. The French artillery and machine guns, now well organized, staggered the attackers by the weight of their fire. The Germans gained two slight successes only. South of Ypres they drove in the British outpost line. At one point they gained ground from the French, penetrating to the Scherpenberg, the next hill behind Kemmel in the chain of the Flanders heights. Here was a danger spot and the situation was not made prettier by wild rumors that the dent was deeper than was really the case. Everywhere else the assault was smashed with heavy loss.

It was the end. The Channel ports were saved. Haig might feel dissatisfied with Foch, but the Germans by no means made light of the aid which seven French divisions had afforded the British in Flanders. German opinion has since classed the Battle of the Lys as a *Misserfolg* (failure). Strategically, it was a worse failure than the March offen-

* Edmonds, *Military Operations, France and Belgium, 1918*, II, 473.

sive. At times the Germans fought brilliantly, but on the whole not quite so well as in March. The majority of the divisions from Russia had never faced the British and found them unexpectedly tough. Yet the majority of the British troops were only shadows of the old army: half-trained, immature, weakly led at the lowest level, and often hardly knowing their lieutenant colonels by sight. But for that factor and the failure to relieve the Portuguese in time there would not have been cause for grave anxiety. Even as things were, it must be said that these lads, many of them none too well fed before enlistment, gave a good account of themselves. As in most of the great battles in the west, the losses of the opposing forces, German on one side, British, French, and Belgians, on the other, appear to have been extraordinarily similar, in the two offensives combined about 350,000 on both sides.

The staff work was remarkable. Though the Germans had made many preparations for the Lys offensive, they had to hurry the last stages and they did the job well. It is still more notable, however, how the French D.A.N., none of whose weapons or ammunition were interchangeable with the British, was brought into a British zone, over railways dislocated by the previous German offensive, and so supplied that it could expend artillery and small-arms ammunition on the vast scale which defeated the attack of April 29.

Chapter II

PARIS IN DANGER—
COUNTERSTROKE DELIVERED

THE Germans still entertained hopes of final victory. The Anglo-French allies realized that they still lay in danger of final defeat. Strain and uneasiness were the lot of the leaders on both sides, accentuated by political or semipolitical uncertainties. The German O.H.L. feared that the government was leaning toward peace. Clemenceau's anxiety about the state of industrial France may be gauged by the fact that on March 21 four cavalry divisions, invaluable for their mobility, had been held in the interior in case of revolutionary outbreaks.

Haig was the worst off. The government talked of reducing his strength to twenty-eight divisions, though reinforcements were now arriving from Palestine. Eight divisions had been reduced to cadres. Foch backed Haig here. In the end seven of these divisions were re-created, though in some cases with men of low physical category. On the strategic side the British, and especially the Second Army in the north, were dangerously cramped by the German advance. Ports, depots, railway marshaling yards, reinforcement camps, and hospitals were an easy prey, even for short-range aircraft. Serious loss was caused by night bombing, and among the sufferers were women of the nursing services and Queen Mary's Army Auxiliary Corps, who faced their trial with fine courage.

Ludendorff, though balked in Flanders, was still determined on the destruction of the British forces. He reasoned, however, that he must first prevent the French coming to their aid for a third time. To do this he would launch against the French a great diversionary offensive, give them a terrible mauling, draw their reserves south, and then, as soon as possible, fall upon the British yet again. The very fact that a large proportion of the French reserves were still unusually far to the north would help him. He must strike where it would hurt. He chose the Chemin des Dames sector north of the Aisne, the scene of Nivelle's offensive in 1917. Though mainly a diversion it was to be a very big thing. The code name was "Goerz." Forty-one divisions were assembled. The inevitable and indispensable Bruchmüller came to conduct his hellish orchestra, and the organization of this bombardment was perhaps the supreme triumph of his art. The country lent itself to the concealment of troops and fine weather made bivouacs no hardship.

Now for the defense, which was strangely inept. The threatened front was held by four French divisions and three exhausted British divisions which Haig had agreed to send to this quiet sector as some compensation for the French reserves on or near the British front. In rear were seven French and two other tired British divisions, making a total of sixteen. Foch and Haig were at one in their belief that Ludendorff meant to attack the British again. They were right—but they had not taken into account the intermezzo on the Chemin des Dames. Here the responsibility falls on Foch and the French intelligence services.

Another curious feature was the disposition of the troops. The Chemin des Dames ridge, very narrow and dropping away southward to the Aisne valley, was suitable only for an outpost position. Six to seven miles in the rear was a far better one, an equally obvious main position, between the Aisne and the Vesle. Here the top was broad and the ground sloped back gently, a typical "Wellingtonian" position which would hide the defenders from view while giving them a fine field of fire as the attackers breasted the rise. Surely the line to take was: "Now, my friends, you have stormed the Chemin des Dames. Come on and see how you like this position."

Unhappily, the Sixth Army commander, General Duchêne—Foch's capable staff officer in 1914—kept the bulk of his line divisions much too far forward, despite the protests of the British corps commander, so that they were not only on a bad position and terribly exposed to fire but had behind them two unfordable rivers instead of one. In part he was influenced by the prestige of the name "Chemin des Dames," which had cost so much blood. He disregarded orders to establish his defense in depth. But the responsibility is not his alone. It goes through the hierarchy: Franchet d'Esperey, commanding the

G.A.N.; Pétain, commander in chief; Foch, generalissimo. The biog-
rapher of Franchet d'Esperey asserts that Duchêne appealed to Pétain
and "finally obtained authorization to defend himself on the Chemin
des Dames." Pétain and Franchet d'Esperey blamed Foch for moving
so many reserves northward.*

So Bruchmüller was given every chance. The bombardment was
shattering. Some men went off their heads in that 160 minutes' inferno
before 3.40 A.M. on April 25. At that hour the troops of General
von Boehn's Seventh Army crossed the Ailette brook below the
north face of the Chemin des Dames ridge and swarmed up. Five
divisions crashed into the Allied center, largely upon a single French
division which was practically destroyed at a blow. Much the same
fate met the British left division.

The Allied center was thus a void. The Germans, scenting an
opportunity almost incredible on the Western Front, swept down-
hill to the Aisne. To their delight they found that the bridges had
not been destroyed. Victory was being handed to them on a tray.
The British divisions, reinforced by a fourth, put up a fight remarkably stiff in the circumstances. "The behavior of all arms of the
British forces was magnificent," Haig wrote in his dispatch.† They
were compelled to wheel back till they faced northwest instead of
northeast, but they did prevent an undue widening of the breach.
On the left flank the French were pressed back toward Soissons,
but they still contained the German right at least partially. But in
the center the breach was gaping open and the French forces entering it were brushed out of the enemy's path. By evening he had
reached the Vesle. This was roughly an advance of ten miles. No
such day's work had been done in France since trench warfare had
begun.

The Germans had already accomplished the task they had set
themselves. But could they stop with practically nothing in front of
them and Paris only eighty road miles away? It was not to be thought
of. And the second day was a vast success. Now the pocket was
fifteen miles deep and still resistance was unavailing, though French
reserves were streaming in. In brief, by June 3 the Germans were
once more on the Marne, east of Château-Thierry. Now the road
distance to Paris was fifty-six miles, but Hindenburg and Ludendorff
were beginning to be worried that the sack was so narrow.

* Azan, pp. 167, 172.
† Haig's *Despatches*, p. 254.

Next something astonishing happened. Up to the Marne came marching new men. They were two divisions only, but they strode proudly through the flotsam and jetsam always present on the fringe of a stricken battlefield. Three United States divisions had already been in line on the French front and the First Division in a successful little action at Cantigny, near Montdidier. On June 1 a machine-gun battalion of the Third Division put up a grand defense near Château-Thierry. On June 6 the Second Division launched an attack and captured the village of Bouresches and the southern part of Belleau Wood. The offensive was then virtually over, so it is not correct to say "the Americans stopped it," but their action and demeanor were bracing. Actually on the night of June 3 the German Crown Prince called a halt, though some attacks were to be undertaken to deceive the French.

Ludendorff afterward admitted that the offensive had gone on too long. We must acknowledge that the temptation to continue exploiting success was very strong. The disadvantage was that as the front increased he had to make greater and greater efforts and even then could not widen the breach to his liking. In front of Reims the French had stopped him dead on June 1. On the western flank he was so dissatisfied with the situation that he decided to better it by an entirely new operation at the earliest possible moment. This involved a delay in launching Crown Prince Rupprecht's offensive against the British in Flanders. It cannot be doubted that he was pretty well bound to halt on June 4. His Seventh Army had outrun its transport. On the third the French rubbed out the little German bridgehead over the Marne at Jaulgonne. It may be added that one of the later subsidiary operations, an attack on the heights southwest of Reims, was defeated on the sixth by French and British troops, the latter a crumbled handful of men.

Foch had been caught on the wrong foot on the only occasion during his career as generalissimo. Even so, though twenty-five French and two American divisions had been drawn in, he had not committed the reserves held in his own hand. He had an uncannily good eye for a military situation. On April 14, when Hazebrouck seemed in imminent peril, he had astonished Haig and Milner by the comment: *"La bataille d'Hazebrouck est finie."* He was right then. On the second day of the Aisne offensive he told Clemenceau that he believed it to be a feint.* As has been related, he was correct

* Edmonds, *Military Operations, France and Belgium, 1918,* III, 24.

again, though it was a very unpleasant feint—and many a time in war a successful feint has been developed into the real thing, the main thrust.

The offensive was followed by a conflict between him and Haig. These two men always held firmly to their opinions. And yet, immeasurably to the credit of both, every wrangle between them ended with one or the other deliberately giving way or compromising if that were possible. This time they disputed the stationing of reserves and came to a compromise. The demand of Foch that five American divisions in the British zone should be transferred to the French, was met with Pershing's assent, but they were replaced by five other American divisions. Haig also agreed that three British divisions should be placed behind the junction of the Allied forces, where Foch thought the Germans might be contemplating another strike. The French government dealt summarily with Pétain's complaints that he had been starved in favor of the British. He was placed directly under the orders of Foch, without Haig's right of appeal to his own government.

While the Battle of the Aisne was drawing to its close the French had observed signs of an extension to the north in the Oise valley. The date was divulged to them by a prisoner, so that Humbert, commanding the French Third Army, was ready when Hutier attacked astride the Matz, a tributary of the Oise, on June 9. It was not quite as well-prepared an affair as its predecessors; nor was the numerical superiority as great as usual. Yet it started with another fine success, penetrating six miles on the first day. Thereafter progress became much slower.

That fierce fighting man Charles Mangin, disgraced after the Nivelle offensive, had been given another command, though only that of a corps, now in reserve. He was ordered to launch a counterattack with five divisions, including the splendid First and Second American, on June 11. For lack of time Fayolle was inclined to postpone the operation until next day, but Mangin fought the proposal and Foch supported him. Just before light failed senior commanders were assigned forming-up places and bidden to guide their troops into position after dusk. The counterattack was only a limited affair and was called off when resistance stiffened, but it stopped the Germans. This was satisfactory, as was the fact that the American troops had behaved admirably.

A number of successful small operations were also comforting.

Again the Americans showed their dash and daring in the capture
of Belleau Wood and Vaux, on either side of Château-Thierry. Two
other actions were of exceptional importance. On July 4 an Australian division with a British tank brigade captured Hamel and
Vaire Woods, south of the Somme. This success was won at small
cost in human life. It gave the Australians complete confidence in
tanks, which they had disliked since being, as they thought, let down
at Bullecourt in the spring of 1917. It also inspired the Fourth Army
commander, Rawlinson, to reflect on the possibility of launching
an offensive on a far greater scale on similar lines. Most striking of
all was the blow dealt on June 28 by Mangin, now commanding
the Tenth Army, on the western side of the salient created by the
Battle of the Aisne. The object was to seize high ground overlooking
Soissons and thus to prevent the Germans' making use of its railway
junction. The success was great; the resistance unexpectedly weak.
To Mangin also came the idea of a major offensive which he believed might blot out the whole salient. This was already in Foch's
mind, but he and his lieutenant had to wait.

However, these combats did little to change the gloomy situation.
Foch was in danger. Clemenceau, in whom burned the old republican
ferocity to generals, might strike him down. Pétain was even more
seriously threatened, and Guillaumat was brought home from
Salonika to be ready to replace him. Franchet d'Esperey went there
in his stead, and, even though to an important independent command,
under a cloud. Needless to say Duchêne was thrown out, to be replaced by a younger man in Degoutte. Curiously enough, this phase
of spiritual feverishness was also one of an amazing corporeal fever,
known as "Spanish influenza." It smote down the soldiers by the
hundred thousand, though most were quickly on their feet again,
and after running out by the first days of August it recurred more
viciously in the autumn. In the British armies over 15 per cent
entered hospitals. In the German ranks, where the epidemic was
known as "Flanders fever," the effects were worse. It was feared
that it might cause a postponement of Rupprecht's offensive.* That,
however, was to be postponed *sine die* for quite different reasons.

The Hindenburg-Ludendorff combination was not satisfied that
the Aisne offensive had drawn in enough French reserves. It was
decided to strike yet again on the French front before launching
"Hagen," the code name for Rupprecht's offensive. To the French

* Rupprecht, II, 240.

and British intelligence services it was clear that both were being prepared but hard to say which would come first. On the whole it looked as though it would be that of the German Crown Prince. Foch requested that four British divisions should be moved to the French front. The British government invited a protest from Haig, but he did not accept the invitation and sent the divisions. Not every commander in his place would have done it while Rupprecht's arm was upraised to smite.

On the German side the policy was doubtful because the longer "Hagen" was delayed the better Haig would be prepared to meet it. The new offensive was enormous: three and a half armies and fifty-two divisions; but it was faced by the army groups of Maistre and Fayolle in considerable strength—thirty-four divisions including nine American and two Italian, with the first two British just arriving—and in a state of preparedness. The French command had also divined that the attack would be in two parts: east of Reims with the objective of the Marne, here fifteen miles distant; and west of Reims, where the front was close to the river, to gain a deep bridgehead and unite with the other section.

The eastern attack fell upon the Fourth Army of Gouraud, one of the heroes of Gallipoli, where he had lost an arm and had both legs broken. The orders of Foch on defense in depth had been fulfilled here, and the army commander had made his troops enthusiastic about it. It worked. The Germans were thrown into confusion by artillery fire as they made their way through the thinly held foremost position and were then shattered upon the defenses of the battle zone. All the twenty German tanks were knocked out by the French artillery. It was a grave, very grave defeat.

For a while it looked as though it might be repaired by the quick success west of Reims. Boehn's Seventh Army overwhelmed the French infantry and artillery by a hurricane bombardment and crossed the Marne at Dormans under a smoke screen. On their right they were held by the American Third Division, but they expanded their bridgehead to a depth of some four miles. It was an ugly threat, and endangered Foch in person. Clemenceau declared that he was not the man he had been and spoke of replacing him. Clemenceau would have been astonished to learn that the general in chief was not displeased by the German passage of the Marne. Boehn's six divisions south of the river were soon shaken by the rain of bombs from the air and shells from the ground upon themselves and their bridges. But this was not all.

A big French counteroffensive against the western flank of the great salient had been planned. It was to be launched on July 18 if the Germans had not attacked by then. Visiting Fayolle on the fifteenth Foch learned that Pétain had telephoned an order to suspend this operation; also that Fayolle was thinking of withdrawing troops assembled for it to reinforce the threatened front on the southeast side. Foch directed that the counteroffensive should go forward.

The Germans had warning, but it came too late and they were ignorant of the scope of the counteroffensive. Mangin's huge concentration of eighteen divisions with another seven in reserve and his tanks were hidden in the vast woodlands behind his front. Of the three elements of tactical surprise, place, time and weight, Mangin had secured the first two partially and the third completely. Degoutte's Sixth Army on his right added to the effect by launching his attack three-quarters of an hour earlier. The Germans were already moving northward guns and mortars for "Hagen," the new title of the Flanders project, and at the height of the battle Ludendorff was calmly driving to Mons, headquarters of Rupprecht's army group, to put the final touches to the plans, trying to cook his hare before he had caught it.

Mangin's men and tanks came swarming forward, dipping into the many hollows, scurrying over the dangerous sky line of the hills, going slow or halting in front of centers of resistance, but as soon as might be attacking them in flank or even in rear. The defense collapsed. By the time Ludendorff had finished his conference and was ready for luncheon the penetration of the French Sixth and Tenth Armies amounted to over four miles. Then there was a pause, but the field artillery was moved forward with astonishing speed and the advance was resumed. It continued next day, but now found things altogether less easy, the German machine-guns pouring out death while very hard to locate amid the thickets and high wheat.

The later attack of the French Fifth and Ninth Armies lacked the advantage of surprise and achieved no such success as that on the west side, but they made ground. It is fair to say that the German infantry, after the first breakdown, showed itself most determined in face of this counteroffensive, the first one on a major scale that it had had to face since its series of offensives began on March 21. It did not flinch again, though its communications in the salient were being pounded from all directions. Both sides received reinforcements, those of the French including the second pair of British divisions, which came under Mangin's command, the other two being already engaged under Berthelot on the east side. As the Fifteenth (Scottish) Division relieved the American First, the men were saddened by the sight of dead in American uniforms lying in regular lines. It revealed the fallacy of some of Pershing's ideas. Able man and stalwart soldier though he was, his view that his troops were trained for open warfare, whereas those of their allies were not, was an exaggeration. So far the Americans had done what they had because in defense they were absolutely determined not to yield at any cost and in attack they meant to get through or die. Many died. They were learning the lessons learned by the British at Loos and on the Somme.

Stoutly as their troops fought, the German senior commanders knew it could not go on. They abandoned the bridgehead over the Marne and started a steady retirement, clinging with all their might to the shoulders of the salient in order to extricate the forces at the bottom of the sack. The pressure was, however, strong enough to determine the German command to withdraw across the Aisne at Soissons and its tributary the Vesle above the confluence. Foch, who had other plans in mind, decided not to assault this position.

Nearly 30,000 prisoners and nearly 800 guns were the spoils of the victors. The Second Battle of the Marne bore a certain similarity to the First, in that a fine victory, though in no sense a decisive one, was gained and the effects of a disaster were largely expunged; and that one was as much a turning point as the other in the struggle. It caused "Hagen" to be first postponed, then abandoned, though this Foch and Haig did not know for some time. It raised French spirits immensely. It was good for inter-Allied relations. Whereas the glory of the counterstroke was French and this was appreciated by the British and Americans, the French were grateful to their allies. The American divisions had more than once been the spearheads. The two pairs of British divisions had fought at the shoulders where the German resistance was fiercest and won the admiration of Mangin and Berthelot.

On August 6 Foch was created a marshal of France. As will appear, he was somewhat busy during the next few weeks and did not receive the baton until the twenty-fourth, at his headquarters, the Château de Bombon. A vision of swift victory had flashed before his eyes one day near the end of July.

"What am I risking, after all? I asked myself. You can prepare for the worst and another year of fighting, but there is no crime in hoping for the best—decisive victory within a few months." *

* Falls, *Marshal Foch*, p. 153.

Chapter III

THE UNITED STATES ARMY

As the American troops reached France—and England, where many first landed—everyone was curious about them and eager to lay eyes on them. Few can have been disappointed. They were fine-looking men and even the rawest had a soldierly air. A Briton alleging that the doughboy looked smarter than the G.I. may run into trouble but will take the risk. These men were no more cut to a pattern than men of any other nation, but they exhibited strong characteristics, most of which met with approval. They appeared self-confident and determined to show what they could do, but also reasonably modest. They were friendly to talk to and gay. They were good marchers. Their discipline was, as Pershing remarked, to a large extent self-conceived and self-imposed. On the whole their behavior was remarkably good.

In the trouble on the Mexican frontier and later in the divisional training camps at home, evidence had been provided of a spirit very different from that of the camps of the Spanish-American War, in which the National Guard and the volunteers have often shown themselves undisciplined and intractable. This good spirit was generally maintained during training in Europe, much of it in a hard winter. Yet no good service to the United States was done by bland postwar assumptions that all the troops were consistently heroic and decorous. "Soldiers are no angels, nor yet among men the harmlest creatures," wrote Sir Henry Sidney in the reign of Queen Elizabeth I. It must be confessed that Pershing set a bad example to those who saw nothing but perfection, e.g., in his statement that serious breaches of discipline were rare before the Armistice. In fact, the "straggling," a word often used as a euphemism for "desertion," did amount to serious breaches and there was a good deal of it, mostly in the rawer divisions. Nor could a corps commander in the American army dispense in action, any more than in the French and British armies, with what the former called a *cordon sanitaire* and the latter more bluntly "stragglers' posts," or with a curtain of military police.* American writers did not stand alone in the use of "dope," as bookshelves full of British unit histories bear witness, but British official history was generally candid. In the famous unofficial French history of General Palat are to be found blistering comments on panics at Verdun.

It is interesting to note the impressions, not intended for publication, made on Haig when he, in his thorough, conscientious way, visited two divisions beginning their training in his area. He was not altogether enthusiastic over that first encountered, finding the older officers "ignorant of their duties," though the men and younger officers were "active and keen to learn." He was won over by the next, the 35th. Major General W. M. Wright "had grounded the rank and file well in first principles"; they were "fine big men," from Kansas and Missouri; "drill was extremely good, very quick and smart; I was greatly pleased." † Wright became a corps commander not long afterward. If Haig was pleased he certainly said so, as always. It may be that he did not make an appeal to the men as strong as a Byng, a Maude, or an Allenby would have, but these strangers under his command saw a man carrying his load with no sign of anxiety. He talked to the cooks, who, unawed by the occasion, complained that they had too much meat and no oatmeal or hominy. It is probable that he did not forget his first impressions. In the end only two divisions remained under Haig, but he took a deep interest in all which served in the British zone. He resisted every attempt to throw them into action while unready, feeling that to commit prematurely such fine material would be criminal.

The American divisions crossed the Atlantic in a steady stream, though to begin with not fast—the convoy of June, 1917, had been hastened for moral effect and did not represent the start of the flow. By the end of July, 1918, a host of twenty-seven divisions had arrived, with two more disembarking. The desperate plight of the Franco-British forces during five successive German offensives had led to wide dispersion of these divisions. Five were with the British

* Pershing, *Report*, p. 80; Bullard, p. 266.
† Duff Cooper, p. 291.

and fourteen with the French. Some 300 miles separated four in Lorraine from two near the Channel coast. They were huge, even unwieldy, divisions, with an establishment of 28,000 and very large staffs. Later they were trimmed to the extent of 4,000 men. The reason was lack of manpower, but the effect cannot have been to their disadvantage.

British shipping played a major part in transporting them. In January, 1918, an agreement was concluded that Britain should transport six whole divisions, which would then be given experience in the British zone. In April, however, the United States War Department gave priority to infantry and machine-gun units during the crisis. Britain and France appeared to believe that this state of affairs would continue indefinitely, but Pershing resisted them after May, for which month he was pledged by the War Department to maintain it. Straight talk was exchanged, but too much need not be made of its heat. Relations are always strained when an alliance is under pressure and here tempers were better than usual in such a case. Up to the Armistice 2,086,000 men crossed the Atlantic, about 56 per cent in British ships and 44 in American; but over half the latter were ex-German ships which had been interned in American ports. The American Expeditionary Force then numbered thirty combat divisions, seven depot, and four replacement divisions.

Entering a country which had been using up its resources in long years of war, the Americans had to do a great deal for themselves. This was something they took to quickly, though Pershing had to check the zeal of universal providers at home. To go on with, he said in the autumn of 1917, he did not want bookcases, cuspidors, floor wax, or lawn mowers. On the other hand, he was generally short of horses and had to call heavily on the French, who were none too well off in that respect themselves. Locomotives and rolling stock were shipped in large numbers. Some of the construction undertaken was on a very big scale. As instances may be given the Saint-Sulpice storage depot near Bordeaux, where 107 warehouses had been built by the Armistice, and that at Gièvres, midway between Tours and Bourges, with tanks for two million gallons of gasoline, and a refrigerating plant said when opened to be the largest in the world,* the whole run by 20,000 men.

---

* *Guide to the American Battle Fields* contains a photograph. It is there described (1927) as the third largest in the world.

The American command was hampered by two factors: the distance from its home bases and the dispersion of its troops. Whereas the national bases of its allies were close at hand, the American were between three and four thousand miles from the railheads. So the expeditionary force from time to time ran short even of the most plentiful commodity, men. Seven divisions were "cannibalized" to provide reinforcements (replacements in American usage). The situation with regard to weapons was far worse. It has been mentioned that war production started slowly in the United States, but plenty of material was produced which could not be shipped. Of 3,000 guns used at Saint-Mihiel not one was American-made. The Americans never had standard tanks of their own, though they had some light ones. They did contrive to build up a fine air force, though it was at its best for only a few weeks of the war, but they had to acquire 2,676 aircraft from the French in doing so. The record of industrial France in the First World War was truly astounding. Having lost in battle some of her most valuable mines, France re-equipped the Serbian army, took a large part in re-equipping the Greek, provided the British with thousands of aircraft and a still greater number of engines, and yet played a great role in arming the American, despite the tremendous burden of her own large forces. It must be remembered, however, that a great share of the financial side of this burden was carried on American loans and that the United States made contributions in material before becoming a belligerent. By the year 1918 the country had been largely denuded of silver birches, the best wood for the nacelles of airplanes, but this was to a greater extent on British account than on French.*

The second hampering influence, dispersion, prevented the assembling of an American army until August 21, less than twelve weeks before the end of hostilities. Even then it was absurd to have only one army headquarters to show for a force of over a million men, but a second could hardly be formed until there were troops to put under it. This was the result of the vital dilemma in which Pershing had been constantly placed, dispersing his troops to plug breaches, to relieve French troops, and to raise morale, or risking the defeat of his allies and the loss of the war. The struggle had always gone the same way: he had yielded to the demands for aid, while refusing those for amalgamation, though he

* Jones, *The War in the Air*, VI, 80.

regarded dispersion as against his country's direct interests. His memory should be kept alive for this honorable course of action, even if it had been his only title to fame.

By the end of August, however, he must—for he was observant—have realized the change that had come over the war. By then mainly British efforts had inflicted upon the enemy two heavy defeats. Already it looked as though Haig were on the road to becoming what a German commentator later called him, "master of the field." Foch had saved the Entente from utter defeat; that cannot be doubted. He was still invaluable as a coordinator of effort, a dauntless spirit, and an invigorating influence on Pétain and the French forces. He had also gained high prestige with the British and was much talked of in officers' messes. Yet Haig had twice taken over the direction of strategy: first, by declining to launch an offensive to recover the northern coal fields; second, by insistence on breaking off the Battle of Amiens and switching his thrusts farther north. He was the man, and his armies were the armies, of the moment.

Pershing was certainly filled with an understandable and indeed laudable spirit of emulation. He now became fiercely determined to put an end to the dispersion of his troops—which he had always loathed and always regarded as a temporary expedient—and get going at all costs with an *American* offensive under his own orders. It must have been this sense of urgency that made him rush into the Saint-Mihiel operation, which both Foch and Haig had come to consider redundant in the circumstances. In general it may be said that, despite rows, his relations were good with Foch and excellent with Haig.

The American higher command was sound. Pershing himself was capable, calm, determined, and hard-working. He was also a considerable personality, though he resembled Haig in lacking personal magnetism and inspired more confidence than affection. The right men would seem to have risen to the top. For the last month of the war Hunter Liggett, who had been president of the Army War College, commanded the First Army.* He came up on merit, though he was on the elderly side and portly in the extreme. He would not admit that this was a disadvantage, holding that fat does not matter "if it does not extend above the neck." Robert Lee Bullard—perhaps needless to say a Southerner—commanded a divi-

* His Deputy C.O.S.–G 3 was G. C Marshall, Jr.

sion and a corps with drive and confidence before commanding the Second Army. J. T. Dickman, who commanded the Third Division at Château-Thierry, became an outstanding corps commander. John L. Hines, moved up from command of the Fourth Division to do likewise.

Pershing paid high tributes to his staff and may have made them all the warmer because he knew that it had come in for foreign criticism. The first chief of staff, James G. Harbord, bore the brunt of the organization, and after commanding a division took over the services of supply, a post well suited to his talents. James W. Mc-Andrew, who succeeded Harbord as chief of staff, was an excellent choice. He had already done invaluable service in launching the Staff College at Langres, near Chaumont. The heavy criticism of American staff work had reference to the offensive between the Meuse and the Aisne, when a halt to restore communications had to be made on September 29, and to slow progress later. It should be noted that a halt for the same purpose and at the same time was made by the Anglo-Belgian forces in Flanders. The impression of Foch was that, in view of the strong resistance met, too many troops were thrown in and inexperienced staffs failed to avoid confusion.* Haig was of the same opinion, though with less opportunity to judge. What is certain, and characteristic, is that the Americans learned more from their own adversities than from the experience of others, though they sought this ardently.

Of in round figures 200,000 officers, only 6,000 came from the regular army and 12,000 from the National Guard. The fifteen officers' training camps in the United States furnished 96,000.† They were started as early as 1915 by General Leonard Wood and known as the "Plattsburg schools," from the first model. Here was one of the most valuable steps in "preparedness," taken by a man who was reproved officially and belabored unofficially during the highly emotional phase when it was almost treason to speak of abandoning neutrality. Doubtless he was indiscreet, but people with unpalatable proposals often have to be. A similar system of schools for officers was established in France by Bullard, who had commanded one of the Plattsburg schools at a place little heard of then and much heard of since, Little Rock, Arkansas.

Pershing found the morale of the French Army "distinctly poor."

---

* Falls, *Marshal Foch*, p. 160.
† McEntee, p. 369.

This was after seeing it at its worst in the German Aisne offensive, in which a number of divisions behaved very weakly. He also wrote that men in the British cadre divisions to which American troops were attached for training told them they had come too late and could now only postpone defeat. This camp gossip in skeleton divisions was as unrepresentative as the statement that pre-Armistice breaches of discipline in the American forces were rare. The British soldier had a taste for the lugubrious. A popular marching refrain, chanted by good battalions, ran:

> Take me back over the sea,
> Where the Allemans can't get at me.
> Oh my! I don't wanter die!
> I wanter go 'ome.

Soldiers' humor in the Falstaff-Pistol style!

The frustrations to which Pershing was subjected rendered him somewhat sour and ungenerous to his allies. It is a pity that Bullard saw relatively little of the British, whose discipline he admired. He saw a great deal of the French, and of France while setting up the schools. He was a convinced Francophile, on terms of friendship with nearly all the French generals with whom he had to do, including Pétain, Mangin and Débeney. He realized that the French suffered vast losses in the final offensive and praised their efforts. When he makes an adverse judgment, it is thus weighty. He considers that French morale was down after the Nivelle offensive—as indeed it was; that it was recovering by September, 1917; that it dropped heavily after the German offensives of 1918; that it rose again after the Marne; but that on the offensive the French "fought warily" and put no push into it.* He saw American divisions outdistance French on several occasions, but told his divisional commanders that when this was so, or when the best American divisions outdistanced the less good—that happened too, of course—reserves were there to cover the flanks and no commander was to report that he must halt because his neighbor lagged in rear. He found that this principle worked.

The United States Army first went into action on a small scale a year after the country entered the war. Its troops were fresh, dynamic and enthusiastic, splendid material, but still short of

* Bullard, pp. 71, 173, 240, 241, 244.

training, and the first engagements and movements were carried out under heavy disadvantages. Fortunately, the handful of combat divisions available were grand fighters, under leaders who thought and acted for themselves. The first contribution, in the Aisne defensive and the Marne counteroffensive, was outstanding because there the danger and need of the Alliance were at their gravest. The staffs floundered at first and may have done so again for a few days in the Battle of the Meuse-Argonne, but if so they recovered. That battle, fought in the most vital sector, where the enemy always showed himself peculiarly sensitive to the shortest advance, was the second main contribution. The third was the freedom of action bestowed on the supreme command: American troops set free others even when not engaged themselves, so that the German reserves were run off their feet and exhausted. But the mightiest contribution of all was in the moral sphere, that which Napoleon described as the "divine half," whereas armament, positions and all combinations of material factors were the "earthly half." The coming of the United States Army lightened weary hearts.

Chapter IV

SEA AND AIR

For the British naval staff the year 1918 opened with high hopes. It knew that it was dealing with the submarine menace on the right lines. Losses were still high and technical methods needed improvement, but, whereas every other measure had failed, the convoy system continued to reap favorable results. Sir John Jellicoe's first year of office, which began in agony and by April appeared almost bereft of the last rags of hope, ended with comfort.

This was, however, to be the only year. His anxieties even more than his work had worn him down. Those in contact with him concluded that the strain "could not be further prolonged with justice to himself or advantage to the Service." * During the last days of 1917 he was succeeded as First Sea Lord and Chief of the Naval Staff by Admiral Sir Rosslyn Wemyss, who had distinguished himself in the Gallipoli campaign, though as commander only toward the end. A little earlier the ministerial head of the Admiralty, Sir Edward Carson, had been succeeded as First Lord by Sir Eric Geddes.

The effect of the submarine menace on naval thought was strikingly and for the first maritime nation of the world—rarely beaten at sea in any past war—tragically illustrated by Beatty's proposal at this time. The commander in chief told a conference at the Admiralty on January 2 that he no longer considered it wise to provoke a fleet action if an opportunity occurred. This from the dashing Beatty, who had writhed under Jellicoe's cautious leading at Jutland! He argued that trade came first; that ships detached to protect it must be written off the strength of the Grand Fleet because they could not form part of a quick concentration; that the

* Newbolt, *Naval Operations*, V, 203.

German battle cruiser fleet was now more formidable than his own; and that new types of shell in which the defects revealed at Jutland had been remedied had not yet been issued. The third point was based on false information, since the *Mackensen*, which Beatty believed was in commission, was not in fact completed while the war lasted. But this point was also based on Beatty's view that only the *Lion*, *Tiger*, and *Princess Royal* were fit to fight in the battle cruiser line; the others were either undergunned, too lightly armored, or not fast enough. Now this had nothing to do with the submarine war. It was proof of errors in design, a tribute to the shooting of the German battle cruisers, and a higher one still to German shell.

Admiral Scheer took some time to discover from intelligence reports and wireless signals that the Grand Fleet had been weakened to provide escorts for the Scandinavian convoys. Even then he missed one point on which German consuls in Norway should have been able to inform him: that these convoys sailed at fixed intervals. In April he drew up a plan to catch a convoy bound for the Firth of Forth and destroy both convoy and escort—a double blow, to British trade and, more important still, to the strength of the Grand Fleet. It was a bold design. This was no raid with 34-knot light cruisers or destroyers like the successful attacks on the convoys in October and December, 1917. Scheer was taking the High Seas Fleet up on to the convoy route, say 400 miles from Heligoland Bight in which he first concentrated, with the Grand Fleet, now at Rosyth, well placed to intercept him. He concentrated *before* moving, under the pretext of battle practice, so that no wireless instructions were necessary. Beatty got no word of the concentration in the Bight, nor of the move out in thick fog on the morning of April 23.

Yet the scheme was ruined by two factors, the first surely Scheer's own fault, the second an unlucky accident. He had chosen a bad day: the day before, he might have caught a convoy in one direction; the day after, one in the other. The accident was in the *Moltke*'s engine rooms, forty miles off Stavanger, which resulted in the breaking of wireless silence and Scheer's decision to turn back on the morning of the twenty-fourth, just about the hour at which the Grand Fleet was ordered to sail. The *Moltke* was torpedoed by a British submarine but reached port. The episode showed that it was virtually impossible to ensure the safety of these particular convoys if the High Seas Fleet were used against them. Scheer should, of course, have tried again, but he never did. The German navy was deteriorating in spirit as more and more good men, often much against their will, were transferred to the submarine service.

Simultaneously the British undertook a blocking operation which has become immortal and part of the national heritage. The leader was Rear Admiral R. J. B. Keyes, of Gallipoli fame, who had recently relieved Vice-Admiral Sir Reginald Bacon in command of the Dover Patrol. The ports were Zeebrugge and Ostend and the object was to destroy their value as U-boat bases, or as entries to the canal port of Bruges, where the boats took refuge from naval bombardment. Such ventures are peculiarly hazardous, but these met with exceptional misfortunes, including two last-minute postponements due to the weather, a change of wind which spoiled the effect of the smoke screens at the critical moment, and rain clouds which prevented a preliminary air bombardment.

Keyes planned to storm the head of the immense boomerang-shaped Zeebrugge mole, 2,690 yards, or just over a mile and a half, long: first, as a diversion while the ships destined to block the Bruges Canal went in; second, to capture the mole-head battery to prevent it from sinking the block-ships prematurely. The fleet of seventy-four vessels sailed on April 22 and arrived off Zeebrugge about midnight. It was a dedicated force, hardly a man in which can have failed to realize how formidable was the defense. The light cruiser *Vindictive* (Captain A.F.B. Carpenter) was laid alongside the mole, which was then boarded by marines and seamen under terrific fire, and cut off by blowing up a submarine filled with high explosive against the girders of the inshore viaduct. Two of the three block-ships reached the lock gates and were sunk in the canal entrance. The defenders fought stoutly and their fire was extremely accurate both in the action and during the British withdrawal.

Meanwhile the Ostend action had failed because the shifting of a buoy caused the block-ships to ground. A new attempt on the night of May 9 blocked only one-third of the Channel, the *Vindictive* serving this time as block-ship. It was proclaimed and believed that Zeebrugge was completely blocked, but in fact the number of exits and entrances of U-boats did not decrease throughout May. They did drop in July, and the official historian claims that this was because Zeebrugge's value as a destroyer base had been lessened.*

* Newbolt, *Naval Operations*, V, 275.

It is to be feared that this was unconscious propaganda. Morally, the heroism of the venture was a victory, at a moment when one was sorely needed. The news streamed over the world, everywhere exciting wonderment and re-creating confidence in the fate of a nation which bred such men.

These blocking operations carried out by Keyes were only part of his policy for keeping U-boats out of the Straits of Dover—not merely to protect cross-channel traffic but to stop the most convenient course for boats making for the Channel, the Irish Sea, or the Atlantic. Immediately after assuming command of the Dover Patrol he reorganized the barrage and worked at high pressure on new lines of deep-laid mines. They were moderately but consistently successful. Since the main effort was to confine the Germans to their bases rather than to "seek out and destroy the enemy," mine laying was clearly more important than ever, and not only against submarines. In the Aegean it scored a fine success when the *Goeben* and *Breslau* made a sortie from the Dardanelles on January 20. Between them they struck no less than eight mines. The *Breslau* was sunk, but the *Goeben* was able to run herself aground and, despite heavy—but very inaccurate—bombing by British aircraft, she was salvaged. However, she did not appear again.

Another ambitious undertaking was put in hand: it was nothing less than a barrage of mines between the Orkneys and the Bergen leads, a distance of some 250 miles. It was carried out to a large extent by American mine-laying forces under the command of Rear Admiral J. Strauss. It caught a few U-boats but was never fully tested. The same may be said of a Franco-Italian net barrage across the Straits of Otranto. This brought about one of the most extraordinary naval occasions of the war. On June 9 two Austrian battleships with a destroyer screen put out from Pola. They would almost inevitably have surprised the barrage forces with overwhelming strength. By pure chance, however, two minute Italian motorboats were cruising across their course. The two Davids attacked the two Goliaths, and Commander Luigi Rizzo hit the *Szent-Istvan* with two torpedoes. She sank, the only dreadnought sunk in action throughout the war. What so many great guns and squadrons of destroyers could not accomplish at Jutland had been done by this intrepid Italian officer in his tiny craft.

This was an incident, if one which grips the imagination tighter than the records of mine laying. But mine laying too, though one of the best U-boat killers, was only a valuable adjunct to the battle winner of the submarine war, the convoy system, as were aircraft and such inventions as the paravane—towed from a ship's bows at a wide angle to catch and cut mine moorings—and the hydrophone— an overhearing apparatus also towed. It was the improvement of the system in organization, armament, discipline, but above all by strengthening it that brought victory.

It has been recorded that the losses of Allied and neutral shipping in 1917 rose very sharply to a peak in April, then fell less sharply but steadily to the end of the year.* Nothing of the sort happened in 1918. From January to October losses fluctuated thus: January 96, February 96, March 123, April 80, May 92, June 78, July 81, August 127, September 64, October 42. The August figure was actually the highest since September, 1917. But the total sinkings for the ten months of 1918 were 879 against the 2,122 of the eleven months of unrestricted submarine warfare in 1917. Moreover, in the second and third quarters of 1918 new American and British tonnage largely exceeded that lost. No date can be given for the victory, won chiefly by British forces, but it was a victory on which the fate of the war hung, and it was gained by the ocean convoy system.

Perhaps the success is revealed most clearly, though it had been reached earlier, in the events of the first fortnight of May, 1918. Then the Germans made a "methodical and elaborate" effort against "the mass of shipping steaming in formation" in the western approaches. They sank or damaged five ships. They lost two U-boats. And during this period 183 convoyed ships entered British ports and 110 passed through the danger zone outward bound.†

The scale of this narrative does not permit details of the other side of the victory at sea, the Allied blockade, in which the French, American, and Italian navies bore an honorable part but which was again chiefly a British undertaking. German and Austrian seaborne trade, except in the Baltic and after the fall of Russia to a trifling extent in the Black Sea, as good as ceased altogether.

With regard to goods carried by sea to neutral countries, strong criticism, some of it instructed, afterward appeared. It was asserted that the system of licenses and quotas to neutrals was too tender and that Germany gained the benefit. Doubtless leakages, which

* See p. 292.
† Newbolt, *Naval Operations*, V, 282.

we know were gross to start with, persisted on a smaller scale. Yet this system too worked. The Central Powers were reduced to hunger and suffered many other grave shortages. Every weapon in the naval armory played a part in this pressure, directly or indirectly: the Grand Fleet, the French Mediterranean Fleet, the Italian Fleet, the United States Fleet, devoting its chief energies to the escort of the troops to Europe; cruisers, destroyers, submarines, aircraft, agents abroad, cipher-breakers at home. Word that a single would-be blockade runner was making for a German port set in motion a score of preventive measures. As time went on, however, these could win no more successes because no enemies remained to defeat. For Germany the gates were shut and bolted by a vast concentration of naval power.

The last bold stroke that was to have been struck by the High Seas Fleet when Germany was reeling in defeat never fell. It was prevented by a melancholy, if not shameful, event. Scheer, now chief of the naval staff, directed his successor, Hipper, to strike right through to the Thames estuary, as the Dutch had in 1667. In July and August, 1917, serious disorders had occurred in the High Seas Fleet and had been quieted by concessions. Now, when orders were issued to raise steam, they were disobeyed. In many ships the stokers, on the contrary, drew fires. Hipper could do nothing but disperse the fleet. The leaders of the mutineers had told the crews that they were being taken on a "death ride." The projected sortie was indeed a desperate attempt to bring on a battle with the Grand Fleet, and the morale of the German crews had sunk so low that they could not face it. Here too the blockade had played a part, since the failure of morale was to some extent due to bad and insufficient food. But the main cause was general discontent, resentment of very stiff discipline, and defeatism, worked on by left-wing traitors in their own ranks.

The end of such a fleet as this had been contains an element of pathos after all these years. Some will argue that, the war being as good as over, the admirals had no right to bring on another battle at sea. This is doubtful morality. If German soldiers had to go on fighting, could the sailors with honor refuse to fight?

All through the year 1917 air raids on England had continued, chiefly on London. The German airships were beginning to drop out of the battle, giving place to large airplanes popularly known as "Gothas." The physical effects, measured in terms of war effort, were virtually nil; the moral effects were grave and brought about heavy drops in production. In a populace which had faced the burdens, losses, and privations of war so stoutly an astonishing weakness appeared. The sad truth is that there had been something like a split into two nations, those who fought for a pittance and those who worked at home for such returns as they had never dreamt of. Many of the latter in all ranks of industry had become extremely selfish. When they found that they too could be hit many lost their nerve. The press stormed with rage against the government; the government was distracted by the anger of press and public. Sir William Robertson, after attending a War Cabinet meeting, reflected: "One would have thought the world was coming to an end." On September 23, 1917, the night shift dropped to 27 per cent of its normal total and the output of 303 cartridges—admittedly unpleasant material to handle in an air raid—at Woolwich Arsenal to 19 per cent. Every day shift was down also at this time, though it was long since the Germans had undertaken a daylight raid. In the East End of London there was a tendency to panic, and night after night, raids or not, 300,000 people poured into the underground railways and slept on the platforms.*

The government would, of course, have had to take action in any event, but it was almost certainly pushed by the pressure of public opinion into more extravagant action than it would otherwise have instituted. The results were effective. The last aircraft raid took place on May 19, 1918, when seven planes were shot down by British pilots or anti-aircraft guns. In the course of the war 1,414 people in England were killed by bombs. London was more vulnerable than Paris because the sea favored surprise. Air attacks in Paris were trifling, by two airships and some fifty aircraft in all, and of these one airship and sixteen aircraft were shot down.

It was in retaliation pure and simple—and again in part as a sop to public opinion—that Britain formed the Forty-first Wing near Nancy in October, 1917, to attack industrial traffic. This developed in the summer of 1918 into the "Independent Air Force" to attack industrial targets in Germany. The title was typical of the spirit of the young air staff officers and somewhat impertinent in view of the fact that the force had to operate from Lorraine, far from the British zone. "Independent of God?" asked a French general. Un-

* Jones, The War in the Air, V, 87-89.

fortunately not. By the time the force really got going the weather was unfavorable, poor in September, and really bad in October.

Perhaps the most useful work accomplished was participation at Marshal Foch's bidding in the Franco-American offensive in the Argonne. The most significant feature of the enterprise, however, was the development of the aircraft used in it. The day bombers, D.H.4 and D.H.9 (De Havilland), carried between 500 and 600 pounds weight of bombs, but the big night bombers, Handley Pages, carried sixteen 112-pound bombs and were able to remain in the air for eight hours. The United States Navy also formed the Northern Bombing Group to attack objectives in Belgium. It was in this period that Trenchard, Brigadier General William Mitchell (commanding the United States Army Air Force), and others were first inspired by theories not only then impracticable but which had not caught up with realities a generation later. In the last five months of the war the Independent Air Force dropped in Germany 540 tons of bombs, but the latest Handley Pages, for bombing Berlin, came too late. Only 746 Germans were killed in all air attacks, but, as in Britain, there was a falling off in morale and production, especially by night.

On April 1, 1918, the military and naval forces of the R.F.C. were amalgamated and made independent of the two old fighting services of land and sea. So the Royal Air Force was born, almost exactly forty years before these words were written.

It was formed by Lloyd George on the advice of Smuts. Three months earlier, on January 3, the first step had been taken. An Air Ministry had been set up, with Lord Rothermere, Northcliffe's younger brother and himself a "press baron," as Secretary of State and Major General Sir Hugh Trenchard as Chief of the Air Staff. Major General Sir John Salmond, who had been Director General of Military Aeronautics at the age of thirty-six, became commander in chief of the R.A.F. on the Western Front.

Haig had been a little worried about the formation of the Air Ministry, "uncontrolled by military or naval opinion." In fact, all went well. Whatever might be the future of aircraft in war and whether or not air forces were destined to become predominant, it was clear to the good sense of Salmond and senior R.A.F. officers in the outer theaters that their main role must still be the support of armies in the field. They continued to play that role, and Haig's requests were never refused. Yet the creation of the R.A.F. was symbolic of what was occurring in the design of aircraft, of the vast increase in their number, and of the efficiency of bombing. Much of it was actually more accurate than the general standard of long afterward just because aircraft were slower and flew lower. It was not that they could not fly high. A few could reach 18,000 feet, a remarkable performance, but they took a long time to make half that height. Anti-aircraft guns were indeed baffled by low flying, and small-arms fire, dangerous near the front, was less likely to be thick when an ammunition dump or a railway siding ten miles behind it was the target.

The other belligerents did not imitate Britain in setting up independent air forces, though French officers felt that their organization was handicapped for lack of a ministry.* The French did, however, take a step which in another way showed their appreciation of the advance in the importance of aircraft in war. They formed an "Air Division," which took part in the Marne battle in July. It was next moved northward to fight in the Allied offensive of early August, at which time it consisted of 432 fighters and 193 day bombers.

All the air forces were now undertaking bombing, mainly by night but not infrequently by day, not immediately connected with land or naval operations, though in their interest. French, Americans, Germans, and to a lesser extent Austrians and Italians were realizing that air power was becoming, to a far greater degree than in the early part of the conflict, an independent means of waging war. British veterans of 1918 will assuredly not dispute the statement that the German Air Force made itself very troublesome. On the night of May 19, for example, 182 people, including some women, were killed and 643 wounded by bombs on hospitals and camps. Even when raiders inflicted few losses or none they deprived the resting soldier near the line of his scanty amenities. "In some sectors it (night bombing) became so heavy and frequent that troops could no longer be assembled for entertainment and both concert parties and cinema shows had to be abandoned." †

It would be ridiculous to imagine that all this happened in a flash. Development was gradual and steady. In the German offensive of March, 1918, the attackers started off with terrific verve, but as early as the second day British and French air reinforcements

* Mortane, I, 218.
† Falls, *The Gordon Highlanders in the First World War*, p. 175.

threw themselves into the battle and resistance grew rapidly stiffer. The Germans were outfought in the air long before they were held on the ground. Since the German armies were advancing rapidly and victoriously, the most obvious targets of the German air force were railway stations. Attacks in daylight were fiercely opposed. Day after day it came to fights of hundreds, and the soldier on the ground could see swarms of aircraft twisting in their maneuvers above him, and every now and again a victim spinning earthward. In the Battle of the Lys bad weather limited the activities of both sides, but in that of the Marne "swarms of British, French, and for the first time American packs of from twenty to thirty attacked." They destroyed the Marne bridges and played a very considerable part in the issue of the battle. On July 18, the day of the French counteroffensive, they won, by German admission, a great success.*

The impression of the British—and sometimes of French army officers too—was that the R.A.F. was at this stage of the war more active and bolder than the French and that some of the war-weariness of the French army had penetrated to its air force. In all fairness it should be said that German comments do little to support this view; in fact, they seldom make comparisons between the two in regard to quality. The point they do make—and one about which there can be no doubt—is that the British were particularly active in bombing. *"Besonders die Engländer führten den Bombenkrieg mit grösster Wucht."* † In general, tactical, or short-range, bombing by day could be mastered, especially by the British, French, and American allies who could always assemble far superior strength, from the start when on the offensive and in 1918 within a day or two when on the defensive. Strategic, or long-range, day bombing, usually from great heights for these days, could be hindered, diminished in weight, and made more costly. The losses of the British Independent Air Force were very high. Bombing on these lines could not, however, be completely mastered. Still less could night bombing. That of the British and French contributed to the strain on the German communications which was a big factor in the halting of the offensive of March, 1918. That of the Germans had a high nuisance value. Both sides were compelled to increase their precautions. Ludendorff's orders in June were radical and com-

* Bülow, pp. 107-122.
† Ritter, p. 115.

prehensive. All large troop movements were to be carried out when possible by night; new camps were to be formed with small huts, dispersed to a greater extent than formerly; camouflage was to be put up before, not after, this and other work was taken in hand; camouflage must always be as low as possible to avoid long shadows; every care should be taken to avoid new tracks from camouflaged constructions because they made the camouflage useless.*

It may be added that poled cable from headquarters or administrative offices was a gift to the intelligence officers who dealt with air photographs because even if the poles did not show, the shadows did. Finally, during the victorious offensives of "the Hundred Days" from August 8 to November 11, it cannot be said that German bombing caused the Allied leaders any anxiety, except for one heavy attack on Paris by Gothas in the early hours of September 16.

One formidable and terrifying threat inherent in the new power of aircraft had so far been exercised once only and that on a small scale, in Maude's pursuit of the Turks in Mesopotamia. In countries where roads were few, and especially where such as existed passed through defiles, defeat and hasty retreat were likely to be visited with terrible punishment. The Turks in Palestine, the Bulgarians in Serbia, and to a lesser extent the Austrians in Italy were to suffer in this way before the end.

Though the bomb was the main weapon of the aircraft against troops on the ground, it was not the only one. Low-flying attacks with machine guns were becoming a regular feature of every offensive. They often proved daunting to the enemy and were always very popular with friendly troops, who liked to see aircraft of their own side in action close at hand. Sometimes individual staff officers, in cars, afoot, or on horseback, were coursed like hares by greyhounds.

This expansion of the airman's repertoire, being paralleled by that of the air forces, did not result in any weakening of the tasks of liaison with land forces which at the beginning of the war had been his sole concern. On the contrary, wireless communication between the aircraft and artillery had greatly improved. Photographic aircraft could cover far more ground because their appliances were better. In Palestine and Macedonia they played a leading part in new surveys which furnished the armies with maps superior to any hitherto produced in those regions. Oblique as well as perpendicular

* Mortane, pp. 410-430.

photography gave vivid and accurate knowledge of country which could not be observed from the ground. The practice of general officers making reconnaissances from the air had its origins now, though not many availed themselves of the opportunity. Flying as a passenger was still regarded as an adventure to be undertaken only by those deeply interested in flight or possessed with a devil.

The Germans had made an intense effort to maintain the ascendancy which had been theirs over a great part of the war. With regard to type and performance they were on the whole pretty successful, but by the summer of 1918 their resources had become inadequate to produce more than between one-third and one-half of the aircraft turned out by their enemies. At the end of the war they had about 2,600 first-line aircraft, whereas the R.A.F., the strongest air force in the world, had 3,300. German writers demand sympathy on this score and even go as near as they can venture to declaring that there was something unfair in the situation. Their government and staffs should have thought about it earlier, before they started the war, before they violated the neutrality of Belgium, before they found themselves in the stranglehold of the British naval blockade, before the vast industrial resources of Britain, France, and the United States were geared to war.

Yet up to the end they turned out good aircraft, with good engines. Their experience with high-power engines in Zeppelins helped them as such engines were called for.* The aircraft used by the British and French for artillery liaison and photography were in most cases very poor. Guynemer once remarked that if the Germans had used such machines he would have guaranteed to shoot down one a day. The luckless young British and French airmen engaged on these duties had the highest death-roll of the air forces.

In sum, the air forces of the chief belligerents had about six months at the end of the war in which to show that what had been called "the fifth arm" of the army was no longer an arm, as the word was applied to infantry, cavalry, artillery, and engineers, but a service in its own right.

* Jones, *The War in the Air*, VI, 557.

Chapter V

BLACK DAYS FOR GERMANY

THE Second Battle of the Marne had done more than ward off a peril. It had set the German command sparring for time. Yet Hindenburg and Ludendorff would not want a lot of time. They had decided to go over to the defensive, but were confident that they would be able to return to the offensive without a long delay. They had various projects in mind, but the favorite was still "Hagen" in the region of Ypres, though this would now have to be somewhat reduced in scale. Their foes were thus given the opportunity to get a blow in first. It was a fateful moment in which much depended on the strength of that blow.

For the British the action of Hamel on July 4 afforded a nucleus of ideas, a small-scale model.* The Fourth Army commander, Rawlinson, was eager to expand it into a bigger offensive, with the tank as the predominant weapon. Haig agreed. The area, east of Amiens, appealed also to Foch, who attributed immense importance to the liberation of lateral lines of communication, broken by the German offensives. In this case the Amiens-Paris railway, well known to generations of British holiday-makers, was to be freed. The Germans were not actually sitting astride it, but southeast of the city they were less than four miles from it and Amiens itself came frequently under fire from heavy artillery. Foch directed the French First Army (Debeney) on the British right to take part in the operation and placed it under Haig's orders; but only its two left-hand corps were to attack on the first day.

Then Foch went a step further. He arranged that the French Third Army (Humbert) on the south side of the German salient

* See p. 347.

should strike the enemy's flank in aid of the First Army. He also demanded that the assault should be put forward two days, from August 10 to August 8. That made a lot of work, but it was a welcome change, since practically every big offensive in the war was postponed. The objective was extended to the so-called Roye-Chaulnes line, actually the old, largely decayed, British entrenchments of February, 1917, before the German retreat to the Hindenburg line. This was a maximum distance of nearly fourteen miles.

The main blow was to be struck by the Canadian Corps (Currie). This magnificent body of troops, with many of its battalions two hundred over establishment and no immature men, had taken part in none of the defensive battles because Haig, to his annoyance, was not permitted to use its divisions under any corps commander but their own. It was brought in unobtrusively and none of its troops were permitted to enter the foremost trenches until the night preceding the attack. On its left was the Australian Corps (Monash), equally good troops of a rather different pattern, perhaps even cleverer tactically but at lower levels apt to be less careful of detail. The British contingent comprised the Third Corps (Butler), as virtually a gigantic flank guard; the Cavalry Corps (Kavanagh); a reserve division; a mass of heavy, and a considerable amount of field artillery; and a powerful armored force of twelve tank battalions—324 heavy tanks, 96 light, and twelve armored cars, not including reserves and older types converted to serve as supply vehicles. The United States 33rd Division was in reserve to the Third Corps.

The French First Army began with three corps. So many tanks still remained on the Marne battlefield that only light ones were available, and Debeney judged that they were too few and fragile to be sent over in first line. They were indeed essentially weapons of exploitation. He attached them to divisions destined to take later objectives. Since his leading troops would thus have no armor he considered that a preliminary bombardment would be necessary. This in turn meant that the French First Army would not advance until after the British Fourth, which, on the pattern of Cambrai, was to go forward at the moment the artillery opened fire.

By the morning of August 8 the British had eleven divisions in first line or due to enter the fight on the first day and four in reserve. The French had ten; but their action was to develop from the left and only seven were to be engaged on August 8. The R.A.F. had assembled 374 aircraft. The French strength was greater, but the air division did not come into action until the ninth. The corresponding front of the German Eighteenth Army (Hutier) and Second Army (Marwitz) mustered fourteen divisions against the twenty-one Allied.

Despite the thorough and careful measures to ensure secrecy put into force by Rawlinson and Debeney, this matter caused deep anxiety. A few extracts from notes made in a complex private shorthand by an inconspicuous and youthful British liaison staff officer with the French division on the Canadian right may give a hint of the atmosphere.*

August 6th. Tonight the crowd on the roads was extraordinary, so thick that I was afraid the traffic would be caught by morning light. At times the flood hardly seemed to move for half an hour at a stretch. . . .

So all the old tricks are coming out of the conjurer's box. I have seen it too often before—the Somme, Messines, Ypres, Cambrai—to be fully confident of a great success on this occasion. But one thing is sure: if we take the knock this time after Ludendorff has shown us how it is done, we may as well give up. On the whole I am hopeful. . . .

August 7th. I lay awake in my bunk for some time thinking of the assembly of troops and tanks on the tiny spit of land between the Avre and the Luce, and its dangers. If the Boche were to find it out and launch quite a small attack, or even to deluge that position with high explosive and mustard gas, what hellish confusion and loss there would be!

August 8th. It seemed that I had hardly gone to sleep when a French orderly shook my arm. I went out to find it was still dark and very foggy. . . . Then General Deville took up the telephone and asked to speak to the Corps Commander himself. It appears that this is a sort of ceremony with him before battle. We all stood round waiting patiently for some time, I expect old Toulorge was being hauled out of bed. Then Deville said solemnly: 'My General, I have to report that my troops are in position. The assembly has passed off without hitch. Ah *ça y est!*' While he

---

* The diary is the present writer's. The keeping of diaries was strictly forbidden. Despite the shorthand, this was never taken forward of divisional headquarters.

was speaking there was an almighty crash. It was exactly 4.20. Zero! Now all our hopes were launched.

General Deville read us a little homily which we have heard from him already half a dozen times. 'Liaison, messieurs!' Liaison first and last and always. . . . The old boy's face was radiant. During the past few days his nerves have been a nuisance; he has screamed with impatience and nearly driven his Chief of Staff mad. Now the impatience has passed, and though the excitement remains it is the right kind. He is simply keyed up to concert pitch.

The Germans were surprised. In all their discussions about possible attacks this front had not been mentioned. On the front of the Canadian Corps the success was overwhelming. The tanks unsettled the Germans' spirit and the Canadian soldiers killed them, rounded them up, or chased them back in flight. All the hard fighting was for the villages. The exploitation was not as successful as it might have been because it was difficult to harmonize the action of tanks and cavalry, and even when chances of doing so occurred they were not always accepted intelligently. Just a little more elasticity and enterprise might have brought about a much deeper advance, but at its best it was seven miles. The left did not make equal progress. This was because a German division had attacked a couple of days before just north of the Somme, gained a little ground, and inflicted a considerable number of casualties. The result was that dispositions, start-line, and barrage tables had to be changed in haste. After the first day two regiments of the American division were attached to British brigades and behaved with the expected spirit and enterprise. The French did well, but Deville's splendid Forty-second Division, with no tank support, ended up about a mile in rear of the Canadian right. The air forces, attacking the Somme bridges with magnificent courage, had a bad day, suffering heavy loss.

August 9 fell slightly below expectations, like many second days; but the three miles gain in the center was well above their average. And though the Germans were heavily reinforced on the tenth—seven divisions arrived, with seven more moving in—another two, miles was made. This was the day when the French Third Army struck in on the flank, a little late, as the enemy was withdrawing. Fighting went on here and there for over a week, but this was really a four-day battle. As soon as he realized that resistance was stiffening, Haig determined to break off the attack and set his Third and First Armies going southeastward to outflank the resistance to his Fourth and the French First Armies. An angry struggle with the generalissimo followed, the hottest that ever occurred between them. Foch insistently demanded that the advance should continue on the present front. Haig, anxious as always to carry out his behests, ordered local attacks to test the enemy's resistance. Rawlinson and the Canadian Corps commander, Sir Arthur Currie, were so certain this was folly that they actually checked attacks which their subordinates wanted to make. Once indeed they left the French in the lurch. Foch finally gave way. He went further. He agreed that the Canadian Corps, which would be fit for a new offensive after a brief rest, should be relieved by the French and transferred to the First Army.* The greater impetus of the British army made Haig impregnable in such a dispute, though he always avoided one if possible. The language barrier between them put spiritual fraternity out of the question. The Frenchman with whom Haig was on the most affectionate terms was Georges Clemenceau.

The British losses from August 8 to 11 were over 22,000; the French about 20,000; the German, not published, far heavier than both combined.† The British took 18,500 prisoners and the French 11,373. The victors were conscious that they had gained a success unparalleled in their previous offensives within a similar period of time. It came as a stronger tonic than the counteroffensive of the Marne. Optimism swept through their armies. Yet reasons for still greater buoyancy of spirit were hidden from them. In the midst of the battle a German regiment moving up through troops in flight heard a shout: "We thought that we had set the thing going; now you asses are corking up the hole again." The history of the crack Alpine Corps says: "All ranks in large parties were wandering wildly about, but soon for the most part finding their way to the rear." This was on August 10 at a detraining station seven miles from the front, but under air attack. And at a Crown Council on the fourteenth the Emperor said that "a suitable time must be chosen to come to an understanding with the enemy."

* Falls, *Marshal Foch*, p. 154.
† Edmonds, *Military Operations, France and Belgium 1918*, IV, estimates 75,000, which is excessive. Marwitz, commanding the German Second Army, states that on the first day he lost about 700 officers and 27,000 other ranks.

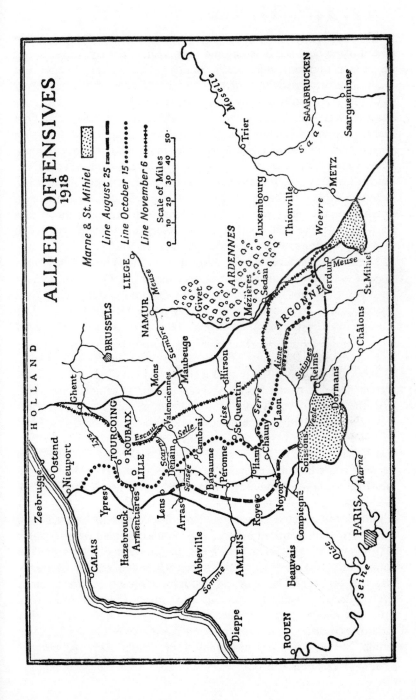

ALLIED OFFENSIVES
1918

Marre & St. Mihiel
Line August 25
Line October 15
Line November 6

Scale of Miles
0 10 20 30 40 50

The next heavy blow was struck on August 20 by Mangin, north of the Aisne between Soissons and Compiègne. Though only two of his twelve divisions were fresh, he overwhelmed the defense and made a maximum advance of two and a half miles. "Another black day!" says Ludendorff. The twenty-first was blacker far. Mangin's advance was deeper than on the twentieth and reached the Oise midway between Chauny and Noyon. The French Third Army on his left took up the offensive with less but not unsatisfactory success. The twenty-first was also signalized by the new offensive of the British Third Army. It merely ambled forward a couple of miles and halted next day to bring up guns and shell. It did no more than brush aside the outer screen of the German defense and move to a start-line for the real operation. The Germans thought they had broken the offensive by the depth of their defense.

They were undeceived on August 23. The Third Army progressed two miles, took 5,000 prisoners and shook Otto von Below's Seventeenth Army in a way to which that successful veteran was unaccustomed. Moreover, the Fourth Army, which had resumed its advance on the twenty-second, had another great day. The First Australian Division shattered two German divisions. These were the sole victories of that day. Mangin was repulsed north of Soissons; Humbert made only a slight advance; and Debeney, not having completed the relief of the British, did not move.* During the next two days the British Fourth and Third Armies pushed on. Again there was only one small French attack and virtually no progress. Next day, however, the battle was expanded, once more by the British. The Canadian Corps, augmented by two fine Scottish divisions, had by now come into line at Arras in Horne's First Army. It dealt the Germans a mighty blow, advancing four miles down the Cambrai road over the old Arras battlefield.

Ludendorff reacted that very night. No sooner had he digested the reports than he issued orders for a withdrawal on a front of some fifty-five miles as the crow flies from the Oise east of Noyon to the Somme at Ham, north along the river to Péronne, east of Bapaume, to south of Lens. This was not enough according to the German Crown Prince. He advised that his army group should retire to the Brunhilde position, up to twenty-five miles north of Reims, and that the groups north of him, Boehn's and the Bavarian Crown Prince's, should fall back to the Hindenburg Line. Prince Rupprecht could

* *Armées Françaises*, VII, 242.

not speak for himself because he was on sick leave.* Ludendorff, always gambling on what he called "the soldier's luck" and not realizing that his had changed for good, would retreat no farther.

The German withdrawal was well conducted and unpleasant for the pursuers, since the guns were not moved back till they had blazed off all their stacked shell. Still the three British armies and the French First on the right followed up at a fair pace and captured a good deal of material.

Haig was by no means at the end of his resources. There was no need now to amass the vastly superior strength called for in British offensives of the past or the German offensives earlier that year. Nor were great tank concentrations required, which was fortunate since the casualties in armor had been enormous. A number of divisions equal to that of the defense and sometimes fewer sufficed. In the most vital task of the next phase three divisions, the First and Fourth Canadian and the British Fourth, were opposed by at least six German divisions. It is true that, though all the British divisions—except the Canadian and the Seventy-fourth from Palestine—were below establishment, the Germans were as a rule still weaker.

In the next phase Haig set Horne's First Army going again. The main operation alluded to above was the breaking of the Drocourt-Quéant Switch, branching northward off the Hindenburg Line. This had called for preparations more like the old ones than was now usual and the Canadian Corps was allotted a generous proportion of the Tank Corps "runners" available. It started on August 30 and was completed with brilliant success on September 3, an outstanding feat of arms. Another as dazzling but briefer was that of the Australians at Péronne, where the Somme was not a river in the literal sense but a great canal, a main stream, minor ones, small lakes and marshes, in all a thousand yards in breadth. Crossing by repaired bridges, they

---

* For long the German front had been organized in three army groups: Bavarian Crown Prince, German Crown Prince, Duke Albrecht of Württemberg. This system of command by royal princes was traditional. However, three groups had proved insufficient. General von Gallwitz had therefore been placed in command of a small group between the Moselle and the Meuse, where he was to have to do with the Americans. Later, at the end of the Battle of Amiens on August 12, General von Boehn had taken over the Bavarian Crown Prince's three southern armies, leaving him two. These changes have provided commentators with witticisms at the expense of the princes, but Rupprecht did not feel slighted. He wrote in his diary that his group had become unwieldy. Rupprecht, II, 437.

took the town and stormed the dominating height of Mont Saint-Quentin, driving off it a fresh German division.

Again O.H.L. ordered a withdrawal, this time to the Hindenburg Line and the Canal du Nord, thus abandoning all the gains of the March offensive. In a period of over a month, from August 5 to September 8, the Germans also abandoned most of those of the Battle of the Lys.

Foch, who had been waspish, though undaunted, in adversity, was beaming now and had made a habit of wearing his cap on one side. Haig was the same as always. He had never showed signs of strain, and he did not become outwardly light-hearted as the peril passed. But he saw his way ahead. He disregarded a singularly defeatist telegram from the C.I.G.S. in the midst of the battle and did not mention its discouraging hint to his army commanders.* It was a little later that his own C.G.S., Lieutenant General Sir Herbert Lawrence, expressed to him some anxiety lest the Germans should launch a counteroffensive, in view of the fact that the British were "doing all the fighting." Haig replied: "We have got the enemy down; in fact, he is a beaten army." † The Germans broke up ten divisions in August to fill gaps in others.

What immediately followed was a closing up to the Hindenburg Line and the Canal du Nord by six Allied armies: Mangin's, Humbert's, Debeney's, Rawlinson's, Byng's, and Horne's. This was partly pursuit, but included some sharp fighting. By the tenth there was a halt. The armies were either up against the Hindenburg Line or, in the center, half a dozen lines of defense held by the British and Germans on March 21.

Meanwhile Pershing had contrived, after much argument, to concentrate a force of army strength in his own hands. The elimination of the Saint-Mihiel salient south of Verdun had been on the generalissimo's program since July. Now, when its turn came, it looked too modest. Surely better use might be made of the American First Army farther west. Haig had suggested to Foch that it should be directed against Mezières, a junction on the only main railway south

---

* Edmonds, *Military Operations, France and Belgium*, IV, 383. "Just a word of caution in regard to incurring heavy losses in attacks on Hindenburg Line as opposed to losses when driving the enemy back to that line. I do not mean to say that you have incurred such losses, but I know the War Cabinet would become anxious if we received heavy punishment in attacking the Hindenburg Line without success. Wilson." (The Drocourt-Quéant Line was meant.)
† Blake, p. 331.

of the Ardennes with a link to Namur on the enemy's main system. It looks fairly obvious strategy, but neither Foch nor Pershing had thought of it. However, it struck Foch forcibly. He told Pershing that he would not mind canceling that Saint-Mihiel offensive, but the American commander in chief was anxious to show what his men could do. It was agreed to limit the offensive and shift the Americans westward as quickly as possible.

Saint-Mihiel did not prove a hard nut to crack. The main attack, by the corps of Liggett and J. T. Dickman, was directed against the southern face; a secondary attack against the western face was made by Cameron's corps; and a purely holding attack between them by a French corps. Fifteen divisions stood in line, with four in reserve. The attack, launched at 5 A.M. on September 12 in dense fog, caught the Germans on the wrong foot because they were just beginning to pull out of the salient. It took just a day and a half to drive them out, leaving 15,000 prisoners and over 450 guns in American hands. At once the artillery started moving a day's march or two westward to its new front. The Americans were pleased by the warmth with which Foch congratulated them and by the arrival of French officers to study their methods.*

It still remained to secure the old fortifications used by the Germans as outworks of the Hindenburg Line, and this entailed hard fighting for the French First and the British Fourth and Third Armies during the fortnight beginning on September 12. Now a really big test was to follow. The battle was becoming more serried as the German salients were eaten up. In fact, owing to the shortening of the front, three French armies had been withdrawn since the counteroffensive on the Marne: the Ninth having disappeared at the end of that battle, and the headquarters of the Sixth and Third coming out in the first half of September.

Inspiring as was the outlook, the losses continued to be very heavy, though small by comparison with those of earlier offensives. Those of the British since August 8 numbered almost exactly 190,000. The French, over 100,000 to the end of August, must have been nearly as high. Over an enormous front every advance left a heavy trail of dead and wounded. The reduction in the rate was welcome of course, but comforting only to a limited extent to nations which had lost in four years of war so high a proportion of their youth and the finest flower of it at that. To individual families, those for instance

* Palmer, p. 296.

which lost a second, or like General de Castelnau, a third son, it could be no comfort at all. This factor accounts for the misgivings of the War Cabinet when Haig closed on the Drocourt-Quéant line. (Wilson would never have sent such a message to Haig had he not been bidden to.) If an assault on the Drocourt-Quéant Line called for reflection, this was far more so when it came to the deep Hindenburg system. Having considered the new plan of Foch, to be given later, Haig came to the conclusion recorded in his dispatch forwarded to the Secretary of State after the war:

> The probable results of a costly failure, or, indeed, of anything short of a decided success, in any attempt upon the main defences of the Hindenburg Line were obvious; but I was convinced that the British attack was the essential part of the general scheme and that the moment was favourable.
>
> Accordingly I decided to proceed with the attack.

Chapter VI

TRIUMPH IN ITALY AND THE BALKANS

FOR just over six weeks during the Austro-German offensive Italy had been a first-class theater of war with all eyes upon it. Seven German divisions had taken part in the "Miracle of Caparetto"; eleven French and British had moved to the aid of the Italians. Counting train journeys, Foch was absent from his post and absorbed in Italian affairs for over a month. Then most of the arrivals departed. Early in the year 1918, Fayolle, soon followed by his successor Maistre, Plumer, and, on the other side, Below, went to France. Four of the six French divisions, two of the British five, and all the German seven made the same journey. Italian protests were received with yawns. Italy had reverted to the status of a second-class theater of war. Two Italian divisions were sent to the Western Front.

The calm was shattered on June 15, when the Austrians launched a great offensive. Though they were without the German aid which had contributed greatly to the Caparetto offensive, their plan this time was actually more ambitious. The Austrian command did not rate the majority of the Italian troops very high, but it was sanguine to undertake offensive on both wings with fewer divisions, guns, and aircraft than the Allies. The main task was allotted to Conrad, who from the mountains was to penetrate to Vicenza; meanwhile Boreović was to cross the Piave, seize Treviso, exploit to Padua, and even to the Adige (65 miles). It was a vast pincer movement, with arms of equal strength. This was a compromise typical of mediocre minds. Conrad, like Schlieffen of old, realized that one arm should be the stronger; he naturally wanted it to be his, and his would come down on the flank of the enemy's communications, whereas the attack across the Piave would push the enemy back upon them. The Archduke Joseph argued that if *either* thrust were made very strong its penetration would ease the attack of the other. They were over-ruled.

Conrad inadvisedly made his heaviest thrust against the British and French on the Asiago plateau. The French shot the attackers to a standstill and lost no ground. Against the British the enemy broke in half a mile on a narrow front, but was thrown out within twenty-four hours. On the Piave it was another matter. The Austrians forced a passage on a 15-mile front and for a time it looked as though an Italian collapse might follow. But for the breaking of pontoon bridges and destruction of boats by the R.A.F., and later the rise of the river, Boreović would have won a signal success. As it was, after a maximum advance of five miles, the Emperor decided on a with-drawal across the river. The Austrians took some 50,000 prisoners, including a few hundred British, against 24,000 captured by the Italians. Yet the failure came as a fearful calamity to Austria. Deser-tion increased and deep depression set in. Conrad was dismissed as a scapegoat, a tragic end to a remarkable soldier. He was succeeded in the command of the western army group by the Archduke Joseph.

Even after the tide turned on the Western Front the Italians took long to make up their minds to pass to the offensive. The British commander, the Earl of Cavan, whose efficiency and loyalty were appreciated by General Diaz, used tactful persuasion. He was sup-ported by the most brilliant officer in the Italian army, the deputy chief of staff, General Badoglio, who became his personal friend. The Supreme War Council, which could play a greater role in Italy than in France, and Foch were active in the same sense. On October 1 Signor Orlando and Diaz agreed that the time was come. Diaz paid a compliment to his allies by creating two new armies, at the head of which he placed Cavan and the French commander Graziani, allot-ting an Italian corps to each. The plan was to break through on the Piave; penetrate to Vittoria Veneto, thus separating the Austrian river front from that in the mountains; and roll up the latter. The strength of the two sides was equal: fifty-six Allied divisions with four cavalry against fifty-five Austrian divisions and six cavalry.

Cavan's Tenth Army on the rough and swollen Piave led off on the night of October 23 by sending a British brigade over in scows poled by expert and gallant Italian boatmen to the big island of Papadopoli, to secure the half upstream. Finding that the Italian troops to take the other half did not appear, this brigade cleared the whole island on the twenty-fifth. There it was temporarily isolated by the rise of the river after heavy rain, and the attack had to be postponed until the twenty-seventh. Meanwhile the Italians had assaulted the Austrian front on the Monte Grappa, between the Piave and the Brenta, on the twenty-fourth, but were held in bloody fighting and lost their small gains to counterattacks. The situation looked rather doubtful.

During the night of the twenty-sixth Graziani's French troops of the Twelfth Army succeeded in crossing the upper Piave fifteen miles above the British front. The bridges were broken by flood and Austrian fire, but French and Italian Alpini battalions pushed boldly out from the north bank and secured a bridgehead. On their right the Eighth Army also got a footing on the north bank but failed altogether on the British left.

Now came the decisive thrust of the battle. By means of boats and footbridges two British brigades joined the two already on Papadopoli Island and the Italians now on it were also reinforced. At about 5.30 A.M. on October 27 the leading British battalions began to creep forward over the shingle. At 6.45 they entered the water, flowing like a torrent, in places in four separate channels. Sections linked arms and dragged their feet on the bottom to avoid being carried away, but a few men were drowned. On the far side they trampled down the wire, swarmed up the ten-foot flood bank, and put the defenders to flight. Then they pushed forward northward. To start with, both their flanks were open, but later on Italian troops came up. There was some fighting in two villages and among isolated houses, but resistance did not last. Meanwhile the French had enlarged their bridgehead and the Italian corps in their army had secured another, but the corps on either side of Cavan's Tenth Army were still stuck. On the following days, while his own advance continued, detachments sent out from both his flanks caused the Austrian fire to cease and assisted his neighbors to cross.

Little remains to be said of the Battle of the Piave. What followed was the pursuit of a beaten army in full retreat and pounded by the air forces of the Allies. The sharpest rear-guard action was on the first considerable river, the Monticano, five miles north of the Piave. Cavan put his two British divisions at this obstacle on October 29 with trifling artillery support, and they did the job against fresh troops. As for themselves, it was only the invigorating wine of victory that kept them on their feet. By October 30 the front formed a rough arc on a base of thirty-five miles along the Piave, and, where the Italians stood, north of the now historic site of Vittorio Veneto, a depth of fifteen miles. The advance continued northward and eastward, and by November 2 the Tagliamento was reached. Among the troops which crossed it was the American 332nd Regiment, forming part of an Italian division. The regiment had been sent to Italy at the end of July.

On the mountain front a British and a French division stood side by side south of Asiago, but in different Italian corps. On the initiative of the French commander, whose patrols had found the Austrians withdrawing, both divisions advanced on the morning of November 1, and the movement was quickly taken up by the Italians. Small actions were fought by the Austrians but did not hold up the advance for long. The British division entered the mighty Val d'Assa on the second and by noon had obtained unconditional surrender of the local Austrian forces at Trent.

This bloody war ended with a series of farcical incidents against the somber background of the final break-up of one of the famous armies of history. When the British reached the Tagliamento, the Second Gordon Highlanders in the advanced guard found a "peace conference" in progress on the bank between Italian cavalry commanders and Austrians.* The latter were protesting that an armistice had been signed, the former that they had heard nothing of it. When the British divisional commander arrived he said that anyhow he meant to cross the river, and did so. Much the same scene was enacted at Trent. An armistice, embodying terms approved by the Allied Prime Ministers—Colonel House representing President Wilson—and the Supreme War Council, had in fact been signed on November 3 but did not take effect until 3 P.M. on the fourth. Before that the Hungarian contingents had refused to go on fighting and their country had declared itself a republic.

The total number of prisoners is given as 300,000 but the majority of these must have been lines of communication troops. Just before the end two Italian naval officers achieved an amazing feat. They entered Pola harbor astride a torpedo used as a means of transport and attached a bomb to the dreadnought *Viribus Unitis*. They were captured and informed that the Austro-Hungarian navy was a thing of the past, having been taken over by an independent Yugoslav

* Falls, *The Gordon Highlanders in the First World War*, p. 242.

National Council. They then admitted what they had done. The ship was abandoned and the bomb duly exploded and sank her.

The factors combining to bring about the Austrian rout are many. Chief among them are the defeat of Germany on the Western Front and the surrender of Bulgaria in the Balkans; the failure of Austria's own summer offensive; the disaffection of troops of the subject peoples; hunger; and the Emperor's proclamation of a "federal state," which caused a break-up at home before it occurred in the field. The presence of British and French troops was enormously important. Their prestige counted for even more than their performance, though the latter was splendid and they led the way wherever they were represented. The sight of the leading British battalions waist-deep in fast-running water spread wholesale terror among Hungarians and South Slavs.

The gloomy and highly political Balkan front had taken on a more promising and more military appearance since the arrival of General Guillaumat. Yet still France and Britain—France backed by the extraordinary genius and personality of Venizelos—differed and wrangled. As the divisions of the Greek regular army came up to the forward zone the War Office counted them delightedly in the hope that as soon as there were enough it could withdraw the British and get quit of this bad-tasting *macédoine*.*

Guillaumat himself was anxious for an offensive. The fates ruled that it should be conducted by another hand, yet that he should be its instrument. On May 30 he carried out an operation west of the Vardar to gain valuable ground but still more to test the Greek troops and Bulgarian powers of resistance. He succeeded in every way. The dash with which the islanders of the Archipelago division swarmed up the precipitous flanks of the rocky Skra di Legen came as an eye-opener to spectators. About 2,000 prisoners were taken and counterattacks were repulsed. Then Guillaumat boomed the affair and managed to set a very fair proportion of the world talking of it, even at a moment when the war provided so much to talk of. It was assuredly a brilliant feat of arms, but the infantry engaged was only that of one division and a regiment of another (the Crete), so that but for Guillaumat's skilled publicity it would have been overlooked. Though the losses were heavy, the incident was a wonderful

* The stock joke about the Macedonian campaign, always good for a grin or a growl. One translation is "hotchpotch."

stimulus to the Greek forces and made the other national contingents realize that a valuable reinforcement had joined their ranks, just when they were getting rid of the Russians, rendered useless by Bolshevism. Ten days later Guillaumat left for France in haste and secrecy.* His departure was regretted by all, but he was not done with the Macedonian theater of war.

Franchet d'Esperey came bustling in, hurried round to see everybody—and found his attention gripped by the Serbian front east of the Crna. Nothing could have been more unpromising at first sight. The Serbians faced the mountain chain along which was traced the frontier between Greece and their own country. It averaged 4,500 feet, and within a couple of miles from the crest on the Greek side were points less than 600 feet above sea level. But the able Serbian chief of staff and virtual commander in chief, Voivode Mišić, showed Franchet d'Esperey a plan to storm this wall-like ridge and he developed it into one for a major offensive of unquestioned genius. The Serbians would drive northward to the Vardar, cut the railways following its bed, secure a region in the quadrilateral Veles-Stip-Gradsko-Krivolak, where a number of roads converged. They would thus at a blow sever the main Bulgarian communications and split the enemy's armies in two. The commander in chief realized that he had a great asset in the Serbians and would doubtless not have attempted such an undertaking without them. They were first-class mountain troops. They had been brought up to strength by about 16,000 former Austrian soldiers who had served with credit alongside the Russians. Some 6,000 had come via Port Arthur and Dalny, determined to fight again. They were eager to liberate their country and recover their homes. The roles allotted to other forces were stiff, but their chief object was to hold the enemy down. He must not be allowed to concentrate against the Serbians.

Though Franchet d'Esperey at once set about preparations, it was by no means certain that he would be allowed to strike. He received first-class support from his predecessor. Guillaumat put his case to Clemenceau and won him over, though he was little interested in the Balkans. He pleaded the cause to the Supreme War Council, hesitant at first but finally persuaded. Yet on July 25 the British C.I.G.S., Henry Wilson, stated that he was opposed to any offensive in this theater. By early September Guillaumat had leisure to extend his advocacy. He journeyed to London, and there on September 4 Lloyd

* See p. 347.

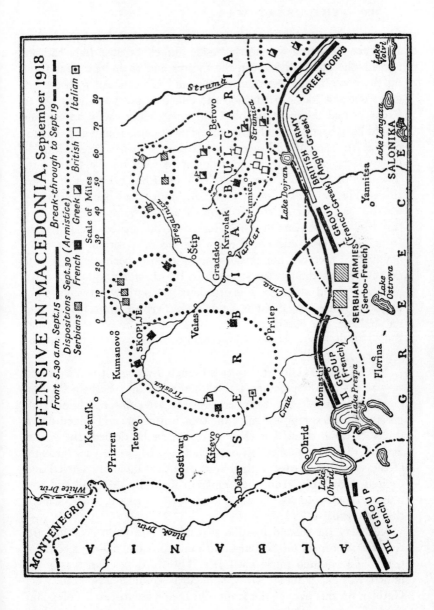

OFFENSIVE IN MACEDONIA, September 1918

Front 5.30 a.m. Sept.15 ▬▬▬ Break-through to Sept.19 ▬▬▬

Dispositions Sept.30 (Armistice) ·········

Serbians ▨ French ▨ Greek ▨ British ☐ Italian ◉

Scale of Miles

0   10   20   30   40   50   60   70   80

George informed him that the government agreed. But by this time Franchet d'Esperey was nearly beside himself because Italy had not agreed—she had a division in the theater and an independent force on the coast facing Austrian troops—and Clemenceau forbade any move without Italian permission and talked of postponement. Off to Rome posted the indefatigable Guillaumat. How useful an airplane would have been! * The Italian government came round and on September 10 Franchet d'Esperey heard that he had a free hand. He ordered the preliminary bombardment to start on the fourteenth. The driving force of the commander in chief had been that of a hurricane. Heavy guns (150 mm. and 105 mm.) had been hoisted by tractors and tackle on to two mountains over 7,000 feet high captured by the Serbians in 1916. Here they dominated the Bulgarian front on the crest and could reach the second position, three miles beyond.† Threefold numerical superiority had been massed at the decisive point, though the strength in the theater was nearly equal in infantry and artillery. The attackers' strength was twenty-eight divisions (nine Greek, eight French, six Serbian, four British, and one Italian), 291 battalions against over 300 in the fewer but larger Bulgarian divisions. About ten German battalions and a great deal of artillery remained.

The assault was entrusted to two French divisions. It was launched at 5.30 A.M. on September 15. With the aid of a Serbian division covering their left, they stormed the crest after fierce fighting. Bulgarian soldiers sprang up on to the trench parapets and rained down grenades upon them, but they were not to be denied. By 6 P.M. Serbian divisions, pushed up on their heels, began to pass through, at the same time crossing their own frontier. Intensely moved and excited, men broke from their ranks to shake by the hand and embrace French soldiers. Then, as they went forward, they chanted the "Marseillaise."

Next day the second position was taken, and from now onward the war weariness in the Bulgarian ranks on which Franchet d'Esperey had counted made itself felt. The third position was abandoned without a fight. Army and corps commanders, who were German on this part of the front, did their best to patch holes, and single German battalions behaved well. But the advance was unre-

---

* Franchet d'Esperey actually sent a staff officer to Guillaumat by air through Italy. It must have been one of the earliest missions of the kind.

† Falls, *Military Operations, Macedonia,* II, 129.

lenting. Before dawn on September 21 the Serbians were looking down into the Vardar valley at Krivolak, watching the glare of burning villages and stores and hearing the explosions of ammunition dumps.

Meanwhile the advance was being extended on both flanks by French and Greek troops, and once more the British attacked, on September 18 and 19, the field fortress west of Lake Doiran which had twice held them up. It did so once again, though Greek troops on the west shore of the lake established themselves nearly a mile within the defenses. Three days later the Bulgarians were in retreat from the lake to Monastir, seventy-five miles, and Franchet d'Esperey was stridently demanding that the retreat should be turned into a rout.

It was, though to an even greater extent by British, French and Greek air forces than by the infantry and cavalry. The bombing of retreating troops in mountain defiles completed the demoralization. On September 30, when Franchet d'Esperey granted an armistice to Bulgarian civil and military plenipotentiaries, the leading Serbian troops were eighty miles from their start-line—and every unit must have marched at least half as far again—and French cavalry was holding Skoplje. By the terms of the armistice all Bulgarian troops blocked west of Skoplje had to lay down their arms and become prisoners of war. The rest of the army was to be demobilized immediately, except for troops required for security. In secret articles it was laid down that Bulgaria should put her railways, roads, and ports at the disposal of her conquerors. To avoid fighting in the country, German and Austrian forces, not participators in the armistice, were given a time limit of four weeks in which to quit it. Those in Serbia had, of course, to take their chance and were soon to find out what this meant.

Franchet d'Esperey—"desperate Frankie," as the British called him in amusement at his methods mingled with admiration for his genius and drive—now took the bit between his teeth. The Supreme War Council and the British War Office had neither cared about the offensive nor taken it seriously. His determination to advance to the Danube was regarded as an extravagant gesture. He was not ordered to stand fast, but Lloyd George turned down his proposal that the British should participate on a large scale. He and Milne had other views for their employment.

Franchet d'Esperey did not greatly mind. He knew this must be a campaign resembling those of the age of Napoleon rather than of the age of railways. Often the troops would have to live on the country, ill stocked after being exploited by the enemy's requisitioning officers. In any case the van must be Serbian, though French and Greek troops would also be employed.

Neither Lloyd George nor Milne was much interested in the Danube, but both were deeply interested in the Dardanelles. They knew that Turkey stood on the brink of capitulation. Her armies had been routed by Allenby in Syria, but it was the collapse of Bulgaria that induced her to sue for terms. Already Anglo-French rivalry was raising its head. The British government felt that, since their country had borne the brunt of the war with Turkey and the armistice with Bulgaria had been arranged without reference to Milne, that with Turkey should be stage-managed by Britain alone. Wemyss, the First Sea Lord, remarked that the Allied fleet must enter the Black Sea under a British admiral, as "a proper recognition of Great Britain's share in the Dardanelles campaign and the final Turkish downfall." * Milne switched forces eastward to the Turkish frontier on the Maritsa, but there was no fighting. Turkish envoys reached Mudros on October 26, to be received by Vice-Admiral Sir S. A. Gough-Calthorpe, British commander in chief in the Mediterranean. The Turks fenced for a time, but on the thirtieth duly signed as bidden. The main clauses of the Mudros armistice were: opening of the Dardanelles and Bosporus, demobilization of the Turkish army, surrender of all warships and all outlying garrisons. The foes were going down like ninepins. On November 12 a vast armada, led by Gough-Calthorpe in the dreadnought *Superb* sailed through the Dardanelles. So long was the naval procession that when the flagship reached Helles, the second fleet, the French, was not yet in sight.

"It was triumphal, yet scarcely a triumph. The memory of the lost chances, of the vast sacrifices of 1915, brooded upon the scene, typified by the hulk of the *River Clyde* and the ruined fort of Sedd el Bahr. The Dardanelles had not been forced; they had survived the war, impregnable." †

Hardly had the other armistice, with Bulgaria, been concluded than the Serbian armies strode northward. They went through the opposition like a scythe through grass. German troops from Russia appeared in strength more than equal to their own, only to be

* Newbolt, *Naval Operations*, V, 351.
† Falls, *Military Operations, Macedonia*, II, 270.

thrashed and hustled out of the way. True, many of them were rotted by communism, but their miserable showing was as big a humiliation as Germany had endured since the flight from Jena. By November 10 French troops had secured a bridgehead over the Danube at Ruschuk. Franchet d'Esperey was prepared to march to Budapest and even Dresden, but there was no need of this. The head of a revolutionary Hungarian government, Count Karolyi, came to Belgrade to sue and was accorded an armistice—yet another. The terms were much the same as the Bulgarian.

It was a marvelous victory. One must doubt whether any leader or any troops other than Franchet d'Esperey and the Serbians who played the major part could have won it. For the British the whole story of this theater of war is sad. The government and general staff hated the venture. The contingent was badly supported from home. Even its mosquito netting arrived late two years running and its modest demands for guns and ammunition for the final offensive were not met. The fine British troops could not win a victory in the series of victories which hastened the end of the war.

Chapter VII

TRIUMPH IN PALESTINE
AND MESOPOTAMIA

SOME critics accuse Allenby of dallying and wasting chances after securing a front north of Jerusalem and Jaffa. Clear evidence would be needed to prove this thrusting man guilty of such an error. Rains, the like of which old men could not recall, had flooded the lowlands. Bridges and culverts had been swept away by wadis in spate. He was compelled to begin the year 1918 by reorganizing his communications. Could he have smashed the Turks in March? Well, in that month he launched a raid beyond Jordan, and had to acknowledge failure in face of Turkish resistance. He tried again in April and again was compelled to withdraw. It looks as though the Turks were then less shaky than the critics allege. In the Jordan valley Allenby even lost guns, from British horse-artillery batteries of the Australian Mounted Division. The Australians, unused to losing guns, were upset.

By the end of March a major offensive was unthinkable for months to come. The great German assault in France was the signal for the War Office to call for troops. It must indeed have felt twinges of conscience over the risk run by keeping so many good British troops in a theater of minor strategic significance. Allenby sent back two divisions and the infantry strength of three more, in all nearly 60,000 men. Numerically he did not suffer. He received two Indian divisions from Mesopotamia and Indian battalions to replace British sent to France, but the single battalions arrived slowly and some were raw. On the other hand, all Indian cavalry regiments in France were sent to him. He could thus create a fourth cavalry division and build up the Desert Mounted Corps to a splendid force. Small French infantry and cavalry detachments, tokens of France's interest in Syria, were embodied. The summer was gone before Allenby was ready to strike again.

By then the Turkish armies had greatly deteriorated. In infantry divisions the Turks far outnumbered Allenby's seven, but the rifle strength was under half the British, and the artillery about two-thirds. Falkenhayn had been replaced by Liman von Sanders of Gallipoli fame, a change for the worse. Liman was a stout and capable soldier. He knew the Turkish army and was more popular than his predecessor. However, whereas Falkenhayn favored an elastic defense, Liman closed up his troops and bade his subordinates fight it out where they stood. This was asking for trouble. Unluckily for Liman the Taurus tunnel was shut for ten days in September, to convert the narrow gauge to standard. The troops thus went hungrier than ever at the critical time. They were afflicted with disease and their lines of communication swarmed with deserters.

They were not left undisturbed during the summer. Minor operations took place, especially in the Jordan valley. The heaviest pressure, however, was exerted against them far from the main front, mostly on 600 miles of the Hejaz Railway, which terminated at the sacred city of Medina, where the southernmost Turkish garrison was entrenched. Murray had consistently supported the Arab revolt; Allenby, whose vivid imagination belied his conventional air, saw still more in it and gave it even more potent aid. The link between him and the Arabs was a little body of British officers, most notable of whom was T. E. Lawrence, who had a spiritual affinity with the Bedouin and was a master of guerrilla tactics and strategy. By the time Allenby arrived the Turks were confined to the railway, which they held by a series of blockhouses at the stations. From Ma'an to Medina, where the two largest garrisons lay, they had about 25,000 troops.

Allenby provided British forces, including armored cars with 10-pounder guns and machine guns. An Arab "regular army" of some five battalions and light artillery was formed under ex-prisoner of war Ja'far, captured at Agagiya.* Bedouin and later settled fellahin were recruited as needed. They could not be kept out for long or indeed brought out without high pay. It was a grand war for them: free arms and a well-paid war of liberation. And these simple-

* See p. 161. Ja'far became Iraqi ambassador in London and Prime Minister of Iraq. His end was assassination, the not uncommon fate of Arab notables.

minded sons of the desert must have foreseen currency inflation, for they insisted on payment in gold sovereigns.

In April the line on either side of Ma'an was utterly destroyed over a long stretch. This finally isolated Medina because the Turks no longer possessed spare rails to replace those destroyed with explosives or removed. Medina continued to be besieged by the Arab southern army, but otherwise the war had left the Hejaz far behind. The northern army was under the command of the Emir Feisal, third son of Sherif Hussein, who had assumed the title of King of the Hejaz. It took its general directions from Allenby. Feisal and Lawrence were ready to call out thousands of nomads and villagers and to march north on Allenby's right flank when he took the offensive.

The Hejaz, on the other hand, was war-weary and King Hussein was angry. The famous Balfour Declaration of November 1917, promising a "national home" for the Jewish people in Palestine, had greatly disquieted him. He had learned also of a secret pact, the Sykes-Picot Agreement, nearly two years older, and disliked it at least as much. It provided for French occupation of part of Syria and influence in another. Hussein considered that both the Declaration and the Agreement, especially the latter, conflicted with the pledges made to him before he raised the standard of revolt at Mecca. Britain's part was curious. It looks utterly dishonest, but it would seem that stupidity and lack of coordination were most to blame. The government could legitimately support the interest of France in Syria, where her scholars, her doctors, her teachers, and her monks had accomplished honorable work. It could reasonably make an offer to Jews calculated to rally to its cause the power of international Jewry. But to hand negotiations, as happened, to different representatives aware only of the pledges they themselves were giving was unworthy of the traditions of the country.

Allenby's plan was entirely his own. No staff officer would have dared to put it up because it involved the cavalry outmarching its supply vehicles and living on the country. Allenby would mass his main infantry strength in the coast plain to wheel forward, the left wing moving fastest, as though he were opening a gate in the Turkish front. Through the gate, he would pass the Desert Mounted Corps of three cavalry divisions—the other being intended to act on the right flank beyond the Jordan. The cavalry would ride fast northward, cross the hill chain which ends in Mount Carmel, descend into the Plain of Esdraelon, and push eastward to the Jordan

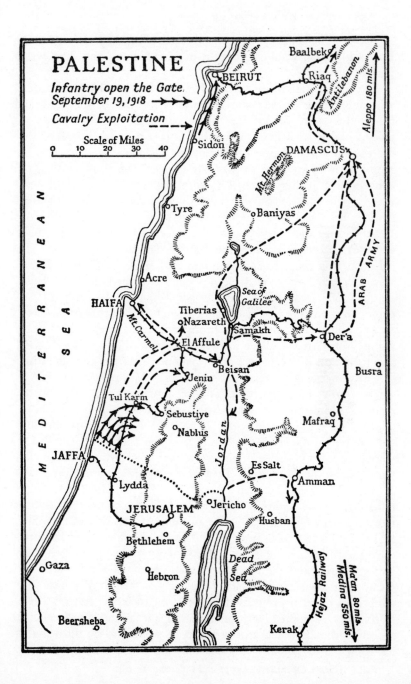

PALESTINE

Infantry open the Gate,
September 19, 1918 →→→
Cavalry Exploitation --->

Scale of Miles
0   10   20   30   40

MEDITERRANEAN SEA

Baalbek
BEIRUT
Riaq
Antilebanon
Aleppo 180 mls.

Sidon

DAMASCUS

Mt. Hermon

Tyre
Baniyas

Acre
Sea of Galilee

HAIFA
Mt. Carmel
Tiberias
Nazareth
El Affule
Samakh
Der'a
ARAB ARMY

Beisan
Busra

Jenin

Tul Karm
Sebustiye
Nablus
Mafraq

JAFFA
Jordan
Es Salt
Amman

Lydda
JERUSALEM
Jericho
Husban

Bethlehem
Dead Sea

Gaza
Hebron

Beersheba
Ma'an 80 mls.
Medina 550 mls.
Hejaz Railway

Kerak

at Beisan. The Turks, toiling northward after their defeat by the British infantry, would be caught in a wide-flung net. This was a plan of genius.

The concentration was screened by the R.A.F. which, reinforced with up-to-date aircraft, drove the Germans out of the skies, and hidden by every device that ingenuity could suggest. Ruses included camps with lines of dummy horses to make it appear that the cavalry was still near Jerusalem and elaborate arrangements for a race meeting on the great day. At 4.30 A.M. on September 19 the concentrated artillery opened its bombardment. The Turkish reply was ragged and quickly declined. A few minutes after the first British shells had dropped the infantry of Bulfin's five divisions swarmed into the Turkish trenches, covered by a cloud of smoke and dust not yet pierced by the light of dawn.

Liman was caught napping. Here and there Turkish resistance was gallant, but every obstacle was quickly turned from the flanks. The advance went almost entirely according to plan, and signs of demoralization appeared as the attack reached the artillery positions. At one point where the enemy brought forward a team, hooked up a gun, and started to drive it away, a British officer swung himself into the saddle of a captured pony, galloped after the gun, and made the drivers turn it back and surrender.* Meanwhile the R.A.F. spread terror and destruction. The rail junction at El Affule in the plain of Esdraelon was temporarily put out of action. The headquarters of the Seventh Army (Mustapha Kemal Pasha, Britain's old foe on the Gallipoli Peninsula) and the Eighth (Jevad Pasha) were bombed, and the latter never afterward had any communication with Liman at Nazareth. Transport retreating northward was smashed, blocking the road out of Tul Karm, which the Turks failed to clear by nightfall. The great wheel was completed. Bulfin's front, facing nearly north in the morning, faced due east at midnight, and his left wing stood at Tul Karm, fourteen miles from the start-line. Fourteen miles in a day's fighting was good going by any standards, and the Londoners who took Tul Karm may have set up a British record to date. (Let Second World War men contemptuous of such progress think of it on their flat feet on a hot, stuffy, day, weighted with ammunition and rations, in face of a foe unexpectedly stubborn just when he seemed to be throwing in his hand.) The infantry had not only opened a corridor for the

* Falls, *Military Operations, Egypt and Palestine*, II, 482.

cavalry but covered its right for these first fourteen miles of its ride.

The two Turkish divisions in the plain were reduced to bands of terrified fugitives seeking only escape and already doomed, since the cavalry was entering the passes in the Carmel range in their rear. In the Judean Hills the Turks remained nearly intact because Chetwode * was too weak to do them great harm, but their escape routes were about to be cut likewise.

The two leading cavalry divisions went forward about 7 A.M., one through a flagged gap cut in the Turkish wire, the other along the beach. To start with there was no resistance because the area had been cleared by the infantry. Any that occurred later on was trifling because the sight of the plain alive with horsemen proved too much for the nerves of the small parties of Turks encountered. The leading regiment of the Fourth Cavalry Division entered the Musmus pass through the Carmel chain in the darkness, trotting twenty minutes, walking twenty, and halting five in its hurry to make up for a hitch which had caused a delay. It emerged in the early hours of September 20 in the plain of Esdraelon. There the first fight occurred, a charge that routed a Turkish regiment which had arrived too late to block the pass. Then the division took El Affule, where many engines and trucks lay in the railway sidings. After a brief halt it moved down to the Jordan at Beisan. It had covered over seventy miles in thirty-four hours and foundered only twenty-six horse, though all were somewhat distressed. Few finer examples of horsemastership can be found than that of these Indian and British yeomanry regiments and the horse artillery.

The troops were inspired and delighted by their feat. The days of cavalry were not over—anyhow not quite. It is true that cavalry had always played a more striking role in Palestine than in other theaters, but the Indian regiments, the largest element, had seen no great success since their arrival and recalled the frustration of the mounted arm in France. Now all felt on top of the world. For the moment the Fourth Division could rest weary horses and wait for thousands of Turks, dazed with fatigue, to march into its arms, sometimes after a short struggle to get through.

The Fifth Cavalry Division crossed the plain of Esdraelon, climbed up to Nazareth, just missed capturing the enemy's commander in chief after fierce street fighting, but sent him off as a fugitive to

* Chetwode's senior general staff officer was now one Brigadier General A. P. Wavell, who was to cause some stir in the next war.

Tiberias. The Australian Mounted Division, following the Fourth Cavalry, sent a brigade eastward on an air report that large bodies of the enemy were retreating north from Jenin. The brigade captured the town, blocked the main Nablus-Nazareth road, and by the morning of the twenty-first took 8,000 prisoners. As these were marched out the highly disciplined Germans at the head of the column goose-stepped when a general's car passed.

The rest of the battle must be briefly recorded. Bulfin's and Chetwode's infantry kept up the pressure, gradually disintegrating Mustapha Kemal's Seventh Army, capturing many thousands of prisoners and driving the rest into the cavalry net. Mount Carmel and Haifa were captured, Carmel by an extraordinary cavalry charge along the crest. Samakh, on the shore of the Sea of Galilee, was stormed by the Australians after bitter fighting with a handful of dogged German defenders. Allenby had told T. E. Lawrence that the one vital point he could not reach quickly was Dera, the junction of the Palestine railways with the Hejaz line. It was strongly defended, so that the Emir Feisal * and Lawrence did not take it until September 27, but they had already cut the line in several places and gravely interrupted the traffic. The one blot on Allenby's scheme, his failure to block, fifteen miles south of Beisan, Jordan fords toward which a great part of the Turkish Seventh Army was streaming in disorder, was remedied by a single brigade of the Fourth Cavalry Division. Moving down both banks, it boldly went into the attack and by the end of a day of sweat and toil captured about twenty-five times its own strength in prisoners. The R.A.F. had already destroyed the Seventh Army's transport in the Wadi el Fara. Farther south the Australian and New Zealand Division crossed the Jordan, captured Amman, and blocked the path of the Turkish Fourth Army's detachments along the Hejaz Railway. In all it took 10,000 prisoners.

Allenby was not given to opening his mind even to senior subordinates before this became necessary. Not till September 22 did he mention the word "Damascus" to the commander of the Desert Mounted Corps, Sir. H. G. Chauvel, but this warning gave the staff time to think out the problem. Chauvel's telegraphic orders of Sep-

* Feisal's chief of staff was a first-class young Arab officer who had served in the Turkish army, Colonel Nuri Bey. Some weeks before these lines were written, when he was Prime Minister of Iraq, he was murdered in Baghdad, deeply regretted by many British friends.

tember 26 began: "Seventh and Eighth Turkish Armies have been destroyed. Fourth Army is retreating on Damascus via Dera. Desert Mounted Corps will move on Damascus." * The Fourth Cavalry Division was to move east of the Sea of Galilee, the other two west of it, the Australians in the lead. Simultaneously Bulfin's corps was to advance along the coast track, not in those days deserving the name of road, and seize Beirut.

Both goals were reached, Damascus (by the Australians) on October 1, Beirut (by the Seventh Indian Division) on the second, after immense efforts and for the cavalry and the Arabs stiff fighting. In the process about half the remainder of the Turkish Fourth Army was killed or taken. Even this was not the end. Homs was reached by the Fifth Cavalry Division on October 16. Then it was sent on to Aleppo alone, waves of malaria and influenza having put the Fourth Cavalry Division virtually out of action. Aleppo was reached on the twenty-fifth and next day two Indian regiments were checked at Haritan by two new divisions formed by Mustapha Kemal. It was the last action before news of the Mudros armistice with Turkey brought a standstill and the return home of the German troops in the country. The German combatants, two regiments of all arms, had never broken and had won the respect of their foes.

The Fifth Cavalry Division had marched 550 miles in thirty-eight days. This will take some beating, but much more when it is added that it lost only 21 per cent of its horses from all causes and that these included four major actions.

The political situation hardly belongs to the war because it did not bear its poisonous fruits for some time. It was, however, from the first a cause of unending worry to the commander in chief. Briefly, for the purposes of military occupation pending final settlements, he was instructed to set up three zones: one, Palestine itself, administered by the British; one, a Syrian coast strip with Beirut as chief town, administered by the French; and one, a vast zone east of the Dead Sea and the Jordan and including Damascus, Homs, Hama, and Aleppo, to be administered by Arab representatives. These zones represented a modified version of the disastrous Sykes-Picot Agreement, which clashed with British promises to the Arabs. At least Britain had the good sense to keep the French out of Damascus and the Arab zone until Clemenceau overcame their opposition at Versailles, with unhappy results. Cynics say Allenby won fame in

* Falls, *Military Operations, Egypt and Palestine*, II, 723.

an easy task, "a tiger against a tomcat." In truth no other British commander would have set such a goal. He took 75,000 prisoners (3,700 of them Germans and Austrians), for a loss of 5,666, only 650 in the Desert Mounted Corps. Objectives in any way short of those he laid down would have achieved only the sort of victory commonly won by our old friend, *le bon général ordinaire*.

Something has been said about the element of politics in the Mesopotamian campaign. In early 1918 it overshadowed the military element. On the spot the Turks were nearly fought to a finish. They were still capable of a respectable static defense and might prove dangerous foes if attacked frontally, but they crumpled if their flank was turned. On the other hand, in Asia Minor they were whooping like huntsmen at the kill, eager to beat their German allies in a race for the northern oil fields. The British C.I.G.S., Sir Henry Wilson, was a politically minded soldier, a merit in itself but bewildering when—just like a politician pure and simple—he overlooked military problems in seeking political ends. These were: if possible to save Georgia, Russian Armenia, and Russian Azerbaijan from Turks and Germans with the aid of local resistance, and at all events to stop any advance into northern Persia and secure control of the Caspian Sea, partly for the sake of Afghanistan, where the friendly Amir was threatened by a pro-Turkish party.

To do any of these things General Marshall, the commander in chief, had to reinforce north Persia and establish lines of communications to the Caspian. Having sent two divisions to Egypt, he now had to push so many troops and so much transport into Persia that his prospects of defeating the Turks on the Tigris looked distinctly less rosy. Major General L. C. Dunsterville, the model for Rudyard Kipling's Stalky, was appointed chief of a military mission to the Caucasus, but to begin with could not go beyond Hamadan, 200 miles south of Enzeli,* on the Caspian. However, on August 4 the leading troops of "Dunsterforce" reached Enzeli, and by the twentieth a battalion was in Baku. Russian troops there proved better at talking than fighting—resolutions rather than resolution were later to be the great advantage of Soviet Russia in these regions. Three weak British battalions could not keep on stopping the Turkish advance on Baku when their allies, including Bolsheviks, kept on bolting.

* Enzeli, then and again Persian after restoration by Russia, is now Pahlevi.

Dunsterville re-embarked his troops for Enzeli on September 15. That port was held and Baku was reoccupied after hostilities with Turkey had ended. Some extracts from a telegram from Wilson to Marshall of June 28 show how the commander in chief had been repetitively jogged: "H. M. Government are not satisfied that we are taking full advantage of our opportunities or that in north-west Persia and on the Caspian our maximum effort is being made. Whole situation should be reviewed by you in light of more recent information regarding lack of enemy activity in the plains of Mesopotamia. ...In short, a greater and more sustained effort must be made in north-west Persia.... We are confident that you will realize now that your main attention must be directed towards Persia and the Caspian." *

Fortunately, he was a calm man who never argued unnecessarily. The value of the effort is difficult to assess, but historians would doubtless have blamed Britain had it not been made.

To return to Mesopotamia, at the end of March the British had hit the secondary Turkish front on the Euphrates a smashing blow at Khan Baghdadi. While the infantry stormed this strong position a cavalry brigade worked round the flank and boldly placed itself across the Aleppo road in rear, where it foiled a Turkish attempt to break through. Over 5,000 prisoners were taken. Then, however, activities were, as before, laid aside for the hot weather.

At the end of September, when Allenby's forces were sweeping northward, the War Cabinet decided that something should be done in Mesopotamia to exploit the victory in Palestine. Marshall was directed to advance up the Tigris and to study the feasibility of a cavalry thrust along the Euphrates valley. Allenby in fact needed no assistance and anyhow Marshall had not got the necessary transport owing to the quantity working south of the Caspian. He disregarded his instructions about the Euphrates valley and prepared an advance up the Tigris by a corps of all arms under his competent subordinate, Lieutenant General A. S. Cobbe.

There appeared to be no need for hurry until October 13, when the Turkish chargé d'affaires in Madrid sought Spanish good offices in asking the President of the United States to re-establish peace. Then on the twentieth General Townshend, the former commander in Mesopotamia, was brought by the Turks to Mitylene to ask for discussions on the terms of an armistice. This seems to have

* Moberly, IV, 186.

acted as a strong stimulant, a sudden "shot in the arm," in Mesopotamia.

On October 2 the War Office had told Marshall that, in case the Turks should ask for a cessation of hostilities, it was advisable to gain as much ground as possible up the Tigris, but that the work of the line of communication to the Caspian should not be retarded in any way. He had replied that the ruling factor was transport and that "practically all my transport of every description is employed on the Persian road." His first objective would be the Little Zab, an eastern tributary of the Tigris some fifty miles ahead. Further action would "depend upon developments." No signs here of a rush for Mosul, which was eighty miles beyond the Little Zab.*

When it was clear that the Turks were definitely seeking an armistice, Mosul and its oil potentialities at once became an extremely attractive goal. To get it, or get as close to it as humanly possible, was most important, because this would present the world with a *fait accompli*. The operations finally took on the air of a race between Cobbe's troops and the negotiators in the cabin of H. M. S. *Agamemnon* in Mudros harbor. It could not be called immoral, but some foreign observers and historians have found it slightly unseemly.

The strength of the Turkish Sixth Army astride the Tigris was not easy to predict because no one could be sure what troops it would be able to draw in toward the river from a front widely spread, especially eastward. Cobbe expected to encounter two divisions and part of a third, but their rifle strength was considerably lower than that of his own two infantry divisions. His tactics were to be those constantly applied in this theater, in general efficiently and successfuly: frontal attack by infantry combined with flank attack when possible; turning movements and reverse attack by cavalry; artillery cooperation from one bank to the other.

The offensive was launched on October 23. The well-tried formula did not catch the Turks in their outpost position because they cleared out in time, withdrawing to the Little Zab. Despite road demolitions, the British followed closely on both banks of the Tigris, and a cavalry brigade, having marched seventy-seven miles in thirty-nine hours, crossed the Little Zab by a bad ford. Finding his flank turned, the commander of the Turkish Tigris Group, Ismael Hakki, cleverly withdrew all troops on the left (eastern) bank to the right and broke up his floating bridge. But he was not quick enough, and indeed had

* Moberly, IV, 259-260.

not the necessary mobility in transport to escape the net. The same cavalry brigade that had crossed the Little Zab found a ford over the Tigris, thirty miles away, on the twenty-sixth, and made its way to the right bank, though one of the three channels was four and a half feet deep. It was in a risky position because the infantry had been held up. (On this day the armistice commissioners met in Mudros Bay, but a day was gained for the advance on Mosul because the Turkish envoys were too weary or seasick to start work).*

On October 27 Hakki fell back to a position five miles north of Sharqat. Before the main body had closed with him, the cavalry brigade three miles farther north had a tough time of it, but it was reinforced by another brigade and some infantry and the united force held its own in very sharp fighting. This force was indeed an indispensable element in what followed. In the battle of Sharqat, fought on the twenty-ninth, the infantry did not succeed in breaking the Turkish front, but Hakki realized he was bottled up. In the great days of the Turkish army he would have tried to break through the force in his rear, but these days were done. At daybreak on the thirtieth white flags were seen flying all along the Turkish front, and by 7.30 A.M. the Turkish Tigris Group surrendered. For the whole offensive the haul was 11,322 prisoners and fifty-one guns. The British casualties were 1,886. (That night the armistice was signed in the *Agamemnon*, but not to come into force till next day.)

The cavalry brigades were ordered to make for Mosul as soon as possible, feeding on the country, which they duly did. As horse-masters they must have been as good as Allenby's. On November 1, twelve miles south of Mosul, they learned that the armistice had become operative at noon the day before. The Turks expected to be allowed to remain in Mosul and even requested the British to go back to the point reached at noon on October 31. Not at all, wired Marshall when he heard of this pretension: Clause 7 gave the victors the right to occupy any strategic point. Now what Clause 7 actually authorized was such occupation "in the event of a situation arising which threatens the security of the Allies." Here one could not find a threat with the strongest magnifying glass. But the British were going to have Mosul. In the discussions that followed the Turkish government was told that if the Turkish remnant would take itself off quietly the British government would not insist on demanding its surrender under Clause 16, which laid down that all garrisons in

* Newbolt, *Naval Operations*, V, 355.

Mesopotamia, among other districts, must surrender. The Sixth Army commander argued with some point that his army, or what remained of it, was not a garrison but a field force, so that the clause did not apply. But the British were going to have Mosul. In the end the matter was amicably settled. The Turks marched out and the British marched in.

The offensive was a very fine one. It hung upon supply far more than usual. Marshall and Cobbe estimated accurately what they could do and did it. The infantry fought like heroes, had most of the dirty work, and suffered the vast majority of the losses, but the cavalry— two brigades as compared with Allenby's three divisions in his main offensive and four in all—had the *beau role*. It was superbly handled, with a combination of boldness and skill, and fought admirably, mounted and dismounted.*

Mesopotamia cost 92,501 casualties, 15,814 killed in battle, 12,807 dead from disease. It is hard to believe that the oil wells and pipes could not have been protected more cheaply by a force at the head of the Persian Gulf and "judicious subsidies," even what cynics may call bribery.

* Divisional commanders can seldom be named in a single-volume history of this war, still less brigade commanders. Here it may be mentioned that the commander of the Eleventh Cavalry brigade which did the turning movements, and later the commander of the whole force which blocked the rear of the Tigris Group was Brigadier General Cassels and that, as General Sir Robert Cassels, he was commander in chief in India in the earlier part of the Second World War.

Chapter VIII

THE DEFEAT OF GERMANY IN THE WEST

VICTORY was in the air breathed by the Allies in the west. Not even the smell of decay, of high explosive, or the sickening sweetness of mustard gas could disguise it. The tasks ahead were certainly formidable. In addition to a series of prepared defenses, the Germans would make good use of rivers and canals. For the first time since 1914, however, a general offensive, on a vast front, from the Meuse to the Channel, could be launched. Superiority of numbers had been attained, but it was not sensational. The chief factors making such an offensive possible were tanks and superiority in the air, in guns, mechanical and horse transport, food, and, last but not least, fighting spirit.

The German leaders were well aware of their deficiencies, particularly in spirit. Significantly, old Hindenburg, almost a cipher in days of victory, was coming to the front. Intrepidity is more useful than tactical skill in times as ugly as these, and Ludendorff's nerves were breaking. Prince Rupprecht, a courageous man but not like Hindenburg an optimist by nature, wrote on September 27 that peace must be concluded in the winter, even though it should be on hard terms.*

The German defensive tactics were sound. The front was held in six zones: outpost zone, forward battle zone, main battle zone, greater battle zone, rearward position, and rearward battle zone. The first was what its name implies. Its function was to disorganize the attack. Even the forward battle zone was lightly held, by squads, machine guns and single field guns. Only in the greater battle zone was the front line the line of resistance. Yet these high-flown titles often meant little. When driven back to a strong prepared position

* Rupprecht, ñ, 451.

like the Hindenburg Line the Germans obviously had to make it the main line of resistance and fight for it; in fact the campaign developed into retreats from one line to the next. In the intervals defense depended on large numbers of hidden machine guns. The result was that serious breaches in the German array were avoided but ground was steadily lost.

The opposing strengths by divisions were French 102, British 60, American 39, Belgian 12, Italian 2, Portuguese 2, a total of 217; German 193, Austrian 4, a total of 197.

On September 3 Foch had issued a directive which determined the future course of the campaign. The influence of Haig's ideas is marked.

The British, supported by the French left, would attack in the direction of Cambrai and Saint-Quentin.

The French center would drive the enemy beyond the Aisne; the Americans, after the Saint-Mihiel operation, and the French Fourth Army on their left would attack in the direction of Mézières.

Then, on September 8, Foch visited the King of the Belgians and afterward saw Haig and Plumer. As a result, an offensive in Flanders, directed on Ghent and Bruges, was added, for which the British Second Army and a French force were placed under the orders of King Albert, with the French General Degoutte as chief of staff. It was the official version of the catchword of Foch: "*Tout le monde à la bataille!*"

The American First and French Fourth Armies struck first, on September 26. The Americans had, after completing their business at Saint-Mihiel, quickly extended their front to include most of the breadth of the Argonne Forest. Pershing states that he was given a choice between this sector and Champagne, farther west, and chose this because he thought no troops but his possessed the morale or offensive spirit to tackle it.* In his personal account he writes: "Most of the light and heavy guns ... and supply trains ... were provided by the French, some by the British ... and practically none from home. We had 189 light tanks, all of French manufacture, 25 per cent of which were handled by French personnel." †

The Germans were partially surprised, and in any case the system of defense in depth made it likely that the first day's thrust with limited objectives would succeed. Neither Pershing—who was com-

* Pershing, *Report*, p. 41.
† Pershing, *My Experiences in the World War*, p. 608.

bining the functions of commander in chief and commander of the First American Army—nor Gouraud on his left met with serious resistance. The advance averaged nearly three miles.

Next day opposition stiffened, and the Americans were much delayed by the difficulty, of which they had small experience, of getting their guns across a shell-pocked no man's land.* Both armies, however, kept the advance going pretty steadily against tough and skilled resistance from the inner flanks of the army groups of Gallwitz and the German Crown Prince. The trouble was in the Argonne, where lack of artillery observation and barriers created by intermingled fallen trees and brushwood proved heavy handicaps. About October 5 a pause occurred, broken only by minor operations. By then the maximum advance of the Americans and French was over eight miles, but in the forest nowhere much beyond half the distance. Losses were heavy.

On September 27, twenty-four hours after the opening of the Franco-American offensive, the British Third and First Armies launched an attack on a front of eighteen miles with the left flank on the Sensée Canal. It was to be a tremendous offensive, bigger even than the Meuse-Argonne. When the Fourth Army joined in on the twenty-ninth, forty-one divisions (including two American) would be advancing against forty-one German divisions, whereas in the Meuse-Argonne it was thirty-seven American and French against thirty-six German. Whereas the country was by nature the easier on the British front, indeed ideal, the obstacles were forbidding. They included the Canal du Nord and Canal de Saint-Quentin, and on the whole Fourth Army front the intact Hindenburg position, three powerful lines of defenses. It had the biggest task, and was allotted ten of the fourteen tank battalions available. So the first two days were only the prologue. Yet the swift passage of the Canal du Nord and the six-mile advance which brought the inner flanks of Byng's and Horne's armies virtually to the gates of Cambrai alarmed O.H.L. On the evening of the twenty-eighth Ludendorff told Hindenburg that a request for an armistice ought to be made.

The alarm was heightened by the success of Rawlinson's Fourth Army. It crossed the Canal de Saint-Quentin—where this held water, the assault troops used collapsible boats, rafts, and 3,000 life belts borrowed from Channel packets—and breached the first and second Hindenburg systems. Rawlinson, a very good tactician, noting the

* Liggett, p. 82.

obstinacy with which the enemy was now disputing the progress of the Third and First Armies, was convinced that by extending the breach northeastward he could clear their path. On October 4 he smashed a way through the third Hindenburg system. His expectations were fulfilled. The Germans drew back, not only on his front but on that of the Third, First, and even the Fifth Army in the now quiet country between Lens and Armentières.* So three corps, one of which was American, cleared the front of three armies. The incident points to a flaw in Haig's masterful handling of the offensive: he parceled out divisions rather too evenly. This heavy punch on a narrow section of a long front was rarely to be repeated. We must recall, however, that Haig had allotted Rawlinson nearly all the British armor, without which the punch would have lacked its violence.

Haig was dissatisfied with the progress of Debeney, who embarrassed Rawlinson by hanging back on his right. He went so far as to appeal to Foch to urge him on, and the Generalissimo admonished Pétain, and even Debeney directly. The British command believed that Debeney, a first-class soldier, had in mind France's frightful death-roll and waited for the toughest objectives to be breached first by the British. He was certainly slow, but it is only fair to add that his First Army was faced by a higher proportionate German strength than most others.

The Flanders offensive began on September 28. The original forces allotted were ten British, twelve Belgian, and six French divisions. The Belgians had fought only one major battle since those of 1914. Since then 120,000 men, the majority refugees, had joined the army, which was now 170,000 strong. Twenty-two thousand had entered national workshops set up by King Albert. He believed that, with few recruits left, the army was capable of only one great operation. He had avoided taking part in the Flanders offensive of 1917, which he thought would waste away his forces without adequate return, but he had extended his front in order to make the campaign possible. The Belgians had been the first to stop a German offensive dead. The King was a cool, determined soldier and his army was in good form. He suspected that he had been given a French chief of staff in order to rob him of the leadership of his armed forces, of which he could not constitutionally divest himself,

* The Fifth Army, formerly Gough's, had been reconstituted under Birdwood.

and on more than one occasion he asserted his position strongly.*

Despite heavy rain upon the Flanders clay, the first day was a great success. By evening most of the notorious Ypres ridge, wrung from the enemy in the prolonged and bloody struggle of 1917 and afterward perforce yielded without a battle, was in the hands of the Allies. By the following evening that could be said for it all, and at the Anglo-Belgian junction due east of Ypres the progress exceeded nine miles. The defense of the German Fourth Army was a thing of patches, and the infantry was generally ready to flee or surrender. For a moment the vision of a swift advance providing a chance to roll up the German right hung before the vision of the Allies.

It was a mirage. Once again the Ypres plain lived up to its reputation. The conditions differed from those of 1917. The advance had stridden across the old battlefield into unspoiled country and reached firm ground. It was not now the troops who were bogged, but it came to the same thing, except that they were spared the miseries of a year ago. It was the transport that was caught by the rise of the water in the churned ground. The stoppage was most serious behind the Belgians, the largest contingent. On October 2, 15,000 rations for Belgian and French troops were dropped by the Belgian Air Force, with some aid from the R.A.F.† This hold-up came when the Allies stood facing the German Flanders position, had indeed pierced its foremost line, and when fresh German divisions had reached the scene. But for local actions, rarely successful, the offensive was hung up until October 14, while the assailants turned their energies to toil on roads and railways. The convergent operations which Haig had suggested and Foch had decreed were showing no signs of turning the enemy's flanks and meanwhile Haig's armies of the left center had burst into open country.

Thus the plan was not working perfectly. On the other hand, the Allies were clearly marching to victory. Now lift the curtain to survey the German government, G.H.Q. and O.H.L. It is a scene of defeat.

On September 29 Ludendorff stated at a Council of War that an immediate armistice was necessary. The Foreign Minister, Admiral von Hintze, spoke to his brief by suggesting an appeal to President Wilson on the basis of his "Fourteen Points." Hintze, primed here

* Cammaerts, pp. 235-239, 296.
† Jones, *The War in the Air*, VI, 534.

also, advised that the Emperor should initiate democratic government. This would associate the left wing with the defeat and perhaps shift the blame to it. That was only the first of successive efforts by ministers—who behaved from first to last in more dignified fashion than the Hindenburg-Ludendorff duumvirate—to take the responsibility of surrender from the shoulders of the army. The duumvirs of course agreed. Chancellor Hertling now turned up and was shocked by the armistice proposal. He asked for permission to resign, which was granted.

Prince Max of Baden, a Liberal, was offered the appointment, and, after a system of parliamentary government had been decreed, accepted. On October 4 German and Austrian notes requesting an armistice were sent to the President. Ludendorff was naturally influenced by the collapse of Germany's ally in Macedonia and the breach opened in the front of the Central Powers, but he made the most of it. Anything to slide the blame off his own shoulders! We must drop the curtain on him again for a moment.

On October 12 Pershing formed the Second Army under the command of Bullard in the more or less inactive front between the Moselle and the Meuse. He handed over the First Army to Liggett, who seems to have been a better tactician than his chief. Clemenceau the Tiger had been roaring about the check and talked of appealing to Wilson to remove Pershing, a proposal which Foch managed to blanket. The renewal of the offensive on October 14 brought but limited success and was extremely costly. The rawer among the American troops exposed themselves as recklessly as the new British divisions on the first day of the Somme. Liggett, who actually took over on the sixteenth, decided on further reorganization.

Meanwhile Rawlinson's Fourth Army, covered on the right by Debeney and on the left by Byng, advanced to the new German front on the Selle, and Horne fought his way forward to the Sensée Canal. During the pause before the assault on this position the Germans withdrew to the Hunding-Brunhilde fortifications, with the French Fifth and Tenth Armies on their heels. Rawlinson's set attack on October 17 with only four British divisions and two American—the same two as before, the 27th and 30th, with the British forces from the first—broke a reorganized German defense on the Selle. Two days later the Third Army forced a passage of the river lower down, where it was a more formidable obstacle. By the twenty-fourth Boehm's Army Group had taken a dreadful beating and left 20,000 prisoners on the battlefield of the Selle. This great British victory immensely hastened the German slide to perdition. It could not go on much longer because the bottom was all but reached. Meanwhile the First Army reached the Scheldt Canal at Valenciennes and on the Fifth Army front the Germans fell back so fast to this obstacle that the British pursuit involved little fighting. The enemy was by now desperately short of reserves, ammunition, and horses.

In Flanders the British Second Army in King Albert's group forced a passage of the Lys against stiff opposition on October 19 and paved the way for a general Allied offensive toward the Scheldt. The French had now formed an army, the Sixth, including two American divisions, in this group.

What of the French armies between the Americans and the British? Gouraud's Fourth Army on Pershing's left played a full and vital part in the offensive, though so far the depth of its advance was less than that of the First American Army. Of the other three no comment more acute and reasonable has been written than the following: "With shrewd strategic sense the French in the center appreciated that decisive results depended on the rapid penetration and closing of the pincers, and so did not unduly hasten the retreat of the Germans facing them. In their skilful advance they usually kept a step in rear of their allies on either flank. . . . If their commanders had been slow to learn how to economize life, they, and still more their men, had learnt it now. Perhaps a shade too well." *

It may be added in qualification that French casualities in the offensive were very heavy and that from July 18 to the end their haul of prisoners amounted to 74 per cent of the British and three times the American. Their most enterprising army commander was Mangin, who won a fine victory astride the Serre on October 18, but he did not remain to the end.†

The request for an armistice did not make a cessation of hostilities certain. In fact, Ludendorff, typically of a gambler, had changed his mind about this. The Allies could not afford to let up. In this phase Liggett's and Gouraud's armies had heavy fighting. The Americans first broke the German front to the northward, then,

* Hart, *The Real War*, p. 493.
† His army headquarters gave place to that of Humbert's Third Army on the twenty-seventh because Mangin was destined to play the major part in the Lorraine offensive, which the Armistice forestalled.

414   THE GREAT WAR

simultaneously with the advance in that direction, drove the enemy off the dominating Hauts de Meuse, east of the river. In one day, November 1, the defense to northward was cracked. The rest was pursuit against rear guards, except for the clearance of the Hauts de Meuse, in which a French corps under Liggett's command took part. By November 6 the American left was looking down into Sedan,* and Americans and French had closed on the Ardennes. This was the thrust that O.H.L. feared most acutely because it would hasten the growing paralysis of the railways.

The French Fifth and Third Armies made only a slight advance, but on November 2 the progress of the British Third and First was good. On the fourth Rawlinson forced his way across the Sambre-Oise Canal and Debeney followed suit.

Then suddenly everyone was marching. Not very fast, because the German machine gunners were still troublesome and, more important, the communications were feeling the strain. Railheads were far in rear because the Germans had effected demolitions all along the permanent way and planted delayed-action mines under it. Road movement was checked because all bridges had been cut and it needed herculean efforts to push bridging material forward through dense traffic. Food had to be provided for the inhabitants, especially as the Germans had generally taken the cattle and poultry with them. Still, contact was maintained.

At certain points fighting was bitter. The American First Army was still hard at it in the early hours of November 11 and affected crossings of the upper Meuse on a wide front. Bullard's Second Army, having attacked on the ninth, was still advancing slowly. A Canadian battalion cleared the last German machine guns out of Mons just before first light. Foch was shifting strength eastward for an offensive in Lorraine under the orders of Castelnau, in which he hoped Pershing would allow six American divisions to take part under the orders of Bullard.

We return to the German scene. On October 9 President Wilson's reply to the request for an armistice was received in Berlin. As preliminaries he demanded acceptance of his Fourteen Points and the evacuation of all occupied territory. After much wrangling, these terms were accepted, on the twelfth. Then on the sixteenth came a cold douche from the American President: the conditions of an

* One who enjoyed this view was the commander of the Forty-second Division, Brigadier-General Douglas MacArthur.

armistice must be drawn up by the military advisers of the Allied governments. The debate grew hot, Ludendorff making a great show of resisting these conditions. Was it that he could safely do so without preventing an armistice? Prince Max accepted the conditions. On October 27 Ludendorff resigned to avoid formal dismissal. He was succeeded by Groener, who, however, did not return from Russia until the thirtieth.

The victorious Allies had meanwhile given their naval and military representatives the outline of the terms and Wilson's suggestion that all details should be left to them had been accepted. Haig's proposed terms were the mildest. Pétain's line was more severe. Pershing's was extremely so. Foch, the final arbiter, followed a middle course. Wilson's reliance on a military solution had one curious effect. It set up a contrast between his Fourteen Points and the armistice terms, in that the former made no mention of occupation of German territory, whereas the latter provided for it. This gave the Germans an opportunity, eagerly seized, to pretend that they had been tricked. In fact, peace suggestions drawn up in general terms and armistice conditions for a period during which a state of hostilities is only suspended, not terminated, and for which strict and definite precautions are required, are very different matters. It must be added, however, that Foch was careful to provide for German military evacuation of the left bank of the Rhine and bridgeheads on the right, to be held by the victors. This had a political as well as a military object, the former being that if, as he hoped, France were to claim a frontier on the Rhine at the Peace Conference, prior occupation of the bridges was necessary. "Only the sacrifice of territory agreed to by the enemy *at the time of signing the armistice will remain final.*"

Spurred to haste by the Turkish armistice signed on October 30, by the Austrian armistice signed on November 3, and by the naval mutiny beginning on October 29, the German government nominated its delegates. At their head was the Roman Catholic leader, Mathias Erzberger. A representative of O.H.L. was appointed, but at the last moment withdrawn to bolster the fiction that the armistice had not been demanded by the army.

In the early hours of November 7 Foch was informed by wireless of the names of the delegates. The German government also stated that it would be happy if "in the interests of humanity" their arrival were made the signal for a provisional suspension of arms. He disregarded this request, hardly meant to be taken seriously, and simply gave the place and time at which representatives should present themselves at the outposts. Then, accompanied by Admiral Sir Rosslyn Wemyss, head of a British naval delegation, he left by train for Rethondes in the Forest of Compiègne. The train was run on to a gun spur.

Erzberger did some fencing, but obtained only slight technical concessions. It is now known that he was bidden to sign, whatever the terms, and that those offered appeared to him easier than any his highest hopes had envisaged. During the discussions Germany was proclaimed a republic in Berlin on November 9 and Prince Max resigned, to be succeeded by Fritz Ebert, a Socialist. Early on the tenth the Emperor fled to Holland, followed by the Crown Prince. The Germans signed at 5 A.M. on November 11. The essentials were:

> Cessation of hostilities at 11 A.M. that day;
> Evacuation of invaded territory and of Alsace-Lorraine;
> Repatriation of citizens of Allied nations;
> Surrender of vast stocks of war material (including 5,000 guns and 25,000 machine guns);
> Evacuation of the left bank of the Rhine and bridgeheads behind it, to be held by the Allies;
> Repatriation of Allied prisoners of war, without immediate reciprocity;
> Surrender of all submarines;
> Internment of surface vessels as designated by the Allies.

From the Swiss frontier to the Moselle the front had not been affected by the great series of offensives. Thence the armistice line ran by Stenay, Sédan, Mèzieres, Maubeuge, Mons, and Ghent to the Dutch frontier.

That morning the scenes and sounds varied. Here and there a little combat took place even after 11 A.M., but over sections of the front only the occasional thumping of artillery or rattling of machine guns was heard. Some batteries fired final salvos just before the eleventh hour of the eleventh day of the eleventh month. Then a strange silence fell. The victorious troops showed no immediate excitement. Doubtless many thought of lost kinsmen and friends, but the incredible fact that all was over left little room for other reflections. At night bonfires were lit here and there. Very lights and colored rockets were shot into the sky already faintly illuminated by the sickle moon entering its first quarter.

SUMMARY OF PRESIDENT WILSON'S FOURTEEN POINTS, JANUARY 8, 1918

1. Open covenants for peace; no secret diplomacy.

2. Freedom of navigation, even in war outside territorial waters, except when seas closed by international action.

3. Removal as far as possible of economic barriers.

4. Guarantees for reduction of armaments.

5. Impartial adjustment of colonial claims, interests of peoples concerned having equal weight with claims of governments.

6. Russian territory to be evacuated.

7. Restoration of Belgian sovereignty.

8. French territory to be freed and the wrong done by Prussia in the matter of Alsace-Lorraine to be righted.

9. Readjustment of Italian frontiers on lines of nationality.

10. Peoples of Austria-Hungary to be accorded opportunity of national development.

11. Rumania, Serbia, and Montenegro to be evacuated. Serbia to be given access to the sea. Relation of Balkan states to be settled on lines of allegiance and nationality.

12. Non-Turkish nationalities of the Ottoman Empire to be assured of autonomy. The Dardanelles to be free to all shipping.

13. Poland to be given independence.

14. A general association of nations to be formed under covenants to afford mutual guarantees of political independence and territorial integrity, to great and small states alike.

Epilogue

IT has often been called in England the Battle of the Hundred Days, after the Campaign of the Hundred Days which ended so satisfactorily just over a century earlier. The title errs on the side of modesty. The offensive lasted only ninety-six days even with November 11th included. Considering the German strength on the morning of August 8, it was quick work. Yet the strategy did not quite come off. In a convergent offensive the wings should move the fastest. Here the vital right wing had to advance over the ground most favorable to defense, and in consequence moved the slowest. One critic holds that the plan to cut the German rail communications in two at Mézières was "fundamentally unreal," because roads and railways through the Ardennes were capable of carrying more traffic than Haig supposed.[*] They were. Nevertheless, the Germans relied heavily on the lines Luxembourg-Mézières and Namur-Mézières, the latter linking the former with the system radiating from Liège and Namur, through which junctions by far the greater part of their traffic passed. That was why O.H.L. was so sensitive about this sector, why Groener, the railway expert, said in effect that all was up unless the American advance could be stopped. Pressure here did make a strong contribution to victory, but it was applied too slowly to mold its shape.

Moreover, it is startling to note that, while Foch accepted the strategy of Haig, what was foremost in his mind was different. His directives, especially in the earlier phase of the offensive, were in terms of liberating railways and coal mines. He did not believe in the possibility of a break-through on the Western Front and when

[*] Hart, *The Real War*, p. 491.

he found an offensive sticking his policy was to "extend the battle to the flanks." * As for Haig, the apostle of the convergent offensive —in which he may have been influenced by memories of talks with Joffre—he had his best army commander and tactician, Rawlinson, on his right, that is, virtually in the center of the whole drive, and gave him the greatest resources. The British Fourth Army was the most effective force in the offensive. Its success was immense, but it did not contribute to convergence.

The student of war may speculate whether a more crushing defeat might have been inflicted on the Germans by more localized thrusts spaced out but made stronger by concentration of armor and infantry divisions. He will, however, bear in mind that the defense had won its greatest advantage—depth—in the first weeks of the war and that the Germans had had four years in which to construct successive positions of great strength. To win a victory so complete on one position that the next could be overrun without a pause would have been very difficult. Increasing use of mechanical transport to move men, guns, and ammunition was made in 1918, but it could be no more than a useful small-scale makeshift. Foch and Haig had only to look at the map to see what Ludendorff's strategic plan of deep punches followed by rolling up his enemy's front had led to: three great pockets which had rendered his own front far more vulnerable than before. They might well hesitate to run any risk of putting themselves in a similar position. The Lorraine offensive would have introduced variety into the general pattern of a cross-country drive, but would have had to be prepared much earlier. If hostilities had lasted long enough for it to be launched on November 14 it would have been, said Castelnau, only a *coup de main de diversion* because time for preparation had been wholly inadequate.

Foch and Haig emerge as the great captains of 1918: Foch because he held the Allies together, in every sense, by his personality and magnificent fund of will power; Haig because of refusal to admit defeat, his skill on the defensive—shown first at Ypres in 1914 —and then by the way he accepted the main burden of the effort for victory, knowing that his armies would carry it and no one else could. Both were men of unconquerable souls. The third supreme figure, Ludendorff, without their virtues of character, is neverthe-

* Falls, *Marshal Foch*, p. viii.

less the most striking of the whole war in one respect. He realized that this was the first people's war of the industrial age and saw that the efforts of the scientist and the workman and the soldier were all one.

No one man, however, could keep the conduct of the war and the control of the nation at war in his hands. Ludendorff failed to do so. National leadership in the Central Powers was weak. Their foes were more fortunate. Lloyd George proved a great national leader. Clemenceau, later in the field and facing a still heavier task, was at least his equal. Wilson led the United States superbly, but was less sure of his own goal.

Britain started slowly in land warfare, though not in naval. She did not begin to play a great part in the former for two years. France bore the brunt during that period and perhaps the heavier share for another year. She was by then exhausted herself and impatient with her ally because she never realized the extent or the significance of the British naval effort. Exhaustion came to Britain in her turn in the spring of 1918—dates are, of course, merely landmarks in the progress of fatigue, expenditure of capital, and loss of life. Then, from a reserve in the storehouse of will, courage, and energy, she drew enough to break the last German-held barriers and to exert the greatest influence upon the final phase of the war. Much as the United States accomplished in that period, she was then only getting into her stride.

Germany displayed extraordinary endurance, but collapsed in the last weeks. Here and there divisions, on a wider scale artillerymen and machine gunners, were fighting in almost the old style at the end. But the national and military will had cracked.

For long afterward it seemed that the moral effects of the war had cut deeper in Britain than in the peoples of her partners in victory. The flood of antimilitarist literature, for the greater part fiction, which poured from the presses, deriding leadership from top to bottom, treating patriotism as a vice when not as a fraud, as it were bathed in blood and rolled in mud, was astonishing. It was far from being representative but it was assuredly symptomatic of widespread disillusion. It was followed, after the evil spell of Hitler had been laid upon Germany, by incidents which in retrospect appear ridiculous—a fantastic by-election, amazing resolutions—but then shook the nerve of the government. Yet when at last the decision to stand up to Hitler was taken, it was discovered that Britain was sound and France divided, scared, and spiritless.

The forces destined for the occupation of Germany marched unhurriedly to the Rhine. They were held up at first because the Germans, withdrawing to a strict program behind successive lines chalked on maps held by both sides, were physically unable to keep up to schedule. Later the Allies were occasionally delayed by difficulty with their supplies. The Germans had, of course, supplied location lists of unexploded delayed-action mines on the railways, but in many cases they had been so carefully hidden beneath the permanent way that they could not be found even with this aid. The officers responsible were then sent for to find them and, as might be expected of engineers, showed as much enthusiasm—and high courage—in extracting them as they had in laying them.

The trouble was soon over, but it aroused in officers' messes discussions about how hard pursuit could have been pressed had the German armies attempted to retreat to the Rhine without surrender. The occupation began in early December, and the troops destined to hold the bridgeheads crossed the Rhine before the middle of the month. The strength of the contingents varied but was in all cases well under a quarter of the armies represented.

The attitude of the German officials was correct. The people were obedient. A certain number behaved with oily politeness, but that is true of every community under military occupation. The most disturbing element actually divided the Allies rather than brought them into conflict with the Germans. Foch was fighting tooth and nail for a French frontier on the Rhine. He was convinced that the spirit of German militarism was not dead, that it would prove once again a menace to peace, and that the best precaution would be a French hold on the Rhine bridges. The French government accepted his view but felt that it was beaten before the fight began because the United Kingdom and the United States would never agree. Clemenceau, however, was undoubtedly privy to negotiations between French and German advocates of a Rhineland republic, which were fostered by Mangin, commanding the French Army of Occupation at Mainz. The French government, finding that France's allies were indeed inflexibly opposed to the scheme, abandoned and denounced the project, to the regret of the President of the Republic, Raymond Poincaré. The scheme collapsed. There had been rather more in it, however, than derisive comments in the foreign press suggested.

Thus, while all the defeated armies were reduced to mere shells as speedily as possible, the victors demobilized more slowly and kept large forces for purposes of security, not only in Germany but in Eastern Europe. The troops were bored and restless, but steadier than might have been expected. Demobilization proceeded regularly.

The vital Peace Conference at Versailles was delayed, to start with because Lloyd George held an immediate general election to exploit British gratitude. Work did not begin until the latter part of January, 1919. Even then the victors found it more difficult to work in harmony for peace than for victory in war. The German delegates were not summoned for over two months. They proved stubborn in the extreme and refused to sign the dictated treaty. In May it was decided to call their bluff by advancing from the bridgeheads into unoccupied Germany. The resolution was not easily reached and was adopted in the fervent hope that the threat would suffice. It did suffice. The peace terms were signed on June 28, but not ratified until January 10, 1920. Even then the United States had to make a separate peace treaty because his own country had refused to confirm President Wilson's pledges. This treaty was signed on August 25, 1921, and ratified on November 11. It omitted the clauses relating to the League of Nations.

The withdrawal may have been inevitable in the then state of American public opinion, but it was highly unfortunate. This, however, was not the worst. One of the most notable feats of imaginative statesmanship on the part of Clemenceau—there were other feats not to be so described—had been that of obtaining a pledge that Britain and the United States would come to the aid of France if she were unjustifiably attacked, the responsibility of each depending on its acceptance by the other. In the United States, Wilson's obligation went by the board with American participation in the League of Nations. The withdrawal of the American pledge automatically wiped out that of Britain. Automatically? Well, there were not a few who considered that, even if the United States backed out, Britain might have mustered courage to give a single-handed pledge.

The Americans packed up early, departing in January, 1923. The British left in December, 1929; the French and Belgians in June, 1930. Guillaumat was the last commander in chief of troops of occupation on German soil.

Endless statistics relating to the loss of life have been compiled, but some are largely based on guesswork. Accidents and disease are a big factor. The Russian death roll is a matter of speculation but probably exceeds three million. Germany is the most difficult problem. Two million dead was the total announced, but the British official historian, on the basis of regimental rolls of honor, puts it at nearly twice as high.* This may be an exaggeration, but three million is under the mark. The deaths in the British Empire fell just short of a million; those of the British Isles were little under 750,000, of whom 88 per cent were battle casualties. French deaths were over one million, and with African and Asiatic troops upward of 1,400,000. Austria-Hungary stands near the million mark and Italy the half million. The United States lost 81,000. The total death roll of the war may have been as high as twelve million. Some statisticians add several millions more for consequential losses such as civilian deaths from bombardment, drowning, starvation, and disease.

Great wars commonly produce a rank aftermath, as the dragon's teeth sown by Cadmus bore armed men who at once set about slaying each other. This time statecraft provided no Castlereagh, no Talleyrand, no Metternich. Moreover, the revolutionary creed of Bolshevik Russia aimed at world domination. The retreat of the United States into isolation, the dismemberment of Austria-Hungary, the appearance of Mustapha Kemal as dictator of a New Turkey, and the ambitions of Japan were among the factors favorable to chaos. Britain, the solid and secure, faced rebellion on the very soil of the United Kingdom—and threw up the sponge.

The worst and most hideous turmoil and suffering were caused by the struggle between Bolshevik Russia and the various elements opposed to it, from ultra-Tsarist to Radical, supported and supplied by Britain and France. At one moment Lenin and all he stood for faced defeat. The tip of the scales affects us all today and will go on doing so. In 1920 a new name was added to the list of great captains when the Polish commander Pilsudski smote the Red Army hip and thigh and, it may be, prevented the Bolshevization of the greater part of Europe. Yet another dictator, Benito Mussolini, possessed himself of Italy. The Greek army, used as a pawn in the power game, after brilliant victories in Turkey, finally broke under the strain. Most of these wars, those of Russia above all, were fought with repellent savagery. Indiscriminate slaughter of prisoners and of civilians were

---

* Edmonds, *Military Operations, France and Belgium, 1918*, V, 598.

a commonplace. The great scourges of mankind, typhus and starvation, marched with the tattered armies.

The roots of the blame are too tangled to follow. Eventually it can all be traced to Homo sapiens, so named. Yet we cannot forget that the victors had to a large extent a free hand to make a new world. It could never have come up to their hopes. They could have made something better of it than they did.

The world and its civilization have constantly passed through similar trials. Sometimes they have plunged into a dark age before recovering; sometimes they have emerged quickly. Civilization has always survived, though changing its course in some cases and often enough shedding what it could ill afford to lose. This war became known as the first of the total wars. It did not, however, though many then believed the contrary, threaten the existence of civilization itself; indeed, if such a threat has ever existed, it has appeared only in the last few years. Despite many reckless and brutal deeds done in high places, this terrible war of material was for the most part directed by statesmen and conducted by commanders who, for all their faults and errors and despite the trammels of nationalist and racialist bigotry, did not altogether lose their sense of the meaning and value of civilization, and, according to their lights, warred for a future in which civilization should not cease to flourish.

Book List

I make no apology for the brevity of this list. Hundreds of books on the war which I have studied at one time or another are not included here, but their essential contributions to the subject have been embodied in other works, especially official histories, in a good many cases by myself. I consider that it would be mere showmanship to parade a long list of them here.

I have been equally sparing of references in the text. I could have included several times the number that I have actually entered, but to do so would not have been very helpful and would have been confusing to the reader's eye. My aim has been to support the more striking statements and particularly those which may seem open to question, as well as direct quotations, by references.

Where only a single work follows an author's name in the book list, that author's name alone is given in the reference, followed by the volume and page. Where an author is represented by more than one work in the book list, the title of that quoted follows his name in the reference.

Adam, George: *Treason and Tragedy.* (London: Cape, 1922)

Adams, James Truslow, and Coleman, R. V.: *Dictionary of American History*, Vol. IV.

Allen, W. E. D., and the late Paul Muratoff: *Caucasian Battlefields.* (Cambridge University Press, 1953)

American Battle Fields in Europe, Guide to the. (Washington: Government Printing Office, 1927)

Armées Françaises dans la Grande Guerre. (Paris: Imprimerie Nationale)

Aspinall-Oglander, Brig.-General C. F.: *Military Operations, Gallipoli.* 2 Vols. (London: Heinemann, 1929)

Azan, General Paul: *Franchet d'Esperey*. (Paris: Flammarion, 1949)

Barnes, Leonard: *Youth at Arms*. (London: Peter Davies, 1933)

Blake, Robert (editor): *The Private Papers of Douglas Haig, 1914-1918*. (London, Eyre & Spottiswoode, 1953)

Bloch, Camille: *The Causes of the World War*. Translation. (London: Allen & Unwin, 1935)

Brusilov, General A. A.: *A Soldier's Note-Book, 1914-1918*. (New York: Macmillan, 1930)

Bullard, Robert Lee: *Personalities and Reminiscences of the War*. (New York: Doubleday Page, 1925)

Bülow, Karl von. *See* Koeltz.

Bülow, Oberst Freiherr v.: *Geschichte der Luftwaffe*. (Frankfurt-am-Main: Moritz Diesterweg, 1937)

Cammaerts, Emile: *Albert of Belgium*. (London: Nicholson & Watson, 1935)

Churchill, Winston S.: *The World Crisis*. (London: Thornton-Butterworth, 1923 &c)

———: *The World Crisis, Eastern Front*. (London: Thornton-Butterworth, 1931)

Clark, George R. and others: *A Short History of the United States Navy*. (Philadelphia & London: Lippincott, 1927)

Conrad, Feldmarschall: *Aus meiner Dientzeit*. 5 Vols. (Vienna: Rikola, 1921 &c)

Corbett, Sir Julian S.: *History of the Great War, Naval Operations*. Vols. I & II. *See also* Newbolt. (London: Longmans, 1920 &c)

Edmonds, Brig.-General Sir James E.: *A Short History of World War I*. (London: Oxford University Press, 1951)

———: *History of the Great War, Military Operations France & Belgium*, and *Italy*. Volumes from hands other than those of Brig.-General Edmonds are listed under their authors' names. (Macmillan, 1923 &c)

Falkenhayn, General Erich von: *General Headquarters and its Critical Decisions*. Translation. (London: Hutchinson, 1919)

Falls, Cyril: *A Hundred Years of War*. (London: Duckworth, 1953)

———: *Marshal Foch*. (London: Blackie, 1939)

———: *Military Operations, Egypt & Palestine*. 2 Vols. Vol. I with Lieut.-General Sir G. MacMunn. (H. M. Stationery Office, 1928 &c)

———: *Military Operations, France & Belgium, 1917*. Vol. I. (New York: Macmillan, 1940)

———: *Military Operations, Macedonia*. 2 Vols. (H. M. Stationery Office, 1933 &c)

———: *Ordeal by Battle*. (London: Methuen, 1943)

———: *The Nature of Modern Warfare*. (London: Methuen, 1941)

Fay, Sidney Bradshaw: *The Origins of the World War*. 2 Vols. (New York: Macmillan, 1929)

Fayle, C. Ernest: *History of the Great War, Seaborne Trade.* 3 Vols. (London: Murray, 1920 &c)

Fischer, Dr. Eugen (editor): *Die Ursachen des Deutschen Zusammen-bruches.* (Berlin: Deutsche Verlagsgesellschaft fur Politik and Geschichte, 1925 &c)

Foch, Maréchal: *Mémoires,* 2 Vols. (Paris: Plon, 1931)

Forster, Edward S.: *A Short History of Modern Greece.* (London: Methuen, 1958)

François, Gen. der Infanterie v.: *Gorlice 1915.* (Leipzig: Kochler, 1922)

Frost, Holloway H.: *The Battle of Jutland.* (Annapolis: U.S. Naval Institute; London: Stevens & Brown, 1936)

Fuller, Major-General J. F. C.: *The Decisive Battles of the Western World.* Vol. III. (London: Eyre & Spottiswoode, 1956)

Gooch, G. P., and Temperley, Harold: *British Documents on the Origins of the War.* Vol. XI by J. W. Headlam-Morley. (H. M. Stationery Office, 1926)

Gough, General Sir Hubert: *Soldiering On.* (London: Barker, 1954)

Gourko, General Basil: *Memories and Impressions of War and Revolution in Russia.* (London: Murray, 1918)

Grasset, Commandant, later Lieut.-Colonel: *Un Combat de Rencontre, Neufchâteau.* (Paris: Berger-Levrault, 1925)

————: *Le 22 aout 1914 au 4ᵉ Corps d'Armée, Virton.* (Paris: Berger-Levrault, 1926)

————: *Le 22 aout au 4ᵉ Corps d'Armée, Ethe.* (Paris: Berger-Levrault, 1927)

Gretton, R. H.: *A Modern History of the British People, 1910-1922.* (Secker, 1929)

Hart, Captain B. H. Liddell: *Reputations.* (London: Murray, 1928)

————: *The Real War.* (London: Faber & Faber, 1930)

————: *The War in Outline.* (London: Faber & Faber, 1936)

Headlam-Morley, J. W.: *See* Gooch

Hendrick, Burton J.: *The Life and Letters of Walter H. Page.* 3 Vols. (London: Heinemann, 1922 &c)

Herbillon, Colonel: *Du Général-en-Chef au Gouvernement.* (Paris: Taillandier, 1930)

Hordern, Lieut.-Colonel Charles: *Military Operations, East Africa.* (H. M. Stationery Office, 1941)

Jones, H. A.: *History of the Great War, The War in the Air.* Vols. II-VI. *See also* Raleigh. (Oxford: Clarendon Press, 1922 &c)

Kessel, Eberhard: *General Feldmarschall Graf Alfred Schlieffen: Briefe.* (Göttingen: Vandenhoeck & Ruprecht, 1958)

Kluck, Alexander von: *The March on Paris and the Battle of the Marne.* Translation. (London: Arnold, 1920)

Knox, Major-General Sir Alfred: *With the Russian Army, 1914-1917*. 2 Vols. (London: Hutchinson, 1921)

Koeltz, Lieut.-Colonel L.: *Documents Allemands sur la Bataille de la Marne*. Translations of accounts by Bülow and Tappen of their experiences, and by Colonel Müller-Loebnitz of the Hentsch mission. (Paris: Payot, 1930)

Kuhl, Hermann von: *Der Weltkrieg, 1914-1918*. 2 Vols. (Berlin: Kolk, 1929)

Krauss, Gen. der Infanterie, Alfred: *Das Wunder von Karfreit*. (Munich: Lehmann, 1926)

———: *Die Ursachen unserer Niederlage*. (Munich: Lehmann, 1920)

Lansing, Robert: *War Memoirs of Robert Lansing* (Indianapolis: Bobbs-Merrill, 1935)

Larcher, Commandant M.: *La Guerre Turque dans la Guerre mondiale*. (Paris, Chiron, 1926)

Liggett, Hunter: *Commanding an American Army*. (Boston & New York: Houghton Mifflin, 1925)

McEntee, Girard Lindsley: *Military History of the World War*. (New York: Scribner, 1937)

Miles, Captain Wilfrid: *Military Operations, France & Belgium, 1917*. Vol. III. (Macmillan, 1948)

Millis, Walter: *Arms and Men*. (New York: Putnam, 1956)

———: *Road to War*. (London: Faber & Faber, 1935)

Moberly, Brig.-General F. J.: *The Campaign in Mesopotamia*. 4 Vols. (H. M. Stationery Office, 1923 &c)

———: *Togoland and the Cameroons*. (H. M. Stationery Office, 1931)

Mortane, Jacques (pseud. of Lieut. de Romanet): *Histoire de la Guerre Aérienne*. 2 Vols. (Paris: Édition Française Illustrée, N. D.)

Müller-Loebnitz, Colonel. *See* Koeltz.

Newbolt, Sir Henry: *History of the Great War, Naval Operations*. Vols. iii & iv. *See also* Corbett. (London: Longmans, 1920 &c)

Newton, Lord: *Lord Lansdowne, a Biography*. (New York: Macmillan, 1929)

Noyes, Alexander D.: *The War Period of American Finance, 1908-1914*. (New York: Putnam, 1926)

Österreich-Ungarns Letzter Krieg. (Vienna: Verlag der Militärwissenschaftlichen Mitteilungen)

Palat, Général: *La Grande Guerre sur le Front Occidental*. (Paris: Berger-Levrault, 1925 &c)

Palmer, Frederick: *John J. Pershing*. (Harrisburg, Pa.: Military Service Publishing Co., 1948)

Pershing, General John J.: *Final Report*. (Washington: Military Service Publishing Co., 1927)

Pershing, General John J.: *My Experiences in the World War*. (London: Hodder & Stoughton, 1931)

Pierrefeu, Jean de: *French Headquarters 1915-1918*. Translation. (London: Bles, 1924)

Playne, Caroline M.: *Society at War*. (London: Allen & Unwin, 1936)

Pochhammer, Captain Hans: *Before Jutland, Admiral von Spee's Last Voyage*. Translation. (London: Jarrolds, 1931)

Pollen, Arthur Hungerford: *The Navy in Battle*. (London: Chatto & Windus, 1919)

Raleigh, Walter: *The War in the Air*. Vol. I. *See also* Jones. (Oxford: Clarendon Press, 1922 &c)

Regele, Oskar: *Feldmarschall Conrad*. (Vienna & Munich: Verlag Herold, 1955)

Ritter, Gerhard: *The Schlieffen Plan*. Translation. (Oswald Wolff, 1958)

Ritter, Hans: *Der Luftkrieg*. (Berlin: Koehler, 1926)

Rupprecht, Kronprinz von Bayern: *Mein Kriegstagebuch*. 3 Vols. (Munich: Deutscher National Verlag, 1919)

Schmitt, Bernadotte E.: *The Coming of the War*. 2 Vols. (New York: Scribner, 1930)

Schwarte, M. (editor): *Der Grosse Krieg*. 6 Vols. (Leipzig, Barth, 1921 &c)

Scott, James Brown: *President Wilson's Foreign Policy*. (New York: Oxford University Press, 1918)

Sérajevo: La Conspiration Serbe contre la Monarchie Austro-Hongroise. (Berne: Wyss, 1917)

Seymour, Charles: *The Intimate Papers of Colonel House*. 4 Vols. (Benn, 1926 &c)

Sims, Rear-Admiral William Sowden, and Hendrick, Burton S. J.: *The Victory at Sea*. (London: Murray, 1927)

Somervell, D. C.: *The Reign of King George V*. (London: Faber & Faber, 1935)

Stanley, George F. G.: *Canada's Soldiers*. (Toronto: Macmillan, 1954)

Sullivan, Mark: *Over Here, 1914-1918*. (New York: Scribner, 1933)

Supf, Peter: *Das Buch der deutschen Fliegsgeschicte*. (Berlin: Klemm, 1935)

Tappen, Gerhard: *See* Koeltz.

Thurlow, Colonel, E. G. L.: *The Pill-boxes of Flanders*. (London: (Nicholson & Watson, 1933)

United States Army in the World War, 1917-1919. (Washington: Historical Division, Department of the Army)

United States, Papers relating to the Foreign Relations of the, 1917. Supp. I. (United States Government Printing Office)

Weltkrieg, 1914 bis 1918: Die militärischen Operationen zu Lande. (Berlin: Mittler, 1925 &c)

Weltkrieg, 1914 bis 1918: Der Krieg zur See. (Berlin: Mittler, 1920 &c)

Whelply, J. D.: *British-American Relations.* (Grant Richards, 1924)

Wynne, Captain C. G.: *Pattern for Limited Nuclear War.* (Journal of the Royal United Service Institution, February, 1958)

ADDENDA

Falls, Cyril: *The Gordon Highlanders in the First World War.* (Aberdeen: University Press, 1958)

———: *The History of the 36th (Ulster) Division.* (Belfast: M'Caw Stevenson & Orr, 1922)

Hoffmann, Major General Max: *War Diaries.* 2 Vols. Translation. (London: Secker, 1929)

Index